# Tackling Harmful Alcohol Use

ECONOMICS AND PUBLIC HEALTH POLICY

*Edited by Franco Sassi*

OECD
BETTER POLICIES FOR BETTER LIVES

This work is published under the responsibility of the Secretary-General of the OECD. The opinions expressed and arguments employed herein do not necessarily reflect the official views of OECD member countries.

This document and any map included herein are without prejudice to the status of or sovereignty over any territory, to the delimitation of international frontiers and boundaries and to the name of any territory, city or area.

**Please cite this publication as:**
OECD (2015), *Tackling Harmful Alcohol Use: Economics and Public Health Policy*, OECD Publishing.
*http//dx.doi.org/10.1787/9789264181069-en*

ISBN 978-92-64-18085-7 (print)
ISBN 978-92-64-18106-9 (PDF)

The statistical data for Israel are supplied by and under the responsibility of the relevant Israeli authorities. The use of such data by the OECD is without prejudice to the status of the Golan Heights, East Jerusalem and Israeli settlements in the West Bank under the terms of international law.

**Photo credits:** © Derek Hatfield/Shutterstock.com

Corrigenda to OECD publications may be found on line at: *www.oecd.org/about/publishing/corrigenda.htm*.

# Foreword

*In a 1726 pamphlet setting out* A Brief Case of the Distillers, *Daniel Defoe, author of* Robinson Crusoe, *wrote that: "The distilling trade, considered in its present magnitude, is one of the greatest improvements, and the most to the advantage of the publick, of any business now carried out in England". Defoe was writing to defend English producers of spirits who were facing Dutch competition, especially from the newly-fashionable "Geneva water", soon to be known as gin. The English distillers won their case, and soon gin was everywhere, with men and women even drinking together in public for the first time. The authorities soon came to regret their decision (as did Defoe) and over the next 25 years, the UK Parliament would pass no fewer than five Acts to try to put an end to what became known as the Gin Craze (Abel, 2001). The craze died out in the 1750s, although it was revived to some extent in the Victorian "gin palaces" of the following century.*

*This anecdote illustrates a number of themes that will be examined in this book. Drinking habits are often viewed as part of a tradition, but dominant beverages, consumption patterns (including hazardous drinking), and the drinking behaviours of various social groups can change quickly. The Gin Craze also shows that government policy can influence behaviour, but that even when the aim is to reduce harm to individuals or society, policy is only one of several competing factors, ranging from lobbying to personal histories, and will have most success when a number of approaches work together.*

*If we forget for a moment those who become addicted to alcohol, we may say that drinking is largely the result of a personal choice, and governments need a strong justification to intervene to change people's behaviour. But, the principle that "your right to swing your arms ends just where the other man's nose begins" (Chafee, 1919) applies to alcohol as much as to other aspects of human life, and economics holds that principle very dear, as a justification for government action. When individual choices generate social costs, as alcohol does very clearly through road traffic accidents, domestic abuse and other forms of violence, and an increased burden on health services, just to cite the most important harms that may involve non-drinkers, economics predicts two outcomes with certainty. First, more alcohol will be drunk than is socially desirable. Second, by making those responsible for the harms caused to others pay for the full cost of their choices, society will be better off. Taken together, these issues provide strong grounds for government action to address the problem of harmful alcohol use.*

*Often though, objective evidence and analyses on which to base policy decisions is lacking. The purpose of this book is to close that gap. We used computer simulations and analyses of data from different countries to look at the major trends concerning alcohol consumption and examine a number of policy options found in the World Health Organization's Global Strategy to reduce harmful use of alcohol.*

*Economics offers powerful tools to enable decision makers to assess the benefits and costs of trying to change the current situation using different options (or indeed of doing nothing). Ultimately, what policies to use is a political choice, but we hope this book can contribute to making it a better informed one.*

*The work presented here was undertaken by the Organisation for Economic Co-operation and Development (OECD), on behalf of its Health Committee, between 2011 and 2014. It benefited greatly from the inputs and comments received from member states and other stakeholders. However, this book is published under the responsibility of the Secretary General of the OECD, and does not necessarily reflect the views of individual member states. The Health Committee and one of its subsidiary bodies, the Expert Group on the Economics of Prevention, examined working documents, progress reports and overview papers, as well as a full manuscript of this book, at various stages during the course of the project.*

*OECD's institutional stakeholder representative bodies, the Business and Industry Advisory Committee (BIAC) and the Trade Union Advisory Committee (TUAC), did not participate in Health Committee meetings in which this work was discussed, but provided written comments and oral inputs in separate formal consultations. BIAC, in particular, conveyed comments on Health Committee papers from members of the alcohol industry, the pharmaceutical industry, and employers more generally. BIAC members from the above industries participated in meetings of the Expert Group on the Economics of Prevention when the work was discussed, along with other invited stakeholders, including Eurocare, the European Association for the Study of the Liver (EASL), the European Liver Patients Association (ELPA), and the Association of European Cancer Leagues (ECL).*

## Bibliography

Abel, E.L. (2001), "The Gin Epidemic: Much Ado About What?", Alcohol and Alcoholism, Vol. 36, No. 5, pp. 401-405, September.

Chafee, Z. (1919), "Freedom of Speech in War Time", Harvard Law Review, Vol. 32, No. 8, pp. 932-973.

# Acknowledgements

Many more people deserve credit for the work presented in this book than those listed as its authors. The book is the result of laborious efforts made during the past four years by a large number of contributors from within and outside the OECD. These include several OECD interns who have worked in the Economics of Prevention programme at various stages. In particular, Michele Sechi Gatta spent a prolonged period of time at the OECD and made important contributions to the development of the CDP-Alcohol model. Chiara Capobianco gathered and reviewed evidence of the labour market outcomes of alcohol use. Raphaël Andler worked on the analysis of trends and disparities in alcohol consumption. Other colleagues in the Health Division, including Jillian Oderkirk and Aliénor Lerouge, contributed to the work at various stages. We received invaluable editorial and administrative support from Judy Zinnemann, Isabelle Vallard and Anna Irvin during the course of the project, and from Marlène Mohier, Nathalie Bienvenu and Emily Carter in the final stages of the preparation of the manuscript. Patrick Love's editorial work on all chapters and Special Focus contributions has been superb for its quality and efficiency. Kate Lancaster provided valuable editorial inputs throughout, and so did Carol Guthrie and Susan Fridy on the latest versions of the manuscript. Spencer Wilson and Paul Gallagher were of great help in sharpening the key messages from this work.

This book would not have seen the light of the day without staunch support from the entire Organisation. We are especially grateful to Mark Pearson for his leadership, first as Head of the Health Division and then as Deputy-Director of Employment, Labour and Social Affairs; to the Directors, John Martin and then Stefano Scarpetta, who have taken responsibility for this work; and to Francesca Colombo.

The institutional process within which the research was carried out, leading to the publication of this book, involved hundreds of people, most of whom provided comments and contributions. The work was discussed at three meetings of OECD's Health Committee, then Chaired by Jane Halton, whose steer has played a crucial role in improving the quality of the work and in building support from countries. The work was also discussed in detail at two meetings of OECD's Expert Group on the Economics of Prevention, Chaired by Taavi Lai and John Henderson. Independent experts, including Peter Anderson and Alan Brennan, made a difference through their contributions. Country experts and delegates are too many to name individually, but some deserve a special mention: Antero Kiviniemi, for his regular and insightful comments and support; Cath Patterson and Crispin Acton, for helping to find a balance on the most sensitive arguments; Peggy Murray, for having brought to the project precious insights from work undertaken and funded by the US National Institute for Alcohol Abuse and Alcoholism (NIAAA). Other external experts who contributed outside of these meetings include Steve Gribble, who was of great help in the initial design of the CDP-Alcohol model; Ben Baumberg, who helped in the analysis of the distribution of alcohol use; and Colin Angus, who provided advice on the design of the analysis of the impacts of brief interventions in primary care.

The OECD maintains a close partnership with the World Health Organization in its work on the prevention of non-communicable diseases, and we wish to acknowledge a continued, strong collaboration with Jeremy Lauer and Dan Chisholm in the evaluation of alcohol policies, as well as inputs from Vladimir Poznyak and Dag Rekve, including in the form of a Special Focus contribution in this book. We are also grateful to the authors of other Special Focus contributions, Henry Saffer, Anne Ludbrook, Marjana Martinic and Martin McKee for having agreed to share some of the results of their work to complement OECD's own findings.

We are especially grateful to the Business and Industry Advisory Committee to the OECD (BIAC), and particularly to Ali Karami Ruiz, for their efforts to convey in a constructive way multiple and sometimes conflicting inputs from different business stakeholders, despite the great pressures involved. We are also grateful to Alain Sommer, former Chair of BIAC's Task Force on Health Care Policy, for the valuable inputs provided from an employers' perspective.

The work was funded through regular contributions from OECD member countries and received partial support from two grants from the Directorate General for Health and Consumers of the European Commission. The contents of this book do not necessarily reflect the views of individual OECD member countries, or those of the European Commission.

# *Table of contents*

Tables



Figures

## Acronyms and abbreviations

| | |
|---|---|
| AAF | Alcohol-attributable fraction |
| ABV | Alcohol by volume |
| APC | Average per capita alcohol consumption |
| AUDIT | Alcohol Use Disorder Identification Test |
| BAC | Blood alcohol concentration |
| CDM | Chronic Disease Model |
| CDP | Chronic Disease Prevention |
| CI | Concentration index |
| CSEW | Crime Survey for England and Wales |
| CVD | Cardiovascular disease |
| DALY | Disability adjusted life year |
| DSM | Diagnostic and Statistical Manual of Mental Disorders |
| DUI | Driving under the influence |
| EAP | Employee assistance programme |
| GENACIS | Gender, Alcohol and Culture International Study |
| GISAH | Global Information System on Alcohol and Health |
| GSHS | Global School-based Student Health Survey |
| HED | Heavy episodic drinking |
| HILDA | Household, Income and Labour Dynamics in Australia |
| IARC | International Agency for Research on Cancer |
| ICD | International Statistical Classification of Diseases |
| IHD | Ischaemic heart disease |
| MUP | Minimum unit pricing |
| NCD | Non-communicable diseases |
| NHANES | National Health and Nutrition Examination Survey |
| NLSY | National Longitudinal Survey of Youth |
| NSDUH | National Survey of Drug Use and Health |
| PPP | Purchasing power parity |
| QALY | Quality adjusted life year |
| RBT | Random breath testing |
| RCT | Randomised controlled trials |
| SBT | Selective breath testing |

| | |
|---|---|
| SES | Socioeconomic status |
| SHARP | School Health and Alcohol Harm Reduction Project (Australia) |
| SIPS | Screening and Intervention Programme for Sensible drinking |
| VAT | Value added tax |
| WHO | World International Organization |
| WTO | World Trade Organization |

Tackling Harmful Alcohol Use
Economics and Public Health Policy
© OECD 2015

# Executive summary

Alcohol has been an element of human society since the Neolithic period at least, both cherished and vilified for reasons that have remained largely unchanged over time. What is drunk, how much is drunk, by whom and where have been strongly influenced by factors such as culture, economics and social norms.

In the period covered by OECD analyses, per-capita alcohol consumption in OECD countries has declined overall, but within this broad trend, some countries have seen an increase, some a decrease. However, many countries have experienced a significant increase in some risky drinking behaviours (such as binge drinking), particularly among young people and women. Emerging economies have also seen a major relative increase in alcohol consumption, albeit starting from lower levels.

These trends are worrying because some of the harms typically associated with heavy drinking in young age, such as traffic accidents and violence, often affect people other than drinkers themselves, representing an important component of the burden of disease related to alcohol. Heavy drinking at a young age is associated with an increased risk of acute and chronic conditions. It is also associated with problem drinking later on in life, and people who are successful in the labour market may see their long-term career prospects jeopardised.

Alcohol has an impact on over 200 diseases and types of injuries. In most cases the impact is detrimental, in some cases it is beneficial. In a minority of drinkers, mostly older men who drink lightly, health benefits are larger. At the population level, detrimental health effects overwhelmingly prevail in all countries worldwide. Harmful drinking is normally the result of an individual choice, but it has social consequences. The harms caused to people other than drinkers themselves, including the victims of traffic accidents and violence, but also children born with foetal alcohol spectrum disorders, are the most visible face of those social consequences. Health care and crime costs, and lost productivity, are further important dimensions. These provide a strong rationale for governments to take action against harmful alcohol use. The public health consequences of harmful drinking are a major concern, as alcohol ranks among the leading causes of death and disability worldwide. According to OECD estimates, approximately four in five drinkers would reduce their risk of death from any causes if they cut their alcohol intake by one unit per week. There is hence wide scope for improving the welfare of drinkers and society as a whole. Evidence of the magnitude of the risks associated with harmful alcohol use, and of the effectiveness of many policy options to address those harms, has never been so abundant and detailed as it is today.

A wide range of policies to address harmful use of alcohol are available, some targeting heavy drinkers alone, others more broadly based. Selecting an appropriate mix of policies in any given context requires political judgements that individual governments are best placed to make, taking into account the social, cultural and epidemiological characteristics of their respective countries. However, economic analysis based on computer simulations of policy scenarios can help governments compare the health impacts and economic value of different interventions, providing a useful tool to support government decision making. The WHO Global Strategy to reduce the harmful use of alcohol, endorsed by the World Health Assembly in 2010, provides a menu of policy options based on international consensus, which OECD used as a starting point to identify a set of policies to be assessed in an economic analysis. The inclusion or exclusion of policies in the analysis does not imply, *per se*, endorsement or rejection of specific options.

Based on a simulation model, OECD analyses show that several alcohol policies have the potential to reduce rates of heavy drinking, regular or episodic, and alcohol dependence, in three countries, by 5% to 10%. This would take those countries a long way towards achieving the voluntary target of reducing harmful alcohol use by 10% by 2025, a target adopted by the World Health Assembly in 2013 as part of the NCD Global Monitoring Framework. The OECD analysis found that governments' ability to design and implement wide-ranging prevention strategies, combining the strengths of different policy approaches, is critical to success. These may include initiatives promoted by the alcohol industry, although more independent evidence of the impacts of such actions is needed.

Simulation models like the one used in OECD analyses have many strengths. They can provide evidence in areas in which direct empirical investigation may be difficult or impossible. However, they also require assumptions and have to rely on a variety of input data, some of which may be of limited quality. Models can always be improved by refining such assumptions and input data.

## Key findings

- Average annual consumption in OECD countries is the equivalent of 9.1 litres of pure alcohol per capita (down by 2.5%, on average, during the past 20 years).
- Close to 11% of all alcohol consumption is estimated to go unrecorded in OECD countries. Adding this to recorded consumption brings the total to 10.3 litres per capita, substantially larger than the world average of 6.2 litres.
- The majority of alcohol is drunk by the heaviest-drinking 20% of the population in the countries examined.
- Rates of hazardous drinking (a weekly amount of pure alcohol of 140 grams or more for women, and 210 grams or more for men) and heavy episodic drinking ("binge drinking", defined as five to eight drinks in one session depending on the country) in young people, especially women, have increased in many OECD countries.
- The proportion of children aged 15 and under who have not yet drunk alcohol shrank from 44% to 30% of boys and from 50% to 31% of girls during the 2000s. The proportion of children who have experienced drunkenness increased from 30% to 43% (boys) and from 26% to 41% (girls) in the same period.
- People with more education and higher socioeconomic status (SES) are more likely to drink alcohol. Less educated and lower SES men, as well as more educated and higher SES women, are more likely to indulge in risky drinking.
- In general, people from minority ethnic groups drink less alcohol than the majority of the population, but with important exceptions in some countries.

 

- While the impact of heavy drinking on labour outcomes is consistently negative, there is some evidence that moderate drinking may have a positive impact, especially on wages. Existing estimates suggest that productivity losses associated with harmful alcohol use are in the region of 1% of GDP in most countries.
- Alcohol influences the development of a host of diseases and injuries. Harmful consumption of alcohol rose from eighth to fifth leading cause of death and disability, worldwide, between 1990 and 2010.
- If offered systematically in primary care settings, alcohol brief interventions have the potential to generate large health and life expectancy gains in the three countries studied in an economic analysis based on a computer simulation approach in this report (Canada, the Czech Republic and Germany).
- A tax hike leading to an average increase of 10% in alcohol prices, as well as a range of regulatory approaches, would also generate large impacts.
- Combining alcohol policies in a coherent prevention strategy would significantly increase impacts, helping to reach a "critical mass" with greater impact on the social norms that drive harmful drinking behaviours.
- As measured in disability adjusted life years (DALYs, the number of years lost due to ill-health, disability or early death) a package of fiscal and regulatory measures, one of health care interventions, and a mixed strategy would each achieve gains of around 37 000 DALYs per year in Canada; 23-29 000 DALYs in the Czech Republic, and 119-137 000 DALYs in Germany, roughly corresponding to 10% of the burden of disease associated with harmful alcohol use estimated in the three countries in 2010.
- Alcohol strategies combining multiple policies would yield yearly savings in health expenditures of up to USD PPP 4, 8 and 6 per person, respectively, in the three countries.
- Policies delivered in health care settings are the most expensive to implement in the three countries, followed by the enforcement of drink-drive restrictions and workplace programmes. Price and regulatory policies are substantially less expensive.
- Even the most expensive alcohol policies have very favourable cost-effectiveness profiles in health terms, in the three countries.
- Although alcohol policy should target heavy drinkers first, there are few approaches available to do this. Primary care physicians may play an important role in addressing heavy drinking, while police enforcement of existing regulations against drinking-and-driving is key to cutting traffic casualties.
- However, broader policy approaches may be required to complement those solely aimed at heavy drinkers. Raising alcohol prices can improve population health, and doing so in the cheaper segment of the market may be more effective in tackling harmful drinking. Regulating the promotion of alcoholic beverages may provide additional benefits.
- An open dialogue and co-operation with alcohol manufacturers, as well as major retailers and other related industries, may be, and has already been in some countries, part of an effective policy approach in fighting the harms associated with alcohol consumption.
- Surveys of alcohol consumption are key instruments in the design of sound alcohol policies. Countries and their statistical and public health agencies must step up their efforts to improve the consistency and accuracy of such surveys.

Tackling Harmful Alcohol Use
Economics and Public Health Policy


# Chapter 1

# Alcohol: The public health side of a social phenomenon

by
Franco Sassi and Patrick Love

*Alcohol has been present throughout the history of humankind, both cherished and vilified for reasons that have remained largely unchanged over time. Both health benefits and harms are associated with alcohol use, but the underlying evidence of these effects is rarely presented in a policy-relevant way. If appropriately set out, the evidence shows that the health benefits of moderate alcohol use warrant full consideration in the policy process, but they do not weaken the case for addressing harmful use, including when governments opt for policies that affect more people than just the heaviest drinkers. Alcohol use is associated with social welfare benefits for some drinkers, but also with significant welfare losses for other heavier drinkers and many non-drinkers. Alcohol policy is a public health area in which government action has a strong economic justification, primarily because of harms to people other than drinkers, and because of the addictive effects of alcohol. This chapter provides an overview of some of the main findings of OECD analyses presented in the remainder of the book, looking at economic determinants of, and explanations for, alcohol consumption, as well as at some of the cultural, social and psychological dimensions of its use.*

## Key findings

- Alcohol use has both beneficial and detrimental effects on the health of individual drinkers. At the population level, the latter outweigh the former in all countries.
- The risk of death for young male adults and young and middle-aged women increases steadily with alcohol consumption, with no beneficial effects overall, but with relatively low risk from moderate drinking.
- Approximately four in five drinkers would reduce their risk of death from any causes if they cut their alcohol intake by one unit (10 grams) per week.
- Measures of the health benefits and harms associated with alcohol use may need to be designed and communicated differently depending on the audience and purpose they serve (e.g. formulation of drinking guidelines for individual consumers vs. policy support).
- Life years potentially gained, quality of life and individual preferences over the timing of outcomes are important elements in the analysis of policy options.
- Alcohol policies have to balance welfare benefits and losses. Harms to people other than drinkers are more effectively reduced by tackling heavy drinking. Price and regulation policies are more likely to affect consumer welfare.
- Harms to others, addiction, and consumers' inaccurate perception of risk provide strong justification for government action in addressing the problem of harmful alcohol use.

## Alcohol, a common fixture in human societies

Tales of birds and small mammals getting drunk on fermented fruit suggest that alcoholic drinks were probably discovered rather than invented. But archaeological evidence shows that by the Neolithic period, about 10 000 years ago, alcohol was already being brewed deliberately. It is even argued that the Neolithic Revolution, the transition from a hunter-gatherer society to agriculture, was the result of Stone Age societies' efforts to ensure a steady supply of grain to make alcoholic drinks (McGovern, 2010). Beer would have been too complicated to make from cereals at this stage, so the first drinks were probably mixtures of fruit wine and mead (a drink made from fermented honey). Apart from getting the drinkers drunk, this high-sugar content beverage was probably quite nutritious too, and may have helped groups to survive since it could be stored for relatively long periods. The drinks may also have had medicinal uses as well. McGovern (2010) discovered that a drink made in Iran included resin that may have had antibiotic properties.

By the time written records were established, alcohol had probably become part of daily life across the planet. The Old Testament says that the one of first things Noah did on reaching dry land after the Flood was to plant a vineyard. The Egyptian god Osiris was also the god of wine, and other civilisations, including the Babylonians, had similar deities. Indirect evidence suggests that alcohol was present in cultures that left no written record as well, such as those of the pre-Columbian Andes (Pierce and Toxqui, 2014).

With the written record come the first tales of excess drinking. Early societies do not seem to have condemned inebriation as such, but the authorities then, as now, were concerned by excess drinking and activities such as prostitution associated with drinking places (Hanson, 1995). It's hard to tell how much of a problem drunkenness was. Exceptional behaviour, especially if it is bad, has always been more likely to be noted, and probably more so when writing materials were scarce. That said, Hanson mentions over 40 attempts by the Chinese Government to ban alcohol over the period from 1100 BCE to 1400 CE. They all failed. As one commentator he quotes said, "To prohibit it and secure total abstinence from it is beyond the power even of sages. Hence we have warnings on the abuse of it" (Hanson, 1995).

Greek writers, including Plato, criticised drunkenness, but again, this may have been due to the social behaviours and lack of self-control associated with drinking rather than a condemnation of inebriety as such. Drinking a bit too much was common at the *symposion*, an evening of drink and talk for the upper classes that gave us the word "symposium", and in fact the Dionysian cult encouraged excess. However Bacchanalia, the Roman equivalent, were eventually banned after the more traditional Roman virtues of frugality and temperance became undermined by excessive drinking as the Empire spread. Even so, alcohol continued to have a spiritual role, one that Christianity eventually inherited from the Dionysian and other cults (Nancy, 2013).

Alcohol also has a number of symbolic roles on a more mundane level. For instance, in many countries Champagne or other sparkling wines signal that something is being celebrated, and if not, that the drinker belongs to a wealthy social class. At the other end of the spectrum, the term "wino" refers to someone who drinks cheap wine to get drunk. In general, "foreign" drinks have a higher social status than local ones, at least when they are first introduced. Likewise, certain drinks, and drinking behaviours, are seen as "masculine", others as "feminine" (SIRC, 1998).

There are geographical differences in what is consumed too, that can be traced back to the fall of the Roman Empire, even if these differences are less marked now than they used to be. Wine continued to dominate in what are now France, Spain, and Italy, but farther north, various kinds of beer and mead became increasingly popular during the Middle Ages, the period dating roughly from the fall of Rome to the Renaissance. Wine acquired a more pragmatic association with religion since it was the monasteries that preserved viticulture and the secrets of making good quality wines (Million, 2013). Incidentally, the story that sparkling champagne was invented by the French Benedictine monk Dom Pérignon is a myth created by one of his successors, but the monk did make important contributions to improving the quality of wines from the Champagne region at the end of the 17$^{th}$ century. As towns began to grow in importance, so too did the brewing of beers for more than immediate household consumption, but arguably the most significant development during the Middle Ages was distillation.

It's impossible to say when the discovery was made, but there is evidence of distillation at the Salerno medical school in Italy in the 12$^{th}$ century, and possibly in China at roughly the same time (Forbes, 1970; Hamel, 2014). Irish whiskey and German brandy both appeared about this time as well. Distilled alcohols were initially seen as medical products and their consumption expanded significantly in the mid-14th century to ward off the Black Death. By the end of the century, ways to distil spirits from a number of feedstocks were developed, leading to the development of drinks we now associate with particular countries or regions, such as whisk(e)y (Scotland, Ireland) or vodka (Russian Federation), even though they may be manufactured and consumed worldwide.

Other sprits were far more international from the start, with all the advantages and problems that go with globalisation. In a 1726 pamphlet setting out "A brief case of the distillers", Daniel Defoe, author of *Robinson Crusoe*, wrote that: "The distilling trade, considered in its present magnitude, is one of the greatest improvements, and the most to the advantage of the publick, of any business now carried out in England". Defoe was writing to defend English producers of spirits, who were facing Dutch competition, especially from the newly fashionable "Geneva water", soon to be known as gin. Over the next 25 years, Parliament would pass no fewer than five Acts to try to put an end to what became known as the Gin Craze (Abel, 2001). The craze died out in the 1750s, although it was revived to some extent in the Victorian gin palaces of the following century. This illustrates a number of recurrent themes in alcohol policy, discussed elsewhere in this book, and illustrates how the trends described in the following chapter can change relatively quickly – dominant beverages, hazardous drinking and other consumption patterns, and drinking by various social groups – partly as an effect of government policy.

Defoe's century still had what we would now term a fairly lax attitude to drunkenness. But that would change with industrialisation during the 19th century and the need for a more disciplined workforce in the factories. Change was slow though, and at the outbreak of the First World War the UK Government introduced laws allowing pubs to be open for only six hours a day. In Australia and New Zealand, the change was even more drastic, with pubs being forced to close at six in the evening, meaning that many men would rush to drink as much as they could when they left work at five, making the problem of drunkenness even worse (Grundy, 2010).

The Australian and New Zealand "six o'clock swill" at the pub is an example of a phenomenon that the speakeasies that sprang up in the United States during Prohibition (1920-1933) also illustrate. As the Social Issues Research Centre report cited above notes, "where there is alcohol, there is almost always a dedicated environment in which to drink it" (SIRC, 1998). And the place where drinking is done usually represents "a special environment (...) a discrete social world with its own laws, customs and values (...) in which status distinctions are based on different criteria from those operating in the outside world." That may still be largely true, as might the broad division of drinking places into, on the one hand, highly visible and open spaces in countries where alcohol is a morally neutral part of everyday, and, on the other hand, enclosed, secretive environments in societies where drinking is a moral issue. However, that is changing in important ways, with the rise of alcohol consumption at home using drinks bought at a supermarket and more public drinking in societies where it was previously not accepted. The latter can also be excessive, as lurid media reports of drunken, binge-drinking youth testify (Hope, 2009).

## Harmful use of alcohol: The size of the problem

An average adult in an OECD country consumes 9.1 litres of pure alcohol a year. Austria, Estonia and France reported the highest consumption of alcohol, with 12.0 litres or more per adult per year in 2012. Low alcohol consumption was recorded in Israel and Turkey.

Although average alcohol consumption has gradually fallen in many OECD countries over the past two decades, it has risen in several northern European countries (Finland, Iceland, Norway and Sweden) as well as in Israel and Poland. Alcohol consumption in the Russian Federation, as well as in Brazil, India, and China has risen substantially, although in the latter two countries per capita consumption is still low.

The amount of alcohol consumed is only one factor determining whether drinking may cause harm or not. A given amount will probably not have the same effect depending on whether it is consumed in one night or over a number of weeks, alone or at party, with a meal or on an empty stomach. This is what is meant by "pattern of drinking". The pattern of drinking is particularly important because of its relationship with the development of acute effects of alcohol, including injuries and intoxication and other alcohol use disorders. In addition, harmful patterns of drinking cancel out the positive effects of moderate alcohol intake on the incidence of, and mortality from, cardiovascular disease (Roerecke and Rehm, 2014).

Despite the difficulties in data definitions and analysis, the evidence suggests that the distribution of alcohol drinking in a population tends to be heavily concentrated. In virtually all of the countries examined in the analyses presented in Chapter 2, the majority of alcohol is drunk by the heaviest-drinking 20% of the population (see Figure 2.4). Most countries show relatively stable trends of hazardous drinking, although declines were observed in Ireland and Germany, where rates were originally high. Most countries present relatively low rates of heavy episodic drinking (HED) among women. In seven out of nine countries, less than 8% of female drinkers report HED at least once per week, this rate being especially low in France and Switzerland. Rates were broadly constant or slightly increasing over time since the early 1990s, but with noticeable drops in England and in Ireland, where HED rates are highest for both men and women, and a lesser decrease in Germany.

To some extent, differences across countries are diminishing. Although HED was traditionally more common in northern Europe, drinking habits are becoming more homogeneous across European countries.

Binge drinking, i.e. drinking large quantities of alcohol in a single session, is the most visible face of harmful use of alcohol, but as the special contribution from the WHO in this publication points out (see Special Focus I), alcohol influences the development of over 200 disease and injury conditions. Harmful consumption of alcohol rose from eighth to fifth leading cause of death and disability in the world between 1990 and 2010, and is now responsible for a greater proportion of deaths worldwide than HIV/AIDS, violence and tuberculosis together (WHO, 2014).

## Protective and harmful effects: A public health perspective

Years of epidemiological research have led to the unequivocal conclusion that alcohol use has both beneficial and detrimental effects on health. Benefits derive, for some people, from a regularly moderate use of alcohol, in the form of a reduced incidence of, and mortality from, some chronic conditions, mostly cardio-circulatory (Poli et al., 2013). Harms to health derive from an increased incidence of a host of acute and chronic conditions and injuries, following any type of alcohol use but increasing sharply with heavy drinking, regular or episodic (WHO, 2014). The causal nature of most of the above links has been firmly established. A working group convened by the International Agency for Research on Cancer (IARC) in 2007 established that alcoholic beverages are "carcinogenic to humans" (group 1, i.e. "definitely" carcinogenic) (Baan et al., 2007). Beneficial effects prevail in some people, detrimental effects prevail in others. Global burden of disease studies have shown that detrimental effects vastly exceed beneficial effects at the population level, in all countries worldwide (Lim et al., 2012; WHO, 2014).

Translating research findings on the health effects of alcohol use into messages for the general public is a major challenge. Both benefits and harms of alcohol use are linked with conditions that are more likely to develop in certain people than in others, depending on their age, ethnicity, socioeconomic status, and other risk factors. A report on alcohol guidelines by the UK Parliamentary Committee on Science and Technology states that "an inherent difficulty of developing generic guidelines for the public on sensible drinking is the loss of recognition of individual risk factors" (House of Commons, 2011). Communicating the beneficial effects of alcohol use is especially challenging, as acknowledged in some of the main epidemiological studies: "disclosure to the lay public of the available notions between moderate alcohol use and health is debated and calls for caution" (Poli et al., 2013), one reason for caution being "the potential for problem drinking even among individuals at apparently low risk" (O'Keefe et al., 2014). Partly as a result of the above difficulties, existing national guidelines often leave much to be desired in terms of clarity and consistency, as further discussed in Chapter 2. This means that most people remain unaware of what constitutes "low-risk" drinking, or precisely what risks they incur when drinking alcohol (e.g. ONS, 2010), which likely makes them more prone to the influence of messages conveyed by the popular media and commercial advertising.

The challenges involved in crafting a simple and balanced message on the health effects of alcohol use apply also in the synthesis of research findings for policy making, which is the main purpose of this book. The messages that may be relevant in a policy perspective are at least partly different from those aimed at the general public. Policy makers are concerned with a population perspective. They need to know about the distribution of alcohol use in the population and how this relates to possible benefits and harms to health, as a basis for assessing the effects of policies that would change the current distribution of drinking. Policies are assessed not just for their effectiveness in curbing harmful alcohol use, but also for their economic and political viability. In order to support such assessments, certain dimensions of the problem have to be brought to the surface which are not always discussed in the debate on the epidemiology of alcohol and health, including, in particular, the size of the loss of life and health expectancy following the development of alcohol-related conditions and deaths attributable to alcohol, as well as people's preferences for different distributions of health outcomes over time. The impacts of these elements are examined further below in this section.

The most popular summary of the links between alcohol use and health is a classical diagram showing the curvilinear relationship between levels of drinking and risk of death (from all causes) relative to the risk incurred by abstainers. This curve is "j-shaped", meaning that the risk of death is reduced in low to moderate drinkers, compared with abstainers, and increased in heavier drinkers. Many caveats are required for a correct interpretation of the evidence underlying the j-curve – e.g. some abstainers may choose not to drink because their health is impaired or at risk for other reasons, which may inflate the correlation between abstention and death; some studies do not properly account for potential confounding factors, such as socioeconomic status; some age groups, notably younger people, are often under-represented or not represented at all in primary studies; and, all studies rely on self-reported measures of alcohol consumption, which may affect the shape of the j-curve. However, the j-shape itself is largely undisputed so far, as shown in studies that have assessed the sensitivity of the curve to at least some of the factors that may affect its shape (Gmel et al., 2003; Di Castelnuovo et al., 2006).

From an epidemiological perspective, the latest challenge to the j-curve comes from recent studies using genetic profiles associated with different drinking (or abstention) behaviours to disentangle the possible causal effects of alcohol use on health, an approach called "Mendelian randomisation". These studies have so far failed to identify a link between light or moderate alcohol use and improved cardiovascular outcomes, casting doubt on the benefits of moderate drinking (Chikritzhs et al., 2014) and suggesting the conclusion that "reduction of alcohol consumption, even for light to moderate drinkers, is beneficial for cardiovascular health" (Holmes et al., 2014). Future research will have to confirm the extent to which these new findings may override the evidence upon which the j-curve rests.

From a policy perspective, the main limitation of the j-curve, at least in its most popular formulations, is the focus on drinkers' death rates, which are important outcomes for health policy makers but not the only, and probably not the most important, ones.

### A death is a death is a death?

Deaths attributed to alcohol, and those spared by alcohol, are associated with very diverse causes, from cancer to injuries, from cardiovascular to liver disease. Deaths from different causes typically occur at different ages and involve different losses of life expectancy. The j-curve balances out a reduced risk of death from cardiovascular conditions with an increased risk of death from injuries, cancer, and other conditions. The implicit underlying rationale is that "a death is a death is a death", i.e. a death prevented from cardiovascular disease has the same value as one occurred as a consequence of, say, a traffic accident. In fact, the loss of life expectancy involved may be very different. The latest WHO estimates of the global burden of disease indicate that, worldwide, a death from ischemic heart disease is associated with an average loss of 24 years of life, while a death from unintentional injuries is associated with a loss of 51 years and a death from alcohol use disorders with a loss of 39 years (WHO Global Health Estimates, 2012[1]).

If the j-curve were to be redrawn on the basis of life expectancy, instead of death, the curve would still appear j-shaped, but the protective effects of alcohol would be reduced. This is because certain levels of alcohol consumption are associated in the j-curve with a lower risk of death, on average, but also with a shorter life expectancy relative to abstention.

### What health impacts at different ages?

J-curves are rarely presented for specific age groups. The best studies of the relationship between alcohol use and risk of death provide estimates that account for age differences among the people observed in the studies (e.g. see Di Castelnuovo et al., 2006), but this is not sufficient to identify how the relationship varies for people in different age groups. In fact, the j-curve is an average across several variously shaped curves reflecting different relationships between alcohol use and risk of death at different ages. According to a study that does provide a detailed breakdown of that relationship by age group, the curves for young men (up to age 35) and for young and middle-aged women (up to age 55) are not j-shaped, but steadily increasing (White et al., 2002). In these groups, less prone to cardiovascular risk and more prone to injuries, e.g. from traffic accidents and violence, and alcohol use disorders (especially men), the detrimental effects of alcohol prevail at any level of drinking, even when focusing purely on risk of death. The typical j-shape appears gradually in older age groups, as cardiovascular risk increases in men and women, and the beneficial effects of alcohol use become more significant.

The classical j-curve does not convey the important and policy-relevant message that children and young adults, as well as middle-aged women, are exposed to health risks at any level of alcohol consumption, with a larger potential loss of life expectancy and risk to cause harm to others than other groups. Based on the relative risks calculated by White et al. (2002) for England and Wales, young men drinking an average of one unit a day would be exposed, each year, to an extra risk of death of approximately 3.5 in 100 000, compared with abstainers, while young and middle-aged women would be exposed to an extra risk of up to 5 in 100 000 (at age 50). The latter is equivalent to the average risk of death in a road accident in the general population in the United Kingdom. For an average consumption of two units a day, risks would increase to 9 in 100 000 in 30-year-old men, and 15 in 100 000 in 50-year-old women.

However, young people are also the ones who feel most strongly that protection from alcohol-related harms is a matter of individual responsibility, according to a recent Eurobarometer survey (61% among 15- to 24-year-olds; 55% among 25- to 39-year-olds), although a large majority of them support specific policy options such as enforcement of drink-driving regulations; bans on underage alcohol sales; banning of alcohol advertising targeting young people; and warning labels on bottles (Eurobarometer, 2010).

Looking at the age-specific health impacts of alcohol consumption makes it easier to assess what proportion of drinkers would benefit from cutting their own drinking levels. A small proportion of drinkers drink most alcohol in OECD countries, as shown in Figure 2.4. However, a vast majority of drinkers would benefit from a reduction in their consumption. In the three countries on which we carried out detailed analyses of policy impacts – Canada, the Czech Republic and Germany – we calculate that between 78% and 83% of drinkers would reduce their risk of death from all causes if they gave up one unit of alcohol (10 grams) per week, based on levels of consumption reported in national surveys (see Table A.1 in Annex A) and age-specific risks calculated by White et al. (2002). Fewer would benefit if they were to quit alcohol altogether. However, an even larger proportion would benefit over their lifetimes, as for some the life expectancy gained by reducing risk in young age will offset any losses from reduced drinking in older age. This is without considering heavy episodic drinking, not accounted for in the j-curve (including in White et al., 2002) and practiced by a significant proportion of people classified as low-to-moderate drinkers based on their average consumption. When heavy episodic drinking occurs, the beneficial effects of alcohol consumption vanish (Roerecke and Rehm, 2014).

### *Drinkers harming others*

In addition to the deaths and years of life lost by drinkers themselves, drinking is also a cause of adverse health outcomes for non-drinkers, which are not typically accounted for in drawing a j-curve. A comprehensive study estimated the risk of death for non-drinkers, as a result of someone else's drinking, to be slightly below 2 per 100 000 in the Australian population in 2005, but with 70 in 100 000 people being hospitalised the same year to treat the consequences of injuries and violence perpetrated by drinkers (Laslett et al., 2010). Especially if assessing the impacts of drinking on health based on life expectancy, the harms described here do have the potential to change the shape of the j-curve, albeit mostly (but not exclusively) at higher levels of drinking, more often associated with injuries and violence.

### *Quality of life matters too*

Health policy makers have become accustomed to assessing the health impacts of policy options based on multidimensional measures reflecting length and quality of life. The most popular examples of such measures are the quality adjusted life year (QALY) and the disability adjusted life year (DALY), the former most often used in cost-effectiveness analyses of health programmes, the latter in burden-of-disease studies. When assessing the potential health gains from alcohol policies, policy makers may wish to know that not only the numbers of years of life lost, but also the quality of those years of life, may be very different for deaths occurring at different ages and due to different causes. A life cut short by a traffic accident at a young age involves the sacrifice (and, conversely, a gain when the death is prevented) of a larger number of life years, lived at a higher level of quality of life, on average, than the fewer years that would be lost following a death from ischemic heart disease.

Perhaps even more importantly, omitting the quality of life or disability dimension of the impacts of alcohol use means neglecting major disease outcomes, such as neuropsychiatric disorders (mostly alcohol-use disorders) which account for 25% of the global burden of disease, but only 4% of deaths, attributable to alcohol worldwide (WHO, 2014).

If a quality of life (or disability) dimension were taken into account in assessing the health impacts of alcohol consumption, this would likely increase the magnitude of the health hazards associated with alcohol use and reduce the scope of the beneficial health impacts.

In their original formulation, DALYs involved the weighting of years of life lost (or gained) at different ages (the so-called "age weighting"), in addition to the weighting for levels of disability (Lopez et al., 2006). Age weighting, which is rarely applied nowadays, was not meant to reflect quality of life dimensions, but mostly "social preferences", leading to a higher value being assigned to years of life lived by young adults, who tend to be actively engaged in economic production and have responsibilities for dependents, among other things. The application of age weighting further increases the burden of disease associated with alcohol, as shown in early global burden of disease estimates produced by WHO (in the standard version of which age weighting used to be applied), due to the typical age distribution of the beneficial and the detrimental health effects of alcohol use, with a significant proportion of health hams concentrated in young adulthood.

### *Accounting for people's time preferences*

People are not indifferent to the timing of the rewards they expect to enjoy, or the losses they expect to suffer. They generally attach a greater absolute value to rewards and losses occurring at the present time relative to those expected in the future. Therefore, they wish to delay any losses, or undesirable outcomes, and they wish to bring forward any rewards, or desirable outcomes. Policy makers typically account for people's time preferences in their appraisals of alternative health policy options by "discounting" future costs and health benefits according to established procedures (Lipscomb et al., 1996). As a result, health impacts that occur with a certain delay, relative to the time when people drink alcohol or the time when policies are implemented, will be valued proportionately less than immediate health outcomes. Cancers attributable to alcohol, for instance, tend to occur with a delay of several years. This is true, albeit to a lesser degree, also for cardiovascular outcomes, while injury and alcohol-use disorder outcomes are more immediate. If these outcomes are discounted according to the time frame in which they are expected to occur, this will affect the j-curve, with a likely reduction of the size of beneficial effects.

## A social welfare perspective on alcohol policy

Alcoholic beverages are a source of pleasure and social enjoyment for many, but they are also a source of welfare losses in connection with the detrimental health, social, and economic effects of their harmful use. The goal of alcohol policies should be to reduce welfare losses to a minimum and preserve people's freedom to consume alcoholic beverages when these are indeed a source of pleasure, provided no harms are caused to others as a result, and provided that drinkers are able to make a fully informed choice, based on a complete knowledge of the consequences of drinking alcohol.

The welfare impacts of alcohol have been estimated in a number of studies that provide a monetary quantification of the costs associated with alcohol in several countries. At least two reviews of such studies are available. One review shows a large degree of heterogeneity in definitions and methods used in different studies (Thavorncharoensap et al., 2009). A second review focused on a selection of studies adopting more comparable methodological approaches, providing estimates of gross economic costs, such as medical and crime costs (only those associated with the negative consequences of alcohol consumption) for middle- and high-income countries ranging from 1.4% to 3.3% of GDP (Rehm et al., 2009). In the same review, costs associated with production losses caused by workers' harmful alcohol use accounted for a large share of total costs, ranging from 50% in Canada to 95% in Thailand. The cost of alcohol dependence alone, in the European Union, was estimated at 0.65% of GDP (Laramée et al., 2013). Importantly, however, these studies did not account for the monetary value of lives lost and pain and suffering experienced as a consequence of alcohol-related diseases and injuries.

Few studies assessed the costs of alcohol net of any offsets that may derive from beneficial health effects, in countries such as Australia, Germany and Sweden (Collins and Lapsley, 2008; Konnopka and König, 2007; Jarl et al., 2008). These studies show that the value of cost offsets is up to 20% of gross social costs.

A further dimension of the economic impact of alcohol is the contribution of the industry to national economies. This has been estimated in a number of studies, generally funded by the alcohol industry itself. In the United Kingdom, for instance, where alcoholic beverages account for 1.6% of consumer expenditure (OECD.Stat – Final consumption expenditure of households), the combined added value contribution of all sectors of the alcohol industry (beer, wine and spirits), including linked economic activities in upstream and downstream sectors, accounts for approximately 1.7% of GDP (Brink et al., 2011; Ernst & Young, 2013).

The results of above studies are important for policy makers to understand the types and magnitude of the consequences of harmful alcohol use. However, the rationale for government action in alcohol policy depends crucially on people's ability to make choices regarding their own consumption of alcohol that take into account their own and societal welfare. There are several reasons to believe that most people have difficulties in factoring these elements into their choices, as explained in the following sections. This provides a strong rationale for government action.

### *Individual choice and social impacts*

Drinking is an individual choice, but it has social impacts. Among the latter, for instance, are the effects of traffic accidents and acts of violence involving people other than drinkers themselves, but also the social spread of hazardous drinking behaviours through family and peer influences. This is what economists define as externalities, which arguably provide the strongest rationale for government intervention.

When externalities exist, consumers typically do not appreciate the full costs of their consumption, because the price they pay when they purchase a commodity does not reflect the external costs (or value) of its consumption. This means that consumption tends to be greater than socially desirable. In the case of alcoholic beverages, virtually all OECD countries apply excise taxes on alcohol, although some beverages are not taxed in some countries, and taxes are a classical economic instrument for ensuring that at least part of the external costs involved in the consumption (or production) of a commodity are reflected in its market price. However in the United States, alcohol taxes were estimated to be approximately USD 0.14 per drink in 2011 across different beverages, when the external costs of alcohol amounted to approximately USD 1.25 (Naimi, 2011).

As mentioned previously in this chapter, heavy alcohol use is associated with important harms to others, and the costs associated with those harms can be estimated, albeit with some uncertainty because the boundaries between "internal" and "external" costs are not always clear-cut. However, a recent review found that the costs associated with harms to others are generally underestimated (Navarro et al., 2011).

The main externalities associated with alcohol abuse are crime, violence and traffic accidents. Several studies have analysed the costs associated with those externalities. In Australia, the estimated tangible costs of alcohol-related crime for the year 2004-05 were AUD 1.24 billion. For the same year, alcohol-attributable road accident costs were AUD 3.1 billion, of which AUD 1.8 billion were human costs, AUD 821 million vehicle costs and AUD 497 million general costs (e.g. police, property, fire, etc.) (Collins and Lapsley, 2008). In the State of Washington, the estimated cost of crime attributable to alcohol (e.g. law enforcement costs, productivity losses for crime victims, other societal costs, etc.) amounted to USD 128.2 million in 2005, while the estimated costs of motor vehicle accidents were USD 70.7 million for the same year (Wickizer, 2013).

Estimates of drink-drive casualties in the United Kingdom show that there were 6 630 accidents involving 230 deaths and 1 200 serious injuries in 2012. The economic loss to society in connection with these was estimated to be GBP 1.5 billion, approximately 10% of the cost of all traffic accidents, including loss of output due to casualties, ambulance costs and hospital treatments, human costs of casualties (based on a willingness to pay approach), damage to vehicle and property, police costs and administrative costs of accident insurance. In the same year, among the motorcyclists and the vehicle drivers who died in traffic accidents, respectively 6% and 25% of them were found to be over the legal blood alcohol concentration limit (Department for Transport, 2013).

A review of existing European studies estimated the cost of crime and traffic accidents related to alcohol use for the European Union. The total cost of crime (police, courts and prisons, defensive and insurance and property damage) was on average EUR 33 billion (from a range of 23-57 billion) in 2003 and the cost related to traffic accidents caused by alcohol abuse was EUR 10 billion (6-16 billion) in the same year (Anderson and Baumberg 2006).

Alcohol abuse is a contributing factor in domestic violence, sexual assault and child abuse. In Australia, studies have shown that women whose partners are heavy alcohol users are more likely to be the victims of domestic violence (Marcus and Braaf, 2007). The total estimated cost of domestic violence in Australia was AUD 8.1 billion in 2002-03, of which half was borne directly by the victims (Australian Government's Office of the Status of Women, 2004). According to the 2011-12 Crime Survey for England and Wales (CSEW), one in two victims of violent incidents believed the offender to be under the influence of alcohol, and 40% of people over 16 years of age who had experienced serious sexual assault believed that their offenders were under the influence of alcohol. Among the victims, 32% reported being under the influence of alcohol at the time of the most recent incident of serious sexual assault. In England, the overall annual estimated cost of alcohol-related crime and anti-social behaviour was GBP 7.3 billion in 2004. For the same year, the overall annual estimated cost of productivity lost as a result of alcohol misuse was GBP 6.4 billion (Prime Minister's Strategy Unit, 2004).

### *Choice, information and risk perception*

In order to make rational and efficient choices, consumers have to be fully informed about the characteristics and quality of what they consume, about the benefits (utility) they will derive from consumption, and about the costs and risks they will be exposed to as a consequence of their consumption. Imperfect information by consumers on the effects of consumption is another classical market failure that applies to alcohol. Beyond a generic perception that drinking large quantities of alcohol is bad for one's health, consumers have a very imprecise knowledge of the exact modalities in which alcohol poses a risk to humans.

In their analysis of the determinants of higher smoking rates in Europe compared to the United States, Cutler and Glaeser (2005) concluded that popular beliefs were changed in the United States when "substantial information about the harms of smoking" was made available to the public, while the same information was communicated less effectively in Europe.

Awareness of the risks potentially associated with alcohol use is often poor and beliefs inaccurate. Information is not always conveyed effectively by governments or the media. Not all countries have drinking guidelines, and when guidelines are available, these are often poorly understood, especially by heavy drinkers (e.g. Cotter et al., 2013). Awareness of the links between cancer and alcohol use, in particular, remains limited in the general public (e.g. Eurobarometer, 2010; Buykx et al., 2014). The latest (2014) edition of the European Code Against Cancer, developed by IARC and the European Commission, indicates for the first time that no level of alcohol use is safe with respect to cancer risk.[2] Similarly, awareness of foetal alcohol spectrum disorder risks is limited among many pregnant women (Anderson et al., 2012; Dumas et al., 2014).

Understanding how risk increases with increasing quantities of alcohol consumed is even more challenging for the average drinker, as it is also challenging to understand what the extent of the beneficial effects of alcohol on health may be, what types and levels of drinking may be associated with those effects, and who the people who may benefit are.

### *Addiction and rational addiction*

Alcohol has addictive properties that produce dependence in certain consumers. Alcohol dependence represents an important share of the burden of disease attributable to alcohol. Economists have studied alcohol consumption as a "rational addiction" (Becker and Murphy, 1988), due to the strong correlation, or "adjacent complementarity", between present, past and future consumption. Economic theory holds that rational addictions are not incompatible with utility maximisation by consumers, and therefore with operating in a market context, however, there are several reasons for viewing the addictive nature of alcohol consumption as contributing to the justification for government intervention. First, any addiction to substances that are harmful (for consumers themselves and for others) is arguably a justification for external intervention. Moreover, economic theory suggests that rational addictions are compatible with utility maximisation only in the presence of perfect information, which is unlikely to be available to alcohol consumers (as discussed in the previous section). Finally, myopic (present-oriented) consumers are likely to display more strongly addictive consumption, as well as inconsistent time preferences (wanting to change their consumption, but constantly deferring).

Separate from addiction, poor self-control applies to a broad range of health-related behaviours, including alcohol. This relates to individual preferences that heavily penalise future outcomes in decisions that may have an impact on health, such as consuming alcohol, with the result that preferences become inconsistent over time and changes in behaviour, even when perceived as desirable in a long-term perspective, are constantly postponed (Sassi and Hurst, 2008).

## The book's main conclusions

Alcohol consumption is one of those issues on which most people have an opinion and some anecdotal evidence to support that opinion. However, the kinds of data and evidence that policy makers need to assess the importance of the issue and devise strategies to combat harmful alcohol use are often missing. And even when data are available, they often paint only a partial picture of the complexity of alcohol consumption by different groups. A basic figure such as per capita consumption is reassuringly objective, but deeper probing tends to reveal a number of shortcomings. The sales data on which it is based may not include all the sources from which consumers buy alcohol. Per capita consumption lumps together a range of behaviours from abstinence to seriously harmful drinking. Data collection has to be improved therefore – and this implies allocating sufficient means for resource-intensive operations such as personal surveys.

Despite the shortcomings in the data, it is clear that abuse of alcohol can harm the drinker's health, career and personal relationships, and cause harm to others as well, through anti-social and violent behaviour or traffic accidents for example. The drinkers themselves may not be able or willing to change, at least not without help, so there is a strong case for the government and public health authorities to intervene.

The difficulties in measuring consumption and its impacts compound the challenges involved in balancing the benefits and harms associated with alcohol use but more evidence of the impact of alcohol, and of the effectiveness of alcohol policies, is available today than ever before. This is contributing to a new momentum in addressing harmful alcohol use.

The rationale for government intervention to curb harmful alcohol use is strong, with a wide scope for improving the welfare of drinkers and society as a whole, and a wide range of policies available. Governments' ability to design and implement wide-ranging prevention strategies, combining the strengths of different policy approaches is critical to success, including initiatives promoted by the alcohol industry itself. This requires, however, drawing on objective and verified evidence.

### *Consumption trends*

Sensational stories and images in the media about binge drinking and drunkenness can give the impression that there is a growing health and social problem related to alcohol abuse. In reality, while harmful drinking has increased in many countries in certain groups, especially young people and women, average alcohol consumption in most OECD countries has not changed over the past two decades, standing at the equivalent of roughly nine litres of pure alcohol per adult per year, with an average decline of 2.5% in 20 years. Nevertheless, average consumption provides a poor and incomplete picture of trends and patterns of consumption in specific population groups which need to be examined more closely to help design and target alcohol policies.

The cultural and environmental influences linked with historical aspects of drinking still influence the varying social patterns of alcohol use in different countries. Wine, for instance, is traditionally consumed with meals in southern European wine-producing countries and is popular in rural areas, while farther to the north wine tends to be more urban and associated with modern lifestyles. Beer drinking is growing in popularity, however, especially among the young in traditional "wine-drinking" countries (Simpura and Karlsson, 2001). The social norms that determine when, where, and how much people drink still have national characteristics, even if there is some convergence among countries (SIRC, 1998).

Social disparities in alcohol consumption are in some respects similar to those we found for obesity (Sassi, 2010) but with one major difference. Men and women who are more educated or have higher socioeconomic status are less likely to be obese than others, but they are more likely to have drunk alcohol in the past 12 months, and in most of the countries examined more highly educated women were more likely to be indulge in hazardous drinking. However, the propensity to engage in hazardous drinking behaviours, like the likelihood of having other unhealthy lifestyle habits such as being obese or smoking is greater for less-educated men. Explanations range from access to, and understanding of, health information to time preferences (instant gratification versus longer-term harm) and intergenerational transmission of alcohol consumption habits.

People with higher socioeconomic status (SES) and higher incomes tend to consume more alcohol and more frequently than those who are less affluent partly because they are able to afford to drink more. Another explanation is that people of lower SES tend to be less healthy than their higher SES counterparts, and consume less alcohol because of health problems.

The reverse social gradient for women, in particular for hazardous drinking, may be due to the fact that women with higher education may have better-paid jobs involving higher degrees of responsibility and thus may drink more heavily because they have more stress as well as more chances to go out drinking with male colleagues with higher limits of drinking (Com-Ruelle et al., 2008). Alcohol use and abuse may also be more acceptable among women with high SES compared to those with low SES. More years spent in education, improved labour market prospects, increased opportunities for socialisation, delayed pregnancies and family ties, are all part of women's changing lifestyles, in which alcohol drinking, sometimes including heavy drinking, has easily found a place (Huerta and Borgonovi, 2010). It is also possible that some of the difference is simply due to how data are obtained, and women with higher education are less likely to under-estimate their alcohol consumption in surveys than those with lower education.

If being able to afford alcohol is part of the explanation of drinking habits, so is being able to find it. Making alcohol more available increases the chances that it will be bought. Evidence from Australia, New Zealand, and the United States suggests that there are more places to buy alcohol per square mile in more disadvantaged urban areas (Livingston, 2011;

 

Berke et al., 2010; Romley et al., 2007). High outlet densities are also associated with a higher rate of injuries, violence, car accidents, domestic violence and child abuse (Fone et al., 2012) as well as with non-injury health outcomes (Tatlow et al, 2000; Theall et al, 2009).

Ethnicity and genetics may play a role too. For example, some people of Asian origin tend to drink less since genetic predispositions may create unpleasant effects like facial flushing and other symptoms. These genetic factors may influence drinking patterns, and certain genes have protective effects on the risk of alcoholism (Edenberg, 2007). But the relationship between ethnicity and alcohol is not straightforward. Apart from genetics, the differences observed by ethnic group may be associated with strong ethnic identity, strong family and local community ties, continuing links with the country of origin and maintaining religious values for groups whose religion discourages or forbids drinking alcohol (Hurcombe et al., 2010). These influences can fade the longer a person stays in the host country. In the United States, for example, higher acculturation among Hispanics is associated with a greater risk of alcohol abuse as well as heavy episodic drinking in women (Chartier and Caetano, 2010).

One of the most striking findings about disparities in alcohol consumption concerns the age factor and trends observed in younger age groups that have important implications regarding public health and social well-being. The spread of high-risk drinking behaviours is associated with an increase in morbidity and mortality from accidents and injuries (the most common cause of death in adolescents and young adults) as well as violence and social disturbances. In Australia, the number of young women aged 18-24 being admitted to hospital because of alcohol misuse doubled between 1998 and 2006 (Livingston, 2008). In the United States, hospitalisations for alcohol overdoses increased by 25% among 18- to 24-year-olds between 1999 and 2008 and even more dramatically (by 76%) when alcohol use is combined with drugs (White et al., 2011). Early drinkers are more likely to develop dependence on alcohol at some point in their lives, and to have multiple and longer-lasting episodes of dependence (Hingson et al., 2006).

### *Policy responses*

A key question policy makers face, given that resources are limited, is whether they should take a broad-based approach and target the maximum number of people, even those at low risk, or concentrate on high-risk subject, or both. The traditional public health view is that the most effective strategy is the broad-based approach. But the fact that moderate drinking may confer some health benefits is given as a reason for calling this approach into question when dealing with alcohol-related risk, although there is uncertainty about the extent of the beneficial effects. The possibility that potential health benefits from moderate drinking might be forgone, if policies make moderate drinkers drink less alcohol, implies that any choice involves political judgements that only individual governments can make.

In general, while the goal of alcohol policies is to curb the harmful use of alcohol, prevention strategies tend to include population-wide actions affecting all drinkers, as well as actions designed to target heavy drinking alone. Traditional approaches to curb alcohol-related harms include information and education policies, as well as regulatory and fiscal options, traffic enforcement measures and interventions within the health care sector (particularly in primary health care and mental health care). Alcohol taxes are highest in northern European countries, Australia and United Kingdom, and lowest in southern and central European countries.

Recent years have also seen the introduction and testing of innovative approaches. Minimum prices, used in Canada and discussed in several European countries, may overcome some of the limitations of taxes – e.g. they are more effective in tackling heavy drinking – but the extra revenue goes to the seller, while the consumer suffers a welfare loss without government revenues to compensate for it.

There is a broad scope for improving the impact of regulatory actions on harmful alcohol use. Restrictions in alcohol advertising are increasingly challenged by the spread of advertising on the Internet and social media. Regulations to prevent driving under the influence of alcohol are in place in most countries, but are not always tightly enforced.

The OECD has assessed a set of policies from the WHO Global Strategy to Reduce the Harmful Use of Alcohol, using economic analysis based on a computer simulation approach. It examined price policies, regulation and enforcement policies, education programmes and health care interventions in Canada, the Czech Republic and Germany. The results show that policies to increase the prices of alcoholic drinks, regulation and enforcement policies, education programmes, and health care interventions are all effective and efficient means of curbing alcohol-related harms and improve population health, though to varying degrees.

The largest gains in health and life expectancy can be obtained through brief interventions in primary care, typically targeting high-risk drinkers, and tax increases leading to an average increase of 10% in alcohol prices, which affect all drinkers. Next for health impact are regulation and enforcement policies as well as health care treatment of alcohol dependence. School-based programmes show less promise.

Most alcohol policies are estimated to cut overall health care expenditures to the extent that their implementation costs would be more than offset. Health care interventions and enforcement of drink-drive restrictions are more expensive, but they still have very favourable cost-effectiveness profiles.

Combining alcohol policies in a coherent prevention strategy would significantly increase impacts, helping to reach a "critical mass" with greater impact on the social norms that drive drinking behaviours. OECD analyses conclude that a package of fiscal and regulatory measures, one of health care interventions, and a mixed strategy would each achieve gains of around 37 000 DALYs per year in Canada; 23-29 000 DALYs in the Czech Republic and 119-137 000 DALYs in Germany. Alcohol strategies combining multiple policies would yield yearly savings in health expenditures of up to USD PPPs 4, 8 and 6 per person per year, respectively, in the three countries. And hundreds of thousands of working-age people would avoid alcohol-related disabilities and injuries, with major potential gains for themselves in terms of their health well-being and for society in terms of reduced negative social impacts and positive economic outcomes such as increased productivity.

## Overview of the remaining chapters

Chapter 2 analyses trends in overall and hazardous forms of alcohol consumption in 13 OECD countries. Data are drawn from a number of sources, including individual-level health and lifestyle survey data, as well as aggregate national-level estimates of sales and "disappearance". The chapter provides a comparison of average alcohol consumption in OECD countries and major emerging economies and describes changes in alcohol consumption in the past 30 years as well as how alcohol is purchased in different countries. The chapter includes a detailed discussion of the challenges of measuring alcohol use.

 

A main message of the book is the importance of targeting at-risk individuals, so Chapter 2 reviews the key elements to understanding individual patterns of alcohol use, including how hazardous drinking is defined. It underlines again the importance of looking beyond average consumption figures, and shows that a few drinkers drink the most alcohol. This chapter also looks at young people's drinking behaviours and drinking patterns in different cohorts.

The data from the 13 countries examined in Chapter 2 are combined in Chapter 3 with evidence from previous studies undertaken in OECD countries to analyse differences in drinking patterns and behaviours across socioeconomic groups and between people with different levels of education. Apart from the social disparities mentioned above, Chapter 3 also looks at the impact of alcohol on various aspects of employment such as wages, productivity and workplace safety.

Chapter 4 reviews policy approaches to tackling alcohol-related harms. Governments have powerful incentives to intervene to change behaviours that are both socially and personally harmful but there is a lively debate about the strategic approach they should adopt. Is overall welfare increased more by a broad approach or by one that focuses on those at highest risk? If the welfare of moderate drinkers is reduced by campaigns, is this a price worth paying? Who responds most to different interventions? As well as looking at the different types of policy, the chapter considers the role of different stakeholders, notably the drinks industry, in reducing harmful use of alcohol.

Chapter 5 examines the health and economic impacts of key policy options for addressing alcohol misuse. The OECD developed a microsimulation model to assess the expected impacts of a full-scale implementation of a range of policy options in three OECD countries. How would these options affect mortality and life expectancy improvements, disease incidence and health expenditures, labour market outcomes and productivity? The findings contribute to the policy debate. For example, they suggest that using price policies and other tools to reduce alcohol consumption by less heavy drinkers, including many moderate drinkers, can generate health gains which may be small at the individual level, but become substantial at the population level given the large numbers of people concerned.

Finally, Chapter 6 calls for coherent policies in the face of such a complex issue as alcohol use and misuse. It argues that the deep cultural and economic roots of alcohol consumption, and the inextricable links of drinking behaviours with broader social norms, are such that individual measures will hardly make a dent in the harmful drinking problem on their own. Like other major public health issues in today's world, harmful alcohol use can only be addressed through society-wide efforts.

This book provides evidence of the value of a broad range of measures, potentially involving multiple stakeholders. This is reflected in the Special Focus contributions provided by specialists on their areas of expertise. The views expressed are those of the writers and do not necessarily reflect the positions on the OECD or its member governments. Their purpose is to enrich the debate by hearing what eminent experts have to say about: the health and social burden of harmful alcohol use; alcohol advertising and harmful drinking; how minimum pricing affects different types of drinkers; the business case for reducing alcohol-related harm in the workplace; and making good use of evidence in alcohol policy making.

## Notes

1. Available at: www.who.int/healthinfo/global_burden_disease/en/.
2. Available at: http://cancer-code-europe.iarc.fr/index.php/en/.

## Bibliography

Anderson, P. and B. Baumberg (2006), *Alcohol in Europe*, Institute of Alcohol Studies, London.

Anderson, A.E. et al. (2012), "Determinants of Pregnant Women's Compliance with Alcohol Guidelines: A Prospective Cohort Study", *BMC Public Health*, Vol.12, No. 777.

Australian Government's Office of the Status of Women (2004), "The Cost of Domestic Violence to the Australian Economy: Part 1", Commonwealth of Australia, Canberra.

Baan, R. et al. and WHO International Agency for Research on Cancer Monograph Working Group (2007), "Carcinogenicity of Alcoholic Beverages", The Lancet Oncology, Vol. 4, pp. 292-293.

Becker, G.S. and K.M. Murphy (1988), "A Theory of Rational Addiction", *Journal of Political Economy*, Vol. 96, No. 4, pp. 675-700.

Berke, E.M. et al. (2010), "Alcohol Retail Density and Demographic Predictors of Health Disparities: A Geographic Analysis", *American Journal of Public Health*, Vol. 100, No. 10, pp. 1967-1971.

Brink, M. et al. (2011), *The Contribution Made by Beer to the European Economy*, Report commissioned by the Brewers of Europe and conducted by Ernst & Young Tax Advisors and Regioplan Policy Research, Amsterdam, September

Buykx, P. et al. (2014), "Public Support for Alcohol Policies Associated with Knowledge of Cancer Risk", *International Journal of Drug Policy*, pii: S0955-3959(14)00220-5, 21 August.

Chartier, K. and R. Caetano (2010), "Ethnicity and Health Disparities in Alcohol Research", *Alcohol Research and Health*, Vol. 33, No. 1-2, pp. 152-160.

Chikritzhs, T.N. et al. (2014), "Mendelian Randomisation Meta-analysis Sheds Doubt on Protective Associations between 'Moderate' Alcohol Consumption and Coronary Heart Disease", *Evidence Based Medicine*, pii: ebmed-2014-110086, http://dx.doi.org/10.1136/ebmed-2014-110086 [Epub ahead of print].

Collins, D.J. and H.M. Lapsley (2008), "The Costs of Tobacco, Alcohol and Illicit Drug Abuse to Australian Society in 2004/05", Commonwealth of Australia, Canberra, available from http://www.nationaldrugstrategy.gov.au/internet/drugstrategy/publishing.nsf/Content/mono64/$File/mono64.pdf.

Com-Ruelle, L. et al. (2008), "Les problèmes d'alcool en France : quelles sont les populations à risque ?", *Question d'Économie de la Santé* No. 129, IRDES.

Cotter, T. et al. (2013), "Knowledge and Beliefs About Alcohol Consumption, Longer-term Health Risks, and the Link with Cancer in a Sample of Australian Adults", *NSW Public Health Bulletin*, Vol. 24, No. 2, pp. 81-86.

Cutler, D.M. and E. Glaeser (2005), "What Explains Differences In Smoking, Drinking, and Other Health-related Behaviors?", *American Economic Review*, Vol. 95, No. 2, pp. 238-242, May.

Department for Transport (2013), "The Reported Road Casualties in Great Britain (RRCGB) Annual Report".

Di Castelnuovo et al. (2006), "Alcohol Dosing and Total Mortality in Men and Women: An Updated Meta-analysis of 34 Prospective Studies", *Archives of Internal Medicine*, Vol. 166, No. 22, pp. 2437-2445.

Dumas, A., L. Simmat-Durand and C. Lejeune (2014), "Grossesse et usage de substances psychoactives en France. Synthèse de la littérature", *Journal de gynécologie, obstétrique et biologie de la reproduction*, pii:S0368-2315(14)00142-2.

Edenberg, H.J. (2007), "The Genetics of Alcohol Metabolism: Role of Alcohol Dehydrogenase and Aldehyde Dehydrogenase Variants", *Alcohol Research and Health*, Vol. 30, No. 1, pp. 5-13.

Ernst & Young (2013), "The Wine and Spirit Trade Association – Economic Impact Assessment", December.

Eurobarometer (2010), "EU Citizens' Attitudes Towards Alcohol", *Special Eurobarometer* 331, Wave 72.3 – TNS Opinion & Social, European Commission, Brussels.

Fone, D. et al. (2012), "Change In Alcohol Outlet Density and Alcohol-related Harm to Population Health (CHALICE)", *BMC Public Health*, Vol. 12, No. 428.

Forbes, R.J. (1970), *A Short History of the Art of Distillation: From the Beginnings Up to the Death of Cellier Blumenthal*, Brill, Leiden.

Gmel, G., E. Gutjahr and J. Rehm (2003), "How Stable Is the Risk Curve between Alcohol and All-cause Mortality and What Factors Influence the Shape? A Precision-weighted Hierarchical Meta-analysis", *European Journal of Epidemiology*, Vol. 18, No. 7, pp. 631-642.

Grundy, J. (2010), "'Lloyd George's Beer' or When It Was Illegal to Buy Your Round", The Western Front Association, retrieved 25 October 2014, www.westernfrontassociation.com/component/content/article/160-life-on-the-home-front/1591-lloyd-georges-beer-or-when-it-was-illegal-to-buy-your-round.html.

Hamel, G. (2014), *Alcohol in World History*, Routledge, Oxon.

Hanson, D.J. (1995), *Preventing Alcohol Abuse: Alcohol, Culture, and Control*, Praeger Publishers Westport, United States.

Hingson, R.W., T. Heeren and M.R. Winter (2006), "Age at Drinking Onset and Alcohol Dependence", *Archives of Pediatrics & Adolescent Medicine*, Vol. 160, pp. 739-746.

Holmes, M.V. et al. (2014), "Association Between Alcohol and Cardiovascular Disease: Mendelian Randomisation Analysis Based on Individual Participant Data", *British Medical Journal*, Vol. 10, pp. 349:g4164.

Hope, J. (2009), "British Teenagers Are the Binge-drinking Champions of Europe", *Daily Mail*, 26 March 2009.

House of Commons (2011), www.publications.parliament.uk/pa/cm201012/cmselect/cmsctech/1536/153602.htm.

Huerta, M.C. and F. Borgonovi (2010), "Education, Alcohol Use and Abuse among Young Adults in Britain", *Social Science & Medicine*, Vol. 71, No. 1, pp. 143-151.

Hurcombe, R., M. Bayley and A. Goodman (2010), "Ethnicity and Alcohol: A Review of the UK Literature", Joseph Rowntree Foundation Report.

Jarl, J. et al. (2008), "The Societal Cost of Alcohol Consumption: An Estimation of the Economic and Human Cost Including Health Effects in Sweden 2002", *European Journal of Health Economics*, Vol. 9, No. 4, pp. 351-360.

Konnopka, A. and H. König (2007), "Direct and Indirect Costs Attributable to Alcohol Consumption in Germany", *Pharmacoeconomics*, Vol. 25, No. 7, pp. 606-618.

Laramée, P. et al. (2013), "The Economic Burden of Alcohol Dependence in Europe", *Alcohol and Alcoholism*, Vol. 48, No. 3, pp. 259-269.

Laslett, A.-M. et al. (2010), "The Range and Magnitude of Alcohol's Harm to Others", AER Centre for Alcohol Policy Research, Turning Point Alcohol and Drug Centre, Eastern Health, Fitzroy, Victoria.

Lim, S.S. et al. (2012), "A Comparative Risk Assessment of Burden of Disease and Injury Attributable to 67 Risk Factors and Risk Factor Clusters in 21 Regions 1990-2010: A Systematic Analysis for the Global Burden of Disease Study 2010", *The Lancet*, Vol. 380, No. 9859, pp. 2224-2260.

Lipscomb, J., M.C. Weinstein and G.W. Torrance (1996), "Time Preference", in M.R. Gold, D.L. Patrick, G.W. Torrance et al. (eds.), *Cost-effectiveness in Health and Medicine*, Oxford University Press, New York.

Livingston, M. (2011), "Using Geocoded Liquor Licensing Data in Victoria – The Socioeconomic Distribution of Alcohol Availability in Victoria", Victorian Health Promotion Foundation (VicHealth), Carlton, Australia.

Livingston, M. (2008), "A Longitudinal Analysis of Alcohol Outlet Density and Assault", *Alcoholism, Clinical and Experimental Research*, Vol. 32, No. 6, pp; 1074-1079.

Lopez, A.D. et al. (2006), "Global Burden of Disease and Risk Factors", The World Bank, Washington, DC, and Oxford University Press, New York.

Marcus, G. and R. Braaf (2007), "Domestic and Family Violence Studies, Survey and Statistics: Pointers to Policy and Practice", Australian Domestic and Family Violence Clearinghouse, Sydney.

McGovern, P.E. (2010), "Uncorking the Past: The Quest for Wine, Beer, and Other Alcoholic Beverages", University of California Press, Oakland, United States.

Million, M. (2013), *Wine, A Global History*, Reaktion Books, London.

Naimi, T.S. (2011), "The Cost of Alcohol and its Corresponding Taxes in the U.S.: A Massive Public Subsidy of Excessive Drinking and Alcohol Industries", *American journal of Preventive Medicine*, Vol. 41, No. 5, pp. 546-547.

Nancy, J.-L. (2013), *Ivresse*, Bibliothèque Rivages, Paris.

Navarro, H.J., C.M. Doran and A.P. Shakeshaft (2011), "Measuring Costs of Alcohol Harm to Others: A Review of the Literature", *Drug and Alcohol Dependence*, Vol. 1, No. 114(2-3), pp. 87-99.

O'Keefe, J.H. et al. (20124), "Alcohol and Cardiovascular Health: The Dose Makes the Poison…or the Remedy", *Mayo Clinic Proceedings*, Vol. 89, No. 3, pp. 382-393.

ONS – Office for National Statistics (2010), United Kingdom, www.ons.gov.uk/ons/rel/lifestyles/drinking--adult-s-behaviour-and-knowledge/2009-report/index.html.

Pierce, G. and A. Toxqui (eds) (2014), *Alcohol in Latin America: A Social and Cultural History*, University of Arizona Press, Tucson, United States.

Poli, A. et al. (2013), "Moderate Alcohol Use and Health: A Consensus Document", *Nutrition Metabolism and Cardiovascular Diseases*, Vol. 23, No. 6, pp. 487-504.

Prime Minister's Strategy Unit (2004), "Alcohol Harm Reduction Strategy for England", Prime Minister's Strategy Unit, London, available at http://alcoholresearchuk.org/wp-content/uploads/2014/01/strategy-unit-alcohol-harm-reduction-strategy.pdf.

Rehm, J. et al. (2009), "Global Burden of Disease and Injury and Economic Cost Attributable to Alcohol Use and Alcohol-use Disorders", *The Lancet*, Vol. 27, No. 373(9682), pp. 2223-2233.

Roerecke, M. and J. Rehm (2014), "Alcohol Consumption, Drinking Patterns, and Ischemic Heart Disease: A Narrative Review of Meta-analyses and a Systematic Review and Meta-analysis of the Impact of Heavy Drinking Occasions on Risk for Moderate Drinkers", *BMC Medicine*, Vol. 12, No. 182, available at http://dx.doi.org/10.1186/s12916-014-0182-6.

Romley, J.A. et al. (2007), "Alcohol and Environmental Justice: The Density of Liquor Stores and Bars in Urban Neighborhoods in the United States", *Journal of Studies on Alcohol and Drugs*, Vol. 68, No. 1, pp. 48-55.

Sassi, F. (2010), *Obesity and the Economics of Prevention*: Fit not Fat, OECD Publishing, Paris, http://dx.doi.or/10.1787/9789264084865-en.

Sassi, F. and J. Hurst (2008), "The Prevention of Lifestyle-Related Chronic Diseases: An Economic Framework", *OECD Health Working Papers*, No. 32, OECD Publishing, Paris, http://dx.doi.org/10.1787/243180781313.

Simpura, J. and T. Karlsson (2001), "Trends in Drinking Patterns in Fifteen European Countries, 1950-2000. A collection of country reports", Stakes, Helsinki.

SIRC – Social Issues Research Centre (1998), "Social and Cultural Aspects of Drinking. A Report to the European Commission", SIRC, Oxford.

Tatlow, J.R., J.D. Clapp and M.M. Hohman (2000), "The Relationship Between the Geographic Density of Alcohol Outlets and Alcohol-related Hospital Admissions in San Diego County", *Journal of Epidemiology and Community Health*, Vol. 25, No. 1, pp. 79-88.

Thavorncharoensap, M. et al. (2009), "The Economic Impact of Alcohol Consumption: A Systematic Review", *Substance Abuse Treatment, Prevention and Policy*, Vol. 25, No. 4:20.

Theall, K.P. et al. (2009), "The Neighborhood Alcohol Environment and Alcohol-related Morbidity", *Alcohol Alcohol*, Vol. 44, No. 5, pp. 491-499.

White, I.R., D.R. Altmann and K. Nanchahal (2002), "Alcohol Consumption and Mortality: Modelling Risks for Men and Women at Different Ages", *British Medical Journal*, Vol. 325, No. 7357, p. 191.

White, A.M. et al. (2011), "Hospitalizations for Alcohol and Drug Overdoses in Young Adults Ages 18-24 in the United States, 1999-2008: Results from the Nationwide Inpatient Sample", *Journal of Studies on Alcohol and Drugs*, Vol. 72, No. 5, pp. 774-786.

WHO – World Health Organization (2014), "Global Status Report on Alcohol and Health", World Health Organization, Geneva.

Wickizer, T.M. (2013), "State-level Estimates of the Economic Costs of Alcohol and Drug Abuse", *Journal of Health Care Finance*, Vol. 39, No. 3, pp. 71-84.

Tackling Harmful Alcohol Use
Economics and Public Health Policy


# Chapter 2

# Trends in alcohol consumption in OECD countries

by
Marion Devaux and Franco Sassi

*Levels of alcohol drinking are relatively high in many OECD countries compared with countries in other parts of the world. An average of between 9.1 litres (recorded consumption) and 10.3 litres (including unrecorded consumption) of pure alcohol are consumed annually in OECD countries, compared with an estimate of 6.2 litres worldwide (recorded and unrecorded). Overall, consumption has slightly declined in OECD countries in the past 20 years, and very large relative falls in consumption have been observed in certain countries, but consumption as risen sharply in other OECD countries, as well as in major emerging economies. Alcohol use is very concentrated in the population, with the heaviest-drinking 20% drinking most alcohol, and high-risk drinking behaviours have become more common in recent years in certain population groups. Hazardous and heavy episodic drinking have rapidly gained in popularity among young people, especially women, in countries where they were traditionally less common. At the same time they have decreased in certain countries where they used to be more popular among young people. These trends are especially worrying because they are fuelled by an increasingly early initiation into drinking and drunkenness. The proportion of children who have experienced alcohol at age 15 increased significantly during the 2000s, even faster among girls than boys.*

## Key findings

- At 9.1 litres per capita, average annual consumption is substantially higher in OECD countries than in other parts of the world.
- A 2.5% decline in OECD average alcohol consumption during the past 20 years results from a combination of dramatic falls in consumption in southern European countries and substantial increases in some northern and central-eastern European countries.
- Alcohol consumption has also risen dramatically in major emerging economies, key partners of the OECD, albeit starting from lower levels.
- Changes in the types of beverages typically drunk in countries have accompanied changes in overall levels of consumption, with a weakening of drinking cultures dominated by a single beverage and the development of more mixed and uniform patterns.
- About 11% of all alcohol consumption is estimated to go unrecorded in the OECD area.
- Although typical patterns of alcohol consumption in OECD countries are not among those at highest risk, most alcohol is drunk by the heaviest-drinking 20% of the population in the countries examined.
- Many OECD countries have seen increasing rates of hazardous and heavy episodic drinking in young people, especially women, and this has translated into a heightened risk of injuries and death from traffic accidents and violence.
- Initiation into alcohol drinking and drunkenness happens at increasingly early ages, and girls have virtually caught up with boys in the past ten years in terms of the age at which they start drinking, on average, in 20 OECD countries.

## Alcohol: How do countries compare?

At first glance, calculating how much alcohol is consumed in a given country appears simple. In reality, it is virtually impossible to obtain objective population-wide measures of alcohol consumption. Sales data provide relatively straightforward estimates of consumption, but they may not be totally accurate because certain types of alcohol go unrecorded and have to be estimated based on empirical investigations and expert judgements. Unrecorded alcohol is defined as "alcohol that is not taxed in the country where it is consumed because it is usually produced, distributed and sold outside the formal channels under government control" (WHO, 2014, p. 30). This refers to homemade or illegally produced alcohol, smuggled alcohol, and alcohol for industrial and medical use. Alcohol consumed by tourists further compounds the interpretation of sales data. For some tourists, alcohol is even the purpose of the trip itself. A whole business has grown, for instance, in and around French ports such as Calais to cater for "booze cruisers" coming over from England for the day to stock up at cheaper French prices. This phenomenon, known as cross-border shopping, as well as other consumption of alcohol by tourists, lead to a potential overestimation of consumption in the countries where alcohol is sold, and an underestimation in the countries of origin of the tourist consumers.

Per capita consumption for a country obtained by simply dividing sales by population also need to be interpreted with caution because of wide demographic (age and sex) differences between countries, and differences in the proportions of teetotallers in the population. In predominantly Muslim countries, for instance, average per capita consumption tends to be low, but average consumption by those who do drink alcohol can be substantial (WHO, 2014).

The data the OECD regularly collects from its member countries on alcohol consumption covers annual sales of pure alcohol in litres per person aged 15 years and over. Data sources are mostly national statistical institutes, except for 11 countries for which data from the WHO Global Information System on Alcohol and Health are used (Belgium, Chile, Germany, Greece, Iceland, Israel, Italy, Luxembourg, Portugal, Spain and United Kingdom). Of course, alcohol sales include a variety of beverages, with vastly different amounts of alcohol for a given volume of liquid (alcohol by volume – ABV). This ranges from some spirits that are 98% pure alcohol to low-alcohol beer that may only have 0.5% ABV. In sales statistics, typically beer is weighted as having 4-5% alcohol content, wine 11-12% and spirits 40%, although the methodology to convert alcoholic drinks to a more readily comparable measure of pure alcohol may differ across countries.

Alcohol consumption, as measured by annual sales, stands at 9.1 litres per adult, on average, across OECD countries, based on the most recent data available (Figure 2.1). Austria, Estonia and France reported the highest consumption of alcohol, with 12 litres or more per adult per year in 2012. Low alcohol consumption was recorded in Israel and Turkey, as well as in two OECD key partner countries included in the figure, India and Indonesia, where religious and cultural traditions restrict the use of alcohol in some population groups.

The WHO provide estimates of average per capita alcohol consumption (APC) as part of the Global Information System on Alcohol and Health (GISAH), which draws upon various data sources, including sales, tax, international trade, and survey data. The WHO made considerable efforts to collect and cross-validate various sources of information, and to estimate unrecorded alcohol consumption, which is likely to account for one in four drinks worldwide. The WHO APC is therefore an estimate of recorded and unrecorded adult per capita consumption of pure alcohol. The WHO estimated APC for the period 2008-10 is 6.2 litres on average worldwide, and about 10.9 litres in the European (WHO) region, which has the highest levels of per-capita consumption.

## Is alcohol consumption falling or rising?

Worldwide, APC by adults has remained relatively stable in the two decades between 1992 and 2012, but increased during the last five years of that period (WHO, 2014). In OECD countries, on average, it decreased by 2.5% in the same period (Figure 2.2). Large and steady decreases were seen in countries where consumption was originally relatively high, such as France, Germany, Italy and Spain. In originally lower-consumption countries, data show a continuous increase, followed in some cases by a downturn in recent years (e.g., Finland, Ireland and the United Kingdom). Consumption rose in Estonia, Finland, Iceland, Israel, Norway, Poland and Sweden, by up to 50%. Alcohol consumption in OECD key partner countries, including the Russian Federation, as well as Brazil, India, and China rose substantially, although in the latter two countries per capita consumption remains relatively low (Figure 2.2).

Figure 2.1. **Alcohol consumption among adults, 2012 (or nearest year)**

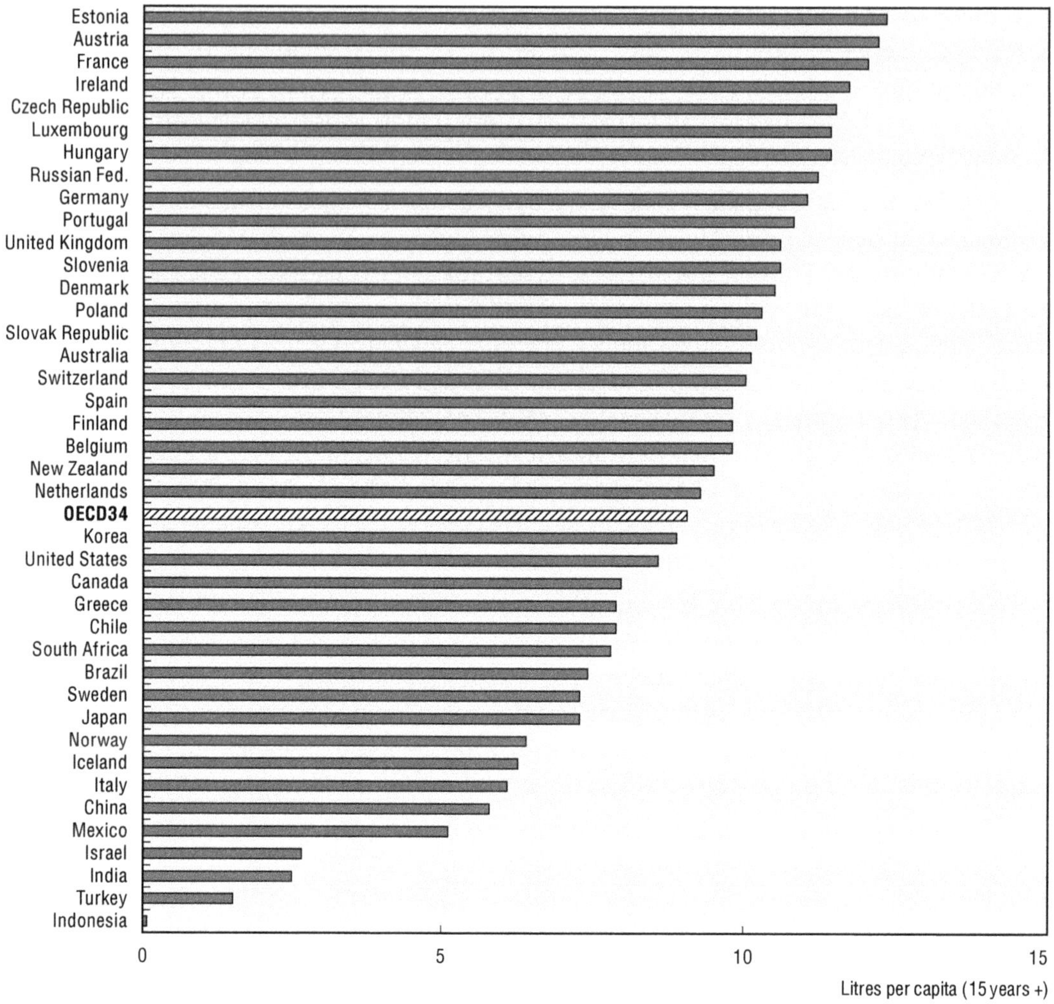


*Source: OECD Health Statistics 2014.*

StatLink http://dx.doi.org/10.1787/888933180256

Alcohol consumption by younger people is growing however. The proportion of adolescent and young adults who drink alcohol has been increasing in low and middle income countries (GSHS, 2004; WHO, 2011). In OECD countries, children are taking up drinking at increasingly earlier ages, as shown below in Figure 2.9. In Europe, the ESPAD study shows small decreases between 2003 and 2011 in the proportion of students who consume alcohol, but it also finds increases in heavy episodic drinking from 1995 to 2007 with some signs of a downturn in 2011 (Hibell et al., 2012).

Some of the reasons suggested for increased drinking by young people include the low cost of alcoholic beverages, the wider availability of alcohol, forms of alcohol promotion designed for younger drinkers and changes in the acceptability of drinking in many societies. Burki (2010) discusses possible causes for the increases in average consumption and highlights a correlation between consumption and affordability (and availability) of alcohol, citing a report by the British Medical Association which shows a higher affordability of alcohol in the United Kingdom between 1980 and 2006, and an increase in per capita alcohol consumption of 1.5 litres during the same period of time. It is worth noting that changes in affordability and availability can have significant impacts

Figure 2.2. **Change in alcohol consumption among adults, 1992-2012 (or nearest year)**

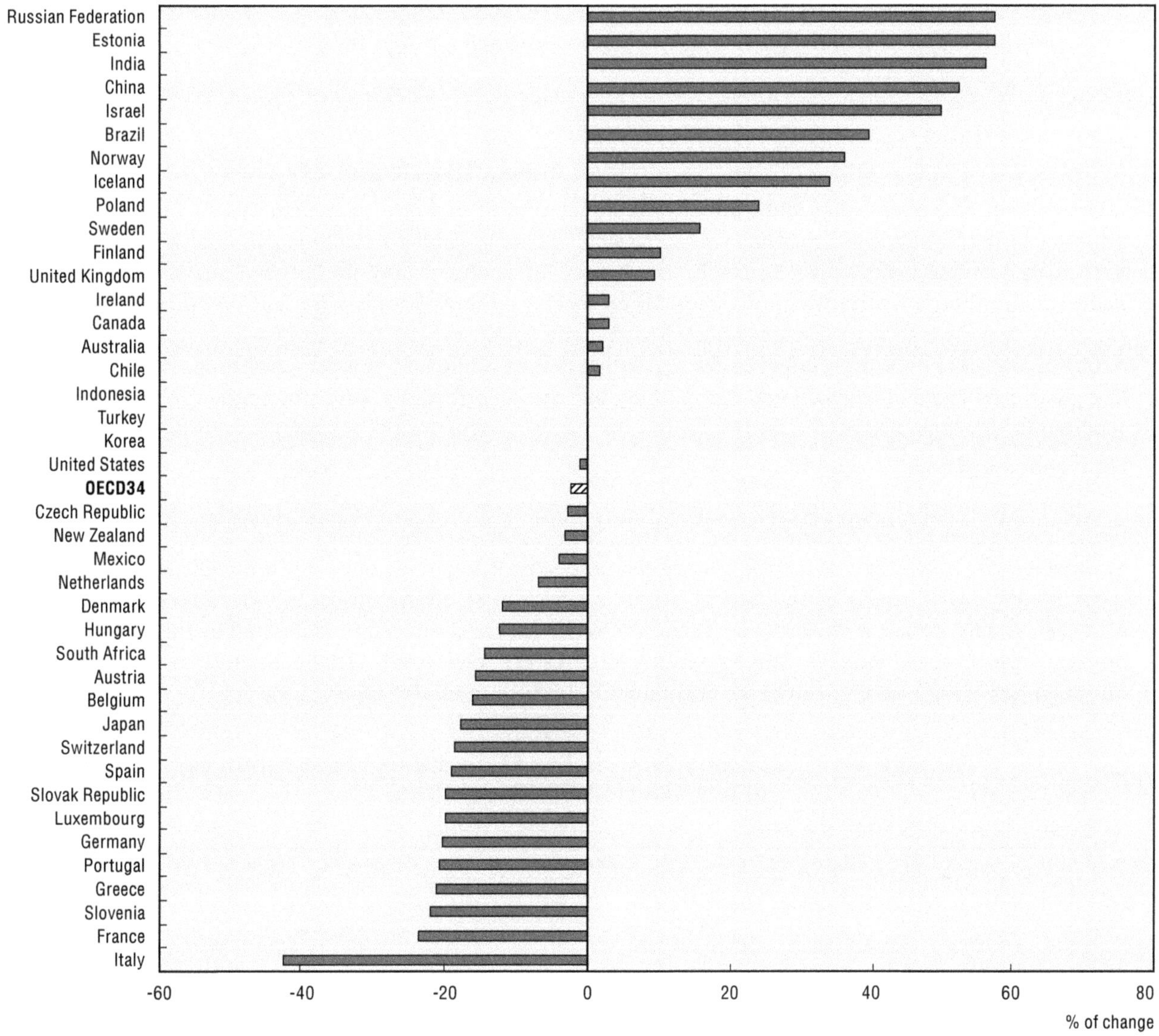


*Source: OECD Health Statistics 2014.*

StatLink http://dx.doi.org/10.1787/888933180261

not just on how much alcohol is consumed, but where it is consumed. In the United Kingdom, the local pub is often described as a national institution, but pubs are closing at the rate of 31 a week, in part because supermarkets are now the main source of beer for many drinkers (Eads, 2014).

Aggregate sales data are a good indicator for monitoring broad national trends and drawing country profiles for population-wide policies on price and availability. Also, there is some evidence of existing correlations between total per capita alcohol consumption and excessive consumption, and its related harms (Leifman et al., 2002). However, the aggregate data do not permit identification and examination of individual patterns of drinking. To design appropriate policies, we need to understand how harmful forms of drinking have evolved over time and to identify which population groups are most likely to engage in problem drinking, and which are most affected by it. Such analyses help policy makers to tailor strategies to reduce harmful drinking to the circumstances of specific populations.

Population health and lifestyle survey data providing information on alcohol consumption and individual characteristics are best suited for assessing drinking behaviours across different sub-groups of the population, although these surveys do suffer from important limitations (see Box 2.1).

### Box 2.1. **The challenge of measuring alcohol use**

Limitations of survey-based data on alcohol consumption are due to measurement bias, including underreporting by surveyed respondents and selection bias in survey sampling. Drinking levels reported in surveys have been shown to account for only 40-60% of alcohol sales (Midanik, 1982; WHO, 2014). OECD analyses based on quantitative approaches for correcting survey estimates for self-report bias (Rehm et al., 2010), suggest that large discrepancies exist in some countries. OECD estimates show varying degrees of bias in different countries, larger in countries like France, Chile and Hungary, and smaller in countries like Japan and England (Devaux and Sassi, 2015), but these corrections were not applied in the analyses reported in this publication.

**Main sources of bias**

Alcohol consumption is typically self-reported by respondents in surveys, and self-reports are prone to bias, most often downward (Boniface and Shelton, 2013; Meier et al., 2013; Rehm et al., 2010; Ely et al., 2001; Stockwell et al., 2004). There is some evidence that underreporting may not be uniformly distributed across respondents, e.g. it is likely to be larger in hazardous drinkers (Townshend and Dukat, 2002; Lemmens et al., 1988). The figure below shows a comparison of WHO data and estimates calculated by the OECD based on data from national surveys. Survey-based estimates are lower than WHO estimates in all countries, although trends over time are quite consistent, with the exception of France.

**Average per-capita consumption based on different data sources, in five selected OECD countries**

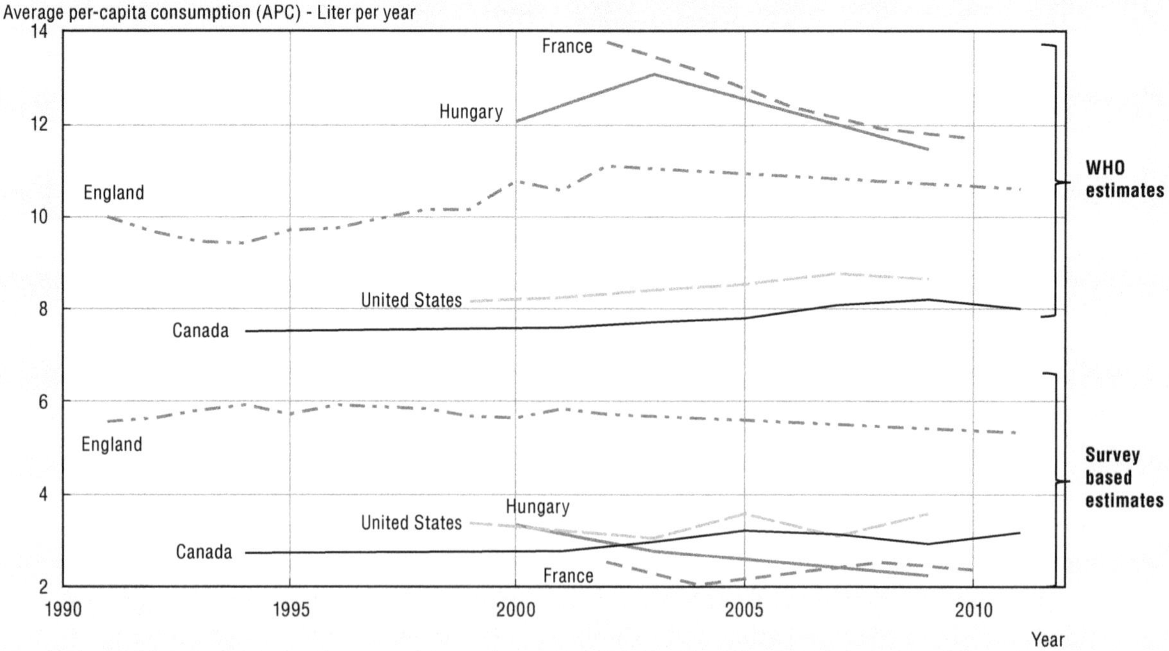


*Source:* WHO Global Information System on Alcohol and Health, National Health Surveys and OECD estimates.

StatLink http://dx.doi.org/10.1787/888933180271

Box 2.1. **The challenge of measuring alcohol use** *(cont.)*

Some people at high risk of heavy drinking may be under-represented in the sampling frames typically used in health and lifestyle surveys (e.g. students, people with alcohol dependence), and some may not be represented at all, including the homeless, or people in institutions (Stockwell et al., 2004; Boniface and Shelton, 2013; Meier et al., 2013).

On the other hand, sales and excise duty clearance data may also misestimate alcohol consumption due to unrecorded alcohol but also due to wastage and consumption by tourists. A recent study in the United Kingdom estimates that the total amount of alcohol not captured in alcohol sales statistics (between 2.1 and 2.9 litres per capita) outweighs the quantity of alcohol not captured in surveys (between 1.9 and 2.1 litres per capita) without accounting for under-reporting (Boniface and Shelton, 2013).

**Correction of bias**

Identifying the size of self-report bias would require, ideally, a data source in which self-reports are available alongside more objective measures of alcohol consumption for a representative sample of a given population. Similar data exist for height and weight, for instance, and have enabled researchers to devise algorithms for correcting body mass index and obesity estimates for self-report bias (Cawley, 2000; Lakdawalla and Philipson, 2002). To the best of our knowledge, such sources do not exist for alcohol, and the idea itself that alcohol consumption can be measured objectively is questionable.

A study of 1 300 adults compared alcohol consumption reports based on seven-day recall questions with more accurate seven-day food diaries, providing some evidence of self-report bias (Ely et al., 2001). The proportion of hazardous drinkers was found to vary between recall and diary from 21% to 35% for men and from 6% to 15% for women. And, the extent of underreporting was large: 20% of male and 11% of female drinkers classified as moderate drinkers based on their recall were reclassified as hazardous drinkers based on diary declarations. And, 31% of male and 5% of female drinkers classified as hazardous drinkers based on recall were classified as harmful drinkers based on diary declarations. Similar attempts to combine recall and diary data exists (e.g. Hill-McManus et al., 2014), but are rare. Surveys of household expenditures often provide reasonably reliable estimates, but usually these are not linked with self-reports of consumption.

Of the datasets used in our analysis, NHANES (United States) provides, in addition to the number of drinks on a typical drinking day and the number of drinking days in the past 12 months, a 24-hour dietary recall and a secondary 24-hour dietary recall 3 to 10 days later. However, estimates of alcohol consumption based on two single-day recall questions provide a weak basis for a correction for underreporting, as this would miss the fact that drinking patterns vary strongly by day of the week.

The most credible approach so far to correct for self-report bias in estimates of alcohol consumption is at the aggregate level, and relies on the triangulation of survey data with recorded aggregate per capita consumption data by modelling an upshifted distribution of alcohol consumption (Rehm et al., 2010). The self-reported levels of alcohol consumption are inflated after correction (technically, the statistical distribution of consumption is shifted to the right), reflecting the fact that people consume more than they declare. According to this method, the proportion of hazardous drinkers in Canada, for instance, would increase from 5% to 20% after correction in men and from 1% to 6% in women (Shield and Rehm, 2012).

New OECD analyses of alcohol consumption undertaken as part of the work presented in this book are based on information from individual-level surveys. However, although surveys provide detailed information on actual consumption, they have to rely on self-reports that can be biased, deliberately or not, in a number of ways that are discussed in detail in Box 2.1. Drinking levels calculated from surveys are often only about half what would be expected from alcohol sales (Midanik, 1982; WHO, 2011). Nevertheless, by combining all types of data sources, it is possible to draw a picture of alcohol drinking in a country that is accurate enough to guide policy making.

## Dominant beverages and patterns of drinking

Supposed drinking habits are an integral part of national stereotypes and these may be exploited for marketing purposes through events like beer festivals, for instance, in Germany or the arrival of Beaujolais nouveau in France. While these clichés have some grounding in national and local cultures and traditions, drinking habits have been converging across the OECD, with wine consumption increasing in many traditional beer-drinking countries and vice versa. Wine-producing countries like France, Greece, Italy, Portugal, Spain, as well as Hungary, the Slovak Republic and Switzerland, have seen per capita consumption of wine fall by 20% or more since 1990.

About one third (3.8 litres per capita) of the alcohol drunk in OECD countries, according to WHO data, is from beer, and 25% is from wine (2.8 litres per capita), while the remaining recorded consumption is from spirits or other alcoholic beverages (Figure 2.3). Unrecorded alcohol may account for a substantial part of total alcohol intake. On average, 1.14 litres of unrecorded alcohol per capita, corresponding to 11% of total alcohol intake, are estimated to be drunk every year in the OECD, but the share is substantially higher in countries like Turkey (29%) or Mexico (25%). The highest consumption figures in volume terms for unrecorded alcohol are about three or more litres per capita in South Africa and the Russian Federation (WHO, 2014).

The type of alcohol consumed (e.g. beer, wine, spirits), whether alcohol is available from institutional or illegal channels, and the patterns of consumption of alcohol, all have an influence on the potential for alcohol control policy to be effective. Therefore, they should be taken into consideration in the design and selection of appropriate policies. For instance, a prevention strategy largely based on taxation will be less effective in countries where consumption of illegal, or informally produced, alcohol is more widespread or where it is cheap and easy to cross the border to buy alcohol at a lower price.

The amount of alcohol consumed is only one factor determining whether drinking may cause harm or not. A given amount will probably not have the same effect depending on whether it is consumed, for instance, in one night or over a number of weeks, alone or at party, with a meal or on an empty stomach. This is what is meant by "pattern of drinking". The pattern of drinking is particularly important because of its relationship with the development of acute effects of alcohol, including injuries, intoxication and other alcohol use disorders. In addition, harmful patterns of drinking cancel out the positive effects of moderate alcohol intake on the incidence of, and mortality from, cardiovascular disease (Rehm et al., 2003; Murray et al., 2002).

The number next to each country in Figure 2.3 indicates the prevailing pattern of drinking (WHO, 2014). On a scale from 1 (least risky behaviour) to 5 (most risky behaviour), OECD countries have a pattern of drinking that ranges from 1 (least risky behaviour) to 3 (medium risk). This indicator is based on a number of dimensions, reflecting the likelihood of harmful drinking (high usual quantity of alcohol per occasion; frequency of festive drinking at fiestas or community celebrations; proportion of drinking occasions when drinkers get drunk; distribution of the same amount of drinking over several occasions); whether drinking is associated with meals; and whether drinking occurs in public places.

Figure 2.3. **Consumption levels by type of alcohol, and country drinking score**

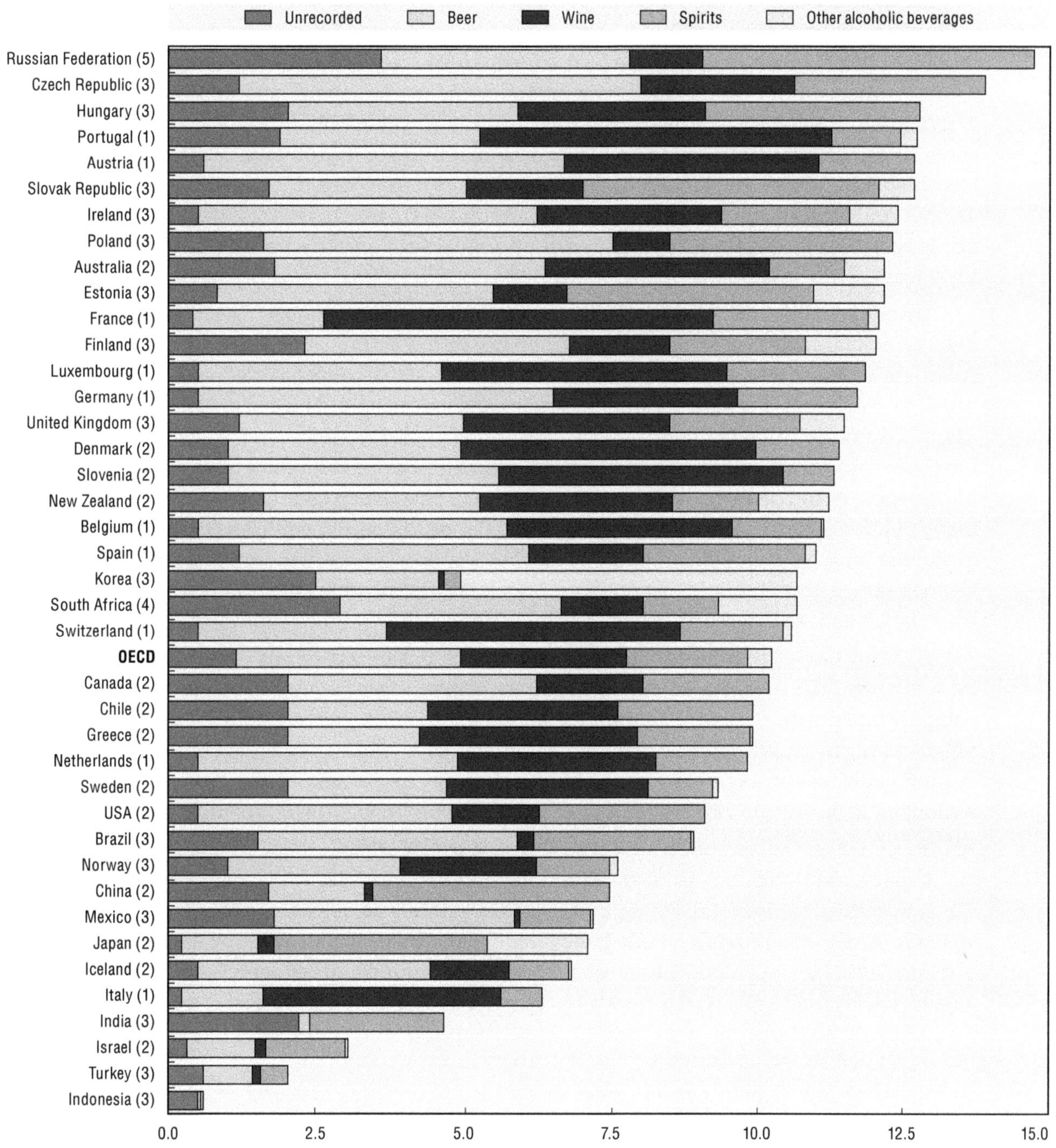


*Note:* The drinking score is defined as 1 least risky, 2 somewhat risky, 3 medium risky, 4 very risky, 5 most risky.

*Source:* WHO GISAH database, 2014.

StatLink http://dx.doi.org/10.1787/888933180287

## Identifying hazardous drinkers

International comparisons need to rely on common measures of alcohol use. Each country has its own definition of a standard drink (how much pure alcohol a drink contains) and its own recommendations for hazardous drinking limits (defined as number of glasses or amount of pure alcohol per day or per week). No international consensus in drinking guidelines exists. While some countries set national guidelines for maximum weekly and/or daily consumption, either expressed in standard drinks or grams of pure alcohol, others do not have official recommendations (Furtwaengler and de Visser, 2013). A summary of what constitutes a standard drink and guidelines for determining what constitutes hazardous drinking and heavy episodic drinking in different OECD countries is available in Table A.2 in Annex A. What constitutes a standard drink varies twofold in alcohol content across OECD countries. The variation in thresholds for defining hazardous drinking is even larger, from 20 to 52 grams of pure alcohol per day for men, and from 10 to 39 grams for women.

Communicating drinking guidelines is a challenge for public health and law enforcement agencies, and the lack of consistency in definitions across, and often within, countries makes the task even more difficult. Many OECD countries define a standard drink as containing between 10 and 12 grams of pure alcohol, and hazardous drinking as approximately three (men) or two (women) drinks per day. However, translating these numbers into actual quantities of different alcoholic beverages is not something that most people would be in a position to do, despite the visual aids created and promoted by many public health agencies. A similar issue applies, of course, to people answering survey questions on their own consumption of alcohol. Visual aids are not always provided by interviewers, in this case, and respondents' understanding of what constitutes a drink may vary (which adds to a potentially biased recollection).

Defining heavy episodic drinking is even more of a challenge, given that the scientific evidence of the risks associated with such pattern of drinking is strong, but builds on studies using different measures and definitions. Most countries do not have official guidelines for discouraging heavy episodic drinking, but many have ongoing debates with a view to issuing guidelines in the near future. For instance, in the context of the European Joint Action on "Reducing alcohol-related harm" (RAHRA), started in 2014, EU member states are trying to build consensus around low-risk drinking guidelines.

Despite the difficulties in data definitions and analysis, the evidence suggests that the distribution of alcohol drinking in a population tends to be heavily concentrated. In virtually all of the countries examined, the majority of alcohol is consumed by the heaviest-drinking 20% of the population. In most countries, the latter drink between 50% and 75% of all alcohol. Figure 2.4 shows the relevant proportions in 13 OECD countries.

## Tracking changes in alcohol consumption over time

We analysed alcohol consumption in 20 OECD countries selected on the basis of data availability (Australia, Canada, Chile, the Czech Republic, England, Finland, France, Germany, Hungary, Ireland, Italy, Japan, Korea, New Zealand, Portugal, the Slovak Republic, Slovenia, Spain, Switzerland and the United States), in order to explore trends in different types of alcohol use over time; social disparities by education and socioeconomic status; and differences by age and sex in alcohol drinking.

Figure 2.4. **Share of total alcohol consumed by the 20% of the population who drink the most**

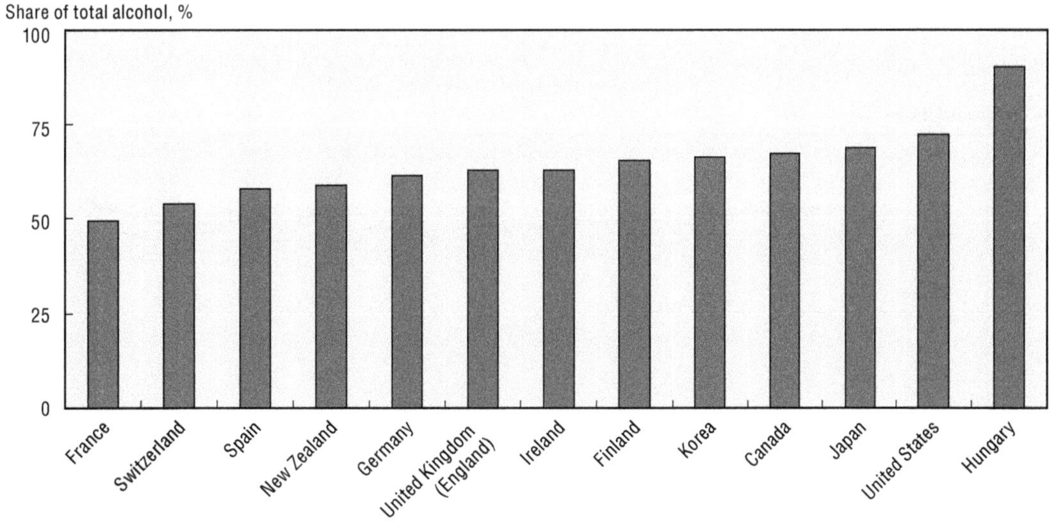


*Source:* OECD estimates based on national surveys, latest available year (details in Table A.1 in Annex A).

StatLink http://dx.doi.org/10.1787/888933180291

Individual-level alcohol consumption data were obtained from national health and lifestyle surveys, or alcohol and drug use surveys. These surveys provide the most detailed information currently available on individual socio-demographic characteristics combined with alcohol drinking patterns, assessed either over the week prior to the interview in nine countries (Australia, Canada, the Czech Republic, Finland, Hungary, Japan, the Slovak Republic, Slovenia and Switzerland) or based on questions on drinking frequency and quantity on a typical drinking day in the 11 remaining. Moreover, some countries' questionnaires use standard scales to measure drinking behaviours such as the Alcohol Use Disorder Identification Test (AUDIT) in Chile, France, Ireland (2007) and Korea (2008). The AUDIT questionnaire includes questions covering alcohol consumption, alcohol-related problems and abnormal drinking behaviour. It was developed by the WHO as a screening tool for health professionals to identify people at risk of developing alcohol problems.

Analyses of trends in alcohol consumption over time used multiple waves of survey data available in 12 OECD countries: Australia, Canada, England, Finland, France, Germany, Ireland, Italy, Korea, New Zealand, Switzerland and the United States, providing a variable temporal coverage starting from as far back as the late 1980s, and ending in 2012, with the longest series covering 18 years (England). The national surveys used and the number of waves available for each country are listed in Table A.1 in Annex A.

Figure 2.5 presents the proportions of people who report having drunk (any) alcohol in the past 12 months in the adult population, standardised to the age structure of the OECD population. In all countries, rates are higher among men than women. Rates of male alcohol consumption are around 90% in most countries whereas female drinking rates are more variable. Rates are relatively stable over time, once sampling variation is accounted for.

Figure 2.5. **Drinking in the past 12 months, population aged 15-74**

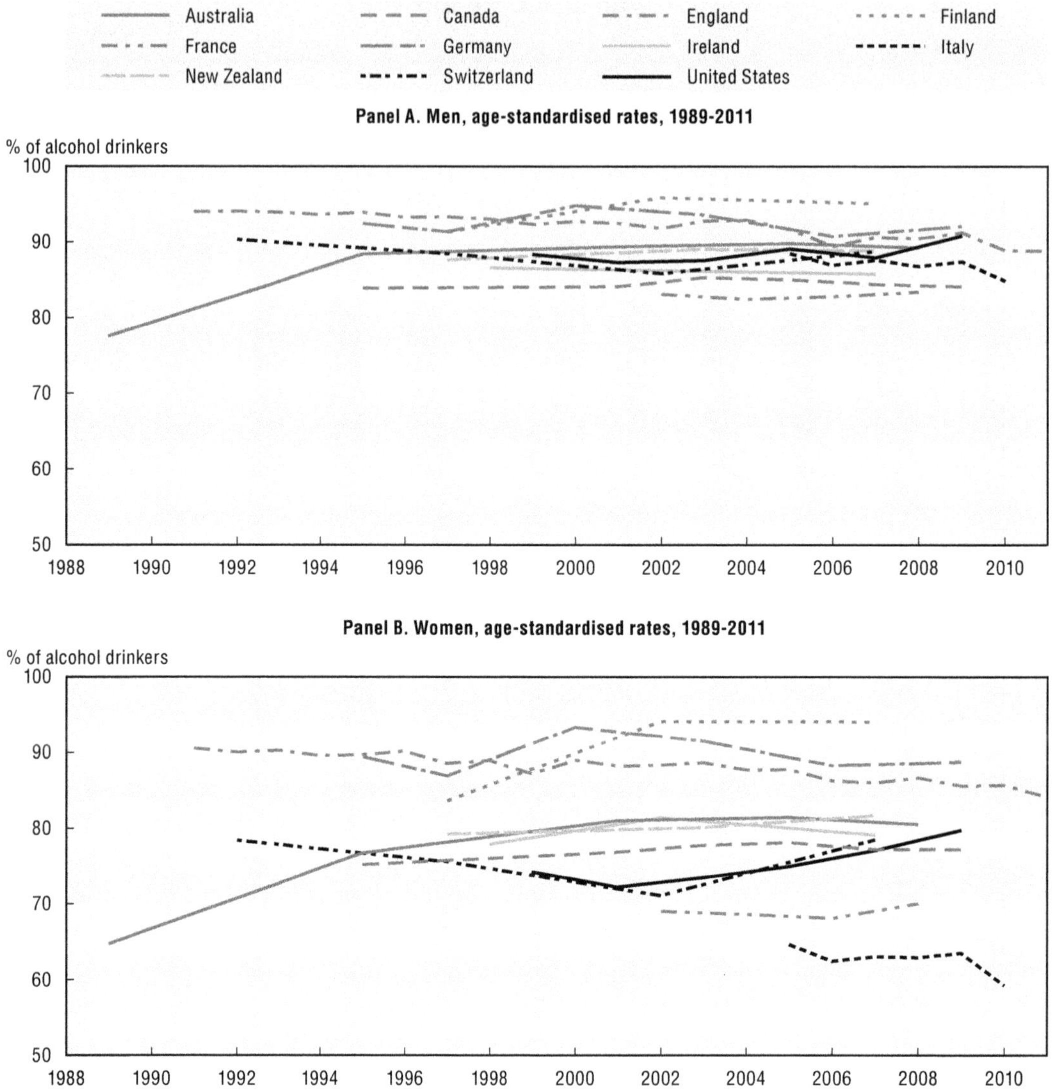


*Note:* Age 25+ in Finland.

*Source:* OECD estimates based on national health surveys, most recent years (details in Table A.1, Annex A), age standardisation based on OECD standard population.

StatLink http://dx.doi.org/10.1787/888933180308

## Changes in hazardous and heavy episodic drinking

National health survey data provide information on individual quantity and frequency of drinking. The definitions used in surveys to identify patterns of drinking vary, and so do interview approaches. As far as possible, comparable measures of risky drinking behaviours were derived from the surveys. These include:

- Hazardous drinking, defined by WHO as "a pattern of substance use that increases the risk of harmful consequences for the user" and is "of public health significance despite the absence of any current disorder in the individual user".[1] In the analyses presented here, thresholds for hazardous drinking were set at weekly amounts of pure alcohol of 140 grams or more for women, and 210 grams or more for men. The thresholds adopted are specific to this study and in line with those observed in most countries, but other studies have used different thresholds (e.g. Rehm et al., 2002).

- Heavy episodic drinking (HED), commonly called binge drinking, recorded in most of national surveys through questions such as: "In the past 12 months, how often did you have (n) or more drinks on one occasion?" (five drinks in Canada, Germany and the United States; six drinks in Chile, France, Hungary, Ireland, Italy and Switzerland for instance; seven drinks for men and five drinks for women in Australia (see more details in Table A.2 in Annex A). In order to increase comparability across countries, our analyses focused on regular HED, i.e. at least once a week. This is a different time frame relative to that used, for instance, by the WHO (once a month, see WHO, 2014).

Rates of hazardous and heavy episodic drinking display a relatively large degree of variation, partly caused by differences between surveys, which exist not only across countries, but also across surveys undertaken in the same countries. Despite efforts to standardise definitions in the analyses presented here, differences remain in the information provided by different surveys, which suggest that the value of these analyses is more in the assessment of trends over time than in the comparison of rates across countries.

Most countries show relatively stable trends of hazardous drinking between 1991 and 2011, although rates declined in Ireland and Germany, where they were high in the 1990s, and more than doubled in England in men between 1991 and 2011, although figures for 2011 are not entirely comparable with previous ones (Figure 2.6). These findings are in line with national trends reported elsewhere (e.g. Morgan et al., 2008; Pabst et al., 2010). Most countries present low rates of HED by women (Figure 2.7). In seven out of nine countries, less than 8% of female drinkers report HED at least once per week, this rate being especially low in France and Switzerland. However, rates grew during this time in most countries with originally low levels of HED, while they dropped in countries where they were originally high, especially in England, Ireland and, to a lesser extent, in Germany.

To some extent, rates of hazardous and heavy episodic drinking have tended to converge over time, and differences across countries are diminishing. These changes are associated with changes in the types of alcohol consumed. In Europe, regional differences in dominant beverage types remain, with more wine drinkers in France and Switzerland, and more beer drinkers in central Europe, but Nordic countries are no longer predominantly spirit-drinking (Mäkelä et al., 2005). Geographical differences in the types of alcohol consumed are diminishing (WHO, 2011), and so are differences in drinking patterns, especially in Europe, where HED is no longer a peculiarity of northern countries, and drinking habits are becoming more homogeneous throughout the continent.

Figure 2.6. **Hazardous drinking rates, drinkers only, population aged 15-74**

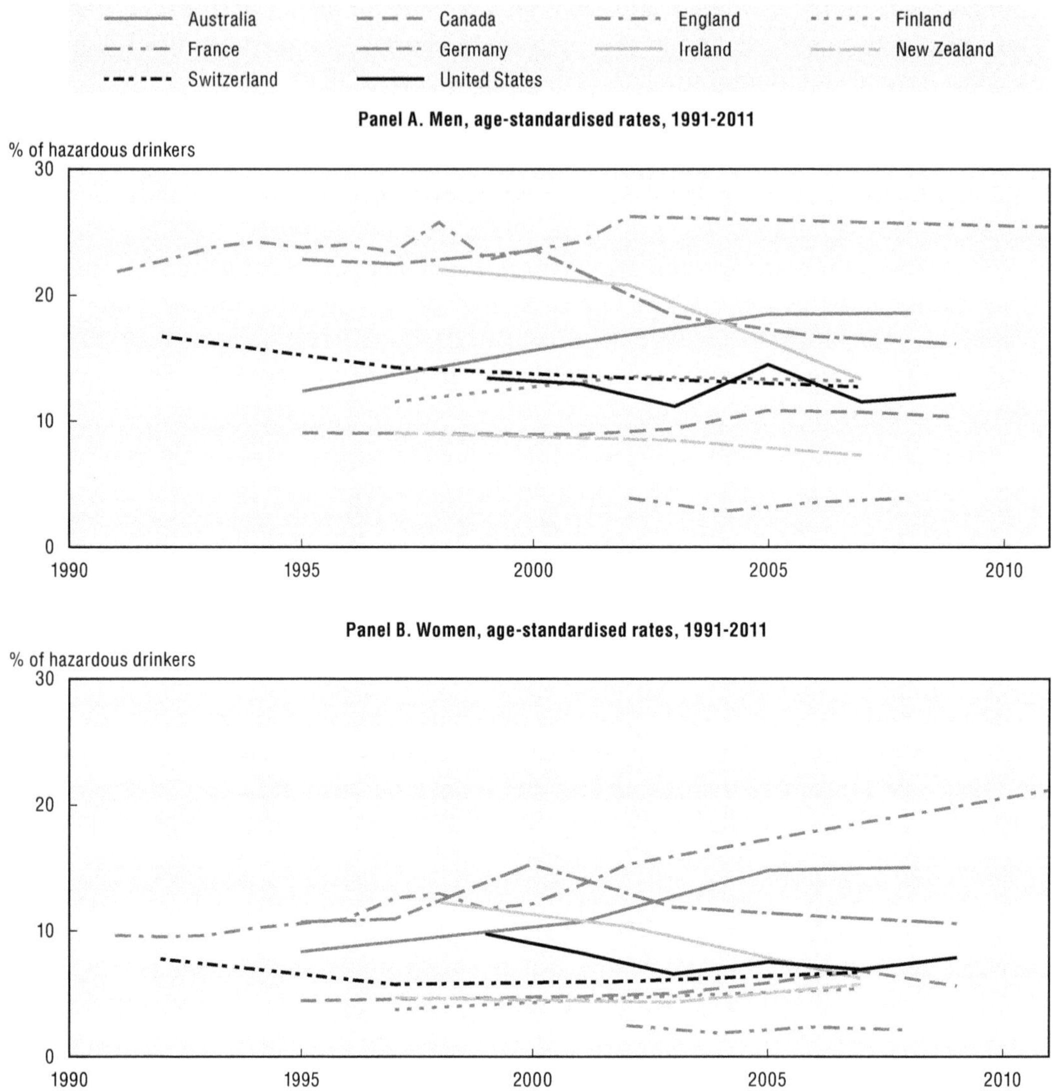


*Note:* Non-drinkers in the past 12 months are excluded from the denominator. Age 25+ in Finland. In England, estimated rates of hazardous drinkers up to 2002 may not be strictly comparable with 2011 rates due to changes in survey methods.

*Source:* OECD estimates based on national health surveys, most recent years (details in Table A.1, Annex A), age standardisation based on OECD standard population.

StatLink http://dx.doi.org/10.1787/888933180314

## Drinking initiation and alcohol use by young people

The picture drawn in Figures 2.6 and 2.7, however, does not tell the full story about trends in harmful drinking. Changes in population rates often hide different and sometimes diverging trends in subgroups of the population. This is clearly the case in many of the countries examined when trends are assessed for specific age groups. During the 1990s and 2000s, younger age groups, generally up to age 35, have tended to display increasing trends in risky drinking behaviours (both hazardous drinking and HED), while the same behaviours have remained stable, or have decreased, in older age groups.

Figure 2.7. **Heavy episodic drinking rates, drinkers only, population aged 15-74**

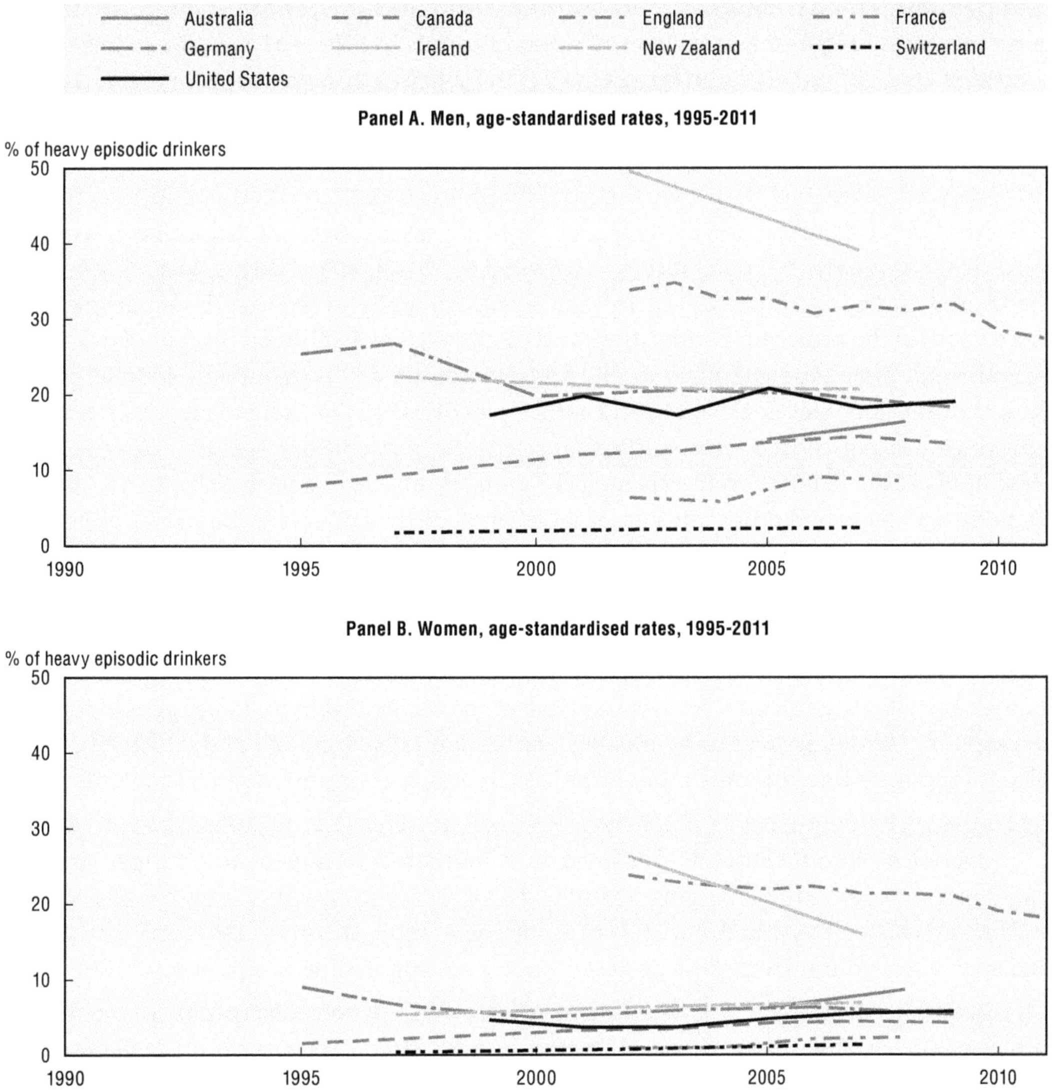


*Note:* Non-drinkers in the past 12 months are excluded from the denominator. HED is at least once per week. Age 25+ in Finland.

*Source:* OECD estimates based on national health surveys, most recent years (details in Table A.1, Annex A), age standardisation based on OECD standard population.

StatLink *http://dx.doi.org/10.1787/888933180327*

Proportions of hazardous drinkers have increased among young adults in England (both men and women), in Switzerland and in the United States (men only). In Ireland and Germany, hazardous drinking rates have remained stable in young men and women while they declined in other age groups.

Age differences are even more apparent in HED, with increasing proportions of young adults engaging in weekly HED sessions. Among the eight countries examined in our analysis, HED has declined in young people only in England and Ireland. Rates have been increasing in young women in Canada, Germany, Italy, and New Zealand, while they have increased in young men in Canada, Germany, Italy and France, with rates in older age groups often heading in the opposite direction. In the United States, data from the National Health and Nutrition Examination Survey (NHANES) show clear increases in HED in both young men (up to age 45) and women (up to age 25) with stable rates in other groups, but data from the National Survey of Drug Use and Health (NSDUH) show significantly smaller or no increases.[2] Figure 2.8 provides examples of trends in different age groups in selected countries. Its eight panels show trends in HED in men and women, respectively, in Canada, France, Italy and New Zealand.

In a study of high school seniors (mostly aged 18) in the United States between 2005 and 2011, approximately one in five students reported binge drinking, and one in ten reported "extreme" binge drinking, involving ten or more drinks per session. White boys were the most likely to engage in binge drinking (Patrick et al., 2013). In a separate national survey in the United States, seven percent of 16 year olds (10th graders) reported being drunk six or more times in the previous month (Hingson et al., 2013). The likelihood of alcohol use, heavy episodic and problem drinking is significantly increased when parents provide alcohol to their children (Kaynack et al., 2014), and early onset drinkers are likely to engage in multiple substance use (e.g. tobacco and marijuana) and to do it at an early age (Patrick et al., 2013; Moss et al., 2014). In addition to exposing children to long-term health risks, and to the risk of traffic accidents and other injuries, early alcohol use has effects on cognitive ability and school performance. Even after one month of abstinence, heavy episodic drinkers aged 16-18 performed worse than non-drinkers in a range of cognitive tests (Winward et al., 2014).

An increased affordability is likely part of the reasons for the trends observed in young people. In Finland the rise in drinking among adolescents has been explained with a greater availability of alcohol and an increase in money available to young people for their leisure time activities, including alcohol consumption (Rahkonen and Ahlström, 1989). Alcohol products have become more affordable in many countries, and this is notably true for young consumers (Rabinovich et al., 2009).

Alcohol products expressly designed and marketed to appeal to younger drinkers may have contributed to changing attitudes to alcohol drinking in young people. Alcohol products have been associated with fun, music, seduction, social success, self-confidence, and sports in alcohol advertising targeting young consumers (de Bruijn et al., 2012).

Hazardous drinking in young adults is often a form of socialisation. Drinking alcohol is often seen as the standard way of fitting in with peers. For the younger generations surrounded by "alcohol offers" (e.g. multiple delivery points, price offers, new products), the pursuit of excessive alcohol consumption has become part of a normal experience of young adulthood (Seaman and Ikegwuonu, 2010). This may involve abusing of spirits for the purpose of getting drunk rapidly, unwind and have fun (Pabst et al, 2010). Young people increasingly consume cheap alcohol, often bought in supermarkets, before going out to party, which has contributed to a shift in alcohol consumption from on- to off-trade in many countries (Hughes and Bellis, 2012).

The trends observed in younger age groups are of major public health and social concern. The spread of high-risk drinking behaviours is associated with an increase in morbidity and mortality from accidents and injuries (the most common cause of death in adolescents and young adults) as well as violence and social disturbances, in addition to an increased exposure to the risk of many chronic conditions for young drinkers. In Australia, the number of young women aged 18-24 being admitted to hospitals because of alcohol doubled between 1998 and 2006 (Livingston, 2008). In the United States, hospitalisations for alcohol overdoses increased by 25% among 18 to 24-year-olds between 1999 and 2008 and even more dramatically, by 76%, when alcohol was used in combination with drugs (White et al., 2011).

 

Figure 2.8. **Trends of heavy episodic drinking by age group, in Canada, France, Italy, and New Zealand**

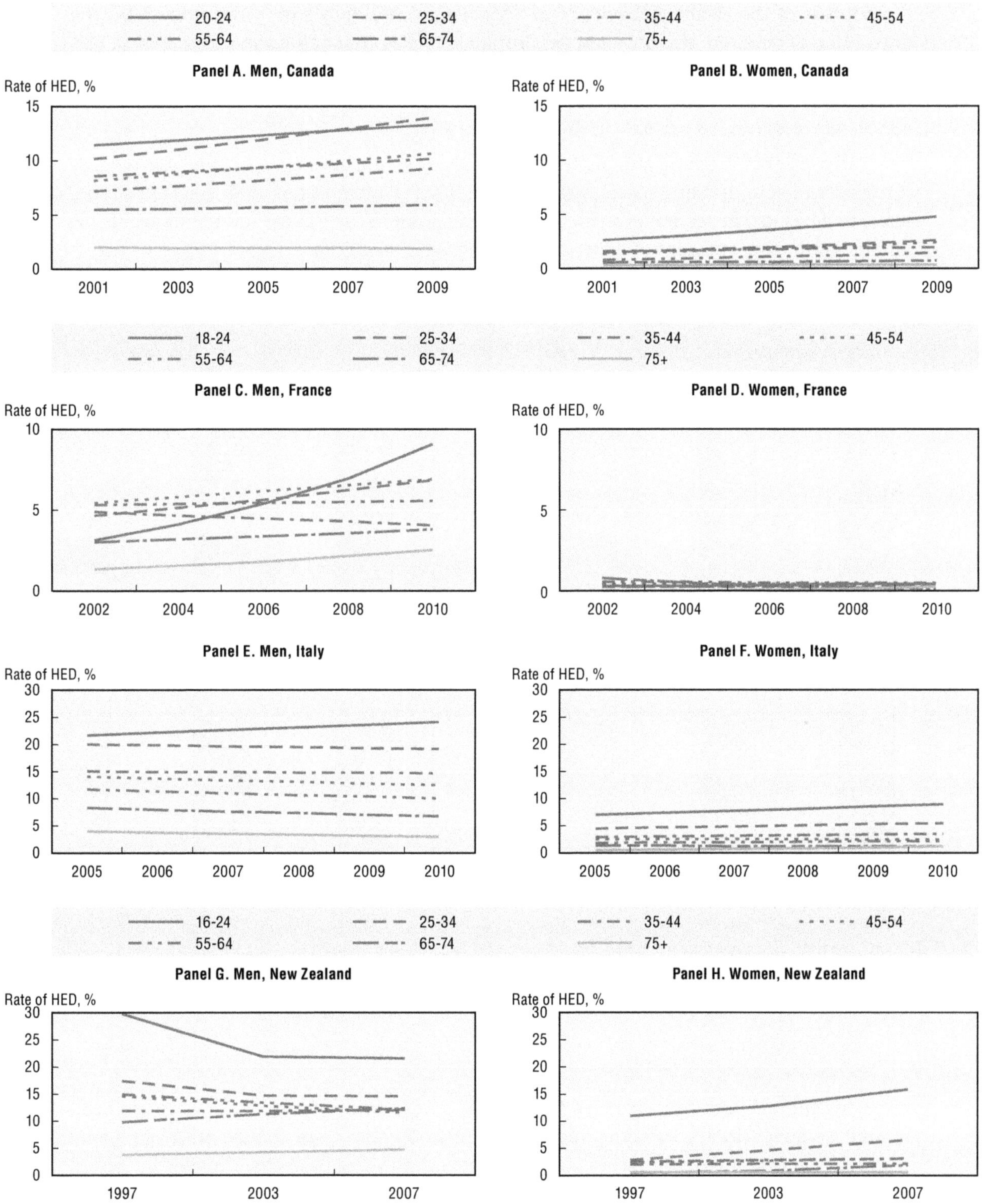


*Note:* HED at least once a week, except in Italy (once a year).

*Source:* OECD estimates based on national health surveys (details in Table A.1, Annex A).

StatLink http://dx.doi.org/10.1787/888933180334

These trends must be read in conjunction with a progressively earlier initiation into drinking and drunkenness in many OECD countries. From 15-year-olds' self-reports in the context of the Health Behaviours in School-aged Children survey, we know that the proportion of children who have not yet drunk alcohol by that age shrank from 44% to 30% (boys) and from 50% to 31% (girls) during the 2000s, as shown in Figure 2.9. Similarly, the proportion of children who had experienced drunkenness by age 15 increased from 30% to 43% (boys) and from 26% to 41% (girls) in the same period.

Early onset of drinking and high-risk drinking at young ages is especially worrying, as it makes problem drinking more likely in adult life. For instance, early drinkers are more likely to develop a dependence on alcohol at some point in their lives, and to have multiple and longer-lasting episodes of dependence (Hingson et al., 2006).

Figure 2.9. **Changes in age of first drink and first drunkenness 2001-2010, average across 20 OECD countries**

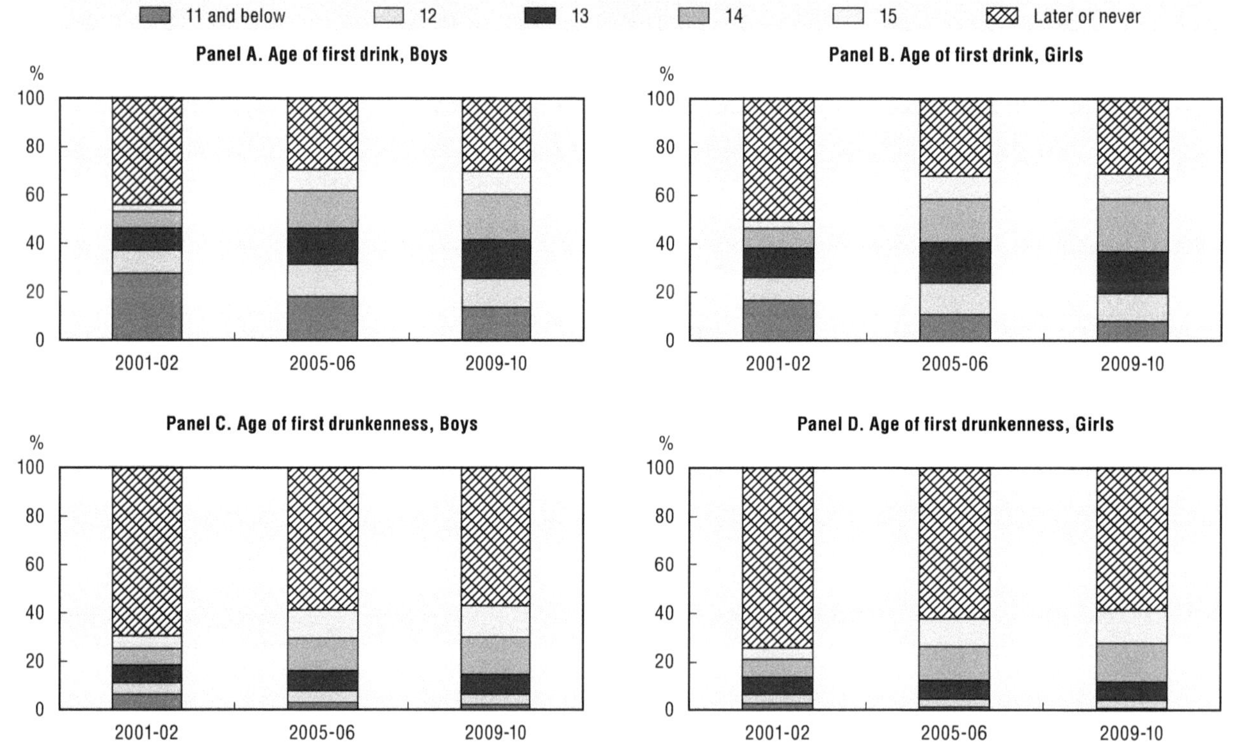


*Note:* Self reports at age 15. Interpretation: in Panel A, 44% of boys aged 15 never drank alcohol in 2001-02, versus 30% in 2009-10.

*Source:* Health Behaviours in School-aged Children survey, 2001-02, 2005-06, and 2009-10. The analysis includes all OECD countries for which data are available in all of the above HBSC waves.

StatLink http://dx.doi.org/10.1787/888933180348

## Cohort patterns in alcohol drinking

Longitudinal data from surveys that follow people over a number of years are used to analyse how drinking patterns and alcohol-related behaviours change with age. Some studies have examined age-period-cohort effects on drinking patterns. On average across age and cohort groups, alcohol consumption has considerably declined over the last 15 years in Germany (Pabst et al., 2010). Cohort effects indicate a decline in alcohol volume from the 1940s to the 1970s birth cohort groups, but a steep increase in younger cohorts. Moreover, cohorts born after 1980 were found to drink to intoxication more often than older cohorts. Likewise, age-period-cohort effects were studied using US and Finnish data, showing evidence of increased alcohol drinking in recent-born cohorts. Average alcohol consumption in US adults aged 26 and over has declined between 1979 and 2005, whereas in the younger age group (18-25) it has increased substantially (William et al., 2008). A Finnish study based on data from the period 1968-2008, found light drinking to have increased over time, and recent-born cohorts, both male and female, increasingly engaging in HED (Härkönen and Mäkelä, 2011).

Our investigation on longitudinal Australian and Canadian data shows that cohort effects exist in hazardous drinking, at least in Canada. Figure 2.10 permits one to follow individuals within the same cohort, and shows that hazardous drinking increases with age and that younger cohorts have higher rates of hazardous drinkers, this being especially the case for women in Canada. For instance, women from birth cohorts 1977-81 display, at the same ages, higher rates of hazardous drinking compared to women from cohorts 1972-76 and 1967-71 (Panel D). The same pattern, however, is not seen in Australian data.

Figure 2.10. **Birth cohort patterns in hazardous drinking**

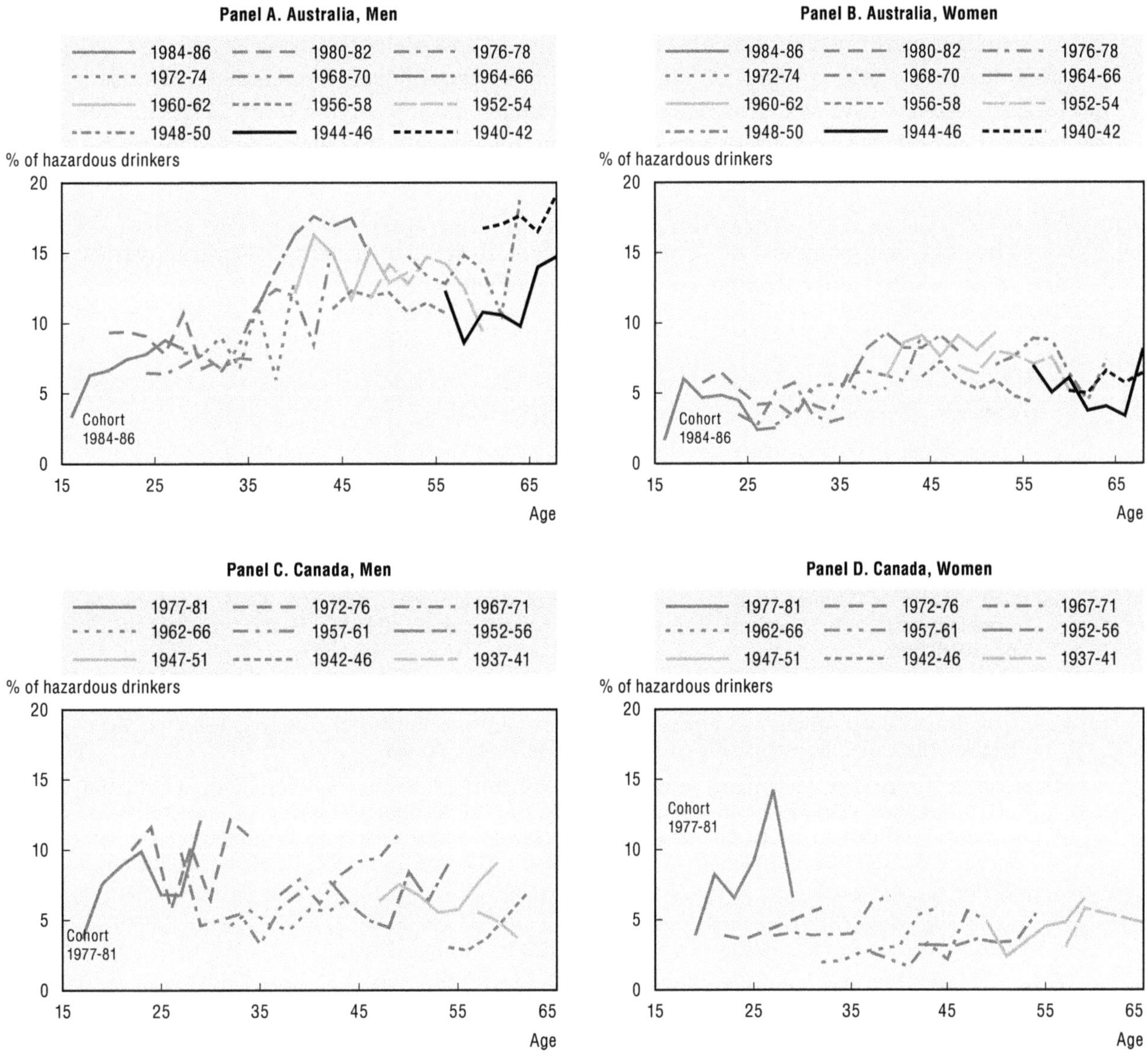


*Source:* OECD estimates based on HILDA (Australia) and NHPS (Canada) surveys.

StatLink http://dx.doi.org/10.1787/888933180358

## Conclusion: Convergence and divergence

Data on the average decline in alcohol consumption over the past 20 years in OECD countries are too broad to provide useful guidance to policy makers and health professionals, and up to a quarter of consumption is probably unrecorded. Moreover, differences in definitions and data acquisition methods across countries, and even for similar studies in a single country, can make it difficult to compare situations. However, some broad trends can be identified. And, while overall drinking patterns in OECD countries tend to range from "least risky" to "medium risk", most alcohol is consumed by a relatively small number of drinkers, so a figure that is reassuring at national level may hide significant problems.

The picture presented here shows a number of trends that are changing over time, but not always in the same direction, trends that vary according to geography, time period, and social and economic characteristics. The WHO European region, for example, has the highest per capita consumption in the world, but consumption has been declining in southern Europe while rising in some northern and central-eastern European countries.

A number of these trends are worrying. The proportion of girls and boys aged under 15 who have consumed alcohol is rising, and girls are now almost as likely as boys to have tried drinking. The proportion of children who have experienced drunkenness has risen for both sexes to over 40%. This risks compounding another worrying trend in the future: levels of hazardous and binge drinking among younger people are rising, notably for young women in some countries, while they have declined or at least remained stable in older age groups.

The following chapter will look in more detail at how drinking behaviour varies according to social and economic group and level of education.

### Notes

1. www.who.int/substance_abuse/terminology/who_lexicon/en/.
2. In our analyses of alcohol use in the United States, we used both NHANES and NSDUH data. When NHANES was used, it was primarily because it provides the longest trend data.

### Bibliography


Boniface, S. and N. Shelton (2013), "How is Alcohol Consumption Affected if We Account for Underreporting? A Hypothetical Scenario", *European Journal of Public Health*, Vol. 23, No. 6, pp. 1076-1081.

Burki, T. (2010), "Changing Drinking Patterns: A Sobering Thought", *The Lancet*, Vol. 376.

Cawley, J. (2000), "Body Weight and Women's Labor Market Outcomes", *NBER Working Paper No. 7841*, National Bureau of Economic Research, Cambridge, United States.

de Bruijn, A., E. van den Wildenberg, A. van den Broeck (2012), "Commercial Promotion of Drinking in Europe: Key Findings of Independent Monitoring of Alcohol Marketing in Five European Countries", Dutch Institute for Alcohol Policy (STAP), available at http://amphoraproject.net/w2box/data/AMPHORA%20Reports/Ammie_repport_2012.pdf?PHPSESSID=35ci20qg5dv9k73h8ugq6dho71.

Devaux, M. and F. Sassi (2015), "Alcohol Consumption and Harmful Drinking: Trends in Social Disparities across OECD Countries", *Health Working Paper*, OECD Publishing, Paris.

Eads, L. (2014), "UK Pub Closures Climb to 31 Per Week", *The Drinks Business*, 12 August 2014 www.thedrinksbusiness.com/2014/08/uk-pub-closures-climb-to-31-per-week/.

Ely, M. et al. (2001), "Methods of Estimating Individual Levels of Alcohol Consumption in the General Population", Alcohol Research, http://alcoholresearchuk.org/downloads/finalReports/AERC_FinalReport_0009.pdf.

Furtwaengler, N. and R. de Visser (2013), "Lack of Consensus in Low-risk Drinking Guidelines", *Drug and Alcohol Review*, Vol. 32, pp. 11-18.

GSHS – Global School-based Student Health Survey (2004), World Health Organization, Geneva.

Härkönen, J. and P. Mäkelä (2011), "Age, Period and Cohort Analysis of Light and Binge Drinking in Finland, 1968-2008", *Alcohol and Alcoholism*, Vol. 46, No. 3, pp. 349-356.

Hibell, B. et al. (2012), *The 2011 ESPAD Report: Substance Use Among Students in 36 European Countries*, Swedish Council for Information on Alcohol and Other Drugs (CAN), Stockholm.

Hill-MacManus, D. et al. (2014), "Estimation of Usual Occasion-based Individual Drinking Patterns Using Diary Data", *Drug and Alcohol Dependence*, Vol. 134, pp. 136-143.

Hingson, R.W., T. Heeren and M.R. Winter (2006), "Age at Drinking Onset and Alcohol Dependence", *Archives of Pediatrics and Adolescent Medicine*, Vol. 160, pp. 739-746.

Hingson, R.W. et al. (2013), "Physician Advice to Adolescents about Drinking and Other Health Behaviors", *Pediatrics*, Vol. 131, No. 2, pp. 249-257.

Hughes, K. and M. Bellis (2012), "Drinking Environments", in P. Anderson, L. Møllers and G. Galea (eds.), *Alcohol in the European Union- Consumption, Harm and Policy Approaches*, WHO, Geneva.

Kaynak, Ö. et al. (2014), "Providing Alcohol for Underage Youth: What Messages Should We Be Sending Parents?", *Journal of Studies on Alcohol and Drugs*, Vol. 75, No. 4, pp. 590-605.

Lakdawalla, D. and T.J. Philipson (2002), "Technological Change and the Growth of Obesity", *NBER Working Paper No. 8946*, Cambridge, United States.

Leifman, H, E. Österberg and M. Ramstedt (2002), "Alcohol in Post-War Europe: A Discussion of Indicators on Consumption and Alcohol-related Harm", European Comparative Alcohol Study (ECAS), European Commission, Stokholm.

Lemmens, P., R.A. Knibbe and F. Tan (1988), "Weekly Recall and Diary Estimates of Alcohol Consumption in a General Population Survey", *Journal of Studies on Alcohol*, Vol. 49, pp. 131-135.

Livingston, M. (2008), "Recent Trends in Risky Alcohol Consumption and Related Harm Among Young People in Victoria, Australia", *Australian and New Zealand Journal of Public Health*, Vol. 32, No. 3, pp. 266-271.

Mäkelä, P. et al. (2005), "Drinking and Gender Differences in Drinking in Europe – A Comparison of Drinking Patterns in European Countries", Chapter 2 in K. Bloomfield et al. (ed.), *Gender, Culture and Alcohol Problems: A Multi-national Study*, Project Final Report, Charité Universitätsmedizin Berlin, January.

Meier, P.S. et al. (2013), "Adjusting for Unrecorded Consumption in Survey and Per Capita Sales Data: Quantification of Impact on Gender- and Age-specific Alcohol-attributable Fractions for Oral and Pharyngeal Cancers in Great Britain", *Alcohol and Alcoholism*, Vol. 48, No. 2, pp. 241-249.

Midanik, L. (1982), "The Validity of Self-Reported Alcohol Consumption and Alcohol Problems: A Literature Review", *British Journal of Addiction*, Vol. 77, No. 4, pp. 357-382.

Morgan, K. et al. (2008), "SLÁN 2007: Survey of Lifestyle, Attitudes & Nutrition in Ireland", Main Report, Department of Health and Children, Dublin.

Moss, H.B. et al. (2014), "Early Adolescent Patterns of Alcohol, Cigarettes, and Marijuana Polysubstance Use and Young Adult Substance Use Outcomes in a Nationally Representative Sample", *Drug and Alcohol Dependence*, Vol. 136, pp. 51-62.

Murray, R. et al. (2002), "Alcohol Volume, Drinking Pattern, and Cardiovascular Disease Morbidity and Mortality: Is There a U-shaped Function?", *American Journal of Epidemiology*, Vol. 155, No. 3, pp. 242-248.

OECD (2014), *OECD Health Statistics 2014*, www.oecd.org/els/health-systems/health-data.htm.

Pabst, A. et al. (2010), "Age, Period, and Cohort Effects on Time Trends in Alcohol Consumption in the German Adult Population", *SUCHT*, Vol. 56, No. 5, pp. 349-359.

Patrick, M.E. et al. (2013), "Extreme Binge Drinking among 12th-grade Students in the United States: Prevalence and Predictors", *JAMA Pediatrics*, Vol. 167, No. 11, pp. 1019-1025.

Rabinovich, L. et al. (2009), "The Affordability of Alcoholic Beverages in the European Union – Understanding the Link between Alcohol Affordability, Consumption and Harms", Rand Europe Report.

Rahkonen, O. and S. Ahlström (1989), "Trends in Drinking Habits Among Finnish Youth from 1973 to 1987", *British Journal of Addiction*, Vol. 84, No. 9, pp. 1075-1083.

Rehm, J. et al. (2010), "Statistical Modeling of Volume of Alcohol Exposure for Epidemiological Studies of Population Health: The US Example", *Population Health Metrics*, Vol. 8, No. 3.

Rehm, J. et al. (2003), "The Global Distribution of Average Volume of Alcohol Consumption and Patterns of Drinking", *European Addiction Research*, Vol. 9, pp. 147-156.

Rehm, J. et al. (2002), "Alcohol as a Risk Factor for Burden of Disease", in M Ezzati, A.D. Lopez, A. Rodgers and C.J.L. Murray (eds.), *Comparative Quantification of Health Risks: Global and Regional Burden of Disease Due to Selected Major Risk Factors*, World Health Organization, Geneva.

Seaman, P. and T. Ikegwuonu (2010), "Drinking to Belong – Understanding Young Adults' Alcohol Use within Social Networks", Joseph Rowntree Foundation Report.

Shield, K. and J. Rehm (2012), "Difficulties with Telephone-based Surveys on Alcohol Consumption in High-income Countries: The Canadian Example", *International Journal of Methods in Psychiatrics Research*, Vol. 21, No. 1, pp. 17-28.

Stockwell, T. et al. (2004), "Under-reporting of Alcohol Consumption in Household Surveys: A Comparison of Quantity –Frequency, Graduated-frequency and Recent Recall", *Addiction*, Vol. 99, No. 8, pp. 1024-1033.

Townshend, J.M. and T. Dukat (2002), "Patterns of Alcohol Drinking in a Population of Young Social Drinkers: A Comparison of Questionnaire and Diary Measures", *Alcohol and Alcoholism*, Vol. 37, No. 2, pp. 187-192.

White, A.M. et al. (2011), "Hospitalizations for Alcohol and Drug Overdoses in Young Adults Ages 18-24 in the United States, 1999-2008: Results from the Nationwide Inpatient Sample", *Journal of Studies on Alcohol and Drugs*, Vol. 72, No. 5, pp. 774-786.

WHO – World Health Organization (2014), "Global Status Report on Alcohol and Health", World Health Organization, Geneva.

WHO (2011), "Global Status Report on Alcohol and Health", World Health Organization, Geneva.

William, C.K. et al. (2008), "Age-period-cohort Modelling of Alcohol Volume and Heavy Drinking Days in the US National Alcohol Surveys: Divergence in Younger and Older Adult Trends", *Addiction*, Vol. 104, pp. 27-37.

Winward, J.L. et al. (2014), "Adolescent Heavy Episodic Drinking: Neurocognitive Functioning During Early Abstinence", *Journal of the International Neuropsychological Society*, Vol. 20, No. 2, pp. 218-229.

Tackling Harmful Alcohol Use
Economics and Public Health Policy


# Chapter 3

# Social disparities in alcohol drinking

*by*
Marion Devaux

*No single variable predicts the likelihood that a person will adopt a given pattern of consuming alcohol. People with more education and higher socioeconomic status are more likely to drink alcohol, but social gradients differ in men and women for hazardous and heavy episodic drinking. Men who are less educated and have lower socioeconomic status, and women who are more educated and have higher socioeconomic status, are more likely to drink at risk in many countries. However, there is a fairly strong trend for women's drinking behaviours to converge to those of men. Heavy drinking is associated with a lesser probability of being in employment, more absence from work, lower productivity and wages, and a greater likelihood of causing accidents and injuries in the workplace. Moderate drinking is associated with improved labour outcomes in many studies; however, these findings are disputed by others due to the potential for selection.*

## Key findings

- People who are better educated and of higher socioeconomic status are more likely to drink alcohol than others.
- In most countries, hazardous drinking is more common among women who are more educated and of higher socioeconomic status, then in women of lower socioeconomic status, but the opposite is true for men.
- For heavy episodic drinking, the link with education and social status varies across countries for both men and women.
- The drinking behaviours of young, better educated, and higher socioeconomic status women are converging to those of men.
- In general, people from minority ethnic groups drink less alcohol than the majority of the population, but there are important exceptions in some countries.
- Alcohol has mixed impacts on labour market outcomes, with results varying according to pattern of drinking and age. However, existing estimates suggest that alcohol-related productivity losses are in the region of 1% of GDP in most countries.
- While the impact of heavy drinking on labour outcomes is consistently negative, there is some evidence that moderate drinking may have a positive impact, especially on wages.

## Identifying social patterns in alcohol drinking

Most people drink alcohol in OECD countries, but a few people drink most of the alcohol, as we have shown in Chapter 2. This suggests that hazardous drinking behaviours are likely to be concentrated in certain population groups, and this may be a source of additional concerns for alcohol policy makers. The work presented in this chapter assesses whether the distribution of hazardous drinking follows systematic patterns within and across countries. We identify the people who are most likely to engage in hazardous and heavy episodic drinking, based on their gender, education, socioeconomic status, racial and ethnic background, and we have compared patterns across countries, assessing differences and similarities.

We have made special efforts to shed light on the complex relationship between alcohol drinking and socioeconomic status, by looking at the links involved in both directions: socioeconomic status as a determinant of alcohol drinking, and alcohol drinking as a determinant of labour market outcomes such as employment, productivity and wages, affecting in turn socioeconomic status.

## The gender dimension: Drinking habits in men and women

Numerous international studies found that men are more often drinkers and consume more alcohol than women. Bloomfield et al. (2006) highlighted gender differences in 13 European countries, as well as in Brazil and Mexico. They found the smallest gender differences in drinking behaviour in northern, followed by western and central European countries, with the largest gender differences in countries with less developed economies. Their results also show that gender differences in drinking behaviour are smaller in countries with greater overall gender equality. Gender differences in drinking are intertwined with educational and socioeconomic gradients in harmful drinking patterns (Bloomfield et al., 2006; Gmel et al., 2005; Huerta and Borgonovi, 2010; Grittner et al., 2013), also discussed in the following sections.

However, the gender gap is tending to narrow as women's drinking behaviours increasingly resemble men's. Surveys and journalist interviews of women convicted of drink and drive offences show how much social attitudes and other contributing factors have changed over the years (Beuret et al., 2014; Rock, 2014). The UK Government's first drink-drive campaign, launched at Christmas 1964, was aimed at women at an office party. But it was based on the assumption that they would not drink and could stop a man who'd had too much from getting behind the wheel. That may or may not have been the case 50 years ago, but greater female labour force participation and greater professional equality has exposed more women to the same work environments and social pressures to drink as men. This is particularly true of professional women, who tend to start families later and continue longer with a lifestyle that features socialising with colleagues both during and after working hours.

### Box 3.1. **Alcohol and women's health**

Maternal alcohol consumption during pregnancy has several adverse consequences on foetal development. The most important of these are Foetal Alcohol Spectrum Disorders (FASD), which include a range of physical, cognitive, behavioural and learning disabilities. A recent systematic review found that mothers of children with FASD have distinctive patterns of alcohol drinking, including an overall higher intake before and during pregnancy; failure to reduce, or abstain from, alcohol use during pregnancy; frequent episodes of binge drinking; a higher number of weekdays with alcohol consumption and an earlier age of initiation into regular alcohol consumption (Esper et al., 2014). The risk of FASD development increases with the duration of alcohol intake during pregnancy, from 12-fold for women who drink only during the first trimester, relative to non-drinking women, to 65-fold for women drinking in all trimesters (May et al., 2013).

Drinking during pregnancy is also a leading risk factor for miscarriage (Feodor Nilsson et al 2014). An increased risk has been found to be associated with an intake of four or more drinks per week, and with drinking only spirits (Avalos et al., 2014). Even small amounts of alcohol use during the early stages of pregnancy can increase the risk of spontaneous abortion (Nybo Andersen et al., 2012), but not alcohol consumption before pregnancy (Lassi et al., 2014). Maternal alcohol use was also found to be associated with an increased risk for both sudden infant death syndrome (SIDS) (McDonnell-Naughton et al., 2012; Van Nguyen and Abenhaim, 2013), and non-SIDS infant death (O'Leary et al., 2013).

Beuret et al.'s findings confirm that the stereotyped image of "Female drinkers" as young, working-class women getting drunk on a night out is often only the most visible aspect of the phenomenon. The highest proportion of hazardous drinkers is to be found among women in the 45-64 age group. The women interviewed by Rock confirm this, but suggest that while their increased drinking compared to previous generations is partly due to increased social acceptability, much of it is done at home, still hidden from public view. These women also illustrate another phenomenon described in more detail in Chapter 2, the shift in type of alcoholic beverage consumed. They mostly drink wine, rather than more traditional "British drinks" like beer or gin. This is partly because it is now so easy to find wine and other drinks at supermarkets, and at far cheaper prices than in previous decades.

A report by the Public Health Foundation of India (PHFI, 2013) argues that: "Wine companies are especially targeting urban women". The PHFI lists other strategies previously deployed elsewhere now being tried in India, such as "ladies nights" where women are given free alcohol, or drinks promoted primarily for women. In OECD countries, these have included "rosé" beers, while women in China are the target for fruit-flavoured "Hello Kitty" beers (Weissmann, 2013), with lower alcohol content and different packaging from traditional products.

There has been a social change too, with wine, and other alcohol readily available at numerous "normal" social occasions and places and no longer reserved for special events and celebrations or specific drinking places.

## Social disparities in any alcohol drinking

Many studies have looked at the association between socioeconomic condition and patterns of alcohol drinking. At first sight, it seems possible to explain alcohol consumption in purely economic terms – the better-off tend to drink more than people with less money because they can afford to. In that, it would be unlike other behaviours such as smoking that are both costly and more frequent in people with lower incomes. However, alcohol consumption is similar to other harmful behaviours as far as abuse is concerned. For instance, there is evidence of a positive association between education and the frequency of consumption but also of a negative association between education and heavy drinking (Bloomfield et al., 2006; Caldwell et al., 2008; Casswell et al., 2003).

In a meta-analysis of 33 countries as part of the GENACIS project (Gender, Alcohol and Culture International Study), women with more education were found to be more likely to consume alcohol than women with less education. The same was true for men in most countries (with the exception of India) (Grittner et al., 2012).

In a number of countries (the Czech Republic, Finland, France, Germany, Hungary, Sweden, Switzerland and the United Kingdom), both men and women with higher incomes were found to be more likely to consume alcohol (Gmel et al., 2005). Similar findings were reported based on data from Estonia, Latvia and Lithuania (McKee et al., 2000), with women in the highest income group being more likely to consume alcohol compared to women in the middle or lowest income group (Figure 3.1.).

OECD estimates show a similar distribution of drinking status: for both genders, adults with higher education and higher socioeconomic status are more likely to consume alcohol in the past 12 months than their lower-education and lower-SES counterparts. This is observed in all countries, although the educational gradient and the socioeconomic gradient are not significant in a few cases, as illustrated in Figures A1 and A4 in Annex A, presenting differences in alcohol drinking rates by education level and by socioeconomic status.

Figure 3.1. **Social disparities in alcohol drinking in the past 12 months**

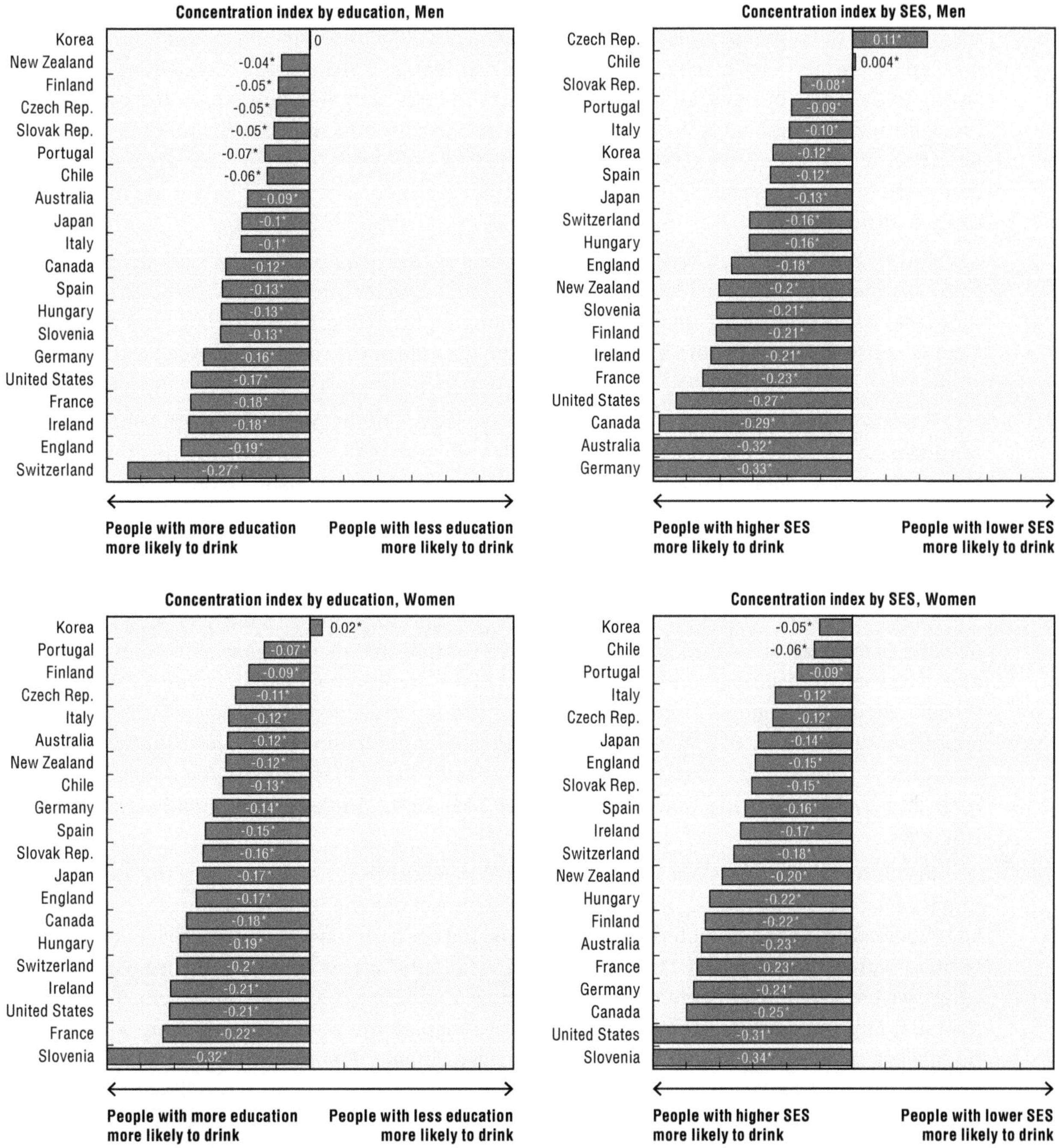


*Note:* Normalised values. Socioeconomic status (SES) is based on occupation in Chile, England, France, Hungary, Italy, Japan, Portugal, Spain, and Switzerland, and on household income in other countries. The analysis covers people 25+ except for the Czech and Slovak Republics and for Slovenia (16+). (*) value of index is statistically significant ($p<0.05$).

*Source:* OECD estimates based on national health surveys, most recent years (details in Table A1).

StatLink http://dx.doi.org/10.1787/888933180363

The "concentration index" shown in Figure 3.1 is a statistical measure used to quantify the degree of inequality in a health variable (in this case drinking any alcohol in the last 12 months) that is related to socioeconomic characteristics (education or socioeconomic status here). Almost all countries display a negative index indicating that people with less education and with lower SES are less likely to consume alcohol in the past 12 months. The magnitude of these inequalities varies among countries. Education-related inequalities are marked in Switzerland in men, and in Slovenia in women. SES-related inequalities are strong in Canada, Germany, and the United States in both men and women. On the other hand, virtually no inequality is detected in men in Korea (by education level) and Chile (by SES). Positive values of the index (e.g. men by SES in the Czech Republic and women by education in Korea) mean that people at the bottom of the socioeconomic ladder are more likely to drink alcohol.

Part of the explanation why people of higher SES drink more often than others may be that drinking is associated with and integrated into a wider range of activities. The fact that rates of abstinence are generally lower among higher SES groups also suggests that alcohol consumption is a more integral part of the lifestyle of the more advantaged (Giskes et al., 2011).

It is also possible that better-educated are more aware of the potential health benefits of moderate drinking, even though some studies suggest that those with the healthiest behaviour profile obtain no additional benefit from moderate consumption of alcohol (Britton et al., 2008).

## Social disparities in hazardous drinking

While the overall trend for any drinking in the past 12 months is fairly clear, social disparities for hazardous drinking present a more complicated picture, especially for men, as can be seen from simply comparing the "look" of the graphs presented in Figure 3.2 with those in Figure 3.1. Figure 3.2 presents the concentration index for hazardous drinking by education level and by SES in 15 OECD countries. As a complement, Figures A2 and A5 in Annex A present the corresponding probabilities of hazardous drinking by education level and by SES, showing that proportions of hazardous drinkers vary greatly across countries.

Moreover, unlike "any drinking" where level of education has practically the same impact everywhere, increasing the probability, the impact of a higher level of education can be to increase the chances of hazardous drinking, reduce it, or have no clear impact at all. In other words, the "direction of the gradient of inequality" varies among countries. Three countries have significantly higher male hazardous drinking rates in the higher-educated (Canada, England, and Germany); seven countries display the reverse relationship – but not always significant; and four countries (Australia, Finland, France and Ireland) have an unclear pattern (see Figure A.2 in Annex A). Men with higher SES are more likely to be hazardous drinkers in six countries (Australia, Canada, England, Finland, Germany, and Ireland), whereas they are less at risk in Hungary, Japan, Korea, Switzerland and the United States (see Figure A.5 in Annex A). Canada, England and Germany therefore show higher hazardous male drinking rates for the two variables studied here.

For women, the picture is less mixed, and more in line with what one might expect from the data on "any drinking". In a large majority of countries, higher-educated and higher-SES women are not only more likely to have drunk in the past 12 months, they are also more likely to be hazardous drinkers (Australia, Canada, England, Finland, France, Germany, Hungary, Ireland, Spain, Switzerland, and the United States).

Figure 3.2. **Social disparities in hazardous drinking**

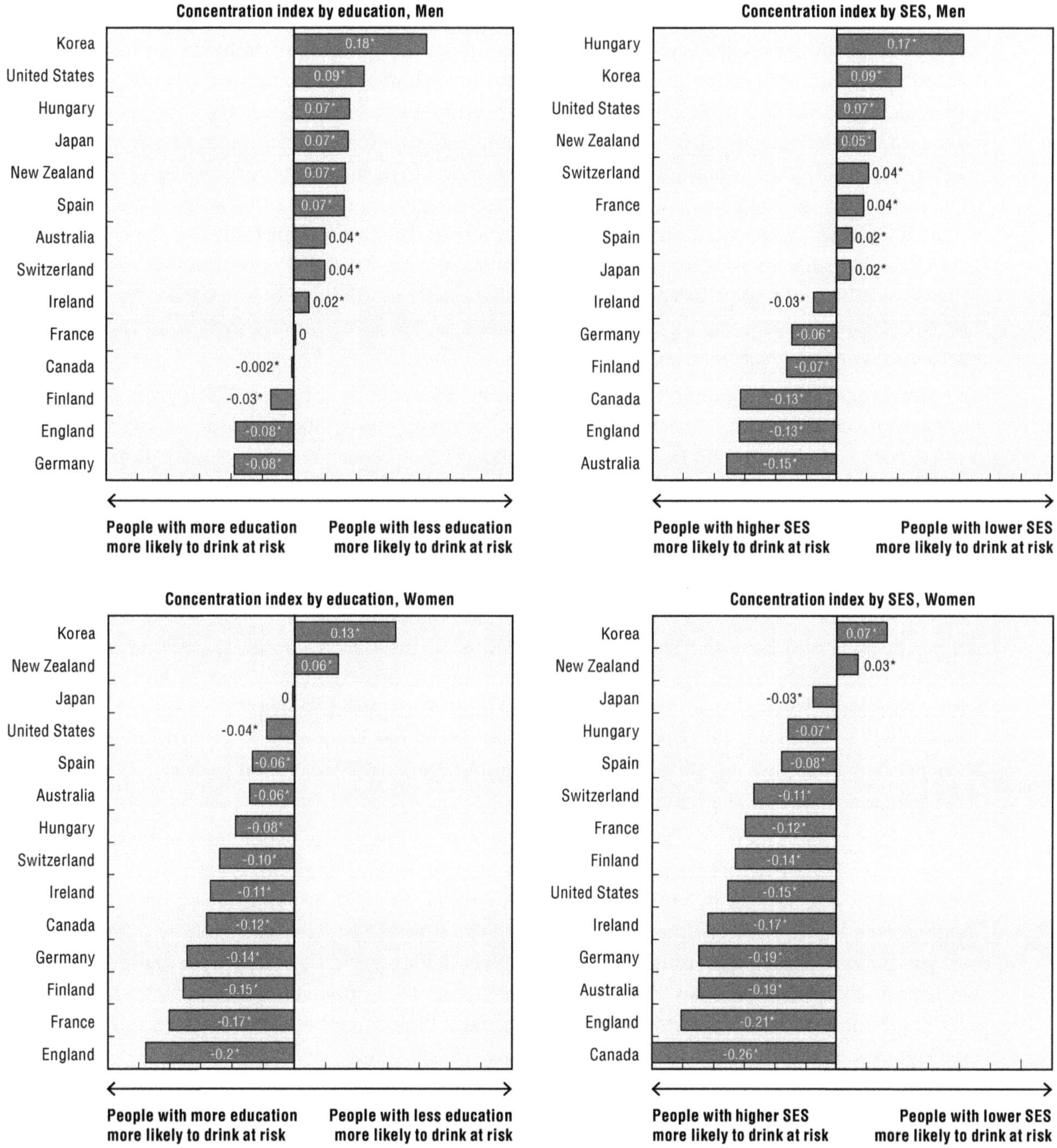


*Note:* Normalised values. Socioeconomic status.(SES) is based on occupation in England, France, Hungary, Japan, Spain and Switzerland, and on household income in other countries. The analysis covers people 25+ (*) value of index is statistically significant (p<0.05).

*Source:* OECD estimates based on national health surveys, most recent years (details in Table A1).

*StatLink* http://dx.doi.org/10.1787/888933180374

For men, most countries show a concentration index above zero in Figure 3.2, indicating that the more educated and the better-off are less at risk. Chile, Hungary, Korea and the United States display the highest degree of inequality in male hazardous drinking. Conversely, for women, most countries show a concentration index under zero, indicating that the more educated and the better-off are more at risk.

## Social disparities in heavy episodic drinking

Heavy episodic or "binge" drinking is probably the most talked-about phenomenon in alcohol consumption in recent years. It differs from other forms of drinking and even hazardous drinking because the intention is to drink harmful amounts of alcohol. The expression was coined in Britain but has been adopted in other languages too as the behaviour spread to countries with less experience of this form of drinking, like France. As Berridge et al. (2007) point out, practices similar to binge drinking have been a feature of British society at least since written records began and binging has not always attracted social disapproval or government intervention. Another constant seems to be the attention given to a particular social group (the poor or industrial workers at different times) whether it deserved the most attention or not. Recent interest seems to have been sparked by the fact that binge drinking was increasingly being seen as a problem among the young and in particular working-class women.

However, the pattern of social disparities in heavy episodic drinking (HED) presented here is more complicated. Once again it is mixed for men, but results for women also show a more complex picture than those for "any drinking" and "hazardous drinking". Figure 3.3 presents the concentration index for HED by education level and by SES in 17 countries for men and 13 countries for women. As a complement, Figures A3 and A6 in Annex A present the corresponding probabilities of HED by education level and by SES.

Rates of HED vary greatly across countries with very low levels of HED in Chile, France, Hungary, Portugal, Slovenia and Switzerland, as shown in Figures A.3 and A.6 in Annex A. Men who have received higher education in the Czech Republic, England, and Italy are more likely to engage in HED whereas they are less likely to do so in Australia, Chile, Hungary, Ireland, New Zealand, Portugal and the United States. The well-off are more at risk in Australia, Canada, and England, while the reverse is true in Chile, Germany, Hungary, Portugal and the United States, although results for the social gradient in the latter countries are not always significant.

Similarly, for women, the direction of the gradient of inequality is not clear-cut within all countries. More highly educated women are more at risk in England, France, Italy, and Portugal, but less at risk in other countries (Australia, Canada, Ireland, Japan and New Zealand; see Figure A.3 in Annex A). The pattern for SES-related inequalities in women is also mixed, but less so, with only women from New Zealand and Germany with lower SES being more likely to drink than women of higher SES, and the opposite in Australia, Canada and England, with other countries showing no clear difference between the two groups (see Figure A.6 in Annex A).

Figure 3.3 presents a cross-country comparison of concentration indexes (CI) in HED in order to gauge inequalities across countries. For men, most countries show a concentration index above zero indicating that the more educated are less at risk to engage in HED, although this is not always verified in the picture of CI by SES. Chile, Portugal and the United States display the highest degree of inequality in male HED. Similarly, for women, the pattern of education-related and SES-related inequalities is unclear. While Japan (CI by education) and New Zealand (CI by SES) have one of the highest degrees of inequality in female HED (where HED is more concentrated among the less educated and the worst-off), at the other end of the scale, in France (CI by education) and Australia (CI by SES) HED is more concentrated among the more educated and the better-off.

 

Figure 3.3. **Social disparities in heavy episodic drinking**

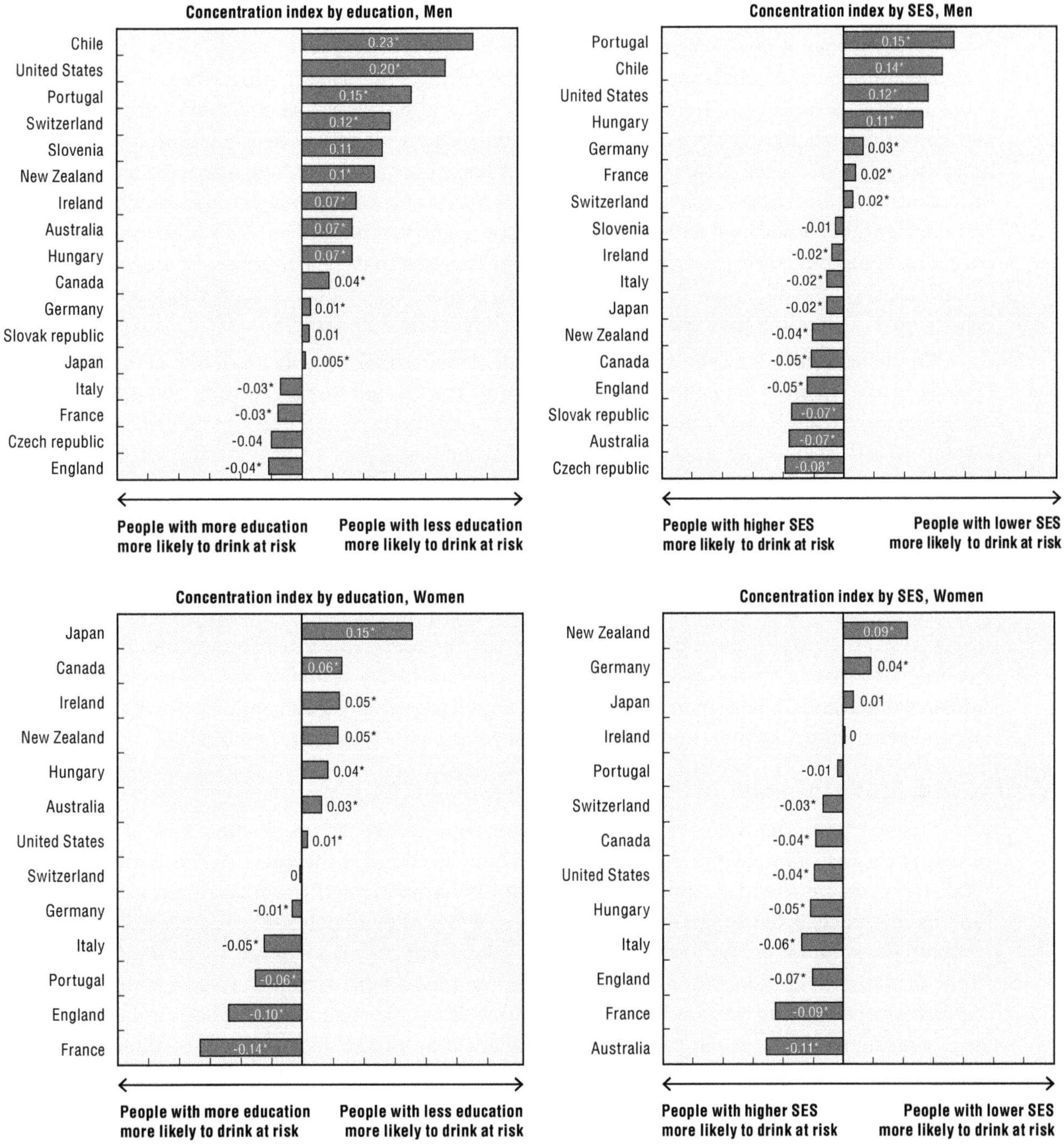


*Note:* Normalised values. Socioeconomic status (SES) is based on occupation in Chile, England, France, Hungary, Italy, Japan, Portugal and Switzerland, and on household income in other countries. The analysis covers people 25+ except for the Czech and Slovak Republics and for Slovenia (16+). Data not shown for women in Chile, Slovenia, the Czech Republic and the Slovak Republic, because of small numbers of observation. (*) value of index is statistically significant ($p<0.05$).

*Source:* OECD estimates based on national health surveys, most recent years (details in Table A1).

StatLink http://dx.doi.org/10.1787/888933180389

## Ethnic disparities in alcohol use

Culture has a strong influence on many aspects of alcohol consumption. For example, in a traditional wine-producing country where wine is a normal part of meals, initiation to the consumption of alcohol may happen as a child during a family gathering, where alcohol consumption is incidental to other activities such as eating. For a teenager from northern Europe on the other hand, if the first drink is tasted at home, it may be secretly, or initiation may be as part of a group of peers going to a bar or pub, or buying drink from a shop, in which cases drinking alcohol is a goal in itself. It seems reasonable to assume that people whose ethnic identity is associated with strong cultural or religious roots will be influenced in their drinking behaviour by their origins. It may even be the case that the culture associated with ethnic origin is the dominant factor in explaining the pattern of alcohol consumption for a given individual, rather than social status, age, or education for example.

The relationship between ethnic status and alcohol drinking was analysed, all other things being equal, in England, New Zealand and the United States. Results show that minority groups generally drink less alcohol than the white population, except in the United States where Mexican-American men have a higher prevalence of any alcohol drinking than non-Hispanic white men. Concerning harmful forms of drinking, results show that in England, white men and women are more likely to engage in hazardous drinking and HED (Figure 3.4), while findings in other countries are seldom statistically significant.

However, while ethnicity may stay fixed, its influence on succeeding generations can change over time, with younger cohorts showing different behaviours to their elders, especially if the latter were immigrants. A study for the Joseph Rowntree Foundation found for example that in the United Kingdom, frequent and heavy drinking has increased for Indian women and Chinese men, and that while any drinking among Sikh girls has increased, second generation Sikh men drink less than first generations (Hurcombe et al., 2010).

## Alcohol and labour market outcomes: A complex link

Slogans from Victorian-era temperance movements like "Drink is the curse of the working classes" (famously inverted by Oscar Wilde as "Work is the curse of the drinking classes") promote the idea that drinking alcohol is harmful for the workers themselves, and by inference, is detrimental to their ability to work. Alcohol policies at the start of the industrial revolution did not try to eliminate drinking, but they were based on attempts to limit alcohol consumption, for example by restricting the length of time licensed premises could stay open during working hours or at night when workers should have been at home recuperating for the next day's shift. The argument that alcohol has a negative influence on the workplace would still receive widespread support today. But while alcohol use is undoubtedly associated with employment and labour outcomes, the influence is not always negative, and it varies according to levels of alcohol consumption, as shown by the evidence of this association from the studies reviewed in this section.

Some of these studies are based on statistical approaches that enable the causal nature of the associations observed between alcohol use and labour market outcomes to be assessed. Other studies simply explore statistical correlations without trying to say if alcohol is the main cause or a significant cause of the observed outcome. The following review does not provide a detailed account and discussion of the methods adopted in each study, but it is safe to say that all of the main findings of the review are supported by at least one econometrically sound analysis confirming the causal nature of the links assessed.

Figure 3.4. **Ethnic disparities in drinking behaviours**

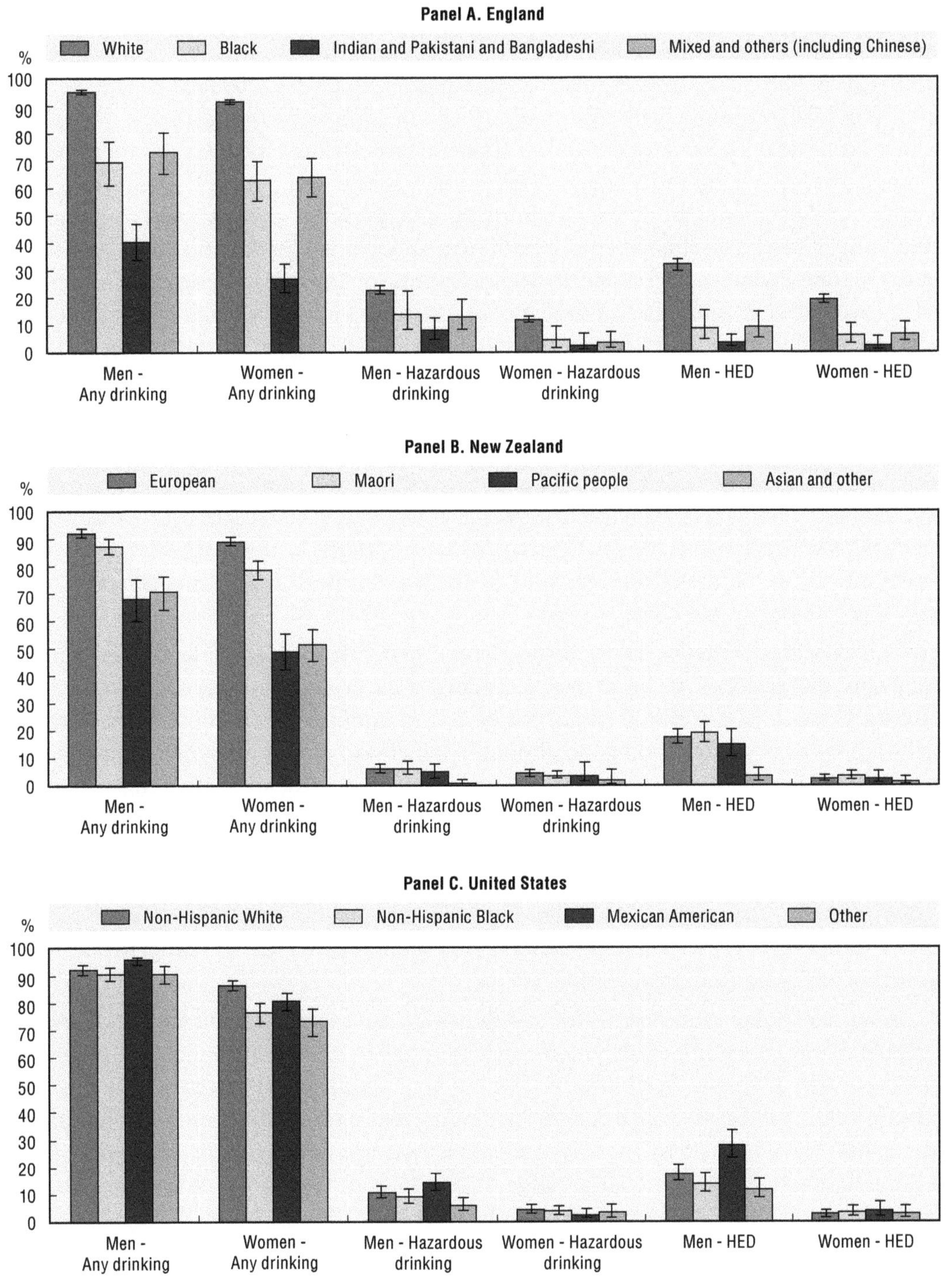


*Note:* Population aged 25+.

*Source:* OECD estimates based on national surveys, latest available years (details in Table A.1 in Annex A).

StatLink http://dx.doi.org/10.1787/888933180396

### *Alcohol and employment*

The impact of alcohol consumption on employment, as well as on other labour market outcomes discussed in the following sections, depends on the quantity consumed and pattern of consumption, and may also be influenced in some cases by factors specific to the country in which the data were collected. In Sweden, long-term light drinkers were shown to have better employment opportunities than any other group, including former drinkers, former abstainers, long-term heavy drinkers and abstainers (Jarl and Gerdtham, 2012). In other studies looking at different countries, heavy drinking was shown to reduce the probability of being in employment for both men and women (Booth and Feng, 2002 for the southern United States; MacDonald and Shields, 2001 for England; Johansson et al., 2008 for the European Union), although a number of other studies found no significant relationship between alcohol abuse and employment (Feng et al, 2001 again for the southern United States; Asgeirsdottir and McGeary, 2009 for Iceland).

The effects of problem drinking on employment appear to vary over the life cycle. Some studies provide surprising evidence that suggests that alcohol-dependent people above age 60 are more likely to be in employment than their non-dependent counterparts (Mullahy and Sindelar, 1993), without however offering any explanation as to why this is the case. The relationship for younger age groups is more in line with what one would expect intuitively, with alcohol-dependence damaging a person's prospects in the labour market (Johansson et al., 2008).

The relationship between problem alcohol drinking and employment is complex. Alcohol consumption may be a way of coping with stress, whether this stress is the result of the financial and others worries linked to unemployment, or the stress related to certain kinds of job or working conditions. An increase in unemployment was found to be associated with higher suicide rates for people below age 65, and with a higher alcohol-related mortality (Stuckler et al., 2009). Working conditions, such as long working hours and job insecurity, have been linked with an increased likelihood of high-risk alcohol consumption (Marchand et al., 2011). Some types of jobs may be affected by problem alcohol drinking more than others. For instance, in England and Wales, higher alcohol-related mortality was found among workers of the broader alcohol industry, including bar managers and staff (Romeri et al., 2007).

Heavy alcohol consumption during early adulthood seems to impact on people's lives in the long run, affecting employment opportunities. A US study found that those who drank regularly during early adulthood (18-30 years old) had lower "occupational prestige"[1] 15 years later, than occasional drinkers. The finding was particularly strong among African-Americans, for whom even moderate alcohol consumption in early adulthood had a negative impact on occupational prestige at age 45 and heavier drinking has an impact also on the probability of being employed (Sloan et al., 2009).

### *Alcohol and wages*

A number of studies suggest that there is some evidence that moderate drinking is positively associated with wages. The arguments put forward to support this claim are based on health and social characteristics. The underlying reason would be that moderate drinkers have better health and better job performance than heavy drinkers and abstainers, and this is reflected in their career prospects and wages (Hamilton and Hamilton, 1997; Barrett, 2002; Peters, 2004; Lee, 2003; MacDonald and Shields, 2001). As well as that, in an economy where "soft" skills such as networking, cooperating with members of a team and other social skills are important, the fact that moderate drinkers may spend more time socialising with their colleagues in and out of working hours, and thanks to this may have more professional contacts and access to more information about job prospects or other professionally relevant factors, positively influences their wages, for example by improving their chances of promotion or finding a better job. They also report a higher degree of life satisfaction than abstainers. A positive impact of moderate drinking on wages was also found in Germany, increasing in size and significance with age, starting from age 35 (Ziebarth and Grabka, 2009).

However, Lye and Hirschberg (2010) reviewed evidence of the labour market outcomes of alcohol consumption and found older studies indicating that alcohol consumption boosted wages, such as those cited above, may be biased in a number of ways. They may omit relevant variables such as personality traits, and the sample of workers studied may be biased by a number of factors, including the lower participation in the labour force by heavy drinkers and abusive drinkers, or classifying former heavy drinkers (whose health may already have been damaged) as abstainers. It is also possible that some drinkers hide their alcohol-related work problems, or that there is "reverse causality", i.e. that moderate drinking is a result of higher earnings and not a contributing factor (for example, if higher earnings also mean better working conditions or less stress outside work).

In contrast, many studies have found heavy drinking to be associated with lower earnings (Mullahy and Sindelar, 1991; 1993). The effects can be direct, for example in physically demanding jobs where earnings are determined by productivity, or indirect, by reducing "human capital" for instance by damaging education and training prospects and outcomes (Williams et al., 2003). Problem drinking impairs people differently depending on their gender and personal traits associated with the propensity to be heavy drinkers (Jones and Richmond, 2006). In a study by Renna (2007), alcoholism,[2] but not alcohol abuse, was found to be linked with reduced earnings, and the mechanism identified was reduced working hours, rather than a lower wage rate.

Some research examined gender differences in the relationship between alcohol use and wages, and found this to be stronger in men and weaker, or absent, in women (Soydemir and Bastida, 2006; Van Ours, 2004). These findings were deemed to reflect differences in the propensity to risk taking as a common determinant of both drinking behaviour and professional success. According to this argument, individuals who are more risk-averse are more likely to be attracted by occupations that pay less but are more stable (Bonin et al., 2007), and a large body of experimental evidence suggests that women are more risk-averse than men (Bertrand, 2010).

### *Alcohol and labour productivity*

#### *Absenteeism*

Alcohol abuse has acute and chronic health consequences such as hangovers, injuries from accidents, and psychiatric and somatic diseases, all of which are likely to increase short- and long-term sickness absences. In a number of countries, there is evidence for a link between high-risk alcohol consumption and sickness absence among men, though not in women (Roche et al., 2008; Norström and Moan, 2009; Norström, 2006; Johansson et al., 2008). For example, Roche et al. found that in Australia, high-risk drinkers were up to 22 times more likely to be absent from work due to alcohol use than low-risk drinkers. However, Roche et al. also stress that alcohol-related absenteeism is not just a problem of a relatively small number of chronic heavy drinkers. A much larger number of workers who drink less frequently at risky levels are still more likely than low-risk drinkers to be absent from work due to any illness or injury (and not just hangovers or other conditions directly related to alcohol).

The relation between alcohol intake and sickness absence is U-shaped rather than linear, that is to say that absence rates do not simply increase in line with the quantity of alcohol consumed, and the curve changes direction at one point. In Finland, for example, medically certified absences were 20% higher among former and heavy drinkers compared with light drinkers, but they were 20% higher for lifetime abstainers too (Vahtera et al., 2002). Additional evidence for the U-shaped relationship between alcohol consumption and sickness absence is found elsewhere in the literature (Salonsalmi et al., 2012). Using Swedish data for women, Jarl and Gerdtham (2012) showed that long-term light alcohol consumption reduces the probability of long-term absenteeism, but that the risk of absenteeism rises by around 10% for long-term abstainers and heavy drinkers. They also found that having changed consumption behaviour to or from abstention (i.e. former drinkers and former abstainers) shows the highest increases in the risk of long-term absenteeism. They do not explain why this should be the case, but it could be that such a change is linked to a relatively traumatic incident that in itself would also have an influence on absenteeism.

A more pronounced association between quantity of alcohol consumed and sickness absence was observed in men with low levels of education (Johansson et al., 2008). Another study suggested that perceived support from co-workers may make a worker who has problems of alcohol abuse less likely to be absent from work (Bacharach et al., 2010). Several factors could explain this. If workmates cover up for the alcohol abusers, then they may judge that the chances of getting fired for taking too much time off, or unannounced time off, are greater than the chances of getting fired for being drunk on the job. The alcohol abusers may also feel a sense of duty towards their helpful co-workers who would have to do extra work if they don't turn up.

### *Presenteeism*

Even so, when they are at work, alcohol abusers may not be as productive as their colleagues, a condition sometimes referred to as "presenteeism" – they are present, but as far as output they are like someone who is absent. Some studies have claimed that the main reason for reduced productivity due to alcohol is not days off work, but lower productivity while present in the workplace (Single et al., 2003). Presenteeism is far more difficult to assess than absenteeism, and there is no agreement on how it should be measured. Estimates are generally based on the costs associated with reduced output, increased number of errors, and failure to meet production targets (Schultz et al., 2009). Alcohol abuse is a cause of presenteeism. The after-effects of heavy drinking include inability to concentrate at work, deterioration in job performance and relationships with colleagues, higher safety risks and reduced overall output. These in turn can lead to disputes, grievances, loss of working time and reduced productivity (ILO, 2012).

### *Early retirement*

In addition to increasing the risk of sickness absence, alcohol abuse may also be a cause of early retirement on disability grounds, with receipt of disability benefits, in middle-aged workers (Upmark et al., 1999). Problem drinking was found to increase the risk of being the beneficiary of a disability pension in Finland, Norway, and Sweden (Salonsalmi et al., 2012; Skogen et al., 2011; Sidorchuk et al., 2012) although there is also evidence for a link between abstinence and receiving a disability pension (Upmark et al., 1999; Skogen et al., 2011; Salonsalmi et al., 2012).

### *Work-related accidents and injuries*

There have been suggestions that 20%-25% of workplace accidents are alcohol related (Henderson et al., 1996). These figures may be an underestimate since the person responsible may hide the involvement of alcohol in the incident if, as is likely, this changes possible compensation or sanctions. Even so, Figure 3.5 below still shows a remarkably high probability of harming the drinker or another person in two of the four countries examined, at over 35% and 25% for hazardous drinkers in Chile and Australia respectively. Even in Germany and Switzerland, however, hazardous drinkers are at least twice as likely as the average drinker to cause harm to themselves or others.

Figure 3.5. **Probability of injury or injuring someone else because of one's drinking**

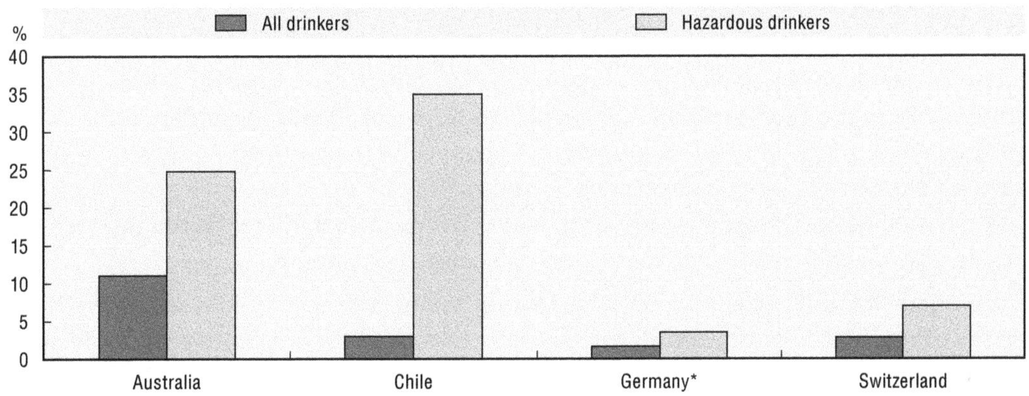


*Note:* (*) Includes only injuries to others.

*Source:* OECD estimates based on national surveys (details in Table A1), latest available years. For Australia: Household, Income and Labour Dynamics in Australia 2012.

StatLink http://dx.doi.org/10.1787/888933180401

### *The value of lost productivity*

A review of 22 studies from different countries observed a substantial economic burden of alcohol on society (Thavorncharoensap et al., 2009). In the United Kingdom, nearly 11 million working days were lost by alcohol-dependent workers in 2001, and the total cost of absenteeism due to alcohol was estimated to be GBP 1.2 billion (UK Cabinet Office, 2003). In the European Union alcohol accounted for an estimated EUR 59 billion worth of lost productivity through absenteeism, unemployment and lost working years through premature death in 2002 (Anderson and Baumberg, 2006). Productivity losses were found to be an important part of alcohol-related costs in Scotland, France and Canada (Rehm et al., 2009). In Ireland, the value of output lost due to alcohol-related absences from work was of EUR 330 million (9% of the total costs of absences from work) and the cost of alcohol related accidents at work of EUR 197 million (5% of total work-related accident costs), in 2007. The total cost of alcohol (EUR 3.7 billion) represented 1.9% of GDP in Ireland in 2007 (Byrne, 2010).

Lost labour earnings were found to account for the largest part of the economic costs associated with alcohol abuse in the Unites States (Harwood, 2000). In 2006, lost productivity represented 72.2% of the total economic cost of excessive drinking. The bulk of the value of lost productivity was attributable to impaired productivity at work (46%) and premature mortality (40%), while absenteeism accounted for 2.6% of the total value (Bouchery et al., 2011). In Australia, based on data from the 2001 National Drug Strategy Household Survey, the cost of alcohol-related absenteeism was estimated to be USD 437 million, or 36% of the cost due to all absenteeism (Pidd et al., 2006).

## Different gradients in consumption and alcohol-related harm?

As mentioned in the first chapter, drinking alcohol is influenced by cultural norms that are relatively straightforward. Per capita consumption is lower in societies where drinking is discouraged or forbidden by the dominant religion for instance. However, as the preceding sections of this chapter show, the impact of social norms on alcohol consumption is more complicated than that of cultural norms, and behaviours related to alcohol do not always show the same characteristics as those associated with other harmful or potentially harmful lifestyle features such as smoking or not doing any physical exercise.

Disparities are apparent in all the combinations of variables studied here, whether social criteria such as level of education, gender, and socioeconomic status; drinking patterns; or geographical location. In some cases or places, the better-off and more highly educated are more likely to drink, elsewhere the opposite may be true. For example, better-educated women of higher socioeconomic status may be more likely to drink, and more likely to indulge in hazardous drinking, while for men hazardous drinking rates vary considerably for these same variables from one country to another.

Women with higher education who end up taking better-paid jobs involving higher degrees of responsibility may drink more heavily because they are exposed to more stress, and have more occasions of socialising and going out with colleagues. Besides, these occasions being typically in masculine work environments, women are confronted with a situation where the limits on drinking are higher than they would be exposed to otherwise (Com-Ruelle et al., 2008). Women of high SES may also wish to engage in heavy drinking as a form of emancipation, similarly to what happened with tobacco smoking in the past century. It is possible that the "innovative" behaviour will then spread to other social groups, eventually reproducing a similar gradient as that observed today in men (Grittner et al., 2012).

Despite the complex relationships between socioeconomic dimensions and alcohol consumption, existing evidence suggests that people in lower socioeconomic groups and ethnic minorities are more prone to alcohol-related harms. The worst-off have higher rates of alcohol-related problems and mortality than the better-off (Najman et al., 2007; Hemstrom, 2002; Harrison and Gardiner, 1999), even for the same levels of drinking (Mäkelä and Paljarvi, 2008; Grittner et al., 2012). Hence, the social gradient in alcohol-related harm is not entirely consistent with the gradient in alcohol use or heavy drinking. This may be due to several factors: a higher-than-reported frequency of HED in low-SES people; the type and quality of alcohol consumed; differences in vulnerability (low-SES people less resilient in coping with stressors, biological vulnerabilities, higher rates of comorbidities – including obesity, mental ill-health, drug use – contributing to disparities in alcohol-related harm); and differences in health care access (financial and non-financial barriers to health care use, differences in treatment within the system) (Loring, 2014).

This complicates the task of the policy maker who has to devise strategies to tackle harmful drinking and the health professionals and others who have to apply them. Possible approaches to solving the dilemmas posed by the variability exposed here will be discussed in the next two chapters.

### Notes

1. "Occupational prestige" was assessed using a scale devised by the US National Opinion Research Center that included jobs ranging from "food preparation occupations" at one end to physicians at the other.
2. Defined on the basis of American Psychiatric Association's *Diagnostic and Statistical Manual of Mental Disorders* criteria: "*A maladaptive pattern of alcohol use, leading to clinically significant impairment or distress, as manifested by three or more of the following seven criteria, occurring at any time in the same 12-month period*":
   1. Tolerance.
   2. Withdrawal symptoms.
   3. Alcohol is often taken in larger amounts or over a longer period than was intended.
   4. There is a persistent desire or there are unsuccessful efforts to cut down or control alcohol use.
   5. A great deal of time is spent in activities necessary to obtain alcohol, use alcohol or recover from its effects.
   6. Important social, occupational, or recreational activities are given up or reduced because of alcohol use.
   7. Alcohol use is continued despite knowledge of having a persistent or recurrent physical or psychological problem that is likely to have been caused or exacerbated by the alcohol (e.g., continued drinking despite recognition that an ulcer was made worse by alcohol consumption).

### Bibliography

Anderson, P. and B. Baumberg (2006), "Alcohol in Europe: A Public Health Perspective", Report for the European Commission.

Asgeirsdottir, T.L. and K.A. McGeary (2009), "Alcohol and Labor Supply: The Case of Iceland", *European Journal of Health Economics*, Vol. 10, pp. 455-465.

Avalos, L.A. et al. (2014), "Volume and Type of Alcohol During Early Pregnancy and the Risk of Miscarriage", *Substance Use and Misuse*, Vol. 49, No. 11, pp. 1437-1445.

Bacharach, S.B., P. Bamberger and M. Biron (2010), "Alcohol Consumption and Workplace Absenteeism: The Moderating Effect of Social Support", *Journal of Applied Psychology*, Vol. 95, No. 2, pp. 334-348.

Barrett, G.F. (2002), "The Effect of Alcohol Consumption on Earnings", *Economic Record*, Vol. 78, No. 240, pp. 79-96.

Berridge, V., B. Thom and R. Herring (2007), *The Normalisation of Binge Drinking? An Historical and Cross Cultural Investigation with Implications for Action*, London School of Hygiene and Tropical Medicine, London

Bertrand, M. (2010), "New Perspectives on Gender", in D. Ashenfelter and D. Card (eds), *Handbook of Labor Economics, Volume 4b*, Elsevier, pp. 1545-1592.

Beuret, K., C. Corbett and H. Ward (2014), *Drinking among British Women and its Impact on their Pedestrian and Driving Activities, Phase 2: Survey Results*, Social Research Associates, London.

Bloomfield, K. et al. (2006), "Social Inequalities in Alcohol Consumption and Alcohol-related Problems in the Study Countries of the EU Concerted Action 'Gender, Culture and Alcohol Problems: A Multi-national Study'", *Alcohol and Alcoholism*, Vol. 41(Suppl. 1), pp. i26-i36.

Bonin, H. et al. (2007), "Cross Sectional Earnings Risk and Occupational Sorting: The Role of Risk Attitudes", *Labour Economics*, Vol. 14, No. 6, pp. 926-937.

Booth, B.M. and W. Feng (2002), "The Impact of Drinking and Drinking Consequences on Short-term Employment Outcomes in At-risk Drinkers in Six Southern States", *Journal of Behavioural Health Services and Research*, Vol. 29, No. 2, pp. 157-166.

Bouchery, E.E. et al. (2011), "Economic Costs of Excessive Alcohol Consumption in the U.S., 2006", *American Journal of Preventive Medicine*, Vol. 41, No. 5, pp. 516-524.

Britton, A., M.G. Marmot and M. Shipley (2008), "Who Benefits Most from the Cardioprotective Properties of Alcohol Consumption: Health Freaks or Couch Potatoes?", *Journal of Epideliology and Community Health*, Vol. 62, No. 10, pp. 905-908, October.

Byrne, S. (2010), "Costs to Society of Problem Alcohol Use in Ireland", Health Service Executive, Dublin.

Byrne, P., S. Jones and R. Williams (2004), "The Association Between Cannabis and Alcohol Use and the Development of the Mental Disorder", *Current Opinion in Psychiatry*, Vol. 17, No. 4, pp. 255-261.

Caldwell, T.M. et al. (2008), "Lifecourse Socioeconomic Predictors of Midlife Drinking Patterns, Problems and Abstention: findings from the 1958 British Birth Cohort Study", *Drugs and Alcohol Dependence*, Vol. 95, pp. 269-278.

Casswell, S., M. Pledger and R. Hooper (2003), "Socioeconomic Status and Drinking Patterns in Young Adults", *Addiction*, Vol. 98, pp. 601-661.

Com-Ruelle, L.et al. (2008), "Les problèmes d'alcool en France : quelles sont les populations à risque ?", *IRDES Question d'Économie de la Santé No. 129*.

Esper, L.H. and E.F. Furtado (2014), "Identifying Maternal Risk Factors Associated with Fetal Alcohol Spectrum Disorders: A Systematic Review", *European Child and Adolescent Psychiatry*, Vol. 23, No. 10, pp. 877-889.

Feng, W. et al. (2001), "The Impact of Problem Drinking Unemployment", *Health Economics*, Vol. 10, pp. 509-521.

Feodor Nilsson, S. et al. (2014), "Risk Factors for Miscarriage from a Prevention Perspective: A Nationwide Follow-up Study", BJOG – *An International Journal of Obstetrics & Gynaecology*, Vol. 121, No. 11, pp. 1375-1384.

Giskes, K. et al. (2011), "Individual and Household-level Socioeconomic Position Is Associated with Harmful Alcohol Consumption Behaviours Among Adults", *Australian and New Zealand Journal of Public Health*, Vol. 35, No. 3, pp. 270–277, June.

Gmel, G. et al. (2005), "How Do Social Roles and Social Stratification Influence Women's and Men's Alcohol Consumption: A Cross-cultural Analysis", Chapter 7 in K. Bloomfield et al. (eds.), *Gender, Culture and Alcohol Problems: A Multinational Study*, Project Final Report, Charité Universitätsmedizin Berlin, pp. 137-161, January.

Grittner, U. et al. (2013), "Alcohol Consumption and Social Inequality at the Individual and Country Levels – Results from an International Study", *European Journal of Public Health*, Vol. 23, No. 2, pp. 332–339.

Grittner, U. et al. (2012), "Social Inequalities and Gender Differences in the Experience of Alcohol-Related Problems", *Alcohol and Alcoholism*, Vol. 47, No. 5, pp. 597-605.

Hamilton, V. and B.H. Hamilton (1997), "Alcohol and Earnings: Does Drinking Yield a Wage Premium?", *Canadian Journal of Economics/Revue canadienne d'économie*, Vol. 30, No. 1, pp. 135-151.

Harrison, L. and E. Gardiner (1999), "Do the Rich Really Die Young? Alcohol-related Mortality and Social Class in Great Britain, 1988-94", *Addiction*, Vol. 94, No. 12, pp. 1871-1880, December.

Harwood, H.J. (2000), "Updating Estimates of the Economic Costs of Alcohol Abuse in the United States: Estimates, Update Methods, and Data", Report prepared by The Lewin Group for the National Institute on Alcohol Abuse and Alcoholism.

Hemstrom, O. (2002), "Alcohol-related Deaths Contribute to Socioeconomic Differentials in Mortality in Sweden", *European Journal of Public Health*, Vol. 12, pp. 254-262.

Henderson, M., G. Hutcheson and J. Davies (1996), "Alcohol and the Workplace", *WHO Regional Publication European Series*, Vol. 67, pp. 1-100.

Huerta, M.C. and F Borgonovi (2010), "Education, Alcohol Use and Abuse among Young Adults in Britain", *Social Science & Medicine*, Vol. 71, No. 1, pp. 143-151.

Hughes, K. and M. Bellis (2012), "Drinking Environments", in P. Anderson, L. Møllers and G. Galea (eds), *Alcohol in the European Union: Consumption, Harm and Policy Approaches*, WHO, Geneva.

Hurcombe, R., M. Bayley and A. Goodman (2010), *Ethnicity and Alcohol: A Review of the UK Literature*, Joseph Rowntree Foundation, York.

ILO – International Labour Office (2012), "SOLVE: Integrating Health Promotion into Workplace OSH Policies – Trainer's Guide", International Labour Office, Geneva.

Jarl, J. and U.-G. Gerdtham (2012), "Does Drinking Affect Long-term Sickness Absence? A Sample Selection Approach Correcting for Employment and Accounting for Drinking History", *Applied Economics*, Vol. 44, pp. 2811-2825.

Johansson, E., P. Böckerman and A. Uutela (2008), "Alcohol Consumption and Sickness Absence: Evidence from Microdata", *European Journal of Public Health*, Vol. 19, No. 1, pp. 19-22.

Jones, A.S. and D.W. Richmond (2006), "Causal Effects of Alcoholism on Earnings: Estimates from the NLSY", *Health Economics*, Vol. 15, pp. 849-871.

Lassi, Z.S. et al. (2014), "Preconception Care: Caffeine, Smoking, Alcohol, Drugs and Other Environmental Chemical/Radiation Exposure", *Reproductive Health*, Vol. 11, pp. S3-S6.

Lee, Y.L. (2003), "Wage Effects of Drinking in Australia", *Australian Economic Review*, Vol. 36, No. 3, pp. 265-282.

Loring B. (2014), "Alcohol and Inequities – Guidance for Addressing Inequities in Alcohol-related Harm", WHO Europe.

Lye, J. and J. Hirschberg (2010), "Alcohol Consumption and Human Capital: A Retrospective Study of the Literature", *Journal of Economic Surveys*, Vol. 24, pp. 309-338.

MacDonald, Z. and M.A. Shields (2001), "The Impact of Alcohol Consumption on Occupational Attainment in England", *Economica*, Vol. 68, pp. 427-453.

Mäkelä, P. and T. Paljärvi (2008), "Do Consequences of a Given Pattern of Drinking Vary by Socioeconomic Status? A Mortality and Hospitalisation Follow-up for Alcohol-related Causes of the Finnish Drinking Habits Surveys", *Journal of Epidemiology and Community Health*, Vol. 62, pp. 728-733.

Marchand, A., A. Parent-Lamarche and M.E. Blanc (2011), "Work and High-risk Alcohol Consumption in the Canadian Workforce", *International Journal of Environmental Research and Public Health*, Vol. 8, pp. 2692-2705.

May, P.A. et al. (2013), "Maternal Alcohol Consumption Producing Fetal Alcohol Spectrum Disorders (FASD): Quantity, Frequency, and Timing of Drinking", *Drug and Alcohol Dependence*, Vol. 133, No. 2, pp. 502-512.

McDonnell-Naughton, M. et al. (2012), "Maternal Smoking and Alcohol Consumption during Pregnancy as Risk Factors for Sudden Infant Death", *Irish Medical Journal*, Vol. 105, No. 4, pp. 105-108.

McKee, M. et al. (2000), "Alcohol Consumption in the Baltic Republics", *Journal of Epidemiology and Community Health*, Vol. 54, pp. 361-366.

Mullahy, J. and J.L. Sindelar (1993), "Alcoholism, Work, and Income", *Journal of Labor Economics*, Vol. 11, pp. 494-519.

Mullahy J. and J.L. Sindelar (1991), "Gender Differences in Labor Market Effects of Alcoholism", *American Economic Review*, Vol. 81, pp. 161-165.

Najman, J., G. Toloo and G. Williams (2007), "Increasing Socio-economic Inequalities in Drug-induced Deaths in Australia: 1981-2002", *Drug and Alcohol Review*, Vol. 27, No. 6, pp. 613-618.

Norström, T. (2006), "Per Capita Alcohol Consumption and Sickness Absence", *Addiction*, Vol. 101, pp. 1421-1427.

Norström, T. and I.S. Moan (2009), "Per Capita Alcohol Consumption and Sickness Absence in Norway", *European Journal of Public Health*, Vol. 19, No. 4, pp. 383-388.

Nybo Andersen, A.M. et al. (2012), "Moderate Alcohol Intake During Pregnancy and Risk of Fetal Death", *International Journal of Epidemiology*, Vol. 41, No. 2, pp. 405-413.

Peters, B.L. (2004), "Is there a Wage Bonus from Drinking? Unobserved Heterogeneity Examined", *Applied Economics*, Vol. 36, pp. 2299–2315.

PHFI – Public Health Foundation of India (2013), *Alcohol Marketing and Regulatory Policy Environment in India*, PFHI, New Delhi.

Pidd, K.J. et al. (2006), "Estimating the Cost of Alcohol-related Absenteeism in the Australian Workforce: The Importance of Consumption Patterns", *Medical Journal of Australia*, Vol. 185, pp. 637-641.

Rehm, J. et al. (2009), "Global Burden of Disease and Injury and Economic Cost Attributable to Alcohol Use and Alcohol-use Disorders", *The Lancet*, Vol. 373, pp. 223-233.

Renna, F. (2007), "The Economic Cost of Teen Drinking: Late Graduation and Lowered Earnings", *Health Economics*, Vol. 16, pp. 407-419.

Roche, A.M. et al. (2008), "Workers' Drinking Patterns: The Impact on Absenteeism in the Australian Work-place", *Addiction*, Vol. 103, pp. 738-748.

Rock, L. (2014), "The Rise of Female Drink-drivers", *Guardian Online*, 9 November 2014, www.theguardian.com/lifeandstyle/2014/nov/09/the-rise-of-women-drink-drivers.

Romeri, E., A. Baker and C. Griffiths (2007), "Alcohol-related Deaths by Occupation, England and Wales, 2001-2005", *Health Statistics Quarterly*, Vol. 35, pp. 6-12.

Salonsalmi, A. et al. (2012), "Drinking Habits and Disability Retirement", *Addiction*, Vol. 107, pp. 2128-2136.

Schultz, A.B., C.Y. Chen and D.W. Edington (2009), "The Cost and Impact of Health Conditions on Presenteeism to Employers: A Review of the Literature", *Pharmacoeconomics*, Vol. 27, No. 5, pp. 365-378.

Sidorchuk, A. et al. (2012), "Alcohol Use in Adolescence and Risk of Disability Pension: A 39 Year Follow-up of a Population-based Conscription Survey", *PLoS ONE*, Vol. 7, No. 8.

Single, E. et al. (2003). *International Guidelines for Estimating the Costs of Substance Abuse (2nd edition)*, WHO, Geneva.

Skogen, J.C. et al. (2011), "Alcohol Consumption, Problem Drinking, Abstention and Disability Pension Award, The Nord-Trøndelag Health Study (HUNT)", *Addiction*, Vol. 107, pp. 98-108.

Sloan, F.A. et al. (2009), "Racial Differences in the Relationship Between Alcohol Consumption in Early Adulthood and Occupational Attainment at Midlife", *American Journal of Public Health*, Vol. 99, pp. 2261-2267.

Soydemir, G.A. and E. Bastida (2006), "Alcohol Use and Earnings: Findings from a Community based Study", *Eastern Economic Journal*, Vol. 32, No. 4.

Stuckler, D. et al. (2009), "The Public Health Effect of Economic Crises and Alternative Policy Responses in Europe: An Empirical Analysis», *The Lancet*, Vol. 374, pp. 315-323.

Thavorncharoensap M. et al. (2009), "The Economic Impact of Alcohol Consumption: A Systematic Review", *Substance Treatment, Prevention and Policy*, Vol. 4, No. 20.

UK Cabinet Office (2003), "Alcohol Misuse: How Much Does It Cost?", Retrieved from http://alcoholresearchuk.org/wp-content/uploads/2014/01/strategy-unit-alcohol-costs-2003.pdf.

Upmark, M., J. Möller and A. Romelsjö (1999), "Longitudinal, Population-based Study of Self-reported Alcohol Habits, High Levels of Sickness Absence, and Disability Pensions", *Journal of Epidemiology and Community Health*, Vol. 53, pp. 223-229.

Vahtera, J. et al. (2002), "Alcohol Intake and Sickness Absence: A Curvilinear Relation", *American Journal of Epidemiology*, Vol. 156, pp. 969-976.

Van Nguyen, M. and H.A. Abenhaim (2013), "Sudden Infant Death Syndrome: Review for the Obstetric Care Provider", *American Journal of Perinatology*, Vol. 30, No. 9, pp. 703-714.

Van Ours, J.C. (2004), "A Pint a Day Raises a Man's Pay; But Smoking Blows that Gain Away", *Journal of Health Economics*, Vol. 23, pp. 863-886.

Weissmann, J. (2013), "The Insidious Genius of Hello Kitty-Branded Beer", *The Atlantic*, 16 Sept. 2013, consulted 10 November 2014, www.theatlantic.com/business/archive/2013/09/the-insidious-genius-of-hello-kitty-branded-beer/279709/.

Williams, J., L.M. Powell and H. Wechsler (2003), "Does Alcohol Consumption Reduce Human Capital Accumulation? Evidence from the College Alcohol Study", *Applied Economics*, Vol. 35, No. 10, pp. 1227-1239.

Ziebarth, N.R. and M.M. Grabka (2009), "In Vino Pecunia? The Association Between Beverage-specific Drinking Behavior and Wages", *Journal of Labor Research*, Vol. 30, pp. 219-244.

Tackling Harmful Alcohol Use
Economics and Public Health Policy


*Special focus I*

# The impact of alcohol consumption on global health

by
Vladimir Poznyak and Dag Rekve,

World Health Organization, on behalf of the authors
of the Global Status Report on Alcohol and Health 2014*

* This contribution was prepared by Vladimir Poznyak and Dag Rekve based on the text and data from the Global Status Report on Alcohol and Health (WHO, 2014). The full list of contributors to the report is provided in the Acknowledgments section of the publication, available at *http://www.who.int/substance_abuse/publications/global_alcohol_report/en/*.

## Introduction

In 2010, only 38.3% of the world population aged 15 years and older had drunk alcohol in the past 12 months. Nevertheless, alcohol's impact on global health is dramatic. In 2012 about 3.3 million deaths were attributable to alcohol consumption, 5.9% of all deaths. This is greater than the proportion of all deaths from HIV/AIDS (2.8%), violence (0.9%) and tuberculosis (1.7%) put together. In terms of the global burden of disease and injury, measured in disability adjusted life years (DALYs), 5.1% of all years of potential life lost in the world in 2012 due to premature mortality and disability were attributable to alcohol consumption (WHO, 2014).

The estimated ranking of harmful use of alcohol as one of the leading risk factors for death and disability in the world rose from eighth place in 1990 to fifth in 2010 (Lim et al., 2012). Moreover, the data suggest that harmful use of alcohol ranks as the leading risk factor for death and disability in large parts of the world, as well as for persons aged 15–49 years.

The *Global Strategy to Reduce the Harmful Use of Alcohol* endorsed by WHO member states in 2010 (WHO, 2010) defines harmful use as "drinking that causes detrimental health and social consequences for the drinker, the people around the drinker and society at large, as well as the patterns of drinking that are associated with increased risk of adverse health outcomes". The Political Declaration of the High-level Meeting of the UN General Assembly on the Prevention and Control of Noncommunicable Diseases (NCDs) included the harmful use of alcohol as one of the four key risk factors for NCDs, and the Global Action Plan for the prevention and control of NCDs 2013-20 calls for at least 10% relative reduction in the harmful use of alcohol (WHO, 2013).

## Pathways and mechanisms of alcohol-related harm

Alcohol consumption increases the risk of developing many conditions, including some cancers, and can have a negative impact on the course of disorders and their outcomes. It may, for example, impair compliance with treatment regimens, or interact with prescribed medicines. Alcohol influences the development of over 200 disease and injury conditions, through toxic effects on organs and tissues; intoxication, leading to impairment of physical coordination, consciousness, cognition, perception, affect or behaviour; and alcohol use disorders including alcohol dependence (WHO, 2004a; Baan et al., 2007; Shield et al., 2013).

The harm from alcohol depends not just on how much is consumed, but on how it is consumed (the "pattern of drinking"), and what is consumed (Rehm et al., 2003). Drinking a given volume in small amounts over a long period will do less damage than drinking the same amount in large doses in a few sessions. Heavy episodic drinking ("binge drinking"), defined by the WHO as "consumption of 60 or more grams of pure alcohol (6+ standard drinks in most countries) on at least one single occasion at least monthly" can negate the cardio-protective benefit from low-risk drinking (Roerecke and Rehm, 2010). And alcohol contaminated with methanol or other poisons can affect health and mortality too.

## Levels and patterns of alcohol consumption

Globally, individuals above 15 years of age drink on average 6.2 litres of pure alcohol per year, which translates into 13.5 grams of pure alcohol per day (Babor et al., 2003; WHO, 2004b; WHO, 2007). However, total consumption and heavy episodic drinking vary widely across WHO regions and member states. The highest consumption levels continue to be found in the developed world, in particular in the WHO European Region and the Rregion of the Americas. Intermediate levels of consumption are found in the Western Pacific Region and African Region, while the lowest levels are in the South-East Asia Region and particularly the Eastern Mediterranean Region (Babor et al., 2003; WHO, 2004b; WHO, 2007).

Globally, 50.1% of total recorded alcohol is consumed in the form of spirits, with beer second at 34.8%. Only 8.0% of total recorded alcohol is consumed as wine, which, however, represents a quarter of total alcohol consumption in the European Region.

## Alcohol-attributable mortality and morbidity

The highest numbers of deaths due to alcohol consumption are from cardiovascular diseases, followed by injuries (especially unintentional injuries), gastrointestinal diseases (mainly liver cirrhosis) and cancers. The highest proportion of alcohol-attributable deaths relative to all deaths for a particular health condition (alcohol-attributable fractions or AAF) is for liver diseases, especially cirrhosis.

Geographical variation in alcohol-attributable deaths is wide (Figure SFI1). The highest AAF is in the WHO European Region, which also has the highest alcohol consumption. However, the high figures are almost entirely driven by Eastern European countries, which report both high-risk levels and patterns of consumption. The lowest AAFs are in the African and Eastern Mediterranean Regions. Low AAFs in the African Region are probably due to high premature mortality, while low AAFs in the Eastern Mediterranean Region are due to high rates of abstinence and very low levels of alcohol per capita consumption.

A quarter of all alcohol-attributable DALYs were due to neuropsychiatric disorders, mainly alcohol use disorders. As liver diseases are relatively prevalent and are among the top 20 causes of death globally, alcohol-attributable liver disease is a major factor in the global alcohol-attributable burden of disease.

Most people are not aware of the health risks of alcohol consumption for diseases other than alcohol use disorders and liver cirrhosis. This is especially true for cancers, with around 4% to 25% of the global disease burden due to specific cancers attributable to alcohol. About 10% of the global burden of disease due to tuberculosis, epilepsy, haemorrhagic stroke and arterial hypertension can also be attributed to alcohol, and recently a causal relationship between the harmful use of alcohol and the course of HIV/AIDS has been established.

There is substantial regional variability in the global alcohol-attributable burden of disease and injury, similar to that observed for alcohol-attributable deaths. In the European Region and particularly in high-income countries within Europe, the alcohol-attributable disease burden is much higher than alcohol-attributable deaths because of the numbers disabled by alcohol use disorders.

Figure SFI1. **Alcohol-attributable fractions for all-cause deaths, 2012**

Alcohol-attributable fractions (AAFs), percentage; all ages

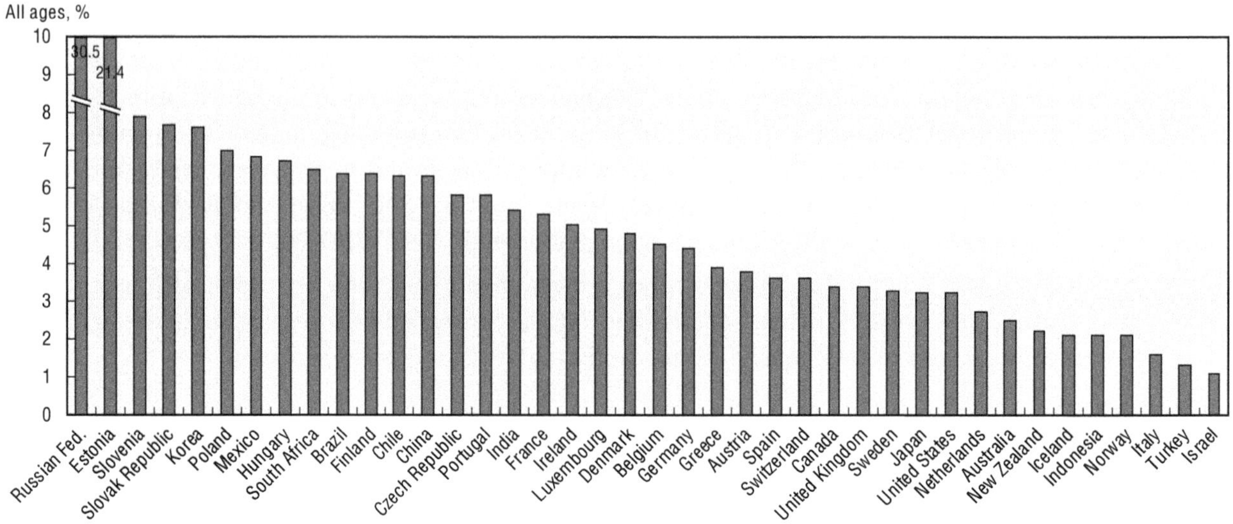


*Source:* World Health Organization (2014), *Global Status Report on Alcohol and Health 2014*, WHO, Geneva.

StatLink http://dx.doi.org/10.1787/888933180565

## Factors impacting on health consequences

### *Age*

Alcohol consumption causes deaths relatively early in life, with alcohol-attributable fractions (AAFs) highest for the 40–49 years age group and relatively lower for those aged over 60 than for younger people. For all age groups aged 15+, the European Region has the highest AAFs, with the Region of the Americas second.

### *Sex*

Men are more likely than women to die from alcohol-attributable deaths. For males, the figure is 7.6% of deaths, with injuries as the main cause, versus 4.0% for females, mainly cardiovascular diseases.

The global burden of disease and injury attributable to alcohol is 5.1% overall from all DALYs lost in the world in 2012, but 7.4% for males and 2.3% for females.

Males in Europe have the highest prevalence of alcohol use disorders (12.6%) while the Region of the Americas shows the highest female prevalence at 3.2%.

### *Economic wealth*

Alcohol consumption and the alcohol-attributable burden of disease are related to economic development, but the relationship is not straightforward. Greater wealth is associated with higher consumption and a higher burden of disease (measured either as deaths or DALYs) but Eastern Europe, has a higher disease burden per litre consumed than might be expected from its level of economic development while the African Region has a lower alcohol-attributable burden of disease than might be expected. Countries with lower economic wealth may have both lower consumption and a higher alcohol-attributable burden of disease per litre consumed because their morbidity and mortality risks are higher.

## Harm to others

Measures of problems from alcohol consumption have primarily focused on the drinker, but harms to others can be associated with serious socioeconomic consequences and substantial health problems.

More than two-thirds of the people who responded to an Australian survey said they had been adversely affected by another person's drinking in the past year, and about half of them had a negative experience due to a stranger's drinking (Laslett et al., 2011). European studies inspired by the Australian work suggest that women suffer more from the drinking of others than men.

In New Zealand, a survey found that others were harmed more than the drinker by drinking (18% versus 12%), particularly among women and young people (Connor and Casswell, 2012). People's scores on measures of personal well-being and health status were lower the more they were exposed to heavy drinkers, the lower (Casswell et al., 2011). Studies of the effects of alcohol on others could benefit from quantitative approaches inspired by work on the effects of passive smoking.

## Policy action to reduce the harmful use of alcohol

Reducing the harmful use of alcohol by 10% by 2025 requires the development and enforcement of comprehensive alcohol policy measures in line with the WHO Global Strategy. To ensure sustained political and societal support, policies have to be based on the best available evidence of effectiveness and cost-effectiveness, and justify measures which could restrict individual choices and benefits for alcohol producers and sellers.

### *References*

Baan, R. et al. (2007), "Carcinogenicity of Alcoholic Beverages", *The Lancet Oncology*, Vol. 8, pp. 292–293, PMID: 17431955.

Babor, T. et al. (2003), *Alcohol: No Ordinary Commodity – Research and Public Policy*, Oxford University Press, Oxford.

Casswell, S., R.Q. You and T. Huckle (2011), "Alcohol's Harm to Others: Reduced Wellbeing and Health Status for Those with Heavy Drinkers in their Lives", *Addiction*, Vol. 106, pp. 1087-1094.

Connor, J. and S. Casswell (2012), "Alcohol-related Harm to Others in New Zealand: Evidence of the Burden and Gaps in Knowledge", *New Zealand Medical Journal*, Vol. 125, pp. 11-27.

Laslett, A.M. et al. (2011), "Surveying the Range and Magnitude of Alcohol's Harm to Others in Australia", *Addiction*, Vol. 106, No. 9, pp. 1603-1611.

Lim, S.S. et al. (2012), "A Comparative Risk Assessment of Burden of Disease and Injury Attributable to 67 Risk Factors and Risk Factor Clusters in 21 Regions, 1990-2010: A Systematic Analysis for the Global Burden of Disease Study 2010", *The Lancet*, Vol. 380, pp. 2224-2260, http://dx.doi.org/10.1016/S0140-6736(12)61766-8 [PMID: 23245609].

Rehm, J. et al. (2003a), "The Relationship of Average Volume of Alcohol Consumption and Patterns of Drinking to Burden of Disease – An Overview", *Addiction*, Vol. 98, pp. 1209-1228.

Roerecke, M. and J. Rehm (2010), "Irregular Heavy Drinking Occasions and Risk of Ischemic Heart Disease: A Systematic Review and Meta-analysis", *American Journal of Epidemiology*, Vol. 171, pp. 633-644, http://dx.doi.org/10.1093/aje/kwp451.

Shield, K.D., C. Parry and J. Rehm (2013), "Chronic Diseases and Conditions Related to Alcohol Use", *Alcohol Research Current Reviews*, Vol. 35, pp. 155-171.

WHO – World Health Organization (2014), *Global Status Report on Alcohol and Health 2014*, WHO, Geneva.

WHO (2013), *Global Action Plan for the Prevention and Control of Non-communicable Diseases 2013-2020*, WHO, Geneva.

WHO (2010), *Global Strategy to Reduce the Harmful Use of* Alcohol, WHO, Geneva.

WHO (2007), "Expert Committee on Problems Related to Alcohol Consumption. Second Report (2007)", *WHO Technical Report Series*, No. 944, WHO, Geneva.

WHO (2004a), *Neuroscience of Psychoactive Substance Use and Dependence*, WHO, Geneva.

WHO (2004b), *Global Status Report on Alcohol*, WHO, Geneva.

Tackling Harmful Alcohol Use
Economics and Public Health Policy


# Chapter 4

# Tackling alcohol-related harms: What policy approaches?

by
Michele Cecchini and Annalisa Belloni

*The target of policies aimed at addressing alcohol-related harms has been the subject of controversy in the policy debate. A traditional public health view holds that policy approaches addressing the entire spectrum of a risk factor, including those who are at low or no risk, are superior to approaches targeting only those at high risk. However, evidence of improved health outcomes in some moderate drinkers, means that potential health benefits might be forgone if policies were to affect consumption by those drinkers. This is a complex policy question involving political judgements that only individual governments can make. Governments have adopted a broad range of policy approaches to curb alcohol-related harms. These include information and education policies, as well as regulatory and fiscal options, traffic enforcement measures and interventions within the health care sector (particularly, in primary health care and mental health care). Especially in recent years, many attempts have been made to develop and test innovative policy approaches, such as minimum prices, education approaches, new measures to prevent traffic fatalities, but also to sharpen existing approaches and make them more effective in curbing heavy drinking. Business stakeholders have stepped up their corporate social responsibility efforts and a number of governments have established a dialogue with them. Multi-stakeholder initiatives have included attempts to reduce the quantity of alcohol on the market by providing incentives for consumers to demand lower-alcohol products.*

## Key findings

- While the goal of alcohol policies is to curb the harmful use of alcohol, most countries' prevention strategies include population-wide actions affecting all drinkers, as well as actions designed to target heavy drinking alone.
- Governments have taxed alcoholic beverages for millennia. Alcohol taxes today are highest in northern European countries, Australia and United Kingdom, and lowest in southern and central European countries.
- Minimum prices, used in Canada and discussed in several European countries, may overcome some of the limitations of taxes – e.g. they may be more effective in tackling heavy drinking – but they generate a loss in consumer welfare without government revenues to compensate for it.
- Restrictions in alcohol advertising are increasingly challenged by the spread of advertising on the Internet and social media.
- Regulations to prevent driving under the influence of alcohol are in place in most countries but are not always tightly enforced.
- Major efforts have been made to improve health care approaches to tackling harmful drinking, particularly through screening and brief intervention programmes, and through pharmacological and psychosocial treatments for alcohol dependence.
- Business stakeholders have engaged in a number of initiatives to promote responsible drinking, some of which in partnership with governments. In the United Kingdom, for instance, they have committed to removing one billion units of alcohol per year from the market.

## One goal, many policy options

The goal of alcohol policies is typically to reduce alcohol-related harms. Many policy approaches are designed to directly address those harms, or the harmful drinking behaviours that generate them. Examples of measures taken by governments seeking to reduce alcohol-related harms include policies to prevent people from driving under the influence of alcohol; policies to restrict opening hours for on-trade outlets such as bars; policies to limit price promotions such as "happy hours" likely to lead people to consume large quantities of alcohol in a single session, and also policies to address heavy drinking as part of primary care and in the workplace (discussed below and in Martinic's Special Focus IV contribution after this chapter).

Other policy approaches taken by governments are targeted more broadly at all consumers of alcohol, on the assumption that the measures implemented would not only deter harmful consumption but also provide benefits to a larger number of moderate drinkers at the same time, and possibly do so more efficiently than approaches targeting harmful drinkers alone. In recent years, attempts have been made to enhance the ability of broadly targeted policy approaches to influence harmful drinkers. For instance, minimum price policies have been at the centre of the alcohol policy debate in several OECD countries. As discussed in Ludbrook's Special Focus III contribution after this chapter, existing evidence suggests that minimum prices have a greater potential to deter harmful drinking than taxation (the most common alcohol policy acting through a price mechanism). Recent evidence discussed in Saffer's Special Focus II contribution suggests that advertising restrictions may also be more effective in curbing harmful drinking than other types of drinking. While policies to limit the availability of alcohol are likely to hit all consumers, they can be tailored in ways that will make them more effective at targeting harmful consumption (e.g. by reducing outlet opening hours at times of the day/week when harmful use is more common).

The approach of targeting all consumption in alcohol policies is in line with an established public health theory, which applies to a broader range of risk factors than just harmful alcohol use. According to this theory, "population" approaches to prevention, involving measures that affect all people (consumers) in a population producing small reductions in levels of risk (consumption) at the individual level, are more effective and efficient at reducing the numbers of people at high risk in the population than policy approaches deliberately targeting those at high risk alone (Rose, 1992). This view has, however, been challenged by the proliferation of evidence of improved health outcomes in moderate drinkers, albeit with controversies on the extent of these effects. This means that potential health benefits from moderate drinking might be forgone if policies were to affect consumption by those drinkers. Whether a population approach or a high-risk approach should be followed is a more complex policy question than it may seem at first sight. Any choice involves political judgements that only individual governments can make. However, it is also possible to inform this decision through a careful consideration of the relative strengths and weaknesses of each approach.

When alcohol policies hit all types of consumption, a number of moderate drinkers (typically, but not exclusively, older men) will benefit from that reduction in terms of a wide range of disease outcomes, such as several types of cancer, and injuries, but will forgo some of the protective effects of alcohol against certain cardiovascular conditions as a consequence of cutting their consumption. OECD analyses of the impacts of alternative policies, quantifying the potentially negative health effects in those consumers, are discussed in Chapter 5. Governments may wish to consider the size of the trade-off involved when implementing policies that are likely to affect all types of consumers, although the key measure of impact they are most likely to be looking at is the overall impact of a policy. The decision on where to strike a balance between population and individual approaches to alcohol policy must be left to individual governments. The work undertaken by the OECD provides detailed estimates of policy impacts at the population level, as well as in specific subgroups, thereby supporting an evidence-based approach to such decisions.

### *Average alcohol consumption and heavy drinking*

Of all major risk factors for health, alcohol consumption displays the most consistent (linear) relationship between average levels of the risk factor (alcohol consumption, in this case) and proportion of people at high risk (heavy drinkers) in the population. Rose (1992) estimated that the relationship between average and heavy alcohol consumption is such that a lower average consumption by 20 ml per week (roughly 1.5 US standard drinks) corresponds to a quarter fewer heavy drinkers, an effect that could hardly be matched by policies targeting heavy drinkers alone. Rose's analysis was mostly based on cross-sectional correlations, so it does not necessarily provide a measure of the changes in consumption that could result from the implementation of specific policies. In particular, an important underlying assumption in Rose's analysis is that population-level prevention programmes would uniformly shift downwards the entire distribution of the relevant risk factor in a population. However, existing evidence shows that each alcohol policy affects certain parts of the alcohol consumption distribution, i.e. certain types of drinkers, more than others.

Rose's theory sets out key principles for public health action, but it should not be interpreted dogmatically. Alcohol consumption is indeed an area in which the correlation between average and harmful consumption is especially strong, but the impacts of specific alcohol policies should be assessed on their own merits, based on the best available evidence of how and to what extent they can be expected to affect different types of consumers.

### *Will moderate consumers be worse off?*

There is established evidence of the benefits of moderate alcohol consumption for certain drinkers, mostly framed in terms of reduced death rates (e.g. Di Castelnuovo et al., 2006). However, as discussed in Chapter 1, comparisons of death rates are not first choice when assessing the effectiveness of different health policies. The slightly premature death of an 80 year old is generally not given the same weight as the death of someone at the age of 40, for example. Hence it is more usual to compare years of life lost, or QALYs/DALYs lost, than death rates. This matters when looking at alcohol-related harm, as excess deaths for moderate drinkers, e.g. from injuries, or cancer, weigh more than deaths that may be spared, typically from ischaemic heart disease (IHD), which tend to occur later in life.

The relationship between alcohol consumption and health outcomes follows a "j-shaped" pattern in men above age 35 and women above age 5, as extensively discussed in Chapter 1, with some moderate drinkers experiencing better outcomes than abstainers, and sharply increasing levels of risk as consumption becomes heavier. However, the fact that some drinkers may enjoy better outcomes than abstainers does not imply that cutting their alcohol intake would always make them worse off, as this depends on their initial level of drinking and on the degree to which they would cut their consumption. In the three countries examined in OECD's analysis of alcohol policies (Chapter 5), Canada, Germany and the Czech Republic, approximately four out of five drinkers would reduce their risk of death by cutting their drinking levels by one unit per week.

### *Do heavy drinkers respond to policy less?*

Some policies targeting all drinkers, such as taxation, may elicit a lesser response from drinkers who are most prone to alcohol-related harms (e.g. young people and heavy drinkers). This lesser response can still produce relatively significant reductions in risk. The shape of the relevant risk functions is such that, for the same reduction in drinking levels, the risk reduction is substantially larger in people at higher risk. For instance, based on the risk functions calculated by Corrao et al. (2004), a 10% across-the-board increase in the prices of alcoholic beverages would produce a 1.5 times larger proportionate reduction in the risk of liver cirrhosis in heavy drinkers than in moderate drinkers, even assuming a smaller proportionate reduction in consumption by heavy drinkers relative to moderate drinkers, (e.g. based on Wagenaar et al., 2009).

To anticipate findings presented in Chapter 5, price policies generate larger reductions in health care expenditure than many other alcohol policies and have a relatively low implementation cost. Therefore, overall, they tend to reduce government spending.

However, policies that increase prices typically cause welfare losses, because some people are no longer able to afford consumption from which they derive pleasure, or have to pay a higher price for it, and these losses tend to be larger in moderate drinkers, who are more responsive to price changes. For instance, alcohol taxation in Australia is estimated to have caused a welfare loss of AUD 612 million in 2007-08, net of AUD 7 426 million of tax revenues generated (Byrnes et al., 2012). Of course, these losses must be assessed against the reduction in harms caused by drinkers to others (e.g. from traffic accidents, crime and violence) which would follow reduced consumption of alcohol. Estimates of the costs associated with harms to others in Australia discussed in Chapter 1 are substantially larger than the welfare loss mentioned above.

### *Are alcohol policies regressive?*

Price policies on alcohol tend to be regressive, although not nearly as much as in the case of tobacco. Expenditure on alcoholic beverages as a proportion of household income is twice as large in low-income households as in high-income households, in countries like the United States and the United Kingdom. Expenditure on alcohol duties in the United Kingdom was 1.6% and 0.9% of disposable income, respectively, for low- and high-income households in 2009-10. Although high-income households purchase a larger share of cheap alcohol than lower-income households (Ludbrook et al., 2012), existing estimates suggest that minimum price policies too would weigh more heavily on the lower-income group, as discussed in Ludbrook's special focus contribution in this volume.

### *The impact of price policies on illicit production and trade*

Increases in tax avoidance and illicit production and trade of alcohol are among the potential consequences of government policies aimed at raising the prices of alcoholic beverages. Cross-border trade, a form of tax avoidance, has a significant impact where large price differentials exist between neighbouring countries. Illicit trade and production of alcohol are important phenomena, including in OECD countries. Recent estimates for the United Kingdom suggest that the illicit market share may be as large as 3% for spirits and 9% for beer, with a loss of tax revenues of just over GBP 1 billion (HMRC, 2013). The size of smuggling and illicit production is even larger in other countries, though by its very nature it is difficult to quantify the effects of alcohol policies on the size of the illicit market. However, more intense efforts by governments in countering these phenomena may generate additional fiscal revenues and contribute to cutting the consumption of relatively inexpensive alcohol. This subject is further discussed in Box 5.2 in Chapter 5.

### *Key messages for alcohol policy makers*

Summarising this section, existing evidence suggests that:

- A more policy-relevant way of framing the health consequences of alcohol consumption would be through more general measures of health outcomes than death rates.
- When assessing the health effects of policies, what matters is whether drinking less is beneficial or not. Most people would be healthier if they drank less.
- The average drop in consumption of alcohol in response to population-based measures may be smaller among harmful drinkers than among non-harmful drinkers. However, the health effects are not proportional to consumption, so even a smaller reduction in consumption is likely to lead to larger health effects.

On the other hand:

- Some people could fall into the category of reduced consumption worsening their health status, which means that governments seeking to address alcohol-related harms must take a political decision about whether the health, employment and wider social effects on the greater part of the drinking population justify the broader approaches.
- There are legitimate concerns about the regressive effects of some alcohol policies.
- Concerns about smuggling and illicit trade need to be taken into consideration.

Several of these issues are further discussed in the context of the analysis of the impacts of specific policy options, presented in Chapter 5.

## Global and national strategies to reduce the harmful use of alcohol

Negative health effects and social harm caused by harmful alcohol consumption can be reduced through effective prevention strategies. In 1979, the World Health Assembly called upon WHO member states to develop and adopt appropriate legislation and measures to tackle alcohol misuse (WHO, 1979). Such efforts culminated with the endorsement, in 2010, of the global strategy on the harmful use of alcohol (WHO, 2011) that supports ten target areas for national actions, including: health sector response; community actions; drinking-and-driving policies; limitation of the availability of alcohol; action on marketing and pricing policies; reducing the negative consequences of intoxication; and reducing the public health effect of illegally and informally produced alcohol.

Policy makers and researchers agree that there is no silver bullet to limit harmful drinking. Rather, countries tend to adopt and combine a range of policies in different areas identified by WHO, with the aim of discouraging harmful drinking. Even though alcohol policies are broadly comparable across countries in terms of the types of measures used, they tend to vary significantly in terms of how they are implemented and in the legal limits for law enforcement. For instance, allowed blood alcohol concentration levels for drivers range from as low as zero (e.g. in Hungary, the Czech and Slovak Republics) up to 0.08% in the United Kingdom and the United States, at the federal level (WHO, 2014). On the other hand, the United States has one of the most restrictive policies for minimum legal drinking age (21 years).

One of the main goals of alcohol policies is to promote public health and social wellbeing. Additionally, policy can address market failures, for example by protecting vulnerable consumers (e.g. children) from exposure to alcohol, protecting people other than drinkers from harms caused by alcohol, and providing all consumers with information about the effects of alcohol. Our analysis is explicitly focused on policies whose primary objective is to reduce harmful alcohol consumption. However, policies in other domains may have important effects on alcohol consumption and alcohol-related harms, although not primarily designed for this purpose. Examples include road safety measures, unemployment and social protection policies. Descriptions of the most common policies in OECD countries are provided in the remainder of this chapter.

### *Influence of trade agreements on national policies*

Policies to control alcohol at the national and the local level have been placed under increasing pressure because of potential conflicts with international trade agreements signed by countries. In such agreements, for example within the European Union or the World Trade Organization (WTO), alcoholic beverages are subject largely to the same rules as other traded commodities. In particular, some have suggested that binding commitments to limit the implementation of protectionist policies, or simply the fear of breaching these commitments, may have weakened national alcohol policies (Grieshaber-Otto et al., 2000). For example, the WTO committee on technical barriers to trade has been discussing concerns expressed by the European Union and Mexico over the recent Russian draft regulation on the safety of alcoholic beverages which, among other things, regulates product marking and labelling (WTO, 2012). Scotland's minimum price policy has been challenged by several European Union Member States on the grounds of alleged restrictions to competition and international trade potentially deriving from the implementation of the policy.

## Main approaches in the alcohol policy toolkit

### *Price policies*

Alcohol prices are altered by governments using taxes or direct price controls, including minimum unit prices, in order to change consumption. Taxation is applied on alcoholic beverages in virtually all OECD countries. Minimum pricing policies, on the other hand, are less common and have only recently attracted the interest of several governments, although a larger number of countries apply measures to prevent the sale of alcoholic beverage at very low prices, as discussed in Box 4.1.

#### *Taxation*

Although taxes on alcohol were originally conceived as a means to raise revenues for the public sector (Smith, 1776), today they are increasingly viewed also as a public health measure (e.g. Rice, 2012). The most common approach is based on a combination of excise duties and value added taxes. Excise duties are applied on alcoholic beverages in two main ways, either or both of which are used in different countries. The excise may be specific to the alcohol content (e.g. percentage of alcohol in the drink) or volume of the product, or calculated as a proportion of the "value" of the product (*ad valorem* excise). The effects of different taxes may vary substantially and changes in taxation require careful planning (e.g. Keen, 1998; Sassi et al., 2013). One important consideration in tax design is substitution effects potentially triggered by price changes. For instance, the introduction of a tax on alcopops in Germany simply shifted consumption from spirit-based to beer-based beverages (Anderson et al., 2012a). A further issue is the potential reduction in the relative weight of alcohol taxes as a proportion of beverage prices, if they are not indexed for inflation, which may diminish their effects on consumption.

Figure 4.1 provides a summary of the relative position of OECD countries in terms of size of excise taxes levied on individual alcoholic beverages, calculated in purchasing power parities, as averages across beverage subtypes (when applicable). Information on alcohol taxation regimes was obtained from OECD's data collection on consumption taxes (OECD, 2014). For each type of beverage, countries are divided into three tertiles in the figure (relatively low, intermediate, and relatively high taxation). Northern European countries, including Finland, Sweden, Norway and Iceland, as well as the United Kingdom and Australia, consistently rank in the upper tertile of taxation for all alcoholic beverages. On the other hand, the mildest alcohol taxation regimes are found in southern European countries, including Italy, France, Spain and Portugal; in central European countries such as Austria, Switzerland and Germany; and in the United States. While beer and spirits are subjected to excise taxation in all OECD countries, a number of countries do not tax wine (only value-added taxes are applied). In particular, countries ranking in the bottom tertile for excise taxes on wine in Figure 4.1 either do not apply, or apply merely nominal, excises.

### Box 4.1. Minimum prices by any other name

The current debate on minimum pricing policies tends to focus on measures to set explicit price thresholds below which alcoholic beverages cannot be sold to consumers. However, governments may employ a range of policy options to selectively raise the prices of cheap alcohol. The main ones are reviewed below.

Minimum pricing policies are currently in use in Canada, albeit with different features in different provinces. In British Columbia, minimum prices for alcoholic beverages have been set since 1989. These have been reviewed over time, but are not indexed for inflation. Minimum prices currently vary from CAD 0.25 per ounce for beer, cider and coolers (alcopops), to CAD 3 per ounce for spirits, not including sales tax, and are not linked with alcohol content. In Saskatchewan, a minimum price policy was adopted in 2003. Since 2010, minimum prices are adjusted for alcohol content, creating a uniform price per standard drink across beverage types and sizes (Stockwell et al., 2012a). Minimum pricing rules were also changed in Ontario in 2010, linking price thresholds for some beverages (e.g. beer) to alcohol content by volume. Prices are also indexed for inflation in Ontario.[1]

The approach adopted in Scotland involves the setting of a minimum price per unit of alcohol across all beverages. Legislation was passed in May 2012, setting a minimum price of GBP 0.50 per unit of alcohol, but legal challenges have so far held up its implementation, as explained in a Special Focus contribution by Martin McKee that follows this chapter. Minimum prices are to be based on the formula MPU x S x V x 100, where MPU is the minimum price per unit, S is alcoholic strength, and V is the beverage volume in litres.[2] For instance, if the minimum price per unit of alcohol is set at GBP 0.50, alcoholic strength is 14%, and the volume is 75 cl, the minimum price at which that alcohol product can be sold is GBP 5.25 (GBP 0.50 x 14% x 0.75 x 100).

The possible adoption of minimum prices for alcohol has been debated in England and Australia (Australian National Preventive Health Agency, 2013), while Ireland is widely expected to introduce minimum unit pricing in a forthcoming Public Health (Alcohol) Bill, along with other measures such as regulation of the marketing and advertising of alcohol, labelling of alcohol products, and the "structural separation" of alcohol from other products in mixed trading outlets.

Evidence of the effects of minimum prices on alcohol consumption is reviewed in Chapter 5, and is primarily based on studies by Stockwell et al. (2012a, 2012b) in the Canadian provinces of British Columbia and Saskatchewan, showing significant reductions in consumption following increases in minimum prices. The same group found direct evidence of health and health care benefits following increases in minimum prices in British Columbia. In particular, a CAD 0.10 increase in average minimum prices was estimated to be able to prevent 166 acute alcohol-attributable hospital admissions in the first year, and 275 chronic admissions two years later (Stockwell et al., 2013). Detailed studies were also undertaken by Sheffield University in the United Kingdom, estimating the potential impact of minimum prices in Scotland and in England, also discussed in Chapter 5, including a reduction of over 480 000 hospital admissions and 15 000 deaths in ten years in England following the introduction of a GBP 0.50 minimum unit price (Brennan et al., 2008).

**Bans on below-cost sales**

Banning below-cost sales means preventing retailers from selling alcoholic drinks at a lower price than the sum of the excise duty and value-added tax payable on the beverage. The principle on which this type of policy is based is that retailers should not use alcohol products and "loss-leaders" by selling them below the cost of doing business, or some proxy measure (Hunt et al., 2011).

Bans on the sale of products below cost, which apply to alcohol products but are not specifically designed for the latter, are in force in several EU member states, including ***Poland***, ***France***, ***Spain***, ***Italy***, ***Belgium***, and ***Luxembourg*** (Hunt et al., 2011). A ban on sales below cost was repealed In ***Ireland*** in 2006 (Rabinovich et al., 2009).

Box 4.1. **Minimum prices by any other name** *(cont.)*

A ban on below-cost sales specifically for alcohol products was recently introduced in ***England and Wales***. The minimum price is calculated by applying the current VAT rate to the excise duty payable on the product, which differs depending on the strength of the alcohol product. Based on this policy, a 440 ml can of beer (4% alcohol by volume – ABV) cannot be sold for less than GBP 0.4; a 750 ml bottle of wine (12.5% ABV) cannot be sold for less than GBP 2.46; and, a 700 ml bottle of spirits (37.5% ABV) for less than GBP 8.89. Retailers can continue to apply promotions on the sale of alcohol (e.g. "buy one, get one free") run promotions in hotels and restaurants, or offer discount coupons for alcoholic drinks, as long as they ensure that the total purchase price is above the permitted price of the products.

In addition to preventing the use of alcohol as loss-leader, bans on below-cost sales can prevent unfair competitive practices by large retailers which could potentially damage small retailers and producers, and could discourage entry into the market by potential new competitors (Hunt et al., 2011). On the other hand, the prices of cheap alcohol are raised only to a modest extent, with uncertain effects on harmful drinking. Researchers at the University of Sheffield estimated a minimal impact of a ban on below-cost sales, "approximately 40 to 50 times smaller than the estimated impact of a GBP 0.45 MUP" (Meng et al., 2013).

**Minimum mark-ups and profit margins**

A further option for governments is to set minimum mark-ups or profit margins for retailers of alcohol products. This policy is based on a similar principle to that underlying below-cost bans, but it goes further than the latter in establishing a deterrent to discourage the sale and consumption of cheap alcohol.

Minimum profit margins are applied in several US States. For instance, the State of Kansas regulates both the price at which alcohol is sold to licensed distributors and the minimum mark-ups on alcohol sold by retailers, "[…] such that they do not unduly stimulate the sale and consumption of alcoholic liquor […]".[3] Similarly, the State of Ohio sets minimum mark-ups for both wholesale prices (33.3%) and retail prices (50%, or 40% for case sales). The wholesale price plus the retail mark-up constitutes the minimum price at which an alcohol product can be sold to consumers.

Minimum mark-ups are also used in Canada. The Province of Alberta applies a flat mark-up varying by type of alcoholic beverage (spirits, refreshment beverages, wine and beer) and alcohol content. Mark-ups currently vary between CAD 0.20 for beer with less than 12% ABV produced by small breweries (less than 20 000 hectolitres per year), to CAD 17.87 for spirits with more than 60% ABV. The Northwest Territories also apply fixed mark-ups. These were increased in 2009 by 10%, with the expectation that this would increase by 7% the prices of spirits and by 5% the prices of other alcoholic beverages, in the "hope that these measures will encourage people to reconsider and reduce their consumption".[4] The Nunavut Liquor Commission also applies flat-rate-per-litre mark-ups in the pricing of alcohol beverage products. An administration fee of CAD 0.27 per litre is also applied. Current mark-ups per litre are CAD 26.11 for spirits, CAD 7.96 for wine, CAD 3.27 for coolers and CAD 2.37 for beer.

**Bans and restrictions on promotions**

Bans, or restrictions, may be imposed on promotional events such as happy hours, ladies' nights, "2 for 1", all-you-can-drink specials, and unlimited beverages at a fixed price for a fixed period of time. Promotions can take a variety of forms, and there is no standard or legal definition of what constitutes a promotion, at least at the European Union level (Rabinovich et al., 2012).

The Canadian Province of Ontario restricts both happy hours and two-for-one drink sales (CCSA, 2012). A recent reform of British Columbia's Liquor Law (June 2014) allowed certain price promotions (e.g. "happy hours") provided beverages are not sold below the minimum price.[5]

### Box 4.1. **Minimum prices by any other name** *(cont.)*

In the United States, legislative provisions are in force in many states limiting or prohibiting practices such as: free distribution of alcoholic beverages; additional servings while previous servings have not been fully consumed; reduced price sales during specified days and times; unlimited beverage offers at a fixed price over a fixed period of time; increasing beverage volume without increasing price; and, using alcoholic beverages as prizes.[6]

A ban on the sale of alcoholic beverages for a fixed price is also in force in France (Law 2009-879) but exceptions have been introduced for fairs or others traditional celebrations (Decree 2011-613). On-trade price promotions (e.g. "happy hours" or "two for one") remain banned in Ireland, despite the repeal of a ban on below-cost sales in 2006 (Rabinovich et al., 2009).

Analyses by Sheffield University researchers have shown that banning off-trade discounts of more than 20% would have a similar effect to the introduction of a GBP 0.35 minimum price in England. Their analyses also found that tight restrictions would affect wine consumption the most and that banning discounts only on lower-priced alcohol (less than GBP 0.30 per unit of alcohol) would not be effective in reducing consumption. A total ban on off-trade discounting was estimated to potentially reduce overall alcohol consumption by 2.8% (Brennan et al., 2008).

A range of studies showing increases in harmful alcohol consumption in connection with various types of promotions provide an indication of the benefits potentially associated with bans and restrictions. On-trade and off-trade price discounts were associated with increased heavy episodic drinking by college students in the United States (Kuo et al., 2003). Drink specials and all-you-can-drink promotions were found to be associated with up to fourfold higher alcohol concentrations in breath tests (Thombs et al., 2008; Thombs et al., 2009). Certain groups (e.g. women, people under age 21, students living on campuses) were found to be more influenced in their drinking behaviour by happy-hour promotions, leading to increased risk of driving under the influence of alcohol and engaging in violent behaviour (Baldwin et al., 2014).

1. www.canlii.org/en/on/laws/regu/o-reg-116-10/latest/o-reg-116-10.html#history.
2. See: www.scottish.parliament.uk/S3_Bills/Alcohol%20etc.%20(Scotland)%20Bill/b34as3-stage3-ml.pdf.
3. See Kansas State Statutes, 41-1114 at: http://kansasstatutes.lesterama.org/Chapter_41/Article_11/#41-1127.
4. See: http://www.fin.gov.nt.ca/press-releases/mar-31-2009/.
5. See: www.pssg.gov.bc.ca/lclb/docs-forms/policy-directive-2014-07.pdf.
6. See NHTSA-Happy hour 2005, available at: http://captus.samhsa.gov/prevention-practice/prevention-approaches/policy-adoption/2.

The impact of changes in the price of alcoholic beverages has been extensively studied and a consistent body of evidence shows that increases in taxation, when passed on to consumers, reduce alcohol consumption. The elasticity of alcohol consumption to price changes tends to be proportionately larger in moderate drinkers than in heavy drinkers (Manning et al., 1995), in women than in men (Elder et al., 2010), in adults than in young people (Gallet, 2007; although a number of studies emphasise that adolescents and young adults do exhibit a strong response to price changes, e.g. Xu and Chaloupka, 2011), and often vary in different ethnic groups (e.g. in the United States, An and Sturm, 2011). Price elasticity also varies for different types of alcoholic beverages, generally with a lower elasticity for beer than wine and spirits (Wagenaar et al., 2009). Variations in average alcohol price elasticity between countries were found to be largely explained by differences in per capita alcohol consumption, beverage mix, and relative ethanol share of beverages (Fogarty, 2006; 2008). In addition, elasticity estimates vary between studies according to the methods used and study design. Much of the effect of increased alcohol taxation on consumption depends on the degree to which the tax is passed on to consumers. In 1991, a nine-dollar increase in the US federal excise tax on beer was found to have produced an almost immediate increase in retail price by USD 15 to USD 17 (Young and Bielinska-Kwapisz, 2002). More recently, a comparison of how taxes on alcohol are passed on to consumers in Ireland, Finland, Latvia and Slovenia showed a more complex and heterogeneous pattern, with a pass-through ratio for beer ranging from 0 (i.e. no change in consumer price) for on-trade sales in Ireland to 2.5 for off-trade sales in Slovenia (i.e. a price increase of 2.5 times the tax increase), and between 0.1 (on-trade in Ireland) and 1.4 (off-trade in Finland) for spirits (Rabinovich et al., 2012).

Figure 4.1. **Alcohol excise taxation levels in OECD countries**

Tertiles

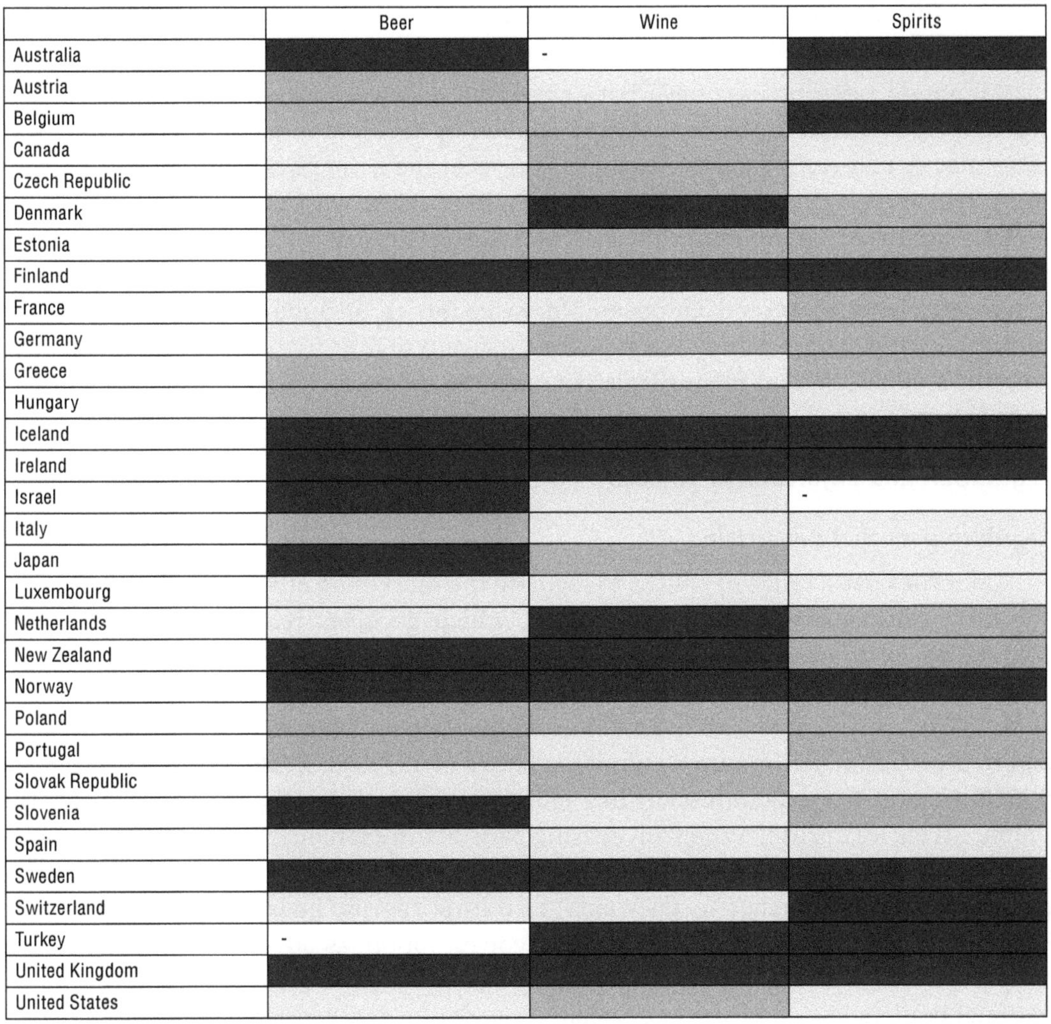


*Note:* Lighter-shaded cells identify the first (lower) tertile of taxation; darker-shaded cells identify the third (higher) tertile of taxation; and, intermediate-shaded cells identify the second tertile. It was not possible to rank Australia for wine taxation, Israel for spirits taxation, and Turkey for beer taxation. In Canada, provincial and territorial governments also impose minimum mark-ups and charge levies on alcohol, which generally exceed rates at the federal level.

*Source:* OECD (2014), *Consumption Tax Trends 2014: VAT/GST and Excise Rates, Trends and Policy Issues*, OECD Publishing, Paris, http://dx.doi.org/ 10.1787/ctt-2014-en.

### *Minimum prices*

Minimum pricing aims at increasing the price of very cheap alcohol, therefore limiting its affordability. Compared to taxation (e.g. sales and excise taxes), setting a minimum price may produce larger effects on drinkers with heavier consumption patterns as they tend to purchase cheaper alcoholic beverages, as discussed in Ludbrook's Special Focus III after Chapter 4. The main impact is typically on supermarket and off-license sales, as prices in the on-trade sector are generally above the minimum levels.

Price increases in compliance with minimum price policies do not constitute fiscal revenues, as the extra money spent on alcohol by consumers would remain with retailers and would not be transferred to the treasury as happens with taxes (Brennan et al., 2008). However, the introduction, or variation, of minimum prices may not be neutral from a fiscal viewpoint, as it would likely alter the tax base for the application of existing taxes.

Minimum price policies have both strengths and weaknesses relative to taxation. Minimum prices have to be consistently applied by retailers in alcohol sales, while tax hikes may or may not translate into higher prices at the point of consumption (Ally et al., 2014). This means that price promotions remain possible with taxation, while they are severely restricted by minimum prices. The larger effects of minimum prices on heavy drinkers represent a further strength of the latter relative to taxation. On the other hand, the governments of several European Union countries, including France, Italy, Spain, Portugal, Poland and Bulgaria, have expressed concern to the European Commission about Scotland's minimum unit pricing legislation, on the grounds of a potential breach of free trade regulations.

## *Regulation and enforcement policies*

### *Regulating alcohol advertising*

Countries use a range of polices to regulate the marketing of alcohol. These are often based on self-regulation and co-regulation, which devolves responsibility for setting boundaries for marketing to the alcohol industry. Existing evidence suggests that the effects of self-regulation of marketing have been disappointing (WHO, 2007; Anderson et al., 2009; Jernigan et al., 2013). This is often due to poor participation and compliance, and to breaches of self-imposed standards (Jones et al., 2008; KPMG LLP, 2008), although the US Federal Trade Commission has found compliance to be generally good in the United States (FTC, 2014). When advertising bans are implemented, they are more likely to be partial, for example for certain products (e.g. only beverages with a higher alcohol content) or certain media (e.g. television) or during specific hours. Partial bans tend to have only limited effects on overall alcohol consumption, as advertising expenditure is simply shifted onto other media or targets. The increasing use of media that reach across national borders (e.g. internet) and social networks for marketing alcohol suggests that governments pursuing marketing regulation may need to consider parallel cross-border measures (WHO, 2014).

Heavy marketing of alcohol is regarded as a causal factor in alcohol consumption, particularly because of its impact on the habits of teenagers and youngsters (Anderson et al., 2009; Snyder et al., 2006). Advertising is a global industry employing increasingly sophisticated marketing techniques in traditional media (e.g. television and print), branding and sponsorship of events, product placement in films and shows, point-of-sale displays and, more recently, new media like Internet, social networks and smartphones. Regulation of advertising is a well-established intervention across the OECD. Most countries implement partial bans preventing the marketing of specific types of alcoholic beverages (e.g. spirits), during certain times (e.g. when a large proportion of the audience is youngsters) or for specific media (e.g. television). Regulation may also target the content and mode of delivery of advertising messages. For instance the EU Council Directive 89/552/EC of October 1989 asserts that television advertising for alcoholic beverages should not be specifically aimed at, or depict minors consuming alcohol, it should not link alcohol to enhanced physical performance, driving, social or sexual success and so on. In a number of cases, these restrictions operate alongside industry self-regulation codes.

### Box 4.2. **Regulation of the marketing of alcohol in France**

In France, alcohol marketing is regulated by the Loi Évin of 1991, often regarded, particularly in its original form, as one of the most comprehensive codes on the topic. It is one of the few policies on alcohol marketing that regulates both the content of the advertisement and the media on which the advertisement appears. This law bans the advertising of all alcoholic beverages containing over 1.2% alcohol by volume on television and in cinemas. Sponsorship of sports or cultural events is also prohibited. For example, the football World Cup that was held in France in 1998 could not be sponsored by any alcohol company. Alcohol advertising is only permitted in the press for adults, on billboards, on radio channels (under certain conditions) and at some special events or places (e.g. wine fairs). In this case, messages and images should not be crafted to appeal to young people and should only have an informative aim. This means that they can only refer to the 'objective' characteristics of the product (e.g. alcohol content, origin, means of production). The advertisement must also carry a health warning ("alcohol abuse is dangerous for health"). The Loi Évin does not regulate mailing of alcohol advertisement or social events (as, for example, the launch of the Beaujolais Nouveau in November).

In 2008, the Loi Évin was amended to cover also alcohol advertising on the Internet and in newspapers and magazine editorials. Alcohol marketing is authorised on the Internet as long as it is neither intrusive nor interstitial (an interstitial ad is one that appears before the actual webpage). In 2012, the appeal court of Paris gave a more restrictive interpretation of alcohol marketing on social networks. Referring to a case of alcohol marketing on Facebook, the court came to the conclusion that marketing on this media should be viewed as intrusive because of the automatic nature of this media (i.e. users do not control the messages shown).

The judgement shed light also on two other modes of diffusion. Mobile applications by alcohol brands are authorised if they are online software (i.e. an internet connection is needed to use the app). Alcohol promotion through movies on the Internet is not prohibited, under the condition that the content respects the law.

Infringements of the law lead to monetary sanctions. Anybody can challenge and bring to the attention of the court an advertisement which is considered as not complying with the law. ANPAA (*Association Nationale de Prévention en Alcoologie et Addictologie*) in particular is actively involved in this. During the first ten years of implementation, 50 advertisements were brought before the French courts and 45 of the complaints were upheld. As an indirect consequence of the law, most of the "seductive" character of alcohol advertisement was lost. An evaluation of the law was published by the office of the Prime Minister in 1999.[1]

1. www.ladocumentationfrancaise.fr/var/storage/rapports-publics/004000708/0000.pdf.

### Box 4.3. **Regulation of the marketing of alcohol in Norway**

Norway may have the strictest regulation of alcohol marketing in the OECD. The policy is defined in the Norwegian Alcohol Act and particularly in Chapter 9, "Prohibition against advertising of alcoholic beverages" and the supplementary regulations in Chapter 14. The Alcohol Act prohibits any form of mass communication on alcohol, including advertisements in printed newspapers, films, radio, television, telephone networks, data networks, illuminated advertisement hoardings, signboards and similar devices, depictions and exhibitions. The distribution of printed matters or trade samples is not allowed. Conversely, editorials are possible as long as the written pieces are not initiated by an alcohol producer or advertiser.

The law is administered by the Ministry of Health and Care Services. The Directorate for Health and Social Affairs supervises and imposes sanctions when the law and regulations have been violated. Complaints about advertisements can be made to the Directorate for Health and Social Affairs by anyone in the country, including private citizens and organisations. Statistics suggest that there has been a rise in the number of complaints over time. If an advertiser is found guilty, usually the Directorate for Health and Social Affairs simply requests the illegal marketing to cease. However, if the illegal marketing continues, sanctions may be imposed. The severity and the character of the sanctions vary from case to case, and depend on the income of the business.

### Box 4.4. **Regulation of the marketing of alcohol in Finland**

In December 2013, the Finnish Parliamentary Social Affairs and Health Committee issued a report to further strengthen the regulation of marketing of alcoholic beverages in public places. The most innovative feature of this law is that, as one of the first in the OECD area, Finland is trying to regulate advertising on the Internet and social media.

Alcohol marketing regulation already in place prohibited the advertisement of strong alcoholic beverages (>22% of alcohol content) with the exception of advertisements in alcohol-shops and restaurants and advertisements aimed at resellers (e.g. restaurant owners). Conversely, the advertisement of mild alcoholic beverages (i.e. alcohol content between 1.2% and 22%) was allowed if it did not target minors, did not suggest an association between alcohol consumption and social or sexual success, and was not shown in cinemas or on TV between 7 in the morning and 9 in the evening.

The new regulation specifically aims at reducing children's exposure to alcohol advertising. For this reason, limitation of radio and TV advertisement is extended to 10 o'clock at night to reflect changes in media usage patterns among youngsters. A new ban on outdoor advertising and on promotion at public events (with the exception of international fairs) is also introduced, as well as a ban on alcohol promotion in games, lotteries and similar activities. However, the most innovative aspect of the new policy is the introduction of restrictive measures of alcohol marketing on social media. The ban includes any textual or visual content which is produced by consumers (i.e. user-generated content) or which is intended to be shared by consumers. The ban does not cover consumer personal areas as, for example, personal Facebook pages.

Research for violation is performed by the National Product Control Agency for Welfare and Health (Valvira) at the national level and by provincial authorities at the sub-national level (e.g. if restaurants or local publications violated the law). In addition, anyone can submit a complaint that is then handled by the Council of Ethics in Advertising. The marketing practice under scrutiny can continue until it is banned by the Control Agency. However, if the violation of the law is particularly evident, the advertiser may be asked to cease the marketing while waiting for the final decision. In most of the cases, the sanction is limited to the ban, but Valvira can also issue fines to, for example, remove the illegal ad. If violations are repeated, the advertiser can be taken to the Market Court which can rule on the amount of the fine.

### Box 4.5. Regulation of the marketing of alcohol in Israel

At the beginning of 2012 the Israeli parliament approved a law, taking effect in mid-2014, that limits the advertising and marketing of alcohol products. The new law was a private member's bill, but was endorsed and promoted by the Ministry of Health. The law contains four elements. First, a total ban on outdoor advertising as well as print items and television ads directed at children and adolescents. Second, forbidding alcohol products as gifts, giveaways or prizes. Third, limitations on advertisement appearance, structure and quantity per printed issue. This limitation included almost unprecedentedly advertising on the Internet, in spite of its complexities.

The fourth element was an obligatory warning notice on alcoholic products and permitted advertisements (print, Internet, television and radio) with defined text, length and size and appearance. Although the original article in the law included a "front of pack" warning-notice, lobbying by the alcohol industry and commerce shifted the warning to a more conservative "back of pack".

The law was accompanied by a reform in taxation of alcohol products that was adopted in 2010 and implemented in mid-2013. The reform increased the tax per litre of alcohol content from NIS 21.28 to NIS 105, irrespective of the pre-tax price of the product, thereby aiming at increasing the price of relatively cheap, high-alcohol products.

The effects of these parallel reforms are to be assessed in the next couple of years.

### *Regulating alcohol product labels*

Product labels are mandated in many countries on certain types of foods to provide consumers with information about the contents (e.g. ingredients), the quantity and the durability of the products, and to warn them about potential health risks (e.g. allergies). According to information collected by WHO (2014), in the vast majority of countries (i.e. 116 out of 167) alcohol content should be reported on the alcohol container. Much less common (i.e. 31 out of 167 reporting countries) is the mandatory requirement for labels to warn consumers about health consequences of excessive alcohol consumption, or messages to discourage the sale of alcohol products to people below the minimum legal age. In the European Union, the labelling of alcoholic beverages is addressed by Regulation 1169/2011, on the provision of food information to consumers, which requires alcohol containers to provide information on alcohol content, but exempts alcohol products from the requirement to list components or to provide nutritional information. France is the only EU member state which mandates the inclusion of a health warning on alcohol product labels.

### *Limiting access to alcohol*

Virtually all countries set a minimum legal age for the purchase of alcoholic beverages. Most of the countries in Figure 4.2 use the same minimum age threshold for both on-trade (e.g. bars, restaurants) and off-trade (e.g. retail) sales. In a few cases age thresholds differ and, normally, are higher for on-trade sales. A second approach to limit alcohol availability is through controls on outlet density, either through State monopolies or commercial regulation. A further approach involves restrictions on licensing and outlet opening hours. Regulation of alcohol availability has the potential to produce significant effects on alcohol consumption (Stockwell and Chikritzhs, 2009; Livingston et al., 2007; Gruenewald, 2007) and health outcomes. However, a stringent policy on alcohol availability should be always coupled with effective enforcement, as informal market activities are likely to develop as a side effect.

### Box 4.6. **Alcohol labelling in the United States**

The United States is one of few countries to have a mandatory labelling policy for alcohol containers. Health warning labels were introduced in 1988 as part of the Alcoholic Beverage Labelling Act which was promulgated as a United States federal law. The health warning reads as follow: "GOVERNMENT WARNING: 1) According to the Surgeon General, women should not drink alcoholic beverages during pregnancy because of the risk of birth defects. 2) Consumption of alcoholic beverages impairs your ability to drive a car or operate machinery, and may cause health problems". According to the regulations implementing the law, the health warning must appear on the brand label or on a separate front or back label of "any alcoholic beverage". The health warning should be, in any case, separate and apart from all the other information contained in the product label. The regulations also make sure that the warning is readable under ordinary conditions by stating that the labelling must appear on a contrasting background and regulating the minimum size of the message according to the size of the containers. The words "government warning" must appear in capital letters and bold type.

Wilkinson and Room (2009) suggest that the introduction of mandatory labelling in the United States led to a significant increase in population awareness of the messages that they contained. The Attorney General is in charge, through the several district attorneys, of enforcing the law. A breach of the law may be brought in front of the relevant district court which has jurisdiction to prevent and restrain the violations. The violation of the law could result in a civil penalty and be subject to a fine of up to USD 10 000 per day of violation (adjusted for inflation).

### Box 4.7. **Alcohol labelling in the United Kingdom**

In 2007, the UK alcohol industry established a voluntary agreement with the Department of Health to introduce health warning labels on alcoholic drink containers by 2008. The agreement aimed at increasing people's awareness and understanding of national drinking guidelines and the risks involved in drinking during pregnancy. Of the five elements included in the labelling scheme, three are "required" (i.e. are taken into account to assess compliance) while two others are "optional". The required elements include: the number of units of alcohol in the container; the UK Chief Medical Officer's daily guidelines for lower-risk consumption (i.e. 3-4 units/day for men and 2-3 units/day for women); and a warning for pregnant women. The optional elements include: a reference to the *Drinkaware* website (an independent charity that promotes sensible drinking) and a responsibility statement (e.g. drink responsibly).

An independent survey carried out in early 2009, found that 85% of labels failed to provide the elements required by the voluntary agreement (Mayor, 2010). The most common failures included changes in the wording of the health warning (e.g. by including the brand name in the warning), poor tonal contrast, or a significantly smaller font size.

In March 2011, the UK Government announced a Public Health Responsibility Deal which included an extension of the voluntary labelling scheme. Under the renewed scheme, the alcohol industry committed to ensuring that over 80% of products on shelf would have a label with the three required elements by December 2013. An independent review was commissioned in early 2014 and results have not yet been published. In December 2013, the Parliamentary Under-Secretary of State, Department of Health, citing evidence provided by the Portman Group (an association of UK's leading alcohol producers), reported that in early 2012 compliance with the voluntary labelling agreement was over 60%. No official authority is designated to enforce the scheme or to sanction violations.

### Box 4.8. **Alcohol labelling in Thailand**

In January 2010, Thailand notified the Committee on Technical Barriers to Trade of the World Trade Organization (WTO) of its intention to introduce a more severe alcohol labelling law. The proposal was based on three elements. The first element was the prohibition of the inclusion on the packaging of words or sentences that may mislead the consumer into believing that alcohol can improve health or that a specific alcoholic beverage is less bad for health than another. The second requirement entailed the inclusion on the package of a warning stating that it is forbidden to sell alcoholic beverages to underage people. The third, and most innovative requirement, was that any alcoholic beverage package should contain a graphic warning similar to those already in place for tobacco products. The warning should be in colour, fixed in a permanent manner to the container and should cover at least 30% of the surface of the package.

The Thai Government presented six warning packages that should be rotated every 1 000 units of production. The images show, for example, a cirrhotic liver and should be associated to a health warning on the potential effects of harmful drinking (e.g. alcohol consumption could lead to cirrhosis of the liver).

A number of member countries of the WTO committee expressed concern about Thailand's proposal on technical and legislative grounds. To date the new alcohol labelling law has not been implemented.

Limiting the physical availability of alcoholic beverages is a policy approach that many governments have used to reduce individual consumption and harm. Interventions in this category may affect retailers (off-trade) as well as bars and restaurants (on-trade), and may use several approaches to reduce alcohol availability. Examples of current measures include: sale bans in specific areas, outlets or circumstances; government monopoly arrangements for retail sales; the setting of a minimum legal age for purchasing or drinking alcohol; restrictions in outlet opening or serving hours; and regulation of the density of outlets through licensing or other means (Anderson et al., 2012b). Three recent systematic reviews provide a comprehensive summary of the evidence available on the effects of these policies (Popova et al., 2009; Hahn et al., 2010; Bryden et al., 2012).

In countries where government monopolies operate, alcohol imports and sales are centrally controlled through direct government ownership of retail outlets, or through strict licensing arrangements, in the interest of public order. There is strong evidence, particularly from northern European countries, that this policy reduces alcohol consumption. It has been estimated that ending monopolies where they exist may significantly increase harmful consumption (Holder, 2008). Partial monopolies (covering only certain types of beverages) can lead to substitution, with an increase in the consumption of other types of beverages (Nelson, 2003). Where monopolies do not exist in the OECD area, their establishment seems an unlikely prospect.

A minimum legal age, as a policy determining the age at which young people may purchase or possess alcohol, is already in place in all OECD countries. Enforcement can be difficult, and underage drinking is common in many countries. The existing evidence suggests that introducing a minimum age improves health outcomes (Carpenter and Dobkin, 2011), although effects may be short-lived (Miron and Tetelbaum, 2009). There seems to be limited scope for a further tightening of this policy in OECD countries. However, countries debating a possible lowering of existing minimum legal drinking age (e.g. the United States) might benefit from an evaluation of the effects of such policies. A summary of minimum legal ages levels in OECD countries is provided in Figure 4.2, while a more detailed account of minimum ages in individual countries is available in Annex A.

Figure 4.2. **National legal minimum age for alcohol sales, OECD countries and key partners**

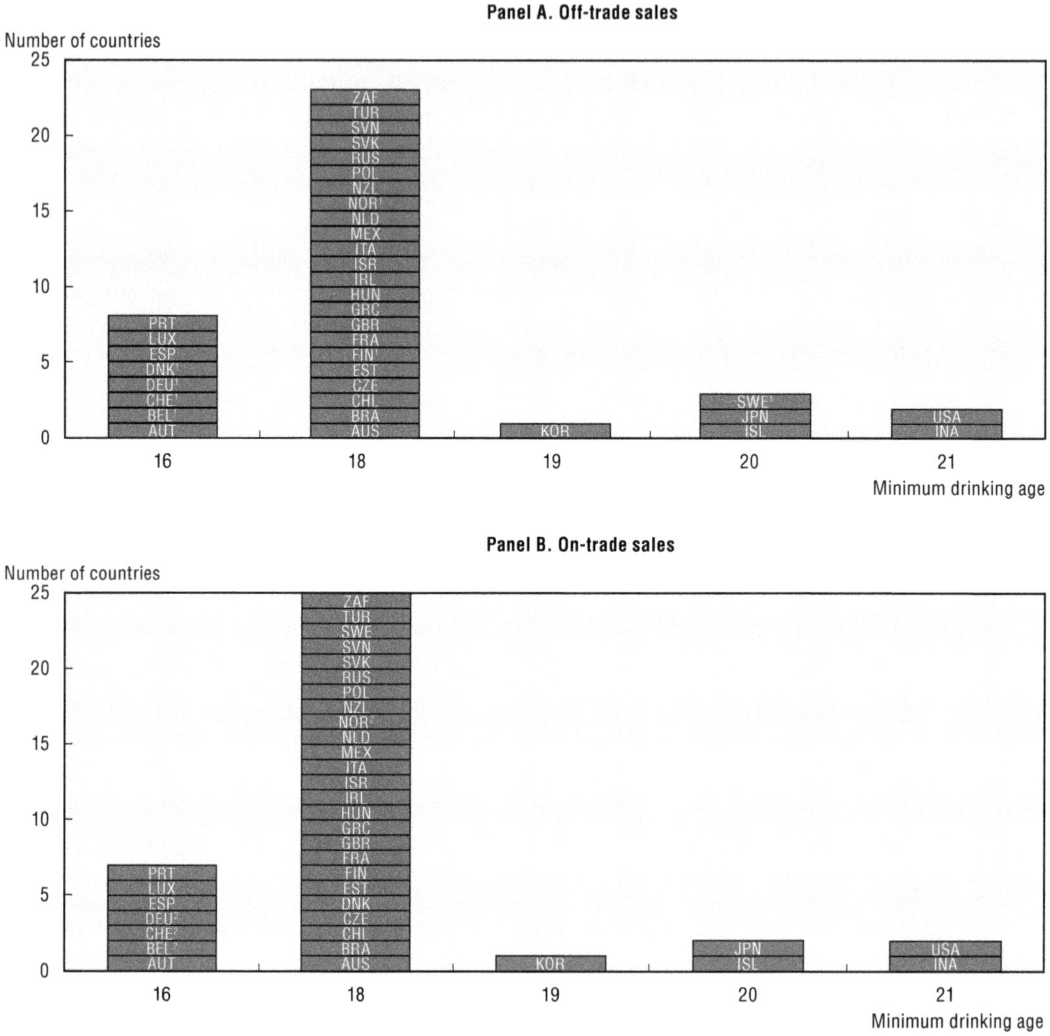


*Note* Panel A: In Belgium, Denmark, Germany, Portugal and Switzerland minimum age of 18 for spirits; in Finland and Norway minimum age of 20 for spirits; in Sweden minimum age of 20 for wine and spirits, 18 for beer.

*Note* Panel B: In Belgium, Germany, Portugal and Switzerland minimum age of 18 for spirits; in Norway minimum age of 20 for spirits.

*Source:* WHO – World Health Organization (2014), *Global Status Report on Alcohol and Health 2014*, WHO, Geneva, and OECD National correspondents, see Table A.3 in Annex A for further details.

StatLink http://dx.doi.org/10.1787/888933180410

A policy approach supported by a relatively broad evidence base, among those used by OECD governments to limit access to alcohol, is the regulation of outlet density and/or opening hours. A large body of evidence is available on the effects of such policies, although studies are highly heterogeneous. A broad variety of measures are assessed, using a variety of outcomes (e.g. reduction in alcohol consumption, violence, assaults, traffic accidents, hospital admissions, etc.), and not all studies show positive and statistically significant effects for these measures. Therefore, making a robust prediction of the likely effects of a given policy, if adopted in a particular setting, may be difficult.

There is clear evidence of an association between outlet density and alcohol-related harm (Babor et al., 2010), but the evidence is mixed on the link between density and alcohol consumption, as illustrated by the opposite findings of Scribner et al. (2000) and Pollack et al. (2005). No statistically significant association was found between density and average alcohol consumption, but an association was found with binge drinking (Connor et al., 2011). Evidence of the effectiveness of restrictions in opening hours is available at the local level in countries like Australia (e.g. Douglas, 1998; Gray et al., 1999), and at the national level in Sweden (Norstrom and Skog, 2005). However, the majority of studies investigate the effects of increases, rather than reductions, in opening hours.

### Box 4.9. **Limiting access to alcohol in Iceland**

Iceland's policy on alcohol is heavily based on regulation of physical availability of alcohol, particularly with the aim of limiting youth access to alcohol. This policy is essentially enforced through a restriction of sales of highly taxed alcoholic products. Sales of alcohol are managed by a state-run monopoly (ÁTVR) that, to date, runs 48 physical liquor-shops (12 in the capital city) and one on-line shop. Shops are generally open between 11 in the morning and six in the evening but some outlets have slightly longer operating hours (i.e. till eight in the evening). Iceland does not adopt any policy to regulate the density of outlet selling alcohol and, in fact, the number of outlets per inhabitants has been increasing over time. In 1922 there was one alcohol store every 13 600 inhabitants, rising to one for every 6 800 inhabitants in 2010. However, since ÁTVR is owned by the Ministry of Finance, the government clearly has strong decisional power on the number of outlets. Conversely, sales of alcohol products for on-trade consumption, as well as the production of alcoholic beverages, are only regulated through licensing. Another characteristic of the Icelandic system is that, although the age of majority is 18, the legal drinking age for purchasing alcohol is 20. The Icelandic Government sees the use of a state-run monopoly as a more effective approach to enforce the minimum legal drinking age. A survey of the attitudes of Icelanders to current arrangements for alcohol sales shows that only about 20% of people are unsatisfied (Jónsson and Kristjánsson, 2013; Ministry of Welfare, 2014). Health care establishments, educational buildings, and public transport are all alcohol-free environments by law. Partial statutory restrictions are in place for government offices and sporting events while voluntary self-regulation applies to other public places (e.g. streets, parks), workplaces and leisure events. In January 2014, the Icelandic Directorate of Health together with the Ministries of Interior, Education and Welfare approved the new alcohol and drug prevention policy to 2020. The policy identifies as its first goal the restriction of access to alcohol. Preventing early drinking initiation is a further goal. Formal actions on how to reach these goals are still under discussion.

### Box 4.10. **Limiting access to alcohol in Italy**

In August 2010, Italy extended the terms of the law prohibiting night sales of alcoholic beverages from petrol stations on highways and motorway service areas. The original law forbade sales of spirits for on-trade consumption between ten at night and six in the morning. The new law extended this ban to spirits for off-trade consumption and banned the sale of any kind of alcohol between 2 and 6 in the morning. Infringements of the law lead to fines of up to EUR 10 500 and, if repeated, to a one month interruption of the licence to sell alcohol. Since the enforcement of the law, the number of car accidents on highways in the hours concerned has decreased substantially. According to the most recent data published by the Italian National Institute of Statistics (ISTAT), car accidents on highways involving at least one injured person or deaths decreased by 15.3% in 2011 relative to 2010, and by a further 14% in 2012 relative to 2011.

### *Policies to prevent drinking and driving*

A high blood alcohol concentration is a major risk factor for traffic accidents, injuries and death. All countries have policies in place to prevent the utilisation of motor vehicles under the influence of alcohol (DUI). A number of countries have different, usually more restrictive, thresholds for professional drivers and young people as they are at higher risk of traffic accidents. Enforcement is usually through check-points and random breath testing. Consequences for drivers identified with levels of alcohol beyond the tolerated threshold vary from fines to suspension or revocation of the driving licence to compulsory treatments for drivers with alcohol dependence. A strict enforcement strategy is key to effective drinking-and-driving policies.

Alcohol is a major contributing factor for traffic fatalities among children and young adults between 5 and 29 years old (Peden, 2004). Usually, the enforcement of laws that prohibit driving under the influence of substances like alcohol has been viewed as an adequate way of limiting harm, but in practice enforcement is often haphazard and punishment is not always timely and commensurate to the offences committed (Babor et al., 2010). As a result, existing policies for countering drinking and driving are not always as effective as they might be, and significant scope remains for improving their ability to reduce traffic accidents and fatalities in many countries. A WHO-Regional Office for Europe (2009) review of policy options to counter drinking and driving and their effectiveness included: the introduction or reduction of blood alcohol concentration (BAC) limits, for all drivers or for higher-risk categories, such as young and professional drivers; designated driver policies; license suspension; and checkpoints and breath tests.

There is consistent evidence that drivers' ability to operate a vehicle is progressively affected by alcohol intake as the concentration of alcohol in their blood increases, therefore the setting of a legal BAC limit was found to have beneficial effects (Mann et al., 2001; Shults et al., 2001; Nagata et al., 2008). Drivers with a BAC of between 0.02 and 0.05 "have at least a three times greater risk of dying in a vehicle crash and this risk increases to at least six times with a BAC between 0.05 and 0.08, and to 11 times with a BAC between 0.08 and 0.10" (Killoran et al., 2010). However, beneficial effects appear to decrease over time due to a diminishing perceived risk of being caught (WHO-Regional Office for Europe, 2009), although at least two studies (Albalate, 2008; Eisenberg, 2003) report no declines after two years or more. BAC control is the most widely adopted intervention in OECD countries and many countries already have lower limits for young and professional drivers (up to "zero tolerance" – e.g. in Australia), which is also a policy of documented effectiveness (Dee, 2001; Shults et al., 2001; Albalate, 2008; Russell et al., 2011). A summary of BAC levels in OECD countries is provided in Figure 4.3, while a more detailed account of limits in individual countries is available in Annex A.

Designated driver programmes, i.e. the selection of a member in a group of drinkers who is designated as sober driver, shows low or marginal effectiveness (Ditter et al., 2005). Education-based interventions, like school-based education, driver training programmes and mass media campaigns were shown to be ineffective or to have mixed results (Novoa et al., 2009; Elder et al., 2004), with more positive findings for road safety campaigns (Phillips et al., 2011). Administrative licence suspension or revocation appears to be an effective policy in reducing drinking and driving where adequate law enforcement is in place (Wagenaar et al., 2007; Babor et al., 2010).

Figure 4.3. **National maximum legal blood alcohol concentration, OECD countries and key partners**

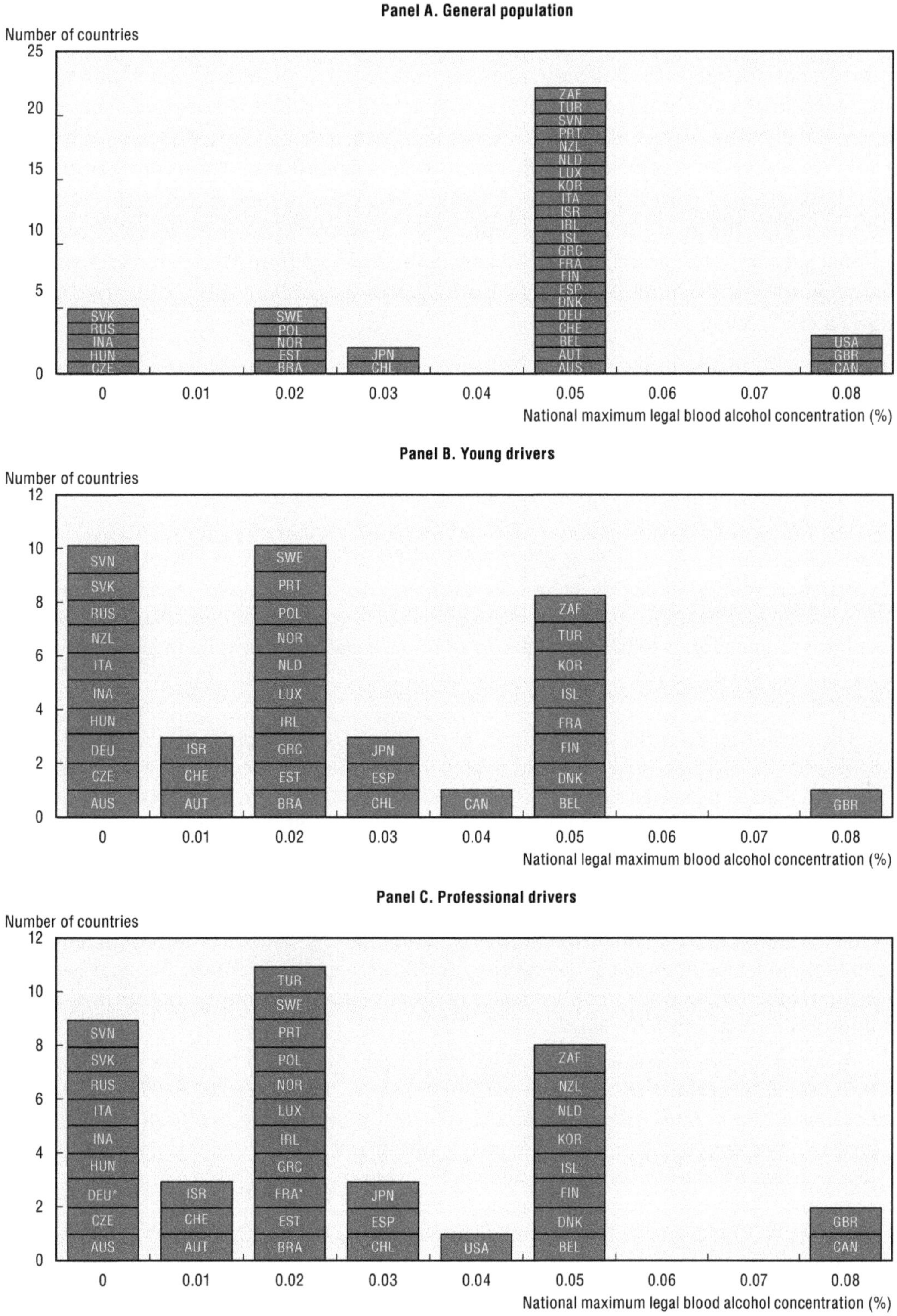


*Note* Panel C: (*) the values reported for France and Germany are for public transportation drivers; in both countries other professional drivers are subject to a limit of 0.05%.

*Source:* WHO – World Health Organization (2014), *Global Status Report on Alcohol and Health 2014*, WHO, Geneva, and OECD National correspondents, see Table A.3 in Annex A for further details.

The European Commission and WHO emphasise the importance of enforcement for the effectiveness of drinking-and-driving legislation, indicating selective breath testing (SBT) and random breath testing (RBT) to test BAC level as the most relevant interventions (Anderson et al., 2012). The first (SBT), more widely used in the United States, involves enforcement officers systematically stopping vehicles at a predetermined location, often during weekends and at night. If an officer suspects that a driver is impaired, a breath test is requested. In the second (RBT), more widely adopted in Australia and Europe, any driver at any time may be stopped and required to take a breath test. These programmes are often implemented with the support of media campaigns to increase drivers' awareness and impact (Shults et al., 2001). Both approaches have been shown to be effective, but a national survey in the United States and anecdotal evidence from other countries suggests that programmes involving checkpoints and breath testing are not deployed systematically (e.g. Fell et al., 2003).

### Box 4.11. **Tackling drinking and driving in Japan**

In the early 2000s Japan started reforms to strengthen its policies against driving under the influence of alcohol. In particular, the following three aspects of the road traffic law were toughened in the two reforms of June 2002 and September 2007.

The first aspect is the definition of DUI. The blood alcohol concentration (BAC) limit was lowered to the current level of 0.3 mg/1 ml for all categories of drivers (i.e. general population, young/novice drivers and professional drivers). Those who obstruct or refuse to undergo an exhalation inspection will be punished by a fine of not more than JPY 500 000 or imprisonment of up to three months. In addition, based on their opinion, police officers have the power to declare a driver as intoxicated (i.e. heavily drunk) independently from the BAC level.

The second aspect is the severity of the punishments when somebody is found driving with a BAC level beyond the threshold or after a road traffic accident. Compared to before 2002, the fine is increased by ten times to up to JPY 500 000 (about USD 5 000) for drivers with a BAC higher than 0.3 mg/1 ml and up to JPY 1 million (USD 10 000) for drivers declared as intoxicated. The pecuniary charge is associated with driving licence suspension or revocation according to the severity of the violation. A driver recognised as intoxicated will incur a fine of no more than JPY 1 million or imprisonment for up to five years, and in cases of DUI, the driver will incur a fine of no more than JYP 500 000 or imprisonment for up to three years. When the driver causes any deaths, being aware of the fact that he/she cannot drive normally due to the influence of the alcohol, the driver will be punished with imprisonment for one to 20 years.

A particular feature of the Japanese legislation is that the similar penalties are extended to those who provided the offender with a vehicle, to those that served the alcoholic beverages, and to other passengers in the vehicle. Unfortunately, no official data on the level of enforcement of the drinking-and-driving law is available. Nakahara and Ichikawa (2010) assert that the level of enforcement did not change substantially, with the exception of periodic crackdown campaigns usually implemented during party seasons (e.g. end of the year). WHO rates the Japanese level of enforcement as one of the highest (8 on a scale between 1 and 10).

Box 4.12. **Tackling drinking and driving in Australia**

Australia has some of the longest-established and most comprehensive regulations against driving under the influence of alcohol. In all states, it is illegal to drive a motor vehicle with a blood alcohol concentration (BAC) of 0.05 g/100 ml or higher. Professional drivers, such as truck and bus drivers, novice drivers and people who previously committed DUI offences are not allowed any alcohol.

Following the adoption of legal limits in the 1980s, the police started large-scale enforcement programmes mainly through sobriety checkpoints and mobile random breath testing. Most Australian states and territories set an annual target for the number of random breath tests equivalent to one-third of the number of licensed drivers within their jurisdiction. Police officers are allowed to stop any vehicle to perform a random breath test on the driver, or other persons in the vehicle if they have reasonable grounds to suspect they were driving.

Australian police can stop a car without any reason or evidence that the driver may be intoxicated. Refusing to take a breath test is treated as a serious offence; for example in Queensland it leads to a fine of AUD 4 000 (USD 3 733) or six months in prison. Giving an unsatisfactory sample (e.g. blowing inadequately into the device) is treated as a refusal to undergo the test. Those caught driving with a BAC over the legal limit face heavy fines and licence withdrawal. The most serious offenders may face imprisonment.

More severe offences significantly increase the amount of the fine and may lead to the withdrawal of the driving licence. In addition, an alcohol interlock may be fitted to the vehicle of drivers who have been convicted of serious DUI offences. An alcohol interlock prevents a vehicle starting if the driver has been drinking. The interlock requires the driver to provide a breath test before starting the vehicle and during the trip.

Over the past 30 years, all jurisdictions have been successful in reducing the contribution of alcohol to road injuries and deaths: in 1980 almost 45% of road traffic deaths involved alcohol, while the most recent data from WHO report a drop to 30%.

### *Education policies*

Education and persuasion strategies are among the most popular approaches to avoid, or at least to delay and reduce, the use of alcoholic drinks in young people. School-based interventions, in particular, are often seen as a potentially effective approach to prevent alcohol-related problems. The principal objective of these interventions is to raise the awareness of students about the dangers caused by alcohol misuse so that young people are less likely to drink in excess. Most interventions address multiple unhealthy behaviours (usually, tobacco, alcohol and narcotics) rather than a specific one. Interventions may include both normative education (i.e. teaching) and resistance-skills training. They may be exclusively directed at the students or include their family or the community in the activities. In general such programmes involve all the students in a class or a school but, in some cases, programmes have been carried out on specific subpopulation groups considered at a higher risk. In some cases, such interventions are implemented as one-off, but the inclusion of "booster" sessions at later stages would seem to favour the maintenance of positive behaviours over time (Foxcroft et al., 2003; Foxcroft et al., 2011).

Campaigns to raise awareness of the risks of excessive drinking are common in OECD countries even outside school settings. Reviews of existing evidence suggest that such campaigns do increase knowledge about the risks of harmful alcohol consumption

(Anderson et al., 2012), but the change in drinking behaviours tends to be limited and short in duration. However, information and education campaigns can contribute to a package of measures to tackle harmful alcohol consumption by generating possible synergies with other measures. The delivery of education messages by private sponsors was found to have no significant public health effects (Christie et al., 2001; Smith et al., 2006; Barry and Goodson, 2010).

***Health care policies for heavy and dependent drinkers***

In most countries, treatments are available within the health sector for those with high levels of alcohol consumption or alcohol dependence problems (WHO, 2010). Two types of intervention are especially common. Brief advice delivered by a trained physician aims at informing the patient about the harms caused by excessive alcohol consumption and providing help in regaining control towards an acceptable use. For patients with more severe problems, such as dependence, interventions usually combine cognitive-behavioural therapies with pharmacological treatment. The main barrier to a greater effectiveness of this approach is represented by difficulties in reaching the target population, which limits overall coverage. A WHO-Europe (2009) review concludes that less than 10% of the population at risk for harmful alcohol consumption are routinely identified, and less than half of those diagnosed are offered advice.

*Brief interventions in primary care*

Counselling services to individuals with harmful alcohol consumption are offered across OECD countries in a number of different ways, for instance, through the medical system (e.g. hospitals, residential facilities, out-patient services) or by social services. General practitioners in particular have a key role as first point of contact both for patients requiring healthcare services and as advisors on lifestyle and prevention for non-treatment seeking patients. Brief intervention in the alcohol domain usually targets this second category of patients with the aim of reducing alcohol consumption among problematic drinkers. A large body of evidence has been developed to assess a number of different approaches or combination of approaches. A number of quantitative and qualitative studies examine the expected effectiveness of brief interventions implemented in different facilities, test the effects of interventions managed by non-physician personnel, and show the importance of the screening component as a complementary part of the intervention. Previous studies also suggest that the small coverage rates granted by this intervention (WHO-Europe, 2009) are the result of lack of time of physicians and obstacles in reimbursement arrangements (NICE, 2010).

Despite findings that support the implementation of routine alcohol screening and demonstrate its advantages, the rate of alcohol screening in health care settings remains relatively low. For example, in the United States, the CDC has calculated that only 1 in 6 people has ever talked with a doctor or other health professional about alcohol use (CDC, 2014a). In England, Wales and Northern Ireland, a third of people admitted to hospitals with known alcohol related liver disease are not referred for support to stop drinking as part of their care (NCEPOD, 2013). In Italy only 15% of people that had contacts with a doctor were asked about their alcohol consumption (CNEPS, 2014).

Several strategies have been found to be effective in promoting the use of screening procedures for other medical problems (e.g., cardiovascular diseases) in health care settings. These strategies can be classified into the following five general categories:

i) group education sessions; ii) education by respected colleagues (i.e., opinion leaders); iii) performance feedback; iv) educational outreach to individual physicians (i.e., academic detailing); v) financial incentives or penalties (Fleming, 1997).

In the United States, the CDC and other US federal agencies support and promote efforts to integrate alcohol screening and brief interventions into primary care settings, including through a guide that provides a process and resources to help primary care facilities to plan and implement screening and brief interventions (CDC, 2014b). Kaiser Permanent has developed a programme based on a user-friendly screening tool that increased uptake rates by patients, up to 90% in centres where the programme has a stronger backing by managers (vs. 65% on average).[1] The "Affordable Care Act" requires new health insurance plans to cover alcohol screening and brief interventions without co-payment.

The UK Government included alcohol screening as one of the five key areas of the Clinical Directed Enhanced Services Project in 2008. In 2012/13 GPs were paid an additional GBP 2.38 to deliver screening and brief intervention to newly registered patients aged over 16 years. Several local commissions increased this economic incentive to assure a wider coverage. A study carried out by Hamilton et al. (2013) came to the conclusion that the financial incentives resulted in a statistically significant increase in the proportion of patients screened for alcohol misuse.

### *Brief interventions in the workplace*

Places of work have the potential to offer all the characteristics needed to carry out successful prevention programmes. The majority of the adult population is employed and spends a significant amount of time at the workplace where the environment and peer-pressure from colleagues shape individuals' behaviours and lifestyles, patterns of alcohol consumption included. From the point of view of the employers, implementing prevention programmes to tackle harmful alcohol consumption may present some positive economic effects. A number of studies emphasize the negative consequences that harmful patterns of alcohol consumption have on absenteeism, "presenteeism", loss of productivity, poor co-worker relations, unemployment and healthcare costs (Anderson et al., 2012). The implementation of prevention programmes could reinforce positive changes in the lifestyle of employees and decrease employers' costs caused by the negative effects of workers' dangerous alcohol drinking behaviours (Dale and Livingstone, 2010). These interventions are further discussed in Martinic's Special Focus contribution IV after this chapter.

### *Drug and psychosocial therapies for alcohol dependence*

Alcohol dependence affects millions of individuals in the OECD area. Dependence is associated with a large burden of disease, and effective treatments are available to reduce this burden. In the European Union alone, it is calculated that between 11 million (Rehm et al., 2012) and 12 million (WHO, 2008) people, in large part males, are affected by this condition, which is deemed responsible for three-quarters of alcohol-attributable deaths and 60% of the social costs of alcohol. Pharmacological treatment is increasingly used, combined with a psychosocial programme, to reduce alcohol consumption or maintain abstinence in the treatment of people experiencing alcohol dependence. The treatment can be delivered in primary and community care, although in practice it is often offered, or at least started, by specialists and in hospital settings.

Several, broadly equivalent, drugs are available, which have been tested in many primary studies and systematic reviews (Rösner et al., 2010; Rösner et al., 2011). Most trials have concluded that the drugs can be effective in treating alcohol dependence, provided they are used in combination with behavioural (psychosocial) interventions. Such interventions have been described and tested in a number of studies (Morley et al., 2006; Baltieri and Guerra de Anchade, 2004; Lui et al., 2008; Mason et al., 2006).

## The role of business stakeholders

As governments have intensified their policy actions along the lines described in this chapter, some business stakeholders, primarily alcohol beverage manufacturers and retailers, also intensified their corporate social responsibility efforts and attempts to engage in a policy dialogue with governments. Large brewers have been especially active in these efforts. The relatively high degree of concentration of the beer sector (compared, for instance, with the wine production sector), and the relatively low alcohol content of many beers, likely place brewers in a better position than other alcohol manufacturers to invest in corporate social responsibility actions.

Many governments have been open to some degree of collaboration with alcohol manufacturers and retailers in designing programmes to reduce the harmful use of alcohol. Product reformulation has been a popular concept in the food sector to decrease the use of less healthy ingredients such as salt (Golan and Unnevehr, 2008; Mozaffarian et al., 2010) in response to demands for quality improvements in nutrition (Sassi, 2010). Increasingly, this concept is being applied to alcoholic beverages.

On the other hand, Alston et al. (2011) suggest that the alcoholic strength of wine steadily increased during the period 1992-2007 mainly due to two reasons. First, wines from non-traditionally wine-producing countries, which have higher alcohol content, are becoming more popular. In addition, the alcohol content of the average bottle increased by about 0.5% each year (i.e. from 12.7% by volume in 1992 to 13.7% in 2007). Winemakers tend to postpone the harvest to obtain more sugary grapes and, therefore, more alcohol, under pressure from consumers who have developed a taste for fuller-bodied wines and for more intense flavours. With appropriate incentives, the reverse process is also possible. In 2012, to avoid an increase in duties, many beer producers in the United Kingdom decreased the alcohol content of their brands sold in the United Kingdom by 0.2% while maintaining the previous strength in other markets (Moylan, 2012). The beer sector has a long tradition of producing and commercialising, among others, low-alcohol and alcohol-free products, but technologies for effectively lowering alcohol content in many wines are also available.

However, persuading consumers to move towards lower-strength beverages is difficult and takes time. Additionally, public health advocates have concerns that the introduction of new low-alcohol drinks instead of decreasing the strength of beverages in the market, may simply add to current consumption, and may encourage drinkers to increase the number of situations in which alcohol is consumed. For instance, there are concerns that the promotion of alcohol-free products may be used as a means to circumvent advertising restrictions on alcohol products, thus promoting brands and corporate image to audiences and in settings that would normally be out of reach for the commercial advertising of alcoholic beverages (de Bruijn et al., 2012).

### Box 4.13. **Public-Private collaboration in England and Denmark**

A prominent example of public-private collaboration is the Public Health Responsibility Deal (for England) struck by the UK Department of Health with a range of business stakeholders. The Deal covers areas, not limited to alcohol, in which commercial interests play a role in shaping people's health through their consumption of specific commodities. The underlying principle of the Responsibility Deal is that business stakeholders make pledges towards goals set by the Department of Health after consultation with stakeholders, and the Department of Health monitors the effects of those pledges in reaching the stated goals. In a recent report on the alcohol pledges and their interim effects, the Department of Health provides the following account of the initiatives undertaken by alcohol manufacturers and retailers as part of the Responsibility Deal (UK Department of Health, 2014):

- Around 125 companies have pledged to help people drink within the guidelines.
- 93 companies are committed to having 80% of bottles and cans displaying unit and health information and a pregnancy warning by the end of 2013.
- 70 pub chains and retailers pledged to display unit and health information.
- 64 companies are funding [the] Drinkaware [alcohol advice website] through financial support (over £5 million a year) and in-kind support.
- 63 companies have pledged to reduce and prevent under-age sales of alcohol, through Challenge 21 and Challenge 25 schemes.
- 92 companies pledged to comply with the latest edition of the Portman Group's Code of Practice, launched in May (2013) that sets the standard for responsible alcohol marketing.
- 57 companies have pledged to support local areas through schemes such as Best Bar None, Pubwatch, Purple Flag, Community Alcohol Partnerships and Business Improvement Districts.
- Over 30 alcohol retailers and producers have pledged to remove 1bn units of alcohol sold annually from the market by December 2015, principally through improving consumer choice of lower alcohol products.

Special emphasis is placed in the Responsibility Deal on reducing alcohol content in beverages, and on ensuring consumers choose lower-alcohol options when available, particularly "by giving consumers a wider choice of lower strength products and smaller servings" (Home Office, 2012).

In 2014 The Danish Government launched the "Healthier life for all" prevention policy framework, supported by a partnership strategy. The framework consists of seven national health targets, one of which aims at reducing the harmful use of alcohol by delaying the uptake of alcohol consumption in young people, and by cutting the number of people who engage in harmful consumption by one third. Among other initiatives, the Danish Government has allocated more than EUR 1 million to fund two partnerships for the next three years to support the implementation of the health target on alcohol. In total, 38 partnerships have received funding, in none of which the government is a partner.

The "Partnership for a responsible alcohol culture" involves business partners, such as beverage trade organizations, the hotel, restaurant and catering sector, the Danish Chamber of Commerce and the Danish Merchants Association. The goals of the partnership are to establish a forum for nationwide coordinated action on alcohol, and create positive incentives for a "responsible alcohol culture" that motivates people to change their behaviour. The partnership focuses on compliance with age limits on the sale of alcohol and on initiatives to change the alcohol culture in bars. On the other hand, the "Partnership for youth and alcohol" involves municipalities and civil society organizations, with the aim to postpone youth alcohol consumption and reduce underage drinking by initiating local activities for young people in collaboration with local authorities and civil society. No assessment has so far been made of the potential or actual impacts of these partnerships.

A number of organisations of the hospitality and retail industries have also developed programmes to raise awareness among their members on how to prevent people from alcohol intoxication and how to deal with people who are intoxicated. Such courses usually include interventions to raise awareness about legal restrictions to the sale of alcohol to minors. The Finnish grocery trade association, which include virtually all grocery sales in Finland, put in place a programme named "age-limit passport" to train all cashiers to verify the age of all customers who appear younger than 30 purchasing alcohol or tobacco products. Cashiers have to follow an on-line course and pass a test.

In some countries interventions also tried to target drink-driving. In Italy, for example, a trade organisation of the nightlife sector joined forces with an organisation of car insurers and with the national police to launch the "drive with caution" strategy. At the entrance of night clubs, groups of friends are encouraged to designate a driver for the night, who should refrain from drinking. The initiative is promoted throughout the evening, for instance, by DJs, and breath analysers are made available free of charge at the exit of the club. The police monitor the implementation of these measures and designated drivers are rewarded for compliance with free entrance tickets for clubs participating in the programme.

### Note

1. http://share.Kaiserpermanente.org/article/heading-off-and-helping-with-unhealthy-alcohol-use/.

### Bibliography


Albalate, D. (2008), "Lowering Blood Alcohol Content Levels to Save Lives: The European Experience", *Journal of Policy Analysis and Management*, Vol. 27, No. 1, pp. 20-39.

Ally, A.K. et al. (2014), "Alcohol Tax Pass-through Across the Product and Price Range: Do Retailers Treat Cheap alcohol Differently?, *Addiction*, http://dx.doi.org/0.1111/add.12590.

Alston, J.M. et al. (2011), "Splendide Mendax: False Label Claims about High and Rising Alcohol Content of Wine", *American Association of Wine Economists Working Paper*, No. 82.

An, R. and R. Sturm (2011), "Does the Response to Alcohol Taxes Differ Across Racial/ethnic Groups? Some Evidence from 1984-2009 Behavioral Risk Factor Surveillance System", *Journal of Mental Health Policy and Economics*, Vol. 14, No. 1, pp. 13-23, March.

Anderson, P., D. Chisholm and D.C. Fuhr (2009a), "Effectiveness and Cost-effectiveness of Policies and Programmes to Reduce the Harm Caused by Alcohol", *The Lancet*, Vol. 373, No. 9682, pp. 2234-2246.

Anderson, P. et al. (2009b), "Impact of Alcohol Advertising and Media Exposure on Adolescent Alcohol Use: A Systematic Review of Longitudinal Studies", *Alcohol and Alcoholism*, Vol. 44, No. 3, pp. 229-243.

Anderson, P., L. Møller and G. Galea (2012), *Alcohol in the European Union Consumption. Harm and Policy Approaches*, WHO Regional Office for Europe, Copenhagen.

Anderson, P., M. Suhrcke and C. Brookes (2012), *An Overview of the Market for Alcohol Beverages of Potentially Particular Appeal to Minors*, HAPI, London.

Australian National Preventive Health Agency (2012), "Exploring the Public Interest Case for a Minimum (floor) for Alcohol", Canberra.

Babor, T.F. et al. (2010), "Alcohol: No Ordinary Commodity", Research and Public Policy, Oxford University Press.

Baldwin, J., J. Stogner and B. Miller (2014), "It's Five O'clock Somewhere: An Examination of the Association Between Happy Hour Drinking and Negative Consequences", *Substance Abuse Treatment, Prevention, and Policy*, Vol. 9, No. 17, pp. 1-12, www.biomedcentral.com/content/pdf/1747-597X-9-17.pdf (retrieved November 1, 2014).

Baltieri, D.A. and A. Guerra De Andrade (2004), "Acamprosate in Alcohol Dependence: A Randomized Controlled Efficacy Study in a Standard Clinical Setting", *Journal of Studies on Alcohol*, Vol. 65, pp. 136-139.

Barry, A.E. and P. Goodson (2010), "Use (and Misuse) of the Responsible Drinking Message in Public Health and Alcohol Advertising: A Review", *Health Education & Behavior*, Vol. 37, No. 2, pp. 288-303.

Brennan, A. et al. (2008), "Independent Review of the Effects of Alcohol Pricing and Promotion. Part B: Modelling the Potential Impact of Pricing and Promotion Policies for Alcohol in England", School of Health and Related Research, Sheffield.

Bryden, A. et al. (2012), "A Systematic Review of the Influence on Alcohol Use of Community Level Availability and Marketing of Alcohol", *Health & Place*, Vol. 18, pp. 349–357.

Byrnes, J. et al. (2012), "The Efficiency of a Volumetric Alcohol Tax in Australia", *Applied Health Economics and Health Policy*, Vol. 10, No. 1, pp. 37-49.

Carpenter, C. and C. Dobkin (2011), "The Minimum Legal Drinking Age and Public Health", *Journal of Economic Perspectives*, Vol. 25, No. 2, pp. 133-156.

CCSA – Canadian Center on Substance Abuse (2012), *Alcohol Price Policy Series: Reducing Harm to Canadians*, Ottawa, www.ccsa.ca/Resource%20Library/CCSA-Alcohol-Price-Policy-Brief-Canada-2012-en.pdf.

Christie, J. et al. (2001), "The Effects of Bar-Sponsored Alcohol Beverage Promotions across Binge and Nonbingers", *Journal of Public Policy & Marketing*, Vol. 20, No. 2, pp. 240-253.

CNEPS – Centro Nazionale di Epidemiologia, Sorveglianza e Promozione della Salute (2014), "La sorveglianza Passi – consumo di alcohol", available at www.epicentro.iss.it/passi/dati/alcol.asp.

Corrao, G. et al. (2004), "A Meta-analysis of Alcohol Consumption and the Risk of 15 Diseases", *Preventive Medicine*, Vol. 38, No. 5, pp. 613-619.

Connor, J.L. et al. (2011), "Alcohol Outlet Density, Levels of Drinking and Alcohol-related Harm in New Zealand: A National Study", *Journal of Epidemiology and Community Health*, Vol. 65, pp. 841-846.

Dale, C.E. and M.J. Livingston (2010), "The Burden of Alcohol Drinking on Co-workers in the Australian Workplace", *Medical Journal of Australia*, Vol. 193, No. 3, pp. 138-140.

de Bruijn, A., E. van den Wildenberg and A. van den Broeck (2011), "Commercial Promotion of Drinking in Europe: Key Findings of Independent Monitoring of Alcohol Marketing in Five European Countries", Dutch Institute for Alcohol Policy (STAP), 2012, available at http://amphoraproject.net/w2box/data/AMPHORA%20Reports/Ammie_repport_2012.pdf?PHPSESSID=35ci20qg5dv9k73h8ugq6dho71.

Dee, T.S. (2001), "Does Setting Limits Save Lives? The Case of 0.08 BAC Laws", *Journal of Policy Analysis and Management*, Vol. 20, No. 1, pp. 111-128.

Di Castelnuovo, A. et al. (2006), "Alcohol Dosing and Total Mortality in Men and Women: An Updated Meta-analysis of 34 Prospective Studies", *Archives of Internal Medicine*, Vol. 166, No. 22, pp. 2437-2445.

Ditter, S.M. et al. (2005), "Effectiveness of Designed Driver Programs for Reducing Alcohol-impaired Driving: A Systematic Review", *American journal of Preventive Medicine*, Vol. 28, No. 5, pp. 280-287.

Douglas, M. (1998), "Restriction of the Hours of Sale of Alcohol in a Small Community: A Beneficial Impact", *Australian and New Zealand Journal of Public Health*, Vol. 22, pp. 714-719.

Eisenberg, D. (2003), "Evaluating the Effectiveness of Policies Related to Drunk Driving", *Journal of Policy Analysis and Management*, Vol. 22, No. 2, pp. 249-274.

Elder, R.W. et al. (2010), "Task Force on Community Preventive Services. The Effectiveness of Tax Policy Interventions for Reducing Excessive Alcohol Consumption and Related Harms", *American Journal of Preventive Medicine*, Vol. 38, No. 2, pp. 217-229, February.

Elder, R.W. et al. (2004), "Task Force on Community Preventive Services. Effectiveness of Mass Media Campaigns for Reducing Drinking and Driving and Alcohol-Involved Crashes", *American Journal of Preventive Medicine*, Vol. 27, No. 1, pp. 57-65.

Federal Trade Commission (2014), "Self-Regulation in the Alcohol Industry", Report of the Federal Trade Commission, March 2014, available at www.ftc.gov/reports/self-regulation-alcohol-industry-report-federal-trade-commission-0.

Fell, J.C. et al. (2003), "Why Are Sobriety Checkpoints Not Widely Adopted as an Enforcement Strategy in the United States?", *Accident Analysis & Prevention*, Vol. 35, pp. 897-902.

Fleming, M.F. (1997), "Strategies to Increase Alcohol Screening in Health Care Settings", *Alcohol Health & Research World*, Vol. 21, pp. 340-347.

Fogarty, J. (2008), "The Demand for Beer, Wine and Spirits: Insights from a Meta-analysis Approach", *AAWE Working Paper* No. 31, American Association of Wine Economists.

Fogarty, J. (2006), "The Nature of the Demand for Alcohol: Understanding Elasticity", *British Food Journal*, Vol. 108, No. 4, pp. 316-332.

Foxcroft, D. et al. (2011), "WITHDRAWN: Primary Prevention for Alcohol Misuse in Young People", *Cochrane Database of Systematic Reviews*, Vol. 9, CD003024.

Foxcroft, D.R. et al. (2003), "Longer-term Primary Prevention for Alcohol Misuse in Young People: A Systematic Review", *Addiction*, Vol. 98, No. 4, pp. 397-411

Gallet, C.A. (2007), "The Demand for Alcohol: A Meta-analysis of Elasticities", *Australian Journal of Agricultural and Resource Economics*, Vol. 7, No. 51, pp. 121-135.

Golan, E. and L. Unnevehr (2008), "Food Product Composition, Consumer Health, and Public Policy: Introduction and Overview of Special Section", *Food Policy*, Vol. 33, No. 6, pp. 465-469.

Government of North West Territories (2009), "Press Release – March 31st, 2009 Tobacco Taxes, Liquor Markups to Increase", 31 March 2009.

Gray, D. et al. (1999), "Beating the Grog: An Evaluation of the Tennant Creek Liquor Licensing Restrictions", *Australian and New Zealand Journal of Public Health*, Vol. 24, pp. 39-44.

Grieshaber-Otto, J., S. Sinclair and N. Schacter (2000), "Impacts of International Trade, Services and Investment Treaties on Alcohol Regulation", *Addiction*, Vol. 95, pp. 491-504.

Gruenewald, P.J. (2007), "The Spatial Ecology of Alcohol Problems: Niche Theory and Assortative Drinking", *Addiction*, Vol. 102, pp. 870-878.

Hahn, R.A. et al. (2010), "Effectiveness of Policies Restricting Hours of Alcohol Sales in Preventing Excessive Alcohol Consumption and Related Harms", *American Journal of Preventive Medicine*, Vol. 39, No. 6, pp. 590-604.

Hamilton, F.L. et al. (2013), "Effect of Financial Incentives on Delivery of Alcohol Screening and Brief Intervention (ASBI) in Primary Care: Longitudinal Study", *Journal of Public Health*, Oxford.

HM Revenue & Customs (2013), "Measuring Tax Gaps 2013 – Tax Gap Estimates for 2011-12", Official statistics release, 11 October 2013, available at www.gov.uk/government/uploads/system/uploads/attachment_data/file/249537/131010_Measuring_Tax_Gaps_ACCESS_2013.pdf.

Holder, H. (ed.) (2008), "Alcohol Monopoly and Public Health: Potential Effects of Privatization of the Swedish Alcohol Retail Monopoly", Swedish National Institute of Public Health, Stockholm.

Home Office (2012), "The Government's Alcohol Strategy", Stationery Office, London.

Hunt, P., L. Rabinovich and B. Baumberg (2011), "Preliminary Assessment of Economic Impacts of Alcohol Pricing Policy Options in the UK", RAND Europe, www.rand.org/content/dam/rand/pubs/technical_reports/2011/RAND_TR858-1.pdf.

Jernigan, D.H. et al. (2013), *CDC MMWR Report*, Vol. 62, No. 44, pp 877-880.

Jones, S.C., D. Hall and G. Munro (2008), "How Effective Is the Revised Regulatory Code for Alcohol Advertising in Australia?", *Drug and Alcohol Review*, Vol. 27, pp. 29-38.

Jónsson R.M. and S. Kristjánsson (2013), "Alcohol Policy and Public Opinion in Iceland, 1989–2012", *Nordic Studies on Alcohol and Drugs*, Vol. 30, No. 6, pp. 539-549.

Kansas Statutes (2010), "Chapter 41: Intoxicating Liquors and Beverages", http://kansasstatutes.lesterama.org/Chapter_41/ (retrieved November 12, 2014).

Keen, M. (1998), "The Balance Between Specific and Ad Valorem Taxation", *Fiscal Studies*, Vol. 19, No. 1, pp. 1-37.

Killoran, A. et al. (2010), "Review of Effectiveness of Laws Limiting Blood Alcohol Concentration Levels to Reduce Alcohol-related Road Injuries and Deaths", National Institute for Health and Clinical Excellence (NICE).

KPMG LLP (2008), "Review of the Social Responsibility Standards for the Production and Sale of Alcoholic Drinks", KPMG, London.

Kuo, M. et al. (2003), "Does Price Matter? The Effect of Decreased Price on Spirits Consumption in Switzerland", *Alcoholism Clinical and Experimental Research*, Vol. 27, No. 4, pp. 720-725, April.

Laming, M.F. (1997), "Strategies to Increase Alcohol Screening in Health Care Settings", *Alcohol Health & Research World*, Vol. 21, No. 4. pp. 340-347.

Lerner, B.H. (2012), "The Art of Medicine – Drunk Driving Across the Globe: Let's Learn from One Another", *The Lancet*, Vol. 379, No. 9829, pp. 1870-1871.

Livingston, M., T. Chikritzhs and R. Room (2007), "Changing the Density of Alcohol Outlets to Reduce Alcohol-related Problems", *Drug and Alcohol Review*, Vol. 26, pp. 553-562.

Ludbrook, A. et al. (2012), "Tackling Alcohol Misuse, Purchasing Patterns Affected by Minimum Pricing for Alcohol", *Applied Health Economics and Health Policy*, Vol. 10, No. 1, pp. 51-63.

Lui, S., M. Terplan and E.J. Smith (2008), "Psychosocial Interventions for Women Enrolled in Alcohol Treatment During Pregnancy", *Cochrane Database of Systematic Reviews*, Vol. 3, Art. No. CD006753.

Mann, R.E. et al. (2001), "The Effects of Introducing or Lowering Legal Per Se Blood Alcohol Limits for Driving: An International Review", *Accident Analysis and Prevention*, Vol. 33, pp. 569-583.

Manning, W.G., L. Blumberg and L.H. Moulton (1995), "The Demand for Alcohol: The Differential Response to Price", *Journal of Health Economics*, Vol. 14, No. 2, pp. 123-148, June.

Mason, B.J. et al. (2006), "Effect of Oral Acamprosate on Abstinence in Patients with Alcohol Dependence in a Double-blind, Placebo-controlled Trial: The Role of Patient Motivation", *Journal of Psychiatric Research*, Vol. 40, pp. 383-393.

Mayor S. (2010), "Ministers May Legislate After Finding 85% of Labels on Alcohol to Be Inadequate", *British Medical Journal*, Vol. 340, p. c966.

Meng, Y. et al. (2013), "Modelled Income Group-specific Impacts of Alcohol Minimum Unit Pricing in England 2014/15: Policy Appraisals Using New Developments to the Sheffield Alcohol Policy Model (v2.5)", Addendum examining the impact of a ban on "below cost selling", ScHARR, University of Sheffield.

Ministry of Welfare, Iceland (2014), "Policy on Alcohol and Drug Prevention, 2020", available at http://eng.velferdarraduneyti.is/newsinenglish/nr/34482, accessed on: 07/04/2014.

Miron, J.A. and E. Tetelbaum (2009), "Does the Minimum Legal Drinking Age Save Lives?", *Economic Inquiry*, Vol. 47, No. 2, pp. 317-336.

Morley, K.C. et al. (2006), "Naltrexone Versus Acamprosate in the Treatment of Alcohol Dependence: A Multi-centre, Randomized, Double-blind, Placebo-controlled Trial", *Addiction*, Vol. 101, pp. 451-1462.

Moylan. J. (2012), "Will Weaker Beers Help the Brewing Industry?", BBC website, London, available at http://www.bbc.co.uk/news/business-17399368 (accessed on 12 November 2014).

Mozaffarian, D., M.F. Jacobson and J.S. Greenstein (2010), "Food Reformulations to Reduce Trans Fatty Acids", *New England Journal of Medicine*, Vol. 362, No. 21, pp. 2037-2039, May 27.

Nagata, T. et al. (2008), "Effectiveness of a Law to Reduce Alcohol-impaired Driving in Japan", *Injury Prevention*, Vol. 14, pp. 19-23.

Nakahara, S. and M. Ichikawa (2010), "Effects of High-profile Collisions on Drink-driving Penalties and Alcohol-related Crashes in Japan", *Injury Prevention*, Vol. 17, No. 3, pp. 182-188.

NCEPOD – National Confidential Enquiry into Patient Outcome and Death (2013), "Measuring the Units: A Review of Patients Who Died with Alcohol-related Liver Disease", NCEPOD, London.

Nelson, J.P. (2003), "Advertising Bans, Monopoly, and Alcohol Demand: Testing for Substitution Effects Using Panel Data", *Review of Industrial Organization*, Vol. 22, pp. 1-25.

NICE – National Institute for Health and Clinical Excellence (2010), "Alcohol-use Disorders: Preventing the Development of Hazardous and Harmful Drinking", NICE Public Health Guidance 24, National Institute for Health and Clinical Excellence, London.

Norstrom, T. and O.J. Skog (2005), "Saturday Opening and Alcohol Retail Shops in Sweden: An Experiment in Two Phases", *Addiction*, Vol. 100, pp. 767-777.

Novoa, A.M., K. Perez and C. Borrell (2009), "Efectividad de las intervenciones de seguridad vial basadas en la evidencia: una revisio´n de la literatura", *Gac Sanit*, Vol. 23, No. 6, pp. 553.e1-553.e14.

OECD (2014), *Consumption Tax Trends 2014: VAT/GST and Excise Rates, Trends and Policy Issues*, OECD Publishing, Paris, http://dx.doi.org/ 10.1787/ctt-2014-en.

Peden, M. (2004), "Global Collaboration on Road Traffic Injury Prevention", *International Journal of Injury Control and Safety Promotion*, Vol. 12, No. 2, pp. 85-91.

Phillips, R.O., P. Ulleberg and T. Vaa (2011), "Meta-analysis of the Effect of Road Safety Campaigns on Accidents", *Accident Analysis & Prevention*, Vol. 43, No. 3, pp. 1204-1218.

Pollack, C.E., C. Cubbin and D. Ahn (2005), "Neighbourhood Deprivation and Alcohol Consumption: Does the Availability of Alcohol Play a Role?", *International Journal of Epidemiology*, Vol. 34, pp. 772-780.

Popova, S. et al. (2009), "Hours and Days of Sale and Density of Alcohol Outlets: Impacts on Alcohol Consumption and Damage: A Systematic Review", *Alcohol and Alcoholism*, Vol. 44, No. 5, pp. 500-516.

Purshouse, R.C. et al. (2010), "Estimated Effect of Alcohol Pricing Policies on Health and Health Economic Outcomes in England: An Epidemiological Model", *The Lancet*, Vol. 375, pp. 1355-1364.

Rabinovich, L. et al. (2012), "Further Study on the Affordability of Alcoholic Beverages in the EU", RAND Europe.

Rabinovich, L. et al. (2009), "The Affordability of Alcoholic Beverages in the European Union – Understanding the Link Between Alcohol Affordability, Consumption and Harms", Santa Monica, RAND Corporation, United States.

Rehm, J. et al. (2012), "Alcohol Consumption, Alcohol Dependence and Attributable Burden of Disease in Europe: Potential Gains from Effective Interventions for Alcohol Dependence", Centre for Addiction and Mental Health.

Rice, P. (2012), "Health Benefits Matter, Not Tax Revenue", *British Medical Journals*, Vol. 344, p. e1781.

Rose, G. (1992). *The Strategy of Preventative Medicine*, Oxford University Press, New York.

Rösner, S. et al. (2011), "Acamprosate for Alcohol Dependence", *Cochrane Database of Systematic Reviews*, Vol. 9, Art. No. CD004332.

Rösner, S. et al. (2010), "Opioid Antagonists for Alcohol Dependence", *Cochrane Database of Systematic Reviews*, Vol. 12, Art. No. CD001867.

Russell, K.F., B. Vandermeer and L. Hartling (2011), "Graduated Driver Licensing for Reducing Motor Vehicle Crashes Among Young Drivers", *Cochrane Database of Systematic Reviews*, No. 10, Art. No.: CD003300

Sassi, F. (2010), *Obesity and the Economics of Prevention: Fit not Fat*, OECD Publishing, Paris, http://dx.doi.org/10.1787/9789264084865-en.

Sassi, F., A. Belloni and C. Capobianco (2013), "The Role of Fiscal Policies in Health Promotion". *OECD Health Working Paper No. 66*, OECD Publishing, Paris, http://dx.doi.org/10.1787/5k3twr94kvzx-en.

Scottish Government (2012), "Final Business and Regulatory Impact Assessment for Minimum Price per Unit of Alcohol as Contained in Alcohol Minimum Pricing Bill. 2012".

Scribner, R.A., D.A. Cohen and W. Fisher (2000), "Evidence of a Structural Effect for Alcohol Outlet Density: A Multilevel Analysis", *Alcoholism Clinical and Experimental Research*, Vol. 24, pp. 188–195.

Shults, R.A. et al. and the Task Force on Community Preventive Services (2001), "Reviews of Evidence Regarding Interventions to Reduce Alcohol-Impaired Driving", *American Journal of Preventive Medicine*, Vol. 21(4S), pp. 66-88.

Smith, A. (1776), *An Inquiry into the Nature and Causes of the Wealth of Nations*, W. Strahan and T. Cadell, London.

Smith, S.W., C.K. Atkin and J. Roznowski (2006), "Are 'Drink Responsibly' Alcohol Campaigns Strategically Ambiguous?", *Health Communication*, Vol. 20, No. 1, pp. 1-11.

Snyder, L.B. et al. (2006), "Effects of Alcohol Advertising Exposure on Drinking Among Youth", *Archives of Pediatrics & Adolescent Medicine*, Vol. 160, No. 1, pp. 18-24, January.

Stockwell, T. and T. Chikritzhs (2009), "Do Relaxed Trading Hours for Bars and Clubs Mean More Relaxed Drinking? A Review of International Research on the Impacts of Changes to Permitted Hours of Drinking", *Crime Prevention and Community Safety*, Vol. 11, pp. 171-188.

Stockwell, T. et al. (2013), "Minimum Alcohol Prices and Outlet Densities in British Columbia, Canada: Estimated Impacts on Alcohol-attributable Hospital Admissions", *American Journal of Public Health*, Vol. 103, pp. 2014-2020.

Stockwell, T. et al. (2012a), "Does Minimum Pricing Reduce Alcohol Consumption? The Experience of a Canadian Province", *Addiction*, Vol. 107, No. 5, pp. 912-920, May.

Stockwell, T. et al. (2012b), "The Raising of Minimum Alcohol Prices in Saskatchewan, Canada: Impacts on Consumption and Implications for Public Health", *American Journal of Public Health*, Vol. 102, No. 12, pp. 103-110.

Thombs, D.L. et al. (2009), "A Field Study of Bar-sponsored Drink Specials and their Associations with Patron Intoxication", *Journal of Studies on Alcohol and Drugs*, Vol. 70, No. 2, pp. 206-214.

Thombs, D.L. et al. (2008), "Drink Specials and the Intoxication Levels of Patrons Exiting College Bars", *American Journal of Health Behavior*, Vol. 32, No. 4, pp. 411-419.

U.K Department of Health, Public Health Directorate, Health and Wellbeing Division, Alcohol and Drugs Branch (2014), "Responsibility Deal Alcohol Network – Pledge to Remove 1 Billion Units of Alcohol from the Market by End 2015", First interim monitoring report, https://www.gov.uk/government/uploads/system/uploads/attachment_data/file/306529/RDAN_-_Unit_Reduction_Pledge_-_1st_interim_monitoring_report.pdf.

Wagenaar, A.C. and M. Maldonado-Molina (2007), "Effects of Drivers' License Suspension Policies on Alcohol-related Crash Involvement: Long-term Follow-up in Forty-six States", *Alcoholism Clinical and Experimental Research*, Vol. 31, pp. 1399-1406.

Wagenaar, A.C., M.J. Salois and K.A. Komro (2009), "Effects of Beverage Alcohol Price and Tax Levels on Drinking: A Meta-analysis of 1003 Estimates from 112 Studies", *Addiction*, Vol. 104, No. 2, pp. 179-190, February.

WHO – World Health Organization (2014), *Global Status Report on Alcohol and Health 2014*, WHO, Geneva.

WHO (2011), *Global Status Report on Alcohol and Health 2011*, WHO, Geneva.

WHO (2010), *Global Alcohol Strategy to Reduce the Harmful Use of Alcohol*, WHO, Geneva.

WHO (2008), *The Global Burden of Disease: 2004 Update*, WHO, Geneva.

WHO (2007), "WHO Expert Committee on Problems Related to Alcohol Consumption (second report)", *WHO Technical Report Series No. 944*, WHO, Geneva.

WHO (1979), "Resolution WHA32.40. Development of the WHO Programme on Alcohol-related Problems", Thirty-ninth World Health Assembly, Geneva, 25 May 1979.

WHO Regional Office for Europe (2009), "Evidence for the Effectiveness and Cost-effectiveness of Interventions to Reduce Alcohol-related Arm", WHO Regional Office for Europe, Copenhagen.

Wilkinson, C. and R. Room (2009), "Warnings on Alcohol Containers and Advertisements: International Experience and Evidence on Effects", *Drug and Alcohol Review*, Vol. 28, No. 4, pp. 426-435.

WTO – World Trade Organization (2012), "WTO 2012 News – Technical Barriers to Trade Formal Meeting. Public Health Regulations Remain High on Members' Agendas", available at http://www.wto.org/english/news_e/news12_e/tbt_20mar12_e.htm, accessed on 14 August 2012.

Xu, X. and F.J. Chaloupka (2011), "The Effects of Prices of Alcohol Use and its Consequences", *Alcohol Research & Health*, Vol. 34, No. 2, pp. 236-245.

Young, D.J. and A. Bielinska-Kwapisz (2002), "Alcohol Taxes and Beverage Prices", *National Tax Journal*, Vol. 55, No. 1, pp. 57-73.

Tackling Harmful Alcohol Use
Economics and Public Health Policy


*Special focus II*

# Alcohol advertising and heavy drinking

by
Henry Saffer,
National Bureau of Economic Research, New York

## Introduction

The alcohol industry spends billions of dollars each year trying to create positive brand images, increase brand name recognition and ultimately increase profits. Advertising Age's list of the top 100 global advertisers in 2012 includes five alcohol companies: Anheuser-Busch InBev, Diageo, Heineken, Pernod Ricard and SABMiller (Advertising Age, 2012). Advertising data show that companies spent about USD 1.1 billion in 2011 on alcohol advertising on TV in the United States alone (WSJ, 2012). Televised alcohol advertising in eight European countries in 2007 accounted for about EUR 750 million (de Bruijn, 2013). Expenditures on other media and other forms of marketing are estimated to be even larger (Anderson et al., 2009; de Bruijn, 2013).

Does all this spending increase total alcohol consumption? In addition, because the adverse consequences of alcohol consumption are associated with heavy drinking rather than moderate or light drinking, what would be the impact on heavy drinking if advertising were reduced?

In the following, I will look briefly at how alcohol is advertised, and then review evidence from psychology, neuroscience and econometrics research suggesting that heavy drinkers are more responsive to alcohol advertising than moderate drinkers, whereas alcohol taxes elicit a greater response from moderate drinkers. I will conclude that limits on alcohol advertising are an underutilised policy for reducing the damage from heavy drinking

## Alcohol advertising

The media employed in alcohol advertising include TV, magazines, point-of-purchase signs and outdoor billboards. The Internet is also important. Alcohol companies offer information on products, events, featured artists, recipes and rebates through Facebook pages and other social media and on their own websites and apps. Alcohol company websites and apps also allow individuals to post their own content relevant to product use, and alcohol companies employ direct marketing by email and other media. Product placement, which is the paid use of a branded product by characters in a film or a TV programme, is another important form of alcohol advertising. Branded merchandise available to retailers and consumers can also be considered advertising and are employed to increase visibility of the brand name and to reinforce the brand image.

Whether the substantial expenditure on alcohol advertising increases total alcohol consumption or simply affects market shares remains controversial. Nelson (2011) questioned the statistical validity of past studies of alcohol advertising and concluded that a causal interpretation between advertising and alcohol consumption may not be justified.[1] However, a growing number of studies conclude that alcohol ads increase alcohol consumption. Gallet (2007) reviewed 132 econometric studies of alcohol demand that included an advertising measure. Economists measure the effect of advertising with a concept known as the advertising elasticity. The advertising elasticity is the percentage change in consumption which results from a percentage change in advertising. Larger values for advertising elasticities represent a greater effect of advertising on consumption. Gallet concluded that alcohol advertising does increase total alcohol consumption and reports a mean value for the advertising elasticity of 0.03.[2]

The public health concern with alcohol is directed at heavy drinkers who are primarily responsible for the social costs of alcohol, but the studies reviewed by Gallet do not distinguish the effects of advertising on heavy drinkers from the effects of advertising on moderate drinkers. Since most drinkers are in the moderate category, the failure to distinguish individuals by consumption level may mask the effects of advertising on heavy drinkers. Although no studies in the older econometric literature address this issue, the psychology and neuroscience literature provide some guidance.

## Psychology and neuroscience research

A cognitive psychology paper by Townshend and Duka (2001) examines whether heavy drinkers differ in their selective attention to alcohol-related stimuli in comparison to a group of moderate drinkers. They assessed selective attention to alcohol-related pictures and words in an experimental setting. Their results showed that heavy drinkers had a greater awareness of alcohol related stimuli than moderate drinkers. The study also suggested that heavy drinkers have greater positive expectations about alcohol and may be less able to self-regulate than moderate drinkers.

Two neuroscience papers, one by George et al. (2001) and the other by Myrick et al. (2004) test whether there are differences in brain activity during alcohol cue exposure between heavy drinkers and moderate drinkers. After a sip of alcohol, only the heavy drinkers had increased activity in regions of the brain associated with addictive substances while viewing alcohol cues compared with viewing other beverage cues. Heavy drinkers also reported higher overall cravings for alcohol than moderate drinkers. These studies suggest that heavy drinkers have a greater response to alcohol cues than moderate drinkers do.

Another neuroscience paper, by Tapert et al. (2003), reports on the extent to which teens with alcohol use disorder and non-abusing teens are reactive to alcohol cues, in this case alcohol adverts. They tested matched samples of adolescents aged 14 to 17. One sample had alcohol use disorders and the other sample consisted of infrequent drinkers. Subjects were shown pictures of alcoholic and nonalcoholic beverage advertisements during functional magnetic resonance imaging. Self-reports of craving were obtained before and after exposure to the pictures. Teens with alcohol use disorders showed substantially greater brain activation to alcoholic beverage pictures than the other group of youths, predominantly in brain regions associated with addictive substances. The degree of brain response to the alcohol pictures was highest in youths who consumed more drinks per month and reported greater desires to drink.

A neuroeconomics paper by Bernheim and Rangel (2004) presents a theory of how cues can affect addictive consumption, based on two key points.

First, the theory argues that the role of cues on addictive consumption is a consequence of the anticipated hedonic effect from the substance, rather than the hedonic effect itself. This is sometimes referred to as Pavlovian conditioning. The hedonic effect is the pleasure derived from consumption. The anticipated hedonic effect is a prediction of how much pleasure will be derived from consumption and is separate from the actual hedonic effect. The hedonic anticipation occurs in a part of the brain that is distinct from the area where the hedonic effect itself occurs. Bernheim and Rangel (2004) report on a series of neuroscience experiments on cues and the level of hedonic anticipation. In these experiments, when subjects are presented with a cue followed by a reward, there is a corresponding level of neural activity. However, as experience with the reward continues, this neural activity occurs in response to the cue rather than the reward.

Second, the theory argues that the forecast of a hedonic effect produced by cues increases as past consumption increases. In the experimental studies, when the reward is increased, but the cue remains constant, the neural activity increases in proportion to the new level of reward. That is, the anticipated hedonic effect is proportional to past levels of consumption rather than proportional to the level of the cue.

### *Econometric research*

Based on the neuroscience and psychology literature, it appears that heavy drinkers subconsciously take more notice of alcohol cues than moderate drinkers and abstainers. Alcohol advertising provides a considerable level of these alcohol cues. However, it is also important to study the effect of actual alcohol ads on alcohol consumption in a non-experimental setting before reaching any policy conclusions. One non-experimental approach is an econometric study. An econometric study analyses a data set that includes alcohol consumption and includes observations on individuals over different time periods and locations. This type of data provides variations in advertising exposure and alcohol prices that occur naturally over different time periods and different geographical units. Advantages of the econometric approach include observations on behaviour outside of a controlled lab environment, considerably larger samples than are used in experimental studies and quantitative estimates of effect sizes. A disadvantage of the econometric approach is that the data employed may include a greater level of measurement error than is found in experimental studies.

Saffer, Dave and Grossman (2012) carried out an econometric study measuring the differential effect of alcohol advertising by consumption level. They employed data for three years from the National Longitudinal Survey of Youth 1997 (NLSY97). The NLSY97 is a data set with repeated annual observations on about 8 000 individuals. The NLSY97 provides information to link individual alcohol use to advertising and prices in geographic locations and specific time periods.

They also developed a behavioural economic model of the response to alcohol advertising and prices based on the neuroscience and psychology literature. The model assumes an analytically convenient fiction of three distinct brain systems that act simultaneously to produce a single decision.

- The *heuristic system* is a subconscious system that can produce rapid decisions with generally beneficial near-term outcomes. It cannot ignore irrelevant past experiences nor adjust forecasts prior to acquiring further experience.
- The *rational system* develops causal models of the world and reasons out the implications of different choices. The Rational system needs time and cognitive resources to reason and make a choice.
- The *governor system* is also energy intensive and can moderate consumption desired by the Heuristic and Rational systems in favor of future goals. This process is called self-regulation.

This behavioural economic model predicts that the effect of advertising on consumption is positive and that this effect increases with the level of past consumption. This implies that heavy drinkers are more responsive to alcohol advertising than are moderate drinkers. The model also predicts that the effect of price on consumption is negative and that as self-regulation decreases, the negative effect of price decreases. Because lower levels of self-regulation are associated with higher levels of consumption, heavy drinkers are less likely to cut consumption due to a price increase than are moderate drinkers.

Saffer, Dave and Grossman (2012) find that advertising elasticities increase as past and current consumption increases. They limit the data to drinkers and estimate an advertising elasticity of about 0.03 for moderate drinkers and about 0.08 for heavy drinkers. The elasticity for moderate drinkers is the same as Gallet's (2007) estimate which included all drinkers and non-drinkers. The results of Saffer, Dave and Grossman (2012) indicate that the alcohol advertising elasticity increases with the level of alcohol consumption as is predicted by the behavioural economic model and suggested by the neuroscience and psychology literature.

They also estimated price elasticities (how consumption reacts to price increases or decreases) that fall within the range of price elasticities for alcohol that are found in prior studies (Wagenaar et al., 2009) and find that price elasticities decline with increased alcohol consumption as was predicted by the behavioural economic model. This decline has also been reported in studies by Manning et al. (1995), Wagenaar et al. (2009) and Ayyagari et al. (2013).

## Conclusions

The combined evidence suggests that alcohol advertising increases total alcohol consumption and that this effect is greater for heavy drinkers. The magnitude of the advertising elasticities estimated by Saffer, Dave and Grossman (2012) can be put into perspective by comparison to alcohol tax elasticities. Tax elasticities are a relevant comparison because taxes are the policy lever by which government can change alcohol prices. An and Sturm (2011) find tax elasticities for light drinkers of about -0.25 and for heavy drinkers of about -0.07, that is, heavy drinkers' consumption is affected less by changes in tax than that of moderate drinkers. Table SF1 presents the predicted changes in alcohol consumption which would result from a 50% decrease in alcohol advertising and a 50% increase in alcohol taxes. The predictions are for both moderate drinkers and for heavy drinkers. These predictions are based on the advertising elasticities reported by Saffer, Dave and Grossman (2012) and the tax elasticities reported by An and Sturm (2011). As shown in the Table SF1 a 50% decrease in advertising would decrease consumption by moderate drinkers by about 1.5% and heavy drinkers by about 4%. A 50% increase in taxes would result in about a 12.5% decrease in consumption by moderate drinkers and about a 3.5% decrease in consumption by heavy drinkers. The data in Table SF1 indicate that both higher taxes and limits on alcohol advertising would reduce heavy drinking. However, higher taxes also heavily impact moderate drinkers while limits on advertising have little effect on moderate drinkers. This suggests that limits on alcohol advertising are an underutilised policy to reduce the damage from heavy drinking.

Table SFII.1. **Predicted reductions in alcohol consumption due to less alcohol advertising and higher alcohol taxes**

| | Light/Moderate drinkers | Heavy drinkers |
|---|---|---|
| 50% decrease in alcohol advertising | -1.5% | -4% |
| 50% increase in alcohol taxes | -12.5% | -3.5% |

## Notes

1. Nelson reports that he has been a consultant to law firms representing SABMiller and Anheuser-Busch and has received funding from the International Center for Alcohol Policies which is funded by the major beverage alcohol producers.
2. Elasticities do not have any metric which allows for comparisons of elasticities across studies which employ different types of data to measure advertising.

## References


Advertising Age (2012), *Top 100 Global Advertisers*, http://adage.com/datacenter/globalmarketers2012.

An, R. and R. Sturm (2011), "Does the Response to Alcohol Taxes Differ Across Racial/ethnic Groups? Some Evidence from 1984-2009 Behavioral Risk Factor Surveillance System", *Journal of Mental Health Policy and Economics*, Vol. 14, No. 1, pp. 13-23.

Anderson, P. et al. (2009), Impact of Alcohol Advertising and Media Exposure on Adolescent Alcohol Use: A Systematic Review of Longitudinal Studies, *Alcohol and Alcoholism* Vol. 44, No. 3, pp. 229-243, doi: 10.1093/alcalc/agn115.

Ayyagari, P. et al. (2013), "Understanding Heterogeneity in Price Elasticities in the Demand for Alcohol for Older Individuals", *Health Economics*, Vol. 22, No. 1, pp. 89-105.

Bernheim, B.D. and A. Rangel (2004), "Addiction and Cue-triggered Decision Processes", *American Economic Review*, pp. 1558-1590.

De Bruijn, A. (2013), Report on the Volume of Youth Eposure to Alcohol Advertisements in European Countries, AMPHORA Deliverable D1.4, available at http://amphoraproject.net/w2box/data/Deliverables/AMPHORA_WP4_D1.4.pdf.

Gallet, C.A. (2007), "The Demand for Alcohol: A Meta-analysis of Elasticities", *Australian Journal of Agricultural and Resource Economics*, Vol. 51, No. 2, pp. 121-135.

George, M.S. et al. (2001), "Activation of Prefrontal Cortex and Anterior Thalamus in Alcoholic Subjects on Exposure to Alcohol-specific Cues", *Archives of General Psychiatry*, Vol. 58, No. 4, pp. 345-352.

Manning, W.G., L. Blumberg and L.H. Moulton (1995), "The Demand for Alcohol: The Differential Response to Price", *Journal of Health Economics*, Vol. 14, No. 2, pp. 123-148.

Myrick, H. et al. (2004), "Differential Brain Activity in Alcoholics and Social Drinkers to Alcohol Cues: Relationship to Craving", *Neuropsychopharmacology*, Vol. 29, pp. 393-402.

Nelson, J.P. (2011), "Alcohol Marketing, Adolescent Drinking and Publication Bias in Longitudinal Studies: A Critical Survey Using Meta-analysis", *Journal of Economic Surveys*, Vol. 25, No. 2, pp. 191-232.

Saffer, H., D. Dave and M. Grossman (2012), *Behavioral Economics and the Demand for Alcohol: Results from the NLSY97*, National Bureau of Economic Research, New York, Working Paper no. 18180.

Tapert, S.F. et al. (2003), "Neural Response to Alcohol Stimuli in Adolescents with Alcohol Use Disorder", *Archives of General Psychiatry*, Vol. 60, pp. 727-735.

Townshend, J.M. and T. Duka (2001), "Attentional Bias Associated with Alcohol Cues: Differences Between Heavy and Occasional Social Drinkers", *Psychopharmacology*, Vol. 157, pp. 67-74.

Wagenaar, A.C., M.J. Salois and K.A. Komro (2009), "Effects of Beverage Alcohol Price and Tax Levels on Drinking: A Meta-analysis of 1003 Estimates from 112 Studies", *Addiction*, Vol. 104, No. 2, pp. 179-190.

WSJ – Wall Street Journal (2012), Liquor Ads Win Airtime, 23 August, available at http://online.wsj.com/news/articles/SB10000872396390444082904577605140973375290.

Tackling Harmful Alcohol Use
Economics and Public Health Policy


*Special focus III*

# How does minimum unit pricing for alcohol affect different types of drinkers?

by
Anne Ludbrook
University of Aberdeen

## Introduction

The Scottish Government passed legislation in 2012 to introduce minimum unit pricing (MUP) for alcohol. The law states that alcohol should not be sold below a price equivalent to 50 pence (EUR 0.615[1]) per unit of alcohol (a unit equals 10 ml of pure alcohol). This has not yet been implemented because a legal challenge is still going through the courts. The Irish Government is also interested in including MUP in its alcohol strategy. The UK Government consulted on MUP but has decided initially to pursue a restriction on below-cost selling – a ban on selling alcohol below a price equivalent to duty plus VAT. As alcohol duties are not levied strictly on alcohol content, this proposal would result in the lowest permitted price varying from 11p or less per unit of alcohol for lower strength still ciders to 42p per unit for higher strength sparkling ciders, with other alcoholic beverages falling between these extremes (Home Office, 2014).

MUP was proposed to tackle a particular set of problems in the UK alcohol market. Low prices, particularly for alcohol sold in supermarkets, shops or other places where it is not consumed (the "off-trade" sector) had helped make alcohol more affordable. Raising alcohol duty was seen to be a less effective response as the impact depended on retailers passing the price increase through to customers. This was uncertain because alcohol products were used as "loss leaders" by supermarkets to encourage customers to enter the store. It was also apparent that the effect on alcohol consumption of average price increases could be weakened by consumers "trading down" to lower cost alternatives. One of the first studies to demonstrate the effect of price increases that targeted different market segments was conducted in Sweden. Using Systembolaget data, Gruenewald et al. (2006) estimated that a 10% price increase on all products would reduce sales by 1.7%, whereas targeting only lower cost brands reduced the total volume of alcohol sold by 4.2%. The largest effect was on low price beer (-11.1%), with the volume of low price spirits also falling (-1.9%). The volume of alcohol from low price wine was estimated to increase (+3.1%) because of the substitution of wine for beer and spirits.

The evidence regarding the relative effectiveness of MUP as an intervention to reduce alcohol related harms is discussed in Chapter 5. However, concerns have been raised about whether minimum pricing may be regressive in its impact on low-income households and about the impact it may have on moderate drinkers, as opposed to those drinking at hazardous or harmful levels. This contribution summarises the evidence available on this issue and places it in the context of the impact of other pricing interventions, such as alcohol duty and restrictions on below cost selling.

## Price effects on population subgroups

The impact of the minimum price intervention on different groups within the population depends critically on who are the main purchasers of cheaper alcoholic beverages, how much they buy, and how responsive they are to a change in price ("price elasticity of demand"). The relative effectiveness of price increases in reducing consumption for heavier drinkers compared with moderate drinkers is subject to some debate in the literature. Much of this discussion has focussed on comparing price elasticities for different groups. However, there are a number of difficulties with this approach.

Whilst there is strong evidence that price has an impact at the population level (Elder et al., 2010; Wagenaar et al., 2009, 2010), estimation of results for population subgroups is subject to a number of methodological issues and problems with data quality. Alcohol is not a single product, and variations in type and quality affect individual willingness to pay for a particular product. The demand for alcohol is, therefore, an aggregation of different relationships, and if different population subgroups favour different alcohol products and face different prices, estimates are likely to be biased. Concentrating more directly on the evidence relating to the choice of products by different population groups and the change in quantity of alcohol purchased or consumed is likely to provide a clearer picture.

One issue that potentially confounds the estimation of price elasticities for different drinking groups is higher volume purchasers searching for lower prices. Black et al. (2011) compared the purchasing behaviour of patients being treated for alcohol related health problems with the general population in Scotland. These patients paid an average price of 43p per unit for alcohol compared with a population average of 71p per unit. Eighty three per cent of units purchased by the patients were priced at below the proposed MUP of 50p.

## Purchasing patterns for low cost alcohol

The purchasing or consumption behaviour of different income groups and different levels of drinking shows a fairly consistent pattern. There is evidence that income affects the probability of purchasing low cost alcohol and the number of units purchased within a given category of drinker (moderate, hazardous, harmful[2]). However, the effects are relatively small compared with the much greater difference between drinking categories.

This is illustrated by our study (Ludbrook et al., 2012), which used three years of data (2006-08) from a UK household survey (Expenditure and Food Survey/Living Costs and Food Survey). Households recorded all their purchases over a two-week sample period. Households were divided into five income quintiles[3] and four categories of household alcohol purchases: zero purchases, and purchasing levels consistent with moderate, hazardous and harmful alcohol consumption. Although the data covered both on-trade and off-trade alcohol purchases, our analysis focussed on off-trade alcohol as this is the category affected by MUP.

Figures SFIII.1 and SFIII.2 summarise the probability of purchasing cheap alcohol and the predicted number of units, respectively, for households who purchased some off-trade alcohol. Income has less effect than drinking category. However, zero purchasers are over-represented in the low-income groups, so if we include households who did not purchase off-trade alcohol in the survey period, then the income effect becomes less apparent and is slightly positive for the harmful category.

Given that the data used were only for a two week period, many of these zero purchasers are more likely to be occasional purchasers. Research by Leicester (2011) using household scanner data analysed purchasing patterns over a year. This found little relationship between the propensity of households to buy cheap alcohol and their income, but cheap units accounted for a larger share of the units purchased by low income households. The proportional effect of MUP on low-income households is therefore larger, but, consistent with earlier findings, MUP makes a bigger difference across the alcohol purchase categories than it does across income groups.

Figure SFIII.1. **Average predicted probability that households purchase low cost (<45p per unit) off trade alcohol by income quintile and purchase level – conditional on purchasing off-trade alcohol**

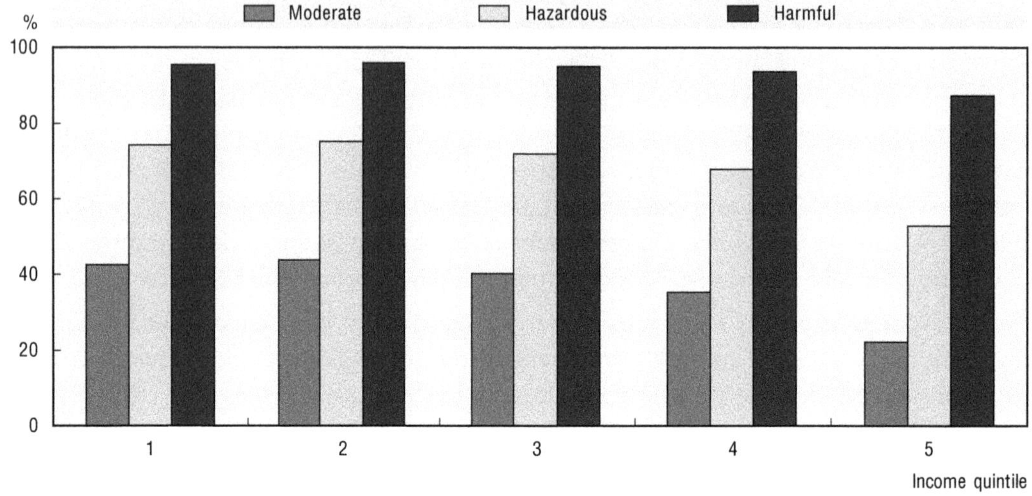


StatLink http://dx.doi.org/10.1787/888933180577

Figure SFIII.2. **Average predicted quantity of low cost (<45p per unit) off trade alcohol by income quintile and purchase level – conditional on purchasing off-trade alcohol**

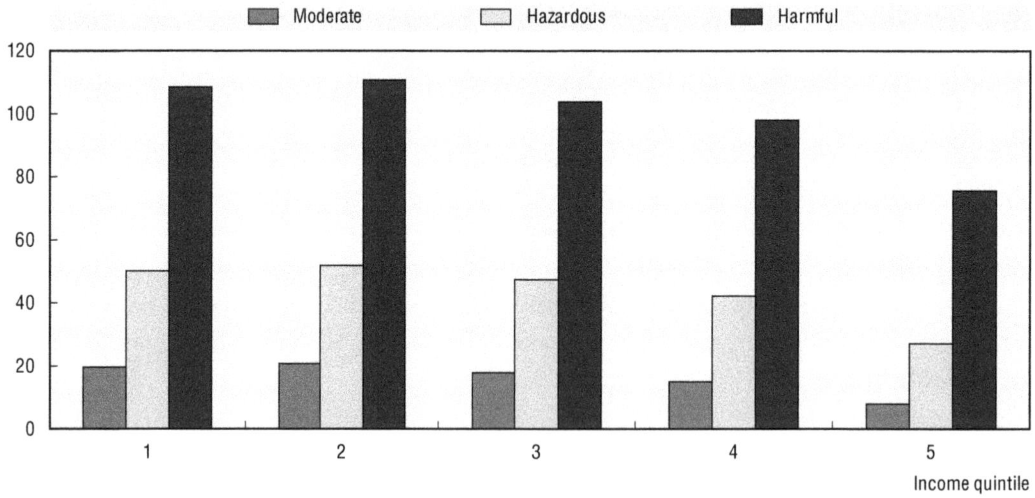


*Source:* Data from Ludbrook, A. et al. (2012), "Tackling Alcohol Misuse: Purchasing Patterns Affected by Minimum Pricing for Alcohol", *Applied Health Economics and Health Policy*, Vol. 10, No. 1, pp. 51-63.

StatLink http://dx.doi.org/10.1787/888933180580

More recently, Holmes et al. (2014) used the Sheffield Alcohol Policy Model to model the effect of MUP by income and drinking category. Their results show that there is more effect on consumption for low-income than for higher-income groups, but also much more effect on harmful drinkers compared with moderate drinkers. With a MUP of 45p, low-income moderate drinkers are predicted to reduce consumption by 29 units per year compared with less than one unit for the highest-income group. Harmful drinkers are predicted to reduce consumption by 138 units per year on average, with a range from 300 units for the lowest-income group to 34 units for the highest-income group. Overall the effect of MUP for those on low-income is concentrated amongst the heaviest drinkers, but low-income, harmful drinkers also have the greatest reduction in alcohol consumption, spend less as a result and have the greatest benefit in terms of health gains. This finding is consistent with other research that suggests that alcohol related harms are disproportionately experienced by deprived groups (Johnston et al., 2012).

## Other pricing interventions

Below-cost selling has recently been prohibited in England but the definition which is used, selling below duty plus VAT, results in only a small proportion of the alcohol market being affected. However, there is some indication that those purchasing the most off-trade alcohol bought a larger proportion of units below cost (Leicester, 2011). The impact of the ban on below-cost selling on average consumption and spending is estimated to be much smaller than MUP and therefore will have relatively little differential effect by income or drinking category.

The effect of increasing alcohol duty differs depending upon whether all households are considered or only those purchasing alcohol. Increasing alcohol taxes is progressive when considering all households but regressive when looking at households who purchase alcohol (Leicester, 2011), although the author notes that the household survey data used may have overestimated the proportion of zero purchasers as it only covers a two-week period. UK duty is complex as it is levied at different rates on different products and not proportional to alcohol content. The impact of duty increases by income group will depend on which product types are affected and by how much and it may be much harder to target drinking categories. In the past, duty increases have been seen as a way of tackling particular "problem" drinks, such as alcopops, but the effect of piecemeal interventions is largely to induce switching to other products rather than reduce alcohol consumption overall.

## Conclusion

MUP has been proposed as a particular policy response to market conditions experienced in Scotland and elsewhere. Concerns about the potential impact on low-income moderate drinkers appear to be unfounded as their levels of purchasing result in relatively small effects. Moderate drinkers across the income distribution will be little affected by MUP. Low-income heavy drinkers appear to be the group that may be most affected in terms of changing consumption, whereas high income heavy drinkers may be able to afford to maintain harmful drinking patterns.

### Notes

1. Exchange rate GBP 1 = EUR 1.23, May 29th 2014.
2. Drinking categories are based on UK guidelines of moderate (up to 14 units for women and 21 units for men); hazardous (14-35 units; 21-50 units) and harmful (over 35; over 50 units). These categories are applied to either quantities consumed or purchased depending on the data available.
3. Based on gross equivalised income.

### *References*

Black, H., J. Gill and J. Chick (2011), "The Price of a Drink: Levels of Consumption and Price Paid per Unit of Alcohol by Edinburgh's Ill Drinkers with a Comparison to Wider Alcohol Sales in Scotland", *Addiction*, Vol. 106; No. 4, pp. 729-736.

Elder, R.W. et al. (2010), "The Effectiveness of Tax Policy Interventions for Reducing Excessive Alcohol Consumption and Related Harms", *American Journal of Preventive Medicine*, Vol. 38, pp. 217-229.

Gruenewald, P.J. et al. (2006), "Alcohol Prices, Beverage Quality, and the Demand for Alcohol: Quality Substitutions and Price Elasticities", *Alcoholism Clinical and Experimental Research*, Vol. 30, No. 1, pp. 96-105.

Holmes, J. et al. (2014), "Effects of Minimum Unit Pricing for Alcohol on Different Income and Socioeconomic Groups: A Modelling Study", *The Lancet*, Published online February 10, http://dx.doi.org/10.1016/S0140-6736(13)62417-4.

Home Office (2014), "Guidance on Banning the Sale of Alcohol Below the Cost of Duty Plus VAT", www.gov.uk/government/uploads/system/uploads/attachment_data/file/311735/Guidance_on_BBCS_3.pdf, accessed 28 April 2014.

Johnston, M., A. Ludbrook and M. Jaffray (2012), "Inequalities in the Distribution of the Costs of Alcohol Misuse in Scotland: A Cost of Illness Study", *Alcohol and Alcoholism*, Vol. 47, No. 6, pp. 725-731, http://dx.doi.org/10.1093/alcalc/ags092.

Leicester, A. (2011), "Alcohol Pricing and Taxation Policies", IFS Briefing Note No. BN124, Institute for Fiscal Studies London, www.ifs.org.uk/bns/bn124.pdf, accessed 28 April 2014.

Ludbrook, A. et al. (2012), "Tackling Alcohol Misuse: Purchasing Patterns Affected by Minimum Pricing for Alcohol", *Applied Health Economics and Health Policy*, Vol. 10, No. 1, pp. 51-63.

Meng, Y. et al. (2013), "Modelled Income Group-specific Impacts of Alcohol Minimum Unit Pricing in England 2014/15: Policy Appraisals Using New Developments to the Sheffield Alcohol Policy Model, (v2.5)", www.shef.ac.uk/polopoly_fs/1.291621!/file/julyreport.pdf accessed 28/04/2014.

Wagenaar, A.C., A.L. Tobler and K.A. Komro (2010), "Effects of Alcohol Tax and Price Policies on Morbidity and Mortality: A Systematic Review", *American Journal of Public Health*, Vol.100, pp. 2270-2278.

Wagenaar, A.C., M.J. Salois and K.A. Komro (2009), "Effects of Beverage Alcohol Prices and Tax Levels on Drinking: A Meta-analysis of 1003 Estimates from 112 Studies", *Addiction*, Vol. 104, pp. 179-190.

Tackling Harmful Alcohol Use
Economics and Public Health Policy


*Special focus IV*

# A business case for reducing alcohol-related harm in the workplace

by
Marjana Martinic,

on behalf of the Business
and Industry Advisory Committee to the OECD (BIAC)

## Introduction

The workplace offers a useful point for interventions addressing alcohol-related problems and related harm because it allows access to a large segment of the working-age population, and can be used to identify individuals who are at increased risk for harm as well as those in high-risk contexts. Focusing on alcohol-related problems in the workplace also makes economic sense for employers and employees alike.

Understanding the relationships between drinking patterns, the contexts for alcohol consumption and associated risks offers options for modifying workplace characteristics associated with problem drinking and tailoring interventions for particular situations where the risk of harm may be increased. Workplace interventions can be used to address drinking in the workplace itself, as well as drinking that occurs outside the workplace but that has an impact on the work environment, productivity, and employee relations.

The complexity of addressing alcohol abuse in, and through, the workplace requires a broad and interdisciplinary approach that brings together the efforts of employers and others. Multi-stakeholder partnerships are desirable, in order to improve current approaches and make their implementation more consistent.

Since the implementation of workplace alcohol policies is often in the hands of individual employers and rarely mandated by governments, the private sector has a unique opportunity to lead the way through engagement and to demonstrate corporate social responsibility.

## The rationale for tackling alcohol-related problems in the workplace

According to some estimates, around 10% of all employed adults may be problem drinkers (Henderson et al., 1996). Drinking on the job can result in injuries, and heavy drinking outside the workplace may result in hangovers and sick days that spill over into working hours (Cook, 1997a and 1997b), contributing to lost efficiency and productivity (Bacharach et al., 2010; Pidd et al., 2006b).

The direct financial cost from illness and death, and the investment needed to replace individuals (and skills) lost is high. Alcohol-related problems also have an impact on the cost of healthcare, sick leave, rehabilitation, redundancy payments for lay-offs, and legal costs. Lost productivity from absenteeism and "presenteeism" (attending work while still under the influence of alcohol) has been identified as the main element of the social cost of alcohol-related harm (Rehm et al., 2006; Rehm et al., 2009; Collins and Lapsley, 2008; Sloan et al., 2000; Anderson et al., 2012).

At the same time, enhanced workplace health and safety have been shown to contribute to worker satisfaction and enhanced productivity, and employers have both a legal and an ethical responsibility to avoid accidents and injuries (Sloan et al., 2000). The investments needed to establish workplace policies and programmes are relatively small for employers compared with the costs of harm, and are more than offset by reductions in these costs (Collins and Lapsley, 2008; Hantula et al., 2001; Oxenburgh and Marlow, 2005).

 

## Workplace interventions: Effectiveness and cost effectiveness

Interventions around alcohol in the workplace range from legal requirements in some countries to full reliance on employer-led programmes and measures in others. However, even where legislation exists, implementation may be largely voluntary and its scope left to the discretion of the employer, particularly in the private sector. A model framework for managing alcohol-related issues in the workplace has been developed by the International Labour Organization (ILO, 1996) in its Code of Practice. Guidance for implementing alcohol prevention interventions is also offered through the European Workplace and Alcohol (EWA) project, co-financed by the European Commission and implemented in 12 EU countries (Dawson et al., 2013).

Other approaches include strategies to help those employees whose drinking may be problematic or puts them at increased risk for harm. The evidence around the effectiveness of various workplace programmes in changing behaviour and reducing harm is mixed (Webb et al., 2009), but some evaluations have found an impact on reducing alcohol consumption and problems (Anderson and Larimer, 2002; Pidd et al., 2006a; Walters and Woodall, 2003), as well as future intentions to engage in heavy drinking (Lapham et al., 2003; Dale and Livingston, 2012). An effect on productivity and cost savings to employers has also been demonstrated (Osilla et al., 2010). Combining various interventions shows better results than single approaches (Osilla et al., 2010; Hermansson et al., 2010).

In some countries, such as the United States, mandatory screening for alcohol, usually combined with screening for drug use, is fairly common, particularly in professions where risk for harm is high. This approach has shown some evidence of effectiveness in reducing injuries in the short-term, although longer-term impact on injury rates was less pronounced (Spicer and Miller, 2005). However, one US-based study shows a 23% reduction in the risk for fatal crashes in the transportation industry following mandatory testing for alcohol among drivers (Brady et al., 2009). Other studies suggest that screening and testing can also improve the effectiveness of other interventions.

Where alcohol-specific programmes are used in the workplace, employee assistance programmes (EAPs), usually including counselling, are common, particularly in large enterprises (Roman and Blum 2002; Hartwell et al., 1996; Jepson et al., 2010), and are often required by company policies. One assessment found EAPs to significantly decrease presenteeism, but not absenteeism (Osilla et al., 2010; Goetzel et al., 2004). However, the resulting improvements in productivity were significant and translated into cost savings of USD 1 200 per employee over the four-week period examined (Osilla et al., 2010).

When applied individually, measures such as counselling, psychosocial skills training, or screening and brief interventions for problem drinkers (SBI) show little or no impact on behaviour (Hermansson et al., 1998; Hermansson et al., 2010), although they can affect individuals' desire to change (Lapham et al., 2003; Matano et al., 2007, Cook et al., 1996; Heirich and Sieck, 2000). However, when a combination of approaches is integrated into EAPs or a more comprehensive programme that positions drinking within a broader context of lifestyle factors and general health risks is applied, the results on reducing alcohol-related harm are promising (Webb et al., 2009).

SBI within EAPs is also cost effective in addressing alcohol-related problems and harm in the workplace, although few studies have been conducted outside of health care settings (Rehm et al., 2006; Rehm et al., 2009; Collins and Lapsley, 2008; Sloan et al., 2000; Bergström et al., 2008; Ames et al., 2000; Frone, 2006, 2008, 2009; Frone and Brown, 2010; Rospenda et al.,

2009). One assessment (Cowell et al., 2011) found SBI costs at the workplace to be significantly lower than in a primary care setting. Employer costs depend, among other factors, on whether programmes are fully supported through employer-based health insurance, as in the United States, or subsidised by government-funded health care systems, as in some European countries. Some employers have implemented peer-based interventions for reducing alcohol-related harm with a focus on changing workplace culture, attitudes, and perceptions around alcohol (Frone and Brown, 2010; Bennett et al. 2004). One programme in the transportation industry showed a 30% reduction in the rate of injuries, which translated into a cost savings of around USD 48 million to the employer for that calendar year (Spicer and Miller, 2005; Miller et al., 2007). The employer avoided USD 1 850 per employee in net injury costs during the year assessed. The ratio of benefits accrued for the employer to the cost of implementing peer-based interventions in this particular programme was estimated at 26:1, lending further support to its cost effectiveness (Miller et al., 2007).

Another promising approach is web-based interventions that include personalised feedback that may be complemented by motivational interviewing sessions. These interventions allow flexibility for employees, allowing them to complete the programme at their own pace and to maintain their privacy. The cost of implementing web-based interventions is relatively low, making them cost effective, and a useful option for employers whose resources are limited. Evaluation of web-based interventions has shown that, in the short term (in some cases up to three months following the intervention), significant reductions in high-risk drinking can be sustained (Matano et al., 2007, Doumas and Hannah, 2008; Hester et al., 2011).

Comprehensive health promotion programmes that also include emphasis on alcohol problems have shown some promise, particularly those emphasizing physical activity. While the evidence overall is still weak, such programmes show higher participation and greater success in reducing risky drinking (Sieck and Heirich, 2010), and hold promise for cost effectiveness (Chapman, 2003, 2005; Baicker et al., 2010).

## Sectoral examples of alcohol-related interventions

Programmes around alcohol are applied to differing degrees in different sectors. While some employers focus primarily on safety, others integrate workplace alcohol problems into efforts around general health and wellness. The steel and iron industries, for example, have long recognised the potential impact drinking on workplace health and safety (ILO, 2005), and their initiatives in many cases predate the establishment of government regulations. The International Civil Aviation Organization sets requirements around alcohol consumption, "bottle-to-throttle" timeframes, and allowable blood alcohol concentration (BAC) limits for pilots, air traffic controllers, or flight attendants in member countries (ICAO, 1995).

Given that alcohol is at the core of their business, alcohol beverage producers devote particular attention to alcohol in the workplace. Interventions for problems include EAPs, counselling and brief interventions, and, where needed, treatment. Education and awareness about alcohol, its relationship with work performance and health, and about country-specific laws are another key component, with training for employees. At a minimum, global producers have policies that apply in all markets in which they operate and that are adapted to local laws.

One example is the Anheuser-Busch InBev Global Standards for Employee Responsible Drinking (ABI, 2008), which apply both to drinking in the workplace and outside of it. Under these standards, some moderate consumption of alcohol within the working context is tolerated under certain circumstances, but alcohol-related impairment is not. Heinken's Cool@Work programme offers different approaches depending on employees' drinking patterns and level of risk (Heineken International, 2005). The French distiller Pernod Ricard has a broader framework within which responsibility and drinking while performing professional duties are positioned (Pernod Ricard, 2006). An unpublished internal evaluation suggests that Diageo's DRINKiQ training programme increased participants' awareness of what constitutes responsible drinking and intention to change drinking patterns.

Pernod Ricard's Road Safety Charter (Pernod Ricard & Délégation Interministérielle à la Sécurité Routière, 2002), requires educating employees about road traffic safety and compliance with laws, as well as the use of breathalysers and sober-designated drivers. According to an internal evaluation, involvement of employees in road traffic crashes (both related to drinking and not involving alcohol) decreased between 2002 and 2006 (Pernod Ricard, unpublished data). It should be noted, however, that other external variables, such as a tightening of French road traffic laws and enforcement during this period may also have contributed to the decline.

## Challenges to workplace interventions

Evidence on the effectiveness and cost effectiveness of different interventions is not robust, due to the barriers to both implementation and evaluation. Evaluation may be hindered by: a lack of consistency across the approaches being assessed and the difficulty of comparing disparate programmes; modest numbers of subjects who may not be representative of the entire workforce; inconsistency regarding the specific outcomes being assessed; and, reliance on self-reporting of outcomes (Webb et al., 2009). Greater consistency across programmes and tools used to measure impact is needed for an improved assessment of what works and what does not.

Ethical considerations around the implementation of workplace programmes to address alcohol abuse and problems present significant challenges, notably privacy and confidentiality issues (Cowell et al., 2011; Verstraete and Pierce, 2001; ILO, 2009; Slavit et al., 2009). To date there are no large-scale studies that assess either the degree to which alcohol is addressed during counselling sessions, or, consequently, the extent of coverage or impact.

Successful implementation of workplace alcohol programmes also faces challenges. In general, larger employers are more likely to implement measures than smaller ones and more likely to have the resources to do so (Linnan et al., 2008). However, the majority of the global workforce is employed by micro, small, or medium enterprises (Eurostat, 2011) that often lack resources to adequately implement workplace alcohol programmes, even though the impact of alcohol misuse in the workplace is relatively higher for smaller businesses.

Another challenge is the increasing tendency in the job market towards outsourcing, subcontracting and short-term contracts. This has resulted in the loss of entitlements and benefits for workers that generally come with full-time employment (OECD, 2002; UNDESA, 2007), including interventions aimed at alcohol misuse. At the same time, state-sponsored social systems have also shrunk in many countries and have not been replaced by effective health care. Ironically, periods of economic downturn, which bring with them job cuts and layoffs, are arguably the very time when efforts around alcohol abuse are particularly needed. While the evidence is mixed (Ruhm, 1995; Ruhm and Black, 2002), studies from the United States (e.g. Bor et al., 2013) and Spain (Gili, 2013) indicate that such periods may coincide with an increase in alcohol problems.

Culture also represents a barrier to workplace policies and interventions by shaping the degree of tolerance towards drinking across societies, as well as, in a more limited way, within the workplace. Workplace culture can be an organisational barrier if management is not inclined to consider alcohol misuse to be a high priority (Bell et al., 1996). Drinking in the workplace may be tolerated as conducive to camaraderie and bonding, and management may turn a blind eye to problems.

### References

ABI – Anheuser-Busch InBev (2008), "Global Standards for Employee Responsible Drinking Policy", Internal communication.

Ames, G., J. Grube and R.S. Moore (2000), "Social Control and Workplace Drinking Norms: A Comparison of Two Organizational Cultures", *Journal of Studies on Alcohol*, Vol. 61, pp. 203-219.

Anderson, B.K. and M.E. Larimer (2002), "Problem Drinking in the Workplace: An Individualized Approach to Prevention", *Psychology of Addictive Behaviors*, Vol. 16, pp. 243-251.

Anderson, P., L. Møller and G. Galea (2012), "Alcohol in the European Union. Consumption, Harm and Policy Approaches", World Health Organization, Copenhagen.

Bacharach, S.B., P. Bamberger and M. Biron (2010), "Alcohol Consumption and Workplace Absenteeism: The Moderating Effect of Social Support", *Journal of Applied Psychology*, Vol. 95, pp. 334-348.

Baicker, K., D. Cutler and Z. Song (2010), "Workplace Wellness Programs Can Generate Savings", *Health Affairs*, Vol. 29, pp. 304-311.

Bell, N.S. et al. (1996), "Workplace Barriers to the Effective Management of Alcohol Problems", *Journal of Occupational and Environmental Medicine*, Vol. 38, pp. 1213-1219.

Bennett, J.B. et al. (2004), "Team Awareness, Problem Drinking, and Drinking Climate: Workplace Social Health Promotion in a Policy Context", *Behavior Change*, Vol. 19, pp. 103-113.

Bergström, G. et al. (2008), "A Comprehensive Workplace Intervention and Its Outcome with Regard to Lifestyle, Health and Sick Leave: The AHA Study", *Work: A Journal of Prevention, Assessment and Rehabilitation*, Vol. 31, pp. 167-180.

Bor, J. et al. (2013), "Alcohol Use During the Great Recession of 2008-2009", *Alcohol & Alcoholism*, Vol. 48, pp. 343-348.

Brady, J.E. et al. (2009), "Effectiveness of Mandatory Alcohol Testing Programs in Reducing Alcohol Involvement in Fatal Motor Carrier Crashes", *American Journal of Epidemiology*, Vol. 17, pp. 775-782.

Chapman, L.S. (2005), "Meta-evaluation of Worksite Health Promotion Economic Return Studies", *American Journal of Health Promotion*, 2005 update, Vol 19, pp. 1-11.

Chapman, L.S. (2003), "Meta-evaluation of Worksite Health Promotion Economic Return Studies", *The Art of Health Promotion*, Vol. 6, pp. 1-16.

Collins, D.J. and H.M. Lapsley (2008), "The Avoidable Costs of Alcohol Abuse in Australia and the Potential Benefits of Effective Policies to Reduce Social Costs of Alcohol", Commonwealth Department of Health and Ageing, Canberra.

Cook, C.C.H. (1997a), "Alcohol and Aviation", *Addiction*, Vol. 92, No. 5, pp. 539-555.

Cook, C.C.H. (1997b), "Alcohol Policy and Aviation Safety", *Addiction*, Vol. 92, No. 7, pp. 793-804.

Cook, R.F., A.S. Back and J. Trudeau (1996), "Preventing Alcohol Use Problems Among Blue-collar Workers: A Field Test of the Working People Program", *Substance Use and Misuse*, Vol. 31, pp. 255-275.

Cowell, A.J., J.W. Bray and J.M. Hinde (2011), "The Cost of Screening and Brief Intervention in Employee Assistance Programs", *Journal of Behavioral Health Services and Research*, Vol. 39, pp. 55-67.

Dale, C.E. and M.J. Livingston (2012), "The Burden of Alcohol Drinking on Co-workers in the Australian Workplace", *Medical Journal of Australia*, Vol. 193, pp. 138-140.

Dawson, J. et al. (2013), "European Workplace and Alcohol Toolkit for Alcohol-Related Interventions in Workplace Settings", Department of Health of the Government of Catalonia, Barcelona.

Doumas, D.M. and E. Hannah (2008), "Preventing High-risk Drinking in Youth in the Workplace: A Web-based Normative Feedback Program", *Journal of Substance Abuse Treatment*, Vol. 34, pp 263-271.

Eurostat (2011), "Structural Business Statistics Overview", European Commission, Brussels, available at http://epp.eurostat.ec.europa.eu/statistics_explained/index.php/Structural_business_statistics_overview.

Frone, M.R. (2009), "Does Permissive Workplace Substance Use Climate Affect Employees Who Do Not Use Alcohol and Drugs at Work? A U.S. National Study", *Psychology of Addictive Behavior*, Vol. 23, pp. 386-390.

Frone, M.R. (2008), "Are Work Stressors Related to Employee Substance Use? The Importance of Temporal Context Assessments of Alcohol and Illicit Drug Use", *Journal of Applied Psychology*, Vol. 93, pp. 199-206.

Frone, M.R. (2006), "Prevalence and Distribution of Alcohol Use and Impairment in the Workplace: A U.S. National Survey", *Journal of Studies on Alcohol*, Vol. 67, pp. 147-156.

Frone, M.R. and A.L. Brown (2010), "Workplace Substance-use Norms as Predictors of Employee Substance Use and Impairment: A Survey of U.S. Workers', *Journal of Studies on Alcohol and Drugs*, Vol. 71, pp. 526-534.

Gili, M. et al. (2013), "The Mental Health Risks of Economic Crisis in Spain: Evidence from Primary Care Centres, 2006 and 2010", *European Journal of Public Health*, Vol. 23, pp. 103-108.

Goetzel, R.Z. et al. (2004), "Health, Absence, Disability, and Presenteeism Cost Estimates of Certain Physical and Mental Health Conditions Affecting U.S. Employers", *Journal of Occupational and Environmental Medicine*, Vol. 61, pp. 219-224.

Hantula, D.A. et al. (2001), "The Value of Workplace Safety. A Time-based Utility Analysis Model", *Journal of Organizational and Behavior Management*, Vol. 21, pp. 79-98.

Hartwell, T.D. et al. (1996), "Aiding Troubled Employees: The Prevalence, Cost, and Characteristics of Employee Assistance Programs in the United States", *American Journal of Public Health*, Vol. 86, pp. 804-808.

Harwood, H.J., D. Fountain and G. Livermore (1998), "Economic Costs of Alcohol Abuse and Alcoholism", *Recent Developments in Alcoholism*, Vol. 14, pp. 307-330.

Heineken International (2005), *Cool@Work. Policy and Guidelines for Implementation*, 2nd edition, Heineken NV, Amsterdam.

Heirich, M. and C.J. Sieck (2000), "Worksite Cardiovascular Wellness Programs as a Route to Substance Abuse Prevention", *Journal of Occupational and Environmental Medicine*, Vol. 42, pp. 47-56.

Henderson, M., G. Hutcheson and J. Davies (1996), *Alcohol and the Workplace*, WHO Regional Publications, European Series, No. 67, WHO Regional Office for Europe, Copenhagen.

Hermansson, U. et al. (2010), "Screening and Brief Intervention for Risky Alcohol Consumption in the Workplace: Results of a 1-year Randomized Controlled Study", *Alcohol and Alcoholism*, Vol. 45, pp. 252-257.

Hermansson, U. et al. (1998), "Feasibility of Brief Intervention in the Workplace for the Detection and Treatment of Excessive Alcohol Consumption", *Journal of Occupational and Environmental Health*, Vol. 4, pp. 71-78.

Hester, R.K., H.D. Delaney and W. Campbell (2011), "ModerateDrinking.com and Moderation Management: Outcomes of a Randomized Clinical Trial with Non-dependent Problem Drinkers", Journal of Consulting and Clinical Psychology, Vol. 79, pp. 215-224.

ICAO – International Civil Aviation Organization (1995), *Manual on Prevention of Problematic Use of Substances in the Aviation Workplace*, ICAO, Montreal.

ILO – International Labour Organization (2009), *Encyclopedia of Occupational Health and Safety*, 4th edition, ILO, Geneva.

ILO (2005), *Code of Practice on Safety and Health in the Iron and Steel Industry*, ILO, Geneva.

ILO (1996), *Management of Alcohol and Drug-related Issues in the Workplace. An ILO Code of Practice*, ILO, Geneva.

Jepson, R.G. et al. (2010), "The Effectiveness of Interventions to Change Six Health Behaviours: A Review of Reviews", *BMC Public Health*, Vol. 10:538.

Lapham, S.C., C. Gregory and G. MacMillan (2003), "Impact of an Alcohol Misuse Intervention for Health Care Workers. 1. Frequency of Binge Drinking and Desire to Reduce Alcohol Use", *Alcohol & Alcoholism*, Vol. 38, pp. 176-182.

Linnan, L. et al. (2008), "Results of the 2004 National Worksite Health Promotion Survey", *American Journal of Public Health*, Vol. 98, pp. 1503-1509.

Matano, R.A. et al. (2007), "A Pilot Study of an Interactive Web Site in the Workplace for Reducing Alcohol Consumption", *Journal of Substance Abuse Treatment*, Vol. 32, pp. 71-80.

Miller, T.R., E. Zaloshnja and R.S. Spicer (2007), "Effectiveness and Benefit-cost of Peer-based Workplace Substance Abuse Prevention Coupled with Random Testing", *Accident Analysis and Prevention*, 39: 565-573.

OECD (2002), *OECD Employment Outlook 2002*, Chapter "Surveying the Jobs Horizon", OECD Publishing, Paris, http://dx.doi.org/10.1787/empl_outlook-2002-en.

Osilla, K.C. et al. (2010), "Exploring Productivity Outcomes from a Brief Intervention for At-risk Drinking in an Employee Assistance Program", *Addictive Behaviors*, Vol. 35, pp. 194-200.

Oxenburgh, M. and P. Marlow (2005), "The Productivity Assessment Tool: Computer-based Cost-benefit Analysis Model for the Economic Assessment of Occupational Health and Safety Interventions in the Workplace", *Journal of Safety Research*, Vol. 36, pp. 209-214.

Pernod Ricard (2006), "Pernod Ricard Sustainable Development Charter", Pernod Ricard, Paris, available at www.pernod-ricard.com/medias/resources/static/Entreprendre/chartegb_def.pdf.

Pernod Ricard & Délégation Interministérielle à la Sécurité Routière (2002), "Charte de sécurité routière", Paris.

Pidd, K., R. Boeckmann and M. Morris (2006a), "Adolescents in Transition: The Role of Workplace Alcohol and Other Drug Policies as a Prevention Strategy", *Drugs: Education, Prevention and Policy*, Vol. 13, pp. 353-365.

Pidd, K.J. et al. (2006b), "Estimating the Cost of Alcohol-related Absenteeism in the Australian Workforce: The Importance of Consumption Patterns", *Medical Journal of Australia*, Vol. 185, pp. 637-641.

Rehm, J. et al. (2009), "Global Burden of Disease and Injury and Economic Cost Attributable to Alcohol Use and Alcohol-use Disorders", *The Lancet*, Vol. 373, pp. 2223-2233.

Rehm, J. et al. (2006), *The Costs of Substance Abuse in Canada 2002*, Canadian Centre on Substance Abuse, Ottawa.

Roman, P.M. and T.C. Blum (2002), "The Workplace and Alcohol Problem Prevention", *Alcohol Research & Health*, Vol. 26, pp. 49-57.

Rospenda, K.M., J.A. Richman and C.A. Shannon (2009), "Prevalence and Mental Health Correlates of Harassment and Discrimination in the Workplace: Results from a National Study", *Journal of Interpersonal Violence*, Vol. 24, pp. 819-843.

Ruhm, C.J. (1995), "Economic Conditions and Alcohol Problems", *Journal of Health Economics*, Vol. 14, pp. 583-603.

Ruhm, C.J. and W.E. Black (2002), "Does Drinking Really Decrease in Bad Times?', *Journal of Health Economics*, Vol. 21, pp. 659-678.

Sieck, C.J. and M. Heirich (2010), "Focusing Attention on Substance Abuse in the Workplace: A Comparison of Three Workplace Interventions", Journal of Workplace Behavioral Health, Vol. 25, pp. 72-87.

Slavit, W., A. Reagin and R.A. Finch (2009), "An Employer's Guide to Workplace Substance Abuse Stratetgies and Treatment Recommendations", Center for Prevention and Health Services, National Business Group on Health, Washington, DC.

Sloan, F.A. et al. (2000), "Drinkers, Drivers, and Bartenders: Balancing Private Choices and Public Accountability", University of Chicago Press, Chicago.

Spicer, R.S. and T. Miller (2005), "Impact of a Workplace Peer-focused Substance Abuse Prevention and Early Intervention Program", *Alcoholism: Clinical and Experimental Research*, Vol. 29, No. 4, pp. 609-611.

UNDESA – United National Department of Economic and Social Affairs (2007), *The Employment Imperative: Report on the World Social Situation 2007*, United Nations, New York.

Verstraete, A.G. and A. Pierce (2001), "Workplace Drug Testing in Europe", *Forensic Science International*, Vol. 121, No. 1-2, pp. 2-6.

Walters, S.T. and W. Woodall (2003), "Mailed Feedback Reduces Consumption Among Moderate Drinkers Who Are Employed", *Prevention Science*, Vol. 4, pp. 287-294.

Webb, G. et al. (2009), "A Systematic Review of Work-place Interventions for Alcohol-related Problems", *Addiction*, Vol. 104, pp. 365-377.

 

Tackling Harmful Alcohol Use
Economics and Public Health Policy


# Chapter 5

# Health and economic impacts of key alcohol policy options

by
Franco Sassi, Michele Cecchini, Marion Devaux, Roberto Astolfi

*Alcohol policies have significant potential to curb alcohol-related harms, improve health, increase productivity, reduce crime and violence, and cut government expenditure. The WHO Global Strategy to reduce the harmful use of alcohol provides a menu of policy options based on international consensus, which the OECD has used as a starting point in identifying a set of policies to be assessed in an economic analysis based on a computer simulation approach. The policies assessed in three country settings – Canada, the Czech Republic and Germany – include price policies, regulation and enforcement policies, education programmes and health care interventions. The results of the OECD analyses show that brief interventions in primary care, typically targeting high-risk drinkers, and tax increases, which affect all drinkers, have the potential to generate large health gains. The impacts of regulation and enforcement policies as well as other health care interventions are more dependent on the setting and mode of implementation, while school-based programmes show less promise. Alcohol policies have the potential to prevent alcohol-related disabilities and injuries in hundreds of thousands of working-age people in the countries examined, with major potential gains in their productivity. Most alcohol policies are estimated to cut health care expenditures to the extent that their implementation costs would be more than offset. Health care interventions and enforcement of drinking-and-driving restrictions are more expensive policies, but they still have very favourable cost-effectiveness profiles.*

## Key findings

- Policies to increase the prices of alcoholic drinks, regulation and enforcement policies, education programmes and health care interventions are all shown to be effective and efficient options for governments seeking to curb alcohol-related harms and improve population health, based on OECD analyses focusing on Canada, the Czech Republic and Germany.
- Several alcohol policies can reduce rates of heavy drinking, regular or episodic, and alcohol dependence, in the above three countries, by 5% to 10%, taking those countries a long way towards achieving the voluntary target of cutting harmful alcohol use by 10% by 2025, part of the Global NCD Monitoring Framework adopted by the World Health Assembly in 2013.
- The WHO Global Strategy to reduce the harmful use of alcohol was used as a starting point in identifying a set of policies to be assessed in an economic analysis. The inclusion or exclusion of specific policies in the analysis does not imply, *per se*, endorsement or rejection.
- If offered systematically in primary care settings, brief interventions have the potential to generate large health and life expectancy gains in Canada, the Czech Republic and Germany; a tax hike leading to an average increase of 10% in alcohol prices would also generate large impacts.
- Combining alcohol policies in a coherent prevention strategy would significantly increase projected impacts, according to OECD analyses.
- A package of fiscal and regulatory measures, one of health care interventions, and a mixed strategy would each achieve gains of around 37 000 DALYs per year in Canada; 23-29 000 DALYs in the Czech Republic and 119-137 000 DALYs in Germany.
- Alcohol strategies combining multiple policies would yield yearly savings in health expenditures of up to USD PPP 4, 8 and 6 per person, respectively, in the three countries.
- Policies delivered in health care settings are the most expensive to implement, followed by the enforcement of drinking-and-driving restrictions and workplace programmes. Price and regulatory policies are substantially less expensive.
- Savings in health care expenditure would be large enough to finance the implementation of several of the policies examined, but even the most expensive alcohol policies have favourable cost-effectiveness profiles.
- Almost 5% of working-age men in the Czech Republic, 3% in Germany and 1.5% in Canada could avoid alcohol-related disabilities each year if brief interventions were systematically offered in primary care settings. Lesser, but still substantial gains can be made with other alcohol policies.

## Assessing the impacts of alcohol policies

The chief goal of governments adopting alcohol policies is to curb the harmful use of alcohol, whether this goal is pursued by trying to prevent high-risk drinking behaviours or through more broadly-based measures affecting all drinkers. This chapter presents the findings of a detailed analysis of the impacts of a range of alcohol policy options in three countries – Canada, the Czech Republic and Germany – based on a computer simulation model described below in Box 5.1.

In this chapter, we first present evidence from previous economic evaluations of alcohol policies and discuss what it is reasonable to expect from model simulations. Consistently, the success of the alternative policy options presented in this chapter has been assessed in our analysis as the policies' ability to reduce the harms that may be caused by alcohol consumption. The main focus of the analysis is on the health impacts of alcohol and alcohol policies, measured in terms of years of life, or disability adjusted life years (DALYs), lived by people in a given national population over a period of 40 years. The forms of disability accounted for are exclusively those caused by the most important alcohol-related diseases and injuries, listed in Box 5.1, whose incidence, prevalence and fatality were also assessed in the analysis.

A brief overview of the alcohol policy landscape in Canada, the Czech Republic and Germany sets the background for our assessment of the impacts of alternative alcohol policies in the three countries, including the prevalence of hazardous and harmful drinkers (as defined by WHO), as well as the prevalence of heavy episodic drinking and alcohol dependence. In the same section, further policy impacts are illustrated in terms of average numbers of life years and DALYs potentially gained each year in the countries examined.

Alcohol policies aim to cut the incidence and fatality of a range of conditions for which alcohol consumption is a risk factor. Our analysis acknowledges that alcohol is only one contributor, and not the sole contributor, to those diseases, which would also exist in the absence of alcohol consumption (with the exception of alcohol use disorders, of course). It also accounts for the loss of some of the protective effects of alcohol on selected cardiovascular conditions when alcohol policies end up reducing moderate alcohol consumption in certain population groups (mostly older men).

A thorough assessment of policy impacts beyond health outcomes (e.g. labour and crime impacts) was not within the scope of our analysis. However, the ability of alcohol policies to increase employment and productivity is reflected in the larger number of years lived without alcohol-related disabilities by people of working age, which was assessed in the analysis.

Effective alcohol policies may prevent or postpone the occurrence of injuries and the onset of a range of chronic diseases linked with alcohol consumption. They may also reduce the likelihood that people who have already developed chronic diseases die because of their conditions. In all cases, there will be impacts on health care expenditure, largely hinging on government funds in most OECD countries, due to changes in the demand for treatments to address alcohol-related conditions and injuries. The sign and size of these impacts depend on the duration of the effects of policies on alcohol consumption, on the likelihood that people who have avoided alcohol-related conditions remain healthy over a prolonged period of time, and on how long people survive with chronic conditions. The combined effects of these factors are difficult to predict, but can be estimated using a simulation model, as we have done in our analysis for a range of alcohol policies. The corresponding estimates are presented in Section 5.8. However, these represent only one side of the expenditure impacts

### Box 5.1. **The CDP-Alcohol model**

The Chronic Disease Prevention, CDP-Alcohol, model was built to simulate population dynamics from individual characteristics and outcomes, including demographic and socioeconomic characteristics, patterns and levels of alcohol consumption, disease incidence and disease-specific mortality. The starting point of each simulation reflects the state of the relevant country in the year 2010, and the simulation projects the population forward for 40 years. In the design of the CDP-Alcohol model, special emphasis was placed on ensuring the relevance of the model to multiple country settings, such as its flexibility and adaptability to alternative demographic, epidemiological and policy contexts, and to different national patterns of alcohol use.

The model is designed as a Montecarlo semi-Markov discrete-event microsimulation model with a dynamic population. It is structured in discrete time and state transitions occur in yearly cycles. The model includes three main modules: a) a demographic module, which simulates births, deaths and migration flows; b) an alcohol consumption module, which simulates individual trajectories of drinking, including both levels and patterns of alcohol use; and c) a disease module, which simulates the onset and natural history of a range of alcohol-related conditions. This modular structure is illustrated in Figure A below. The model was developed using the software TreeAge Pro 2013 (Treeage Software Inc.) and compiled in Java©.

Figure A. **Basic structure of the CDP-Alcohol model**

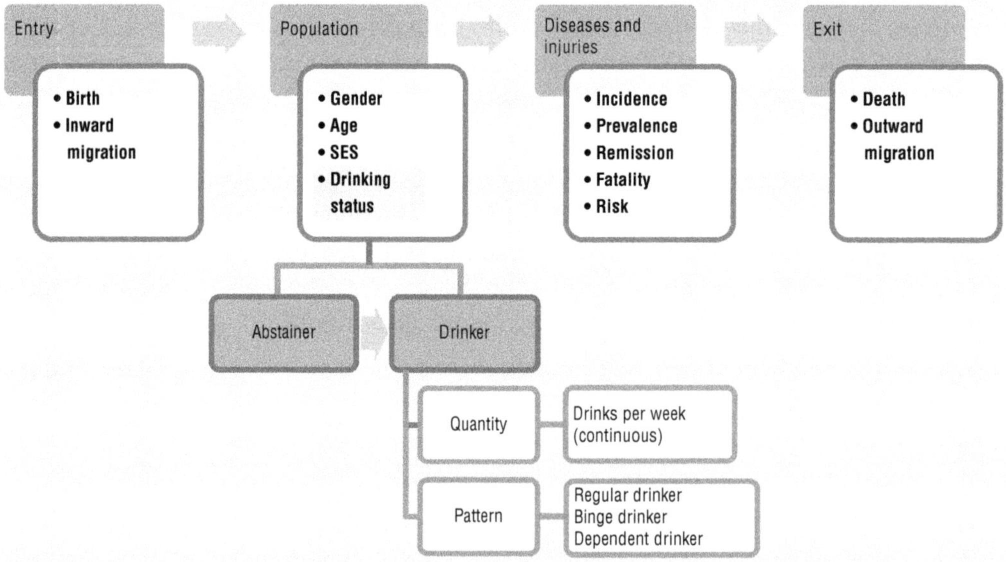


The initial population reflects the age and gender structure of the population in 2010, while population dynamics are based on future rates of birth, migration, and death reflecting official population projections for the country concerned. Alcohol consumption is the only (modifiable) risk factor simulated in the model. This was modelled along two dimensions: quantity of alcohol consumed (continuous number of drinks per week) and pattern of drinking (regular drinker, binge drinker, dependent drinker), based on evidence that patterns of drinking are at least as important as volume of drinking in the development of certain NCDs, such as alcohol use disorders (Rehm et al., 2003) and coronary heart disease (Rehm et al., 2003), as well as injuries. The model randomly assigns drinkers to patterns of drinking based on probability distributions modelled as a function

 

Box 5.1. **The CDP-Alcohol model** *(cont.)*

of age, gender, and quantity of alcohol drunk. All individuals are born abstainers in the simulation and remain such until age 10. Transition from the abstainer to the drinker state starts gradually at age 11 and ceases when age 26 is reached (statistically, drinking onset is very rare after age 25). Once they enter the drinking state, simulated individuals may reduce their alcohol consumption, even to zero, but will never return to the abstainer state. This is based on existing evidence that a large part of the risks (and possible benefits) of drinking persist for a significant period of time in quitters, so the latter cannot be fully assimilated to abstainers. Throughout the simulation, individuals may change their drinking behaviour and, therefore, their risk following country-specific algorithms derived from national survey data. In particular, alcohol consumption in a population is modelled to follow a negative binomial distribution (a zero-inflated negative binomial model was used for Canada), based on a gamma-Poisson mixture. In particular, the number of weekly drinks for each individual is determined on the basis of a Poisson distribution, in which the *lambda* parameter is a random function of the age, sex and socioeconomic status of each individual, following a gamma distribution. The current model does not distinguish between different types of alcohol (e.g. beer, wine, spirits, etc.) and places of consumption (e.g. on- and off-premises).

The CDP-alcohol model explicitly accounts for ten conditions whose incidence is affected by the volume and/or pattern of alcohol consumption. These include: alcohol use disorders; injuries; cirrhosis of the liver; liver cancer; epilepsy; ischaemic heart disease; cerebrovascular diseases; oesophagus cancer; mouth and oropharynx cancers and breast cancer, as shown in Figure B. According to the latest available WHO estimates at the time of designing the model (WHO, 2011) this group of diseases accounts for about 98% of DALYs lost and 93% of alcohol-related mortality

This means that some detrimental effects, as well as some protective effects, of alcohol use on human health have been left out, but the contribution (positive or negative) of these effects to the overall burden of disease is modest. An example of the beneficial effects of alcohol that are not accounted for in the analyses is type II diabetes, which recent evidence has found to be less likely to develop in light to moderate drinkers (Rubin, 2014). However, the latest WHO global burden of disease estimates show that the protective effects of alcohol on diabetes account for less than 0.5% of the burden of disease attributable to alcohol globally, and 1.3% in high-income and upper-middle-income countries, which is significantly less than the detrimental effects of alcohol use not accounted for in the selection of ten conditions included in the model. The beneficial health effects of alcohol that the model does account for are those related to ischaemic heart disease and ischaemic stroke. When alcohol policies affect drinkers' ability to enjoy those beneficial effects, this impact is reflected in the results of the simulations carried out with the CDP-Alcohol model through the relative risks for ischaemic events associated with regularly light and moderate alcohol use (typically smaller than 1). In future CDP-Alcohol analyses, the set of diseases explicitly modelled may be tailored to the disease burden profile of the countries concerned with additional advantages in terms of accuracy of the estimates of policy impacts.

Levels of disability associated with specific conditions are based on the disability weights originally used in the WHO (2008) global burden of disease study. Gender-, age- and disease-specific risks of death (i.e. mortality hazards) are conditional on the quantity and pattern of alcohol consumption, based on relative risks modelled on the basis of the best available evidence (data sources are listed in Annex A). Given the scarcity of evidence from existing epidemiological studies (Holmes et al., 2012), mortality and disease incidence could not be

### Box 5.1. **The CDP-Alcohol model** *(cont.)*

modelled as functions of past, or cumulative, alcohol consumption, but only as functions of current patterns and levels of consumption. For most conditions, this approach is likely to be appropriate (Anderson et al., 2012; Rehm et al., 2012), however, it is less appropriate for conditions like cancers, for which the effects of alcohol consumption, and changes thereof, tend to be delayed by several years. The possible implications of the approach used are briefly discussed in Section 5.4.

A baseline simulation scenario for each country projects current population, alcohol consumption and disease trends into the future, assuming constant policies. On the other hand, a number of policy scenarios project the outcomes of specific policy changes, based on existing evidence of the effectiveness of different policy options in changing individual levels and patterns of alcohol use. Each policy scenario is compared with the baseline scenario to estimate the net effects of policy changes. The model is designed to sample one person every 10 000 in the Canadian population, one in 25 000 in the German population, and one in 3 000 in the Czech population, in each simulation. However, since the degree of stochastic variation in the results generated by the model is large compared with the size of the effects produced by the policies examined, a high number of simulations were run for each country (more for countries with a larger population, i.e. 5 000 for the Czech Republic; 10 000 for Canada, and 20 000 for Germany), in order to increase the degree of confidence around the results estimated. The resulting confidence intervals are displayed in Figure 5.2 for each intervention.

Figure B. **Alcohol-related conditions included in the CDP-Alcohol model**

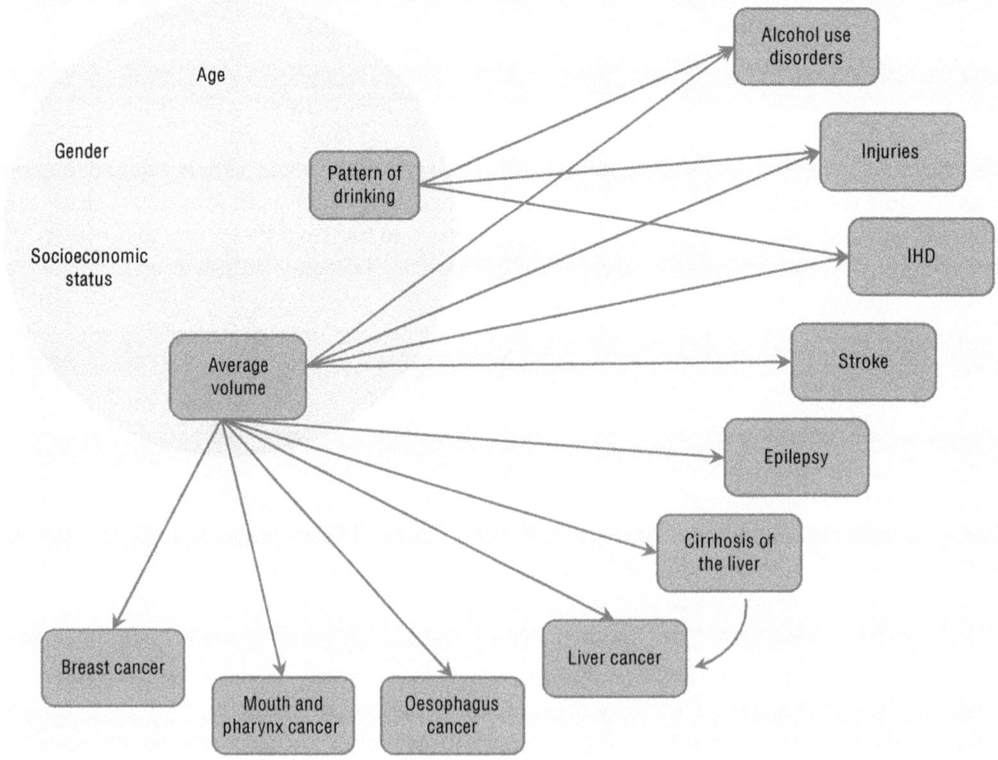


 

of alcohol policies, the other side consisting of the costs that governments typically bear in connection with the implementation of the same policies.

The metric most commonly used to assess the efficiency of government policies in the health sector is cost effectiveness, which provides the means to compare alternative budgetary allocations in terms of the health outcomes produced for the money spent. This approach was used in our analysis to compare alcohol policies between themselves and to other possible uses of health funds. The cost effectiveness of policies was estimated on the basis of implementation costs, net of any possible future savings in health care expenditures, and health outcomes, measured in terms of DALYs gained. A cost-effectiveness profile over time provides additional information for policy decisions, and additional means to compare the relative strengths and weaknesses of alternative policy options. Cost-effectiveness estimates and profiles over time are illustrated below for the alcohol policies examined.

The possible additive impact of combining a number of policies was assessed in the analysis, concluding that the results are broadly additive. The analysis looked at which groups benefit most from alcohol policies. Generally, men benefit more than women, but age also has a significant influence on the impact of various policies. Finally, the robustness of model findings was explored and some of the factors associated with success for alcohol policy are described in the final section of this chapter. In addition to benefits for heavy drinkers, the analysis provides evidence of substantial public health gains at the wider population level.

## What does previous evidence tell us?

In this section we summarise the findings of economic evaluations of alcohol policies available prior to the publication of this book. These evaluations identify price increases, restrictions of availability and bans on advertising as the three most cost-effective policies for reducing alcohol-related harms (Anderson, 2015; World Economic Forum and WHO, 2011). Not all alcohol policies have been found to be cost effective: there is insufficient evidence, in particular, on school-based programmes and mass media campaigns, whose effectiveness is not fully established (Anderson et al., 2009a). Much of the existing evidence, at the international level, is based on a WHO-CHOICE model developed by the World Health Organization in the early 2000s (e.g. Chisholm et al., 2004; Anderson et al., 2009a).

A large number of studies have shown that tax increases have the potential to reduce alcohol-related harms, deaths, costs to the health and criminal justice systems, and lost productivity (Österberg, 2011; Lai et al., 2007; Anderson et al., 2009a; Chisholm et al., 2004; Chisholm et al., 2006). The beneficial effects of tax increases can be diminished by illegal production, tax evasion and illegal trading in some jurisdictions. Reducing this unrecorded consumption via concerted tax enforcement strategies by law enforcement and excise officers has been estimated to cost more than a tax increase, and to produce similar levels of effect (Anderson et al., 2009a). To be effective, tax increases must accommodate changes in the affordability of alcohol compared with other goods (Rabinovich et al., 2009). Targeted taxes on specific types of alcohol are less supported by existing evidence (Anderson et al., 2012). Setting a floor price for alcoholic beverages was also found to be an effective and cost-effective policy option in reducing alcohol-related harm, capable of preventing heavy drinking, both regular and episodic (Purshouse et al., 2010; Stockwell et al., 2012).

Restricting the availability of alcohol by reducing the number of hours alcohol is on sale has been shown to cut violence and damage, assaults and murders, in a cost-effective way (Anderson et al., 2009a; Chisholm et al., 2004; Chisholm et al., 2006). Some economic analyses also show that advertising bans can be effective, provided that these are applied comprehensively (Anderson, 2009; Anderson et al., 2009a; Chisholm et al., 2004; Chisholm et al., 2006).

Brief interventions within the health system have been shown to be cost effective, but more expensive than population-wide strategies (Anderson et al., 2009a; Chisholm et al., 2004, 2006; Vos et al., 2010). Enforcement of drinking-and-driving legislation and measures such as random breath-testing campaigns have also been shown in a number of modelling studies in different country settings to be cost effective (Anderson, 2009; Anderson et al., 2009a; Chisholm et al., 2004; Chisholm et al., 2006; Chisholm et al., 2012; Vos et al., 2010).

A public health alcohol strategy that combines a number of effective interventions is shown to generate additional health benefits while still remaining cost effective (Anderson, 2009; Anderson et al., 2009a; Chisholm et al., 2004, 2006).

### *Previous modelling studies*

An empirical assessment of the impacts of prevention strategies through appropriately designed experimental studies is virtually impossible in most instances. Causal inference based on observational data is also difficult, because of the heterogeneous information on possible interventions contained in such studies and the variety of concurrent factors that confound the possible effects of policies. A data-driven approach that captures the mid- and long-term impacts of prevention strategies, quantifying ranges of uncertainty around them, and isolating these impacts from the effects of potential confounding factors, while at the same time accounting for the heterogeneity of actors, exposures and behaviours, are key steps to an accurate and thorough assessment of the value of prevention. The use of simulation models is especially common in an area in which a large part of policy impacts tend to occur in the medium-to-long term, thus making it difficult, if not impossible, to use an experimental design and empirical observation to ascertain the effects of alcohol policies.

In addition to the WHO-CHOICE model discussed above, the following have been used in the assessment of alcohol policies.

- Australia's ACE-Prevention programme (Cobiac et al., 2009) is aimed at testing a number of primary and secondary prevention policies for major risk factors and diseases in a consistent framework. ACE-Prevention analyses of alcohol policies concluded that taxation policies are supported by strong evidence of effectiveness and can be cost saving. Weaker evidence was found for advertising bans and for an increase in legal drinking age to 21, but, if effective, these would also be cost saving. Brief interventions in primary care, licensing controls and roadside breath testing were found to be effective and cost-effective interventions, whereas evidence in support of mass media campaigns against drinking-and-driving was more limited.
- The Chronic Disease Model (CDM), developed by the Dutch National Institute for Public Health and the Environment, was used to examine the links between alcohol use and a small set of diseases, including CVD and cancer (oral cavity, larynx, oesophagus, breast), and total mortality. Different tax hikes were shown by CDM analyses to be cost effective, relative to taxation levels in use in the Netherlands in 2008, and so was the use of brief interventions, with cost-effectiveness ratios marginally exceeding EUR 5 000 per QALY gained (van den Berg et al., 2008; Tariq et al., 2009).
- Dynamo-HIA is primarily a health impact assessment model. It was used to estimate the impacts of tax increases in EU countries over a ten year period, showing that price increases up to prevailing price levels in Finland would lead to major health gains, but cost effectiveness was not assessed (Lhachimi et al., 2012).

- The Sheffield Alcohol Policy Model was widely used, especially in England and Scotland, for the assessment of the impacts of a range of alcohol policies, including taxation, minimum unit prices, discount bans, brief interventions and others. The Sheffield model has many unique features, including its ability to simulate detailed drinking patterns and their impacts on a variety of chronic and acute diseases. In addition, it accounts for policy effects on domains other than health, including crime and the labour market (e.g. Meier et al., 2010; Purshouse et al., 2010).

## What we can (and cannot) learn from a simulation model

An individual-based, population-wide simulation modelling approach can provide a sound basis for evaluating the relative effectiveness and cost effectiveness of a range of alcohol prevention and control strategies, overcoming the limitations of other approaches. A comprehensive alcohol policy model can generate consistent estimates of resource inputs, costs and outcomes. A case-based microsimulation approach, in particular, offers the best opportunity to model realistic individual life trajectories, taking into consideration the heterogeneity in populations and in individual behaviours that can influence the harm possibly caused by drinking, as well as the relative effectiveness of policies across population groups. Such models capture the complex set of inter-relationships between the prior history and current use of, and demand for, alcohol and the resulting distribution of health, social and economic consequences.

The international dimension of the OECD analysis addresses a broader range of individual, social, environmental and policy factors than any national-level analysis could account for. As in the case of the analyses of policy options to tackle obesity, unhealthy diets and physical inactivity, previously undertaken by the OECD (e.g. Sassi, 2010; Cecchini et al., 2010), a comparison of policy impacts across countries with different characteristics and drinking patterns can provide unique insights on what dimensions are especially likely to determine the returns to be expected from the implementation of those policies. This is particularly important in the case of alcohol policies, because different historical, social and economic factors have led to considerable variability across countries in the treatment of alcohol and the policy approaches used to control alcohol-related harm.

What constitutes the main strength of models, i.e. their ability to separate the effects of policies from potential confounders, may also be seen as a weakness by those who look for predictions in model outputs. Predicting the future is not the purpose of policy models, precisely because many of the factors that are held constant in a simulation, in order to identify policy effects, are bound to change in real life situations, acting as confounders that make real outcomes differ from model outputs. The value of the latter lies in their ability to estimate the incremental effect of policies on the outcomes of interest, independent of the changes that will occur in other factors.

Models typically make the most of available data from a potentially large range of sources, but they cannot replace data when these do not exist. Sometimes assumptions have to be made, which will unavoidably contribute to determining model outputs. In the policy model used here, some of the data that would ideally be used as inputs simply do not exist, and even assumptions would have been difficult to make. For instance, there is no solid evidence of the longitudinal links between consumption of alcohol and many of the diseases considered in the analysis, including time lags between drinking and disease development (as acknowledged in Holmes et al., 2012). Similarly, there is no direct evidence of changes in illicit production and trade of alcohol following changes in market prices of the type and size, for instance, of those caused by tax hikes or the setting of minimum prices. Information on patterns of drinking of different alcoholic beverages, and places of consumption, is also generally unavailable at the individual level, which limits the ability of microsimulation models to capture these dimensions of alcohol use.

In other instances, data may not be available for specific countries or population groups, but reliable proxies can be used instead. An example is relative risks of disease incidence, or fatality, whose best estimates tend to be from meta-analyses of studies typically undertaken in a variety of settings (e.g. Corrao et al., 2004). Although, strictly speaking, these estimates do not reflect relative risks in any specific country, they are dependable proxies, assuming that no major differences exist between countries in such relative risks. A similar reasoning applies, for instance, to alcohol price elasticity estimates, used in the assessment of the impacts of changes in taxation. While country-specific estimates are sometimes available from local studies, the statistical strength of existing large-scale meta-analyses suggests that the latter are more likely to reliably predict the impacts of price changes on alcohol consumption, on average.

Our analysis evaluates alcohol policies over 40 years, which is long relative to the typical time horizon of most policy decisions, but short relative to the time required for some policies to produce their full effects (e.g. policies aimed at children and young adults), so some of the longer-term impacts of the policies examined may not be fully captured in the analysis. Other dimensions of policy impacts that are not captured in our analysis are those related to crime, violence, employment and labour productivity, as well as the possible welfare consequences of policies aimed at changing alcohol consumption by altering market conditions (e.g. prices).

## A new assessment: The policy options

The WHO Global Strategy to reduce the harmful use of alcohol provides a menu of policy options based on international consensus, which OECD used as a starting point in identifying a set of policies to be assessed in an economic analysis based on a computer simulation approach. However, not all types of policies discussed in the Global Strategy lend themselves to a quantitative economic analysis. In particular, certain actions (e.g. monitoring and surveillance) are important in the context of an overall strategy to fight alcohol-related harms, but have only indirect effects on alcohol consumption and harms, and these effects are very difficult to measure or estimate. Other actions have been shown to be effective in reducing alcohol-related harms, but their effectiveness was determined only in qualitative studies, often based on heterogeneous outcomes, not suitable for inclusion in a quantitative modelling framework. Of the remaining actions, some are supported by stronger evidence of effectiveness than others from existing studies.

Therefore, the analysis presented here focuses on a subset of the policy options discussed in the Global Strategy and in the current policy debate, without implying that the inclusion of a policy in the set of those assessed corresponds to an endorsement of the policy. The selection of policies is the result of extended consultations with OECD member countries and relevant stakeholders, primarily within the context of the OECD Expert Group on the Economics of Prevention and the OECD Health Committee. The aim of the selection is not to devise an alternative policy agenda to that endorsed by WHO, but simply to focus the subsequent analysis on policies for which a meaningful assessment can be made. The policy options selected are shown in Table 5.1. The six policy options included in the main analysis, in bold characters in the table, are those for which a stronger and more consistent evidence of effectiveness is available, generally in the form of systematic reviews and meta-analyses of large numbers of high-quality individual studies. The remaining three policy options, assessed in a further analysis, feature prominently in the current debate, but have been assessed in a smaller number of studies (minimum price policies) or in a large number of studies but with inconsistent results (school-based programmes and workplace interventions). Our assessment of the existing evidence builds upon previous comprehensive reviews (e.g. Babor et al., 2010; CDC's Guide to Community Preventive Services[1]), individual studies, systematic reviews and meta-analyses of the effectiveness of alternative alcohol policy options.

Table 5.1. **Alcohol policy options assessed in the analysis**

| *Target* | Price policies | Regulation/enforcement | Education | Health care |
|---|---|---|---|---|
| *All consumption* | **Tax increase** | **Advertising regulation** | | |
| *Heavy use / dependence* | Minimum price | | School-based programmes | **Brief interventions treatment of dependence** |
| | | | | Workplace interventions |
| *Injuries* | | **Drinking-and-driving restrictions** | | |
| | | **Opening hours regulation** | | |

*Note*: Policies in bold are those included in the main analysis; other policies are part of a further analysis.

## *Making alcohol less affordable*

### *Price increases*

Governments wishing to curb alcohol-related harms often choose to employ policies to make alcohol less affordable, including *increasing existing taxes* levied on alcoholic beverages. The policy scenario assessed in the analysis consists of a change in existing alcohol taxation arrangements, which would generate an average price increase of 10% at the point of consumption across all alcoholic beverages. Alcohol taxation systems and rates vary widely across countries; therefore, no specific assumptions were made on how the above price increases would be achieved, e.g. whether by increasing excise duty rates, by modifying other existing taxes, or by introducing new fiscal measures. In the implementation of a similar policy at the country level, multiple changes would likely be required in alcohol taxation in order to obtain a 10% price increase across all alcoholic beverages, given that beverages are often taxed differently, and taxes tend to be passed on to consumers at different rates for different beverages, partly depending on where they are typically or predominantly consumed. The policy scenario also entails increased law enforcement efforts to prevent the spread of tax avoidance and consumption of unrecorded alcohol, including from illicit trade and informal and illicit production. Consistently with available evidence, the tax increase is assumed to translate almost immediately into an increase in the price of alcoholic beverages (Young and Bielinska–Kwapisz, 2002).

Several high-quality systematic reviews and meta-analyses examine the link between alcohol prices and levels of drinking (Dhalwani, 2011; Elder et al., 2010; Gallet., 2007; Fogarty, 2008; Wagenaar et al., 2009; Wagenaar et al., 2010; Nelson, 2013a). The modelling of this intervention in CDP-Alcohol is mainly based on two studies. Price elasticity values are derived from a meta-analysis of 112 studies that took into account more than 1000 different estimates (Wagenaar et al., 2009) while the effect of gender and age groups have been calculated on a different meta-analysis, which provides a more detailed account of the effects of a number of individual characteristics on price elasticity (Gallett, 2007). Based on studies that show a further reduced response of harmful drinkers to price changes (Ayyagari et al., 2013; Nelson, 2013b), an alternative scenario was developed to test the sensitivity of model outputs to assumptions regarding price elasticities.

A 10% increase in the price of all alcoholic drinks sold in a country is assumed to produce a decrease in consumption ranging from 1.7% for young men who drink alcohol at harmful levels, to 6% for adult women (age 25-59) who are moderate drinkers, as shown in Table 5.2. These estimates are at the conservative end of elasticity ranges used in other modelling studies (e.g. Meier, 2008; Lai et al., 2007). Effects on individual drinkers are randomly determined on the basis of a normal distribution, whose mean equals the above elasticities. In the sensitivity analysis scenario, the price responsiveness of harmful drinkers (men and women, of all ages) was cut to one tenth of the values used in the main taxation scenario (e.g. assuming a 0.17% change in consumption for young male harmful drinkers).

Table 5.2. **Price elasticity values used in CDP-Alcohol main analyses**

| Age | Men, not harmful drinkers | Women, not harmful drinkers | Men, harmful drinkers | Women, harmful drinkers |
|---|---|---|---|---|
| Under-25 | -0.029 | -0.042 | -0.017 | -0.024 |
| 25-59 | -0.042 | -0.060 | -0.024 | -0.035 |
| 60 and over | -0.041 | -0.059 | -0.024 | -0.034 |

*Source:* Adapted from Wagenaar, A.C., M.J. Salois and K.A. Komro (2009), "Effects of Beverage Alcohol Price and Tax Levels on Drinking: A Meta-analysis of 1003 Estimates from 112 Studies", *Addiction*, Vol. 104, No. 2, pp. 179-190;, and Gallet, C.A. (2007), "The Demand for Alcohol: A Meta-analysis of Elasticities", *Australian Journal of Agricultural and Resource Economics*, Vol. 7, No. 51, pp. 121-135.

StatLink http://dx.doi.org/10.1787/888933180426

The estimated cost of an increase in taxation (shown in Table A.7 in Annex A) includes basic administration, planning, monitoring and enforcement at the national level, with the latter accounting for most of the total cost. Additional tax revenues are not accounted for in the analysis as they represent transfers rather than costs. Nonetheless, these revenues may be substantial.

### *Minimum prices*

An alternative policy measure taken by some governments to make alcohol less affordable involves the *setting of floor (minimum) prices* for alcoholic beverages. The modelled scenario consists of the setting, or raising (for countries that have already adopted the policy), of minimum prices for all alcoholic beverages. This policy would be designed to produce a 10% increase in current minimum price levels, or in the prices of the lowest-priced alcoholic beverages relative to their prevailing market prices in national markets. The policy is typically designed to affect only the cheapest segment of the alcohol market, unlike tax increases, however, relatively to the latter it would have the additional effect of preventing price promotions below the set minimum price levels. The implementation of this policy includes law enforcement efforts to ensure that minimum prices are consistently applied and to prevent increases in illicit trade and informal and illicit production of alcoholic beverages.

Most of the evidence available on the effectiveness of minimum price policies is from studies carried out in the Canadian provinces of British Columbia (Stockwell et al., 2012a) and Saskatchewan (Stockwell et al., 2012b) exploiting the variation associated with sequential minimum price adjustments over the periods 1989-2010 and 2008-12, respectively. By employing time series and longitudinal models of aggregate alcohol consumption, Stockwell and colleagues estimated by how much a 10% hike in minimum prices decreased the consumption of different alcoholic beverages, as well as alcohol-related deaths (Zhao et al., 2013) and hospitalisations (Stockwell et al., 2013). A study based on the Sheffield Alcohol Policy Model also investigated the effects of changes in minimum prices in British Columbia, producing slightly more conservative estimates than the above studies (Hill-McManus et al., 2012). The Sheffield model, however, was primarily used to predict the impacts of alcohol policies, minimum unit prices, in Scotland and in England. Price elasticities were estimated from survey data for different population groups and alcoholic beverages. Estimates were then used to assess the potential effects of different minimum unit price options, ranging from 0.20 to 0.70 GBP in England (e.g. Purshouse et al., 2010) and Scotland (e.g. Meng et al., 2012).

Stockwell et al. (2012a) estimated that a 10% minimum price increase in British Columbia would produce a decrease in the consumption of spirits and liqueurs by 6.8%, of wine by 8.9%, of alcoholic sodas and ciders by 13.9%, of beer by 1.5%, and of all alcoholic drinks by 3.4 %. Estimates based on data from Saskatchewan (Stockwell et al., 2012b) show that a 10% minimum price increase would produce a reduction in beer consumption by 10.1%, of spirits by 5.9%, of wine by 4.6%, and of all beverages combined by 8.4%. In CDP-Alcohol analyses, the overall effectiveness of this intervention was modelled based on the lower effectiveness estimated in the two Canadian provinces (that of British Columbia). Effects were differentiated by drinking group based on estimates derived from the work of the University of Sheffield on the potential impact of minimum prices in England, particularly with regard to differences in drinkers' responses to a minimum unit price of GBP 0.50, to fit with the average effect calculated for British Columbia. Therefore, the overall reduction in alcohol consumption was assumed to be 1.7% for moderate drinkers, 2.9% for hazardous drinkers, and 6.4% for harmful drinkers.

The estimated total cost for this intervention (shown in Table A.7 in Annex A) includes basic administration, planning, monitoring and enforcement at the national level, with the latter accounting for the largest share of the total cost.

### *Regulating access to, use of, and marketing of alcohol*

#### *Regulating alcohol advertising*

For governments intending to tackle harmful alcohol use, regulating alcohol advertising can be a policy challenge, because of the sheer scale of spending on advertising, and because of the increasing use of media (e.g. Internet, social networks) that tend to fall outside the scope of traditional forms of regulation. The *advertising regulation policy* scenario is not modelled as a comprehensive ban, but as a series of regulatory measures that would lead to a 25% reduction in advertising expenditure, limiting exposure to alcohol advertising for different types of consumers. This regulatory intervention assumes that restrictions would be applied to traditional and new media, sponsorships, branding and point-of-sale displays. Enforcement would be ensured by existing regulatory authorities, as the necessary infrastructures are already in place in most OECD countries.

Five systematic reviews (Anderson et al., 2009b; Bryden et al., 2012; Meier, 2008; Pinsky and El Jundi, 2008; Smith and Foxcroft, 2009) and two meta-analyses (Gallet, 2007; Nelson, 2011) provide ample evidence of the impacts of changes in alcohol advertising. One set of studies calculate the elasticity of alcohol consumption to changes in industry spending on advertising. A second set of studies exploit longitudinal data to estimate how certain groups of people (often teenagers) change their drinking patterns following changes in exposure to alcohol advertising. A new Cochrane systematic review of the effects of restrictions or bans of alcohol advertising concluded that only four studies met the strict methodological criteria required for inclusion. The authors found that these four studies do not provide robust evidence for or against alcohol advertising restriction (Siegfrid et al., 2014).

We modelled this intervention on data from a meta-analysis of 322 estimates of advertising elasticities by Gallet (2007), and from a study by Saffer and Dave (2006). Existing studies indicate that a 25% decrease in advertising expenditure is expected to produce a 0.8% decrease in alcohol demand (Gallet, 2007). However, there is evidence that young people are more responsive to changes in alcohol advertising (Anderson, 2009). So, in CDP-Alcohol analyses, their response was modelled on the basis of a study by Saffer and Dave (2006) reporting elasticities of 0.034 and 0.065, respectively, for any drinking and for binge drinking during the past month. For the modelled intervention, the above elasticities translate into a 0.84% reduction of average consumption in young drinkers, and a 1.6% reduction in the number of binge drinkers (all ages). These assumptions are in line, or more conservative, than those used in previous model-based studies. For instance, Chisholm et al. (2004) assumed that a comprehensive advertising ban would lead to a 2%-4% reduction in the incidence of hazardous alcohol use, while a study using the Sheffield Alcohol Policy Model (Meier, 2008) estimated the effects of partial and total advertising bans assuming 5% and 9% reductions in overall consumption, respectively, in line with Saffer and Dave (2002).

The estimated the cost of this intervention (shown in Table A.7 in Annex A) involves basic administration and planning costs at the national and local levels. In addition, minor training may be required for the regulatory authority staff charged with the task of overseeing the implementation of the scheme. Finally, our estimation includes the cost of monitoring and enforcing the new regulation which is the most expensive component of the intervention.

### *Alcohol limits for drivers*

An area that is heavily regulated in OECD countries is the driving of motor vehicles after drinking alcoholic beverages. However, the enforcement of these regulations is haphazard and varies widely both within and between countries. The policy scenario modelled in the analysis involves a tightening of the *enforcement of drinking-and-driving restrictions*. The design of the policy is based on the example of a sobriety checkpoint programme implemented in Charlottesville (Virgina, United States), thoroughly described and evaluated in a published study (Voas, 2008). The programme involved five-officer checkpoint teams working four hours per night to stop and test drivers on weekend nights (Friday and Saturday) each week. Sites were chosen in advance and signs warned drivers of the checkpoints and breath testing. In one year, 94 checkpoints operations were conducted, for a total of 1 880 hours of work for the officers concerned. Around 24 000 vehicles were stopped and 290 drivers were arrested.

One meta-analysis (Erke et al., 2009) and one systematic review (Shults et al., 2001) provide a basis for modelling the impacts of checkpoint and breath testing programmes. Among the various outcomes reported in existing studies, we selected road traffic fatalities as the main outcome in the analysis of population-level impacts, because evidence of the effects of such programmes on average alcohol consumption is weaker. The meta-analysis by Erke et al. (2009) concludes that both the establishment of new programmes and the strengthening of existing programmes are similarly effective, which indicates that health gains can be made even in countries where programmes are already in place. However, the same meta-analysis also concludes that the effectiveness of these programmes declines over time, from a peak of effectiveness within three months from the start of the programme to progressively weaker effects which tend to stabilise after a few years.

Finally, Erke et al. make a rare effort to correct their findings for publication bias, which leads to lower, but still statistically significant, estimates of effectiveness. Shults (2001) provides estimates of fatal and non-fatal outcomes, as well as an assessment of feasibility and possible unintended effects.

Sobriety checkpoints were found to be most effective in the first half year (Erke et al., 2009). The decline in traffic accidents over time, as estimated in the above meta-analysis, started from 29% after three months, decreasing to 21% at 6 months, and becoming almost stable between years 1 and 8 (with estimates ranging from 13% to 11%). Decreases in fatal crashes and all crashes reported by Erke et al. (15% and 19%, respectively) are broadly in line with those reported by Shults et al. (2001) who estimated decreases of fatal crashes between 20% and 26% with SBT, and between 13% and 36% (median 22%) with random breath testing. In our analysis, a corresponding reduction in traffic-related injuries (fatal and non-fatal, in constant proportions), equivalent to 22% in the first year, 8.9% in the second year, and 7.9% thereafter, was applied assuming coverage of 80% of the population.

The estimated costs of enforcement are shown in Table A.7 in Annex A. The most expensive item is the manning of checkpoints. A media campaign is assumed to be part of the policy intervention.

### *Licensing of alcohol sale outlets*

A further area in which governments currently take measures aimed at reducing alcohol-related harms is the licensing of alcohol sale outlets. Licensing allows governments to control where, when and in what forms alcohol is sold to the public. A policy scenario was modelled, which entails *restrictions in on-trade outlet opening hours* leading to a two-hour reduction, with a view to cutting the incidence of alcohol-related injuries, particularly from assaults and traffic accidents. This policy was assumed to target the most densely populated areas of the countries concerned, corresponding to medium- and large-sized cities. The policy scenario involves increased enforcement efforts by the relevant licensing and law enforcement authorities.

Three systematic reviews are available (Popova et al., 2009; Hahn et al., 2010; Bryden et al., 2012), reporting a variety of study approaches and outcome measures. A modelling study by Chisholm et al. (2004), also used as a basis for modelling the impact of restrictions in opening hours in the context of the ACE Prevention project (Cobiac et al., 2009), quantified the likely effect of this policy on the basis of three northern European studies assessing the effects of Saturday closing (Leppanen, 1979; Nordlund, 1984) or Saturday opening (Norström and Skog, 2003) of (off-trade) outlets in State monopoly settings. A subsequent update of the Norström and Skog study (Norström and Skog, 2005) showed effects in line with their earlier evaluation (an increase in alcohol sales of 3.6%). On average, Chisholm et al. determined that the policy will likely generate a "modest reduction of 1.5%-3.0 % in the incidence of hazardous drinking, and 1.5%-4.0% in alcohol related traffic fatalities". Given the uncertainties in effects on alcohol consumption, our analysis focused on impacts on injuries (traffic- and violence-related), for which the evidence is stronger and more consistent, as shown in a review by Stockwell and Chikritzhs (2009), and by at least two later studies (Kypri et al., 2011; Rossow and Norström, 2011).

Based on the study by Rossow and Norström (2011), the impact of a 2-hour reduction in on-trade outlet opening hours was assumed to be a 34% reduction in assault-related injuries. In addition, a 1.5% reduction in traffic-related injuries was modelled, at the lower end of the range used by Chisholm et al. (2004). The policy was assumed to be implemented in medium- and large-sized cities (with a population of over 30 000), corresponding to an overall population coverage ranging from 68% in Canada to 74% in Germany.

The estimated the cost of this intervention (shown in Table A.7 in Annex A) includes basic administration at local level and law enforcement. Enforcement of the new regulations represents the most expensive component of the intervention.

### *Educating young people*

Educating young people, particularly during their school years, about healthy lifestyles is an established public health priority. The policy scenario modelled in the analysis involves the delivery of a *skill-based educational programme for secondary school students* aged 13, during a period of two years. The scenario is modelled after Australia's School Health and Alcohol Harm Reduction Project (Mc Bride et al., 2000; McBride et al., 2004). During the first year, the programme consists of 17 skill-based activities conducted over 8-10 sessions. This is followed, in the second year, by 12 additional activities over a period of 5-7 weeks. All of the activities involved require active participation and place emphasis on identifying the harms potentially linked with alcohol consumption and ways to prevent them. Approaches used include, among others, the discussion of scenarios and small-group decision making. Students are provided with a workbook and watch a trigger video at the beginning of the second year. School teachers involved in the project undergo a two-day preparatory training. Teachers are also provided with a manual, which contains detailed information on all the activities of the project.

A large body of evidence is available on the effectiveness of this intervention, including nine meta-analyses (Bangert-Drowns, 1988; Bruvold, 1988; Ennet et al., 1994; Rundall and Bruvold, 1988; Tobler, 1986; Tobler, 1992; Tobler and Stratton, 1997; Tobler et al., 2000; Wilson et al., 2001), two Cochrane reviews (Foxcroft et al., 2002; Foxcroft and Tsertsvadze, 2012) and one review of reviews (Jones et al., 2007). Distilling an overall conclusion from this literature is difficult, because studies in this area tend to assess very different outcomes (e.g. knowledge, intention to change, change in behaviour), and interventions tend to tackle harmful alcohol use along with other unhealthy behaviours (usually tobacco and/or drugs). Overall, the existing evidence provides relatively weak support for the use of school-based programmes, although programmes centred on enhancing basic skills such as critical thinking and resistance to social influences (e.g. Spoth et al., 2008) show greater promise (Foxcroft and Tsertsvadze, 2012; Scott-Sheldon et al., 2014)). The final intervention was modelled on the School Health and Alcohol Harm Reduction Project (SHARP), an Australian skill-based programme (McBride et al., 2000; McBride et al., 2004).

The modelled approach was shown to be effective in improving risk awareness and drinking attitudes, with a reduction in alcohol consumption, heavy episodic drinking (more than 2/4 standard drinks per occasion for girls/boys) and harm (Mc Bride et al., 2000; McBride et al., 2004). Effects were assumed to peak at age 14 (-36% in alcohol consumption and -35% in heavy episodic drinking) and to taper off and disappear by age 17. Other studies have suggested that school-based programmes may have some longer-term effects (e.g. Skara and Sussman, 2003), but, overall, the evidence remains weak (Strøm et al., 2014).

The estimated cost of the modelled programme (shown in Table A.7 in Annex A) reflects the cost of scaling up an intervention like SHARP at the national level. The single largest cost item is extra teaching hours (based on an average of seven hours of extra teaching per class of 26 students), followed by equipment for skill-based activities. Teachers are assumed to be trained at the beginning of the project, with booster sessions every five years.

 

## *The role of health professionals*

### *Screening and brief interventions*

Effective health care services are available for heavy drinkers, to prevent them from developing dependence and further adverse health outcomes. A *programme of screening and brief interventions in primary care* was assessed as part of the analysis. The programme is assumed to target harmful drinkers (regular or episodic), but who are not alcohol dependent, aged 18-70 (Kaner et al., 2009). Dependent users, eligible for the drug and counselling intervention, or patients already on a treatment programme are not eligible (Anderson et al., 2012). The intervention typically targets people who are not seeking treatment for alcohol abuse, therefore recruitment typically occurs opportunistically by screening patients who visit a health care facility for a non-alcohol-related problem (Kaner et al., 2009). Significant barriers exist currently in many countries that limit a widespread adoption of brief interventions. These barriers need to be addressed in order for these interventions to have a greater impact on harmful alcohol use at the population level.

Screening is by questionnaire (AUDIT or equivalent) requesting information on health status and alcohol consumption, either delivered on the spot or mailed to the patient's address. Given levels of health care coverage and the likelihood of regularly seeing a general practitioner in the countries concerned, it is assumed that, each year, people in the relevant age group would have a 40% probability of being asked to complete a screening questionnaire, if the programme were offered systematically at all general practices in the country. After accounting for non-compliance with screening or intervention (based on Kaner et al., 2009), it is estimated that each year 30% of those who meet the criteria will receive the intervention, corresponding, for instance, to 6.2% of all men and women in the age group 18-70 in Canada (and larger proportions in Germany and the Czech Republic, where harmful drinking is more common).

The intervention was modelled after the "brief lifestyle counselling" option in the English Screening and Intervention Programme for Sensible drinking (SIPS) trial (Kaner et al., 2013). During an initial five-minute session, a general practitioner explains the potential harm caused by drinking and suggests practical strategies to reduce alcohol consumption highlighting the benefits of the recommended behaviour change. Printed materials (self-help leaflet, booklet to report consumption and a visual to compare own consumption with the average) are handed to participants. Structured lifestyle counselling would be delivered during a 20-minute follow-up appointment with a trained health professional.

At least two, partly overlapping, systematic reviews and meta-analyses provide solid evidence of the effectiveness of brief interventions in primary care (Kaner et al., 2009; Jonas et al., 2012). The primary care setting has been selected based on the availability of stronger evidence of effectiveness than for emergency care (Nielsen et al., 2008), general hospital settings (McQueen et al., 2011), e-interventions (Khadjesari et al., 2010; Sullivan et al., 2011) and obstetric or antenatal care (Doggett et al., 2009). Our analysis focuses on brief interventions, as opposed to extended interventions, because the latter were found to produce a non-significantly larger reduction in alcohol consumption (Kaner et al., 2009), and on non-dependent drinkers, as the effectiveness of brief interventions in dependent drinkers has not been established (Saitz, 2010).

During the course of a brief intervention, male drinkers are assumed, for the purpose of the modelling exercise, to reduce their alcohol consumption by 57 grams/week (i.e. about six standard drinks) and female drinkers by ten grams/week, in line with

Kaner et al. (2009). Evidence about the long-term effectiveness of the intervention suggests a limited persistence. A Cochrane review of studies in hospital settings (McQueen et al., 2011) found "no significant difference between the groups at one year follow up". Likewise, other studies (Burge et al., 1997; Wutzke et al., 2002) found a benefit until the 9th month after the intervention but no significant difference after 12-18 months. Based on these studies and a recent meta-analysis (Jonas et al., 2012), we modelled a linearly declining effectiveness, vanishing one year after the end of the intervention.

The estimated costs of screening and brief interventions (shown in Table A.7 in Annex A) include health professionals' time (general practitioners and nurses), delivery of printed materials, basic administration, monitoring, and training for doctors and nurses delivering the intervention.

### *Increase coverage of alcohol dependence treatment*

Alcohol dependence is associated with a large burden of disease, and effective treatments are available to reduce this burden. The modelled intervention is designed to *increase the coverage of alcohol dependence treatment*, based on a combination of pharmacological and psychosocial therapy, targeting people aged between 18 and 65 who fulfil the diagnostic criteria of alcohol dependence or alcohol abuse according to the Diagnostic and Statistical Manual of Mental Disorders (DSM) or the International Statistical Classification of Diseases (ICD). Candidates are recruited on an opportunistic basis (Morley et al., 2006).

It is currently estimated that only between 10% and 20% of individuals with alcohol dependence are diagnosed and, of these, only 10% receive treatment (WHO, 2008; VisionGain, 2008). The intervention is assumed to raise the probability of receiving treatment for someone who develops alcohol dependence by 8%, representing at least a twofold increase in current levels of medical treatment of alcohol dependence. For instance, the number of people with alcohol dependence currently receiving treatment in Germany is estimated at 297 000 (Kraus et al., 2014), while the modelled intervention would initially increase this number by approximately 250 000, with further increases in subsequent years.

When treated once, patients are assumed to have three in four chances of receiving treatment again in case of a new episode of alcohol dependence. Dependent drinkers undergoing the treatment are first detoxified and must avoid alcohol intake for a period of three to seven days. After this, they undergo a three-month therapy with the drug Naltrexone (50 mg/day) combined with a psychosocial programme. The first, 20 minute-long, psychosocial intervention is carried out by a specialist doctor in a primary care setting and involves a medical assessment and a motivational interview (Lui et al., 2008). This is followed by five additional visits of ten minutes each at weeks 1, 2, 4, 12 and 26, provided by a trained nurse. Patients receive a booklet with information on how to avoid drinking triggers and enhance medication compliance (Morley et al., 2006). About 30% of patients decide to withdraw before the end of the treatment (Baltieri and Guerra de Andrade, 2004).

The effectiveness of pharmacological therapies for alcohol dependence is documented by two Cochrane reviews (Rösner et al., 2010; Rösner et al., 2011), a WHO report (Anderson et al., 2012) and Centre for Addiction and Mental Health report (Rehm et al., 2012). Priority was given to Cochrane reviews and to the drug Naltrexone (rather than Acamprosate) based on its lower cost, shorter treatment duration and equivalent effectiveness in terms of "return to any drinking, return to heavy drinking and cumulative abstinence duration" (Rösner et al., 2010). The delivery of the behavioural component was based on the description of the interventions carried out in four clinical trials (Morley et al., 2006; Baltieri and Guerra de Andrade, 2004; Lui et al., 2008; Mason et al., 2006), whose results were included in the Cochrane review.

Based on the above evidence built on the combination of results from 50 RCTs (Rösner et al., 2010 and 2011), this intervention, for instance, reduces the risk of return to heavy drinking by 17% during treatment and 14% shortly thereafter. In addition, during treatment, the amount of alcohol consumed per drinking day decreases by 11%; the number of drinking days by 4% and the number of heavy drinking days by 3%. However, there is limited evidence of a longer-term effectiveness of Naltrexone. A systematic review by Roozen et al. (2006) concluded that "moderate evidence" is available of a lack of long-term effects of Naltrexone on "percentage of drinking days and time to first relapse". Based on this data, the intervention is modelled on the assumption that half of the effectiveness is retained during the first year after the intervention, with no positive effect thereafter.

The estimated treatment costs are shown in Table A.7 in Annex A. A large share (approximately one third) is represented by the drug (three-month course). The psychosocial programme, primary care visit and follow-up visits managed by a nurse, account for about 20% of the total cost. The remaining costs are for materials handed to patients and programme organisation.

### *Workplace interventions to reduce harmful use of alcohol*

Interventions to address the harmful use of alcohol can also be delivered in the workplace. A policy of *screening and brief interventions in the workplace* (employers with at least 50 employees) was included in the analysis. Participation is assumed to be voluntary and anonymous for workers reporting excessive levels of alcohol consumption or heavy episodic drinking (Richmond et al., 2000; NHMRC, 1992). Patients with a diagnosis of alcohol dependence are excluded from this intervention but are referred to an appropriate treatment centre. This intervention would reach 12.3% of the Tpotential target in participating workplaces (Richmond et al., 2000).

The intervention consists of three phases plus a "kick off" period to promote participation by distributing brochures and posters. The initial screening process is carried out during the first phase that lasts four to five months. Workers are administered a questionnaire about their health and weekly alcohol consumption during the previous three months. Those reporting a high daily intake of alcohol (NHMRC, 1992), are asked to fill a more comprehensive questionnaire (phase two) whose results are used to tailor a subsequent brief intervention (one 20-minute visit) delivered by a general practitioner. During the visit the patient is provided with a booklet and receives information about the health effects of harmful alcohol consumption and advice on how to reduce consumption. Ten months after the start of the programme, a final assessment is carried out with a procedure similar to phase one. One in five employees beginning the programme does not complete it (Webb et al., 2009).

A systematic review by Webb et al. (2009) identified ten, mainly US-based, studies that assessed a heterogeneous set of interventions ranging from peer support programmes to brief interventions and counselling-based interventions. Only brief interventions showed a small but clear positive effect (Cook et al., 1996; Richmond et al., 2000). A literature review by Ames and Bennett (2011) also found the evidence base to be relatively weak for several types of interventions. In our analysis, a brief intervention programme in the workplace is modelled, based on the experience of a large Australian postal network (Richmond et al., 2000). This experience was selected because of the relatively large sample size of the evaluation. Other studies had poor participation rates (e.g. Matano et al., 2007) or did not show statistically significant results (e.g. Hermansson et al., 2010).

The modelled workplace intervention is assumed to decrease the consumption of alcohol in men and women by, respectively, 4.8 and 0.7 standard drinks per week during the course of the intervention, consistently with Richmond et al. (2000). Evidence of long-term effectiveness is weak. Consistently with the modelling of brief interventions in primary care, the effectiveness of workplace interventions in changing alcohol consumption was assumed to decline by half in the year following the end of the intervention and to wane thereafter.

The estimated costs of workplace programmes are shown in Table A.7 in Annex A. Although the intervention is delivered in the workplace, it is assumed to take place as part of a government-sponsored programme. However, the time spent in the programme by participating employees is not assumed to be subsidised. The most expensive single component of this intervention is the brief intervention delivered by a medical doctor, which accounts for about 25% of the cost. Other cost items include printed materials (booklet, leaflet, posters, questionnaire) and administrative support.

## The countries examined: Canada, the Czech Republic and Germany

Germany has, by a wide margin, the largest population of the three countries examined, counting over 81 million people. Canada follows with 34 million, while the Czech Republic has a population of about 10 million. The Canadian population is projected to grow over the next 40 years, mainly due to migration, unlike those of Germany and the Czech Republic, which are projected to decline. The German population has the oldest age structure, followed by the Czech and Canadian populations. Life expectancy at birth is similar in Germany and Canada, around 81 years on average, but three years lower in the Czech Republic. Cardiovascular mortality is over twice as large in the Czech Republic as in Germany and Canada. Mortality from traffic accidents is higher than the OECD average in the Czech Republic and Canada, but significantly lower in Germany.

Beer drinking accounts for the largest proportion of alcohol consumption in all three countries, with spirits coming second in the Czech Republic and Canada, and wine in Germany. Average (recorded) alcohol consumption is among the highest in the OECD area in Germany (11 litres) and the Czech Republic (11.6 litres). Consumption per capita is significantly lower in Canada, with an average of 8.1 litres, although WHO holds that roughly 20% of all alcohol consumption in Canada is unrecorded, while the corresponding estimates for Germany and the Czech Republic are proportionally less than half (4% and 9%, respectively). The levels of risk associated with typical patterns of drinking, as estimated by WHO on a five-point scale (from 1 – lowest risk – to 5 – highest risk) are 1 for Germany, 2 for Canada and 3 for the Czech Republic. However, based on national survey data, Germany appears to have higher rates of hazardous and harmful drinking, as well as heavy episodic drinking, than Canada, while the Czech Republic outpaces the other two countries on all measures.

Taxation rates are somewhat milder in Canada (at the federal level), higher in Germany and higher yet in the Czech Republic. In Canada, provincial and territorial governments also impose minimum prices and mark-ups, which contribute to moderating alcohol consumption by raising prices. Blood alcohol concentration limits for drivers are also milder in Canada (0.08, reduced to 0.04 for young drivers), while the Czech Republic has a zero tolerance policy for all drivers, and Germany has zero tolerance for young drivers, and a limit of 0.05 for other drivers. Other regulatory policies are more haphazard, with access to alcoholic beverages limited only for intoxicated persons in Germany and the Czech Republic and limited bans in connection with special events in the Czech Republic. Regulation of alcohol promotion is mostly limited to advertising in the three countries. Germany has a low minimum legal age for purchasing alcohol (16, raised to 18 for spirits), while the Czech Republic has a minimum age of 18 and Canada has different age limits in different provinces.

With some notable exceptions, such as minimum price policies in Canada and low blood alcohol concentration (BAC) limits in the Czech Republic and Germany, the policies currently in place in the three countries are not amongst the most restrictive in the OECD area. The analyses presented in this section provide an assessment of the impacts to be expected from developments in a number of policy areas in each of the three countries. Policy developments are generally assessed incrementally, as a scaling up, or tightening, of existing policies. One partial exception is minimum price policies, currently in place in only one of the three countries. These have been assessed as an increase (by 10%) of existing minimum price thresholds in Canada, and as a new policy possibly to be introduced at the national level in Germany and the Czech Republic, based on a minimum price set at a level that would cause a similar average price increase (10%) in the cheaper segment of the respective national alcohol markets.

## Policy impacts on harmful alcohol use, longevity and disability

### *Reducing harmful drinking*

The CDP-Alcohol model allows the impacts of alcohol policies on drinking patterns to be compared. The largest reduction (10%) in hazardous (including harmful) drinking is seen for a tax increase in Germany. Price policies (especially tax increases), brief interventions and advertising restrictions are all shown to have strong potential effects. Advertising restrictions have a lesser potential effect in Canada on hazardous drinking overall, but model outputs show that a relatively large proportion of the heaviest drinkers would cut their consumption to some degree. School-based programmes lag behind, due to their targeting of a population group with comparatively low rates of high-risk drinking, and due to the temporary nature of the effects assumed for these programmes. Limitations in opening hours and enforcement of drinking-and-driving restrictions were not assumed to impact consumption in this analysis, hence the lack of effects shown in Figure 5.1 (Panels A, B and C, respectively, for Canada, the Czech Republic and Germany).

Brief interventions, when offered systematically to all eligible patients at all general practices, are shown to have the potential to prevent a significant number of cases of alcohol dependence (as many as 17% in the Czech Republic, 10.5% in Germany and 6.5% in Canada, as shown in Figure 5.1). Brief interventions are also shown to be effective, albeit to a lesser extent, when delivered in the workplace. In addition, important reductions in the prevalence of alcohol dependence can be obtained with price policies, pharmacological and psychosocial treatment of dependence, and advertising regulation. These effects on alcohol dependence compound the interpretation of the changes observed in heavy episodic drinking (HED). In particular, in countries where a larger reduction in alcohol dependence is obtained (typically countries where dependence is more widespread), the analysis predicts that a number of people who would have become dependent otherwise will still drink heavily on an episodic basis, thus partially or entirely offsetting the reduction in HED obtained by lowering the quantity of alcohol drunk by other heavy drinkers. This is the main reason why we see larger reductions in HED in Figure 5.1 for Canada (where reductions in dependence are less pronounced) than for the other two countries. Regulation of advertising and school-based programmes have more consistent effects on HED across the three countries, because of the nature of the effects of these interventions.

Figure 5.1. **Decrease in prevalence rates at the population level over the simulation period**

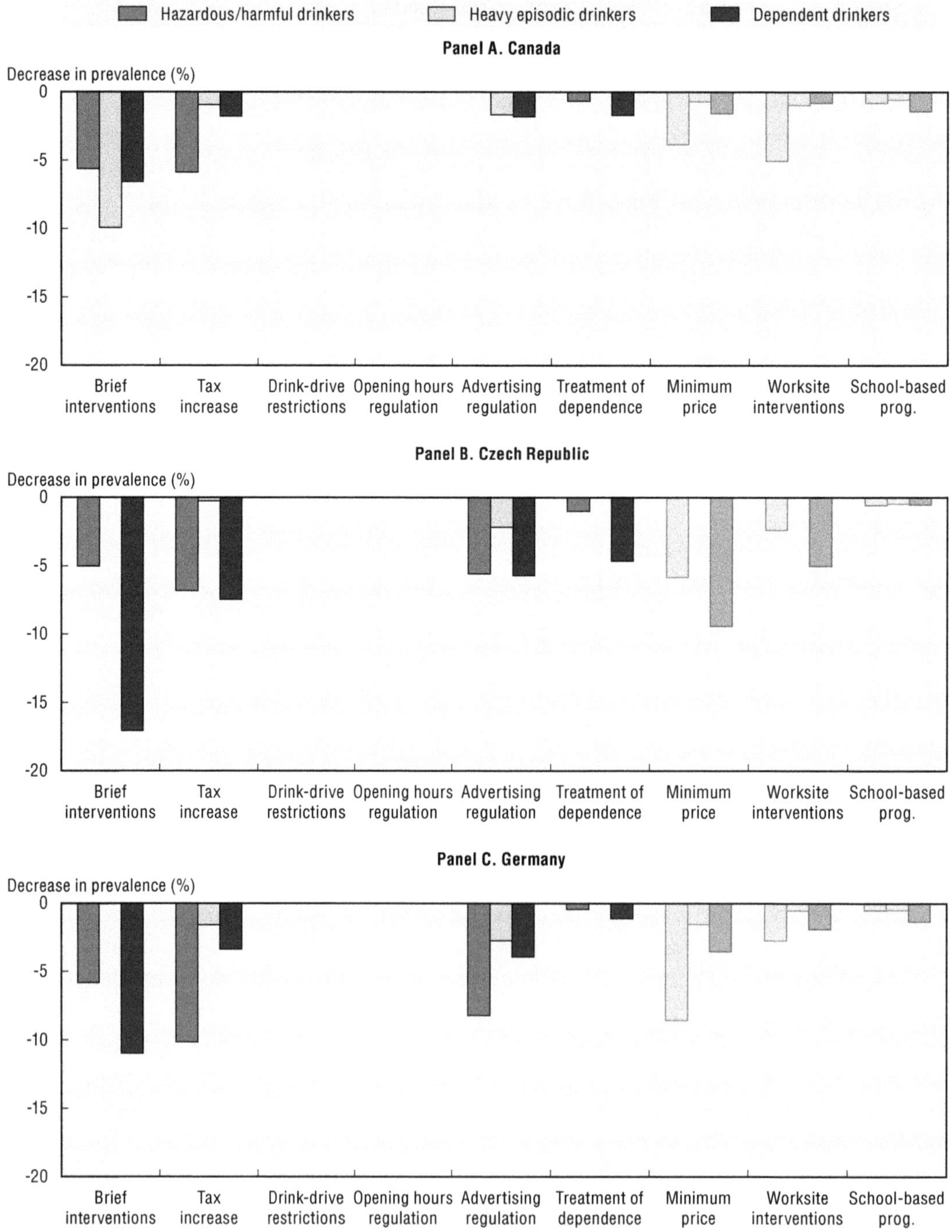


*Note:* Darker-shaded bars, main analysis; lighter-shaded bars, further analysis.

*Source:* CDP-Alcohol analysis relying on input data from multiple sources, listed in Tables A.4 to A.6 in Annex A.

StatLink http://dx.doi.org/10.1787/888933180438

Coverage is as important as the ability to change drinking behaviours at the individual level in determining the overall (i.e. population-level) effects of an intervention. So, for instance, changes in taxation tend to have only mild effects on individual alcohol consumption, but they target large shares of the population (virtually everyone) resulting in large overall effects. On the other hand, brief interventions have larger effects on a smaller number of people.

### *Health gains*

Figure 5.2 shows the average yearly numbers of life years and disability adjusted life years (DALYs) to be gained during the simulation period by implementing individual alcohol policies. Policies are listed in Figure 5.2 in order of decreasing effectiveness (main and further analyses), but the graphs should not be read strictly as a ranking. Results for each policy should be interpreted in the light of the assumptions spelled out above on coverage and effectiveness at the individual level.

Brief interventions in primary care have the potential to produce relatively large health gains at the population level, although it is worth emphasising again that the findings presented here are based on the assumption that brief interventions would be offered systematically by all general practices in a country, throughout the duration of the simulation period, which means that each year approximately 13% of adults in Germany, for instance, would receive brief alcohol advice from their general practitioners. This would involve major efforts to overcome capacity constraints, incentivise and train health professionals. Relatively large health gains are also associated with price policies and advertising regulation (with smaller effects predicted for the latter in Canada). Opening hours regulation and drinking-and-driving enforcement policies, as well as treatment of alcohol dependence and brief interventions at the workplace, are likely to generate smaller but meaningful gains at the population level. Finally, the impacts of school-based programmes are small or not statistically significant in the time frame of the analysis (40 years).

### *Employment and productivity*

A particularly important dimension of the health gains produced by alcohol policies in the analysis is the impact these may have on employment and productivity. While a detailed evaluation of these impacts was beyond the scope of the analysis presented here, the results shown in Figure 5.3 reflect the extent to which alcohol policies could improve labour outcomes. In particular, the figure shows the numbers of life years free of alcohol-related disabilities gained by working-age people as a result of the implementation of the alcohol policies examined. Essentially, the analysis shows that, every year, hundreds of thousands of working-age people could avoid alcohol-related disabilities (injuries and their sequelae, chronic diseases linked with alcohol) in the three countries. For instance, with a tax increase leading to a 10% hike in alcohol prices 168 000 working-age people in Germany, 45 000 in the Czech Republic and 53 000 in Canada would avoid alcohol-related disabilities each year. The gains estimated for brief interventions would be even larger, although less evenly distributed between men and women than with taxation, due to a larger prevalence of high-risk drinking behaviours and alcohol dependence in men. Larger benefits in men are also observed in connection with alcohol policies whose main effects are on alcohol-related injuries, as these are more common in men than in women.

Figure 5.2. **Health outcomes at the population level, average number per year**

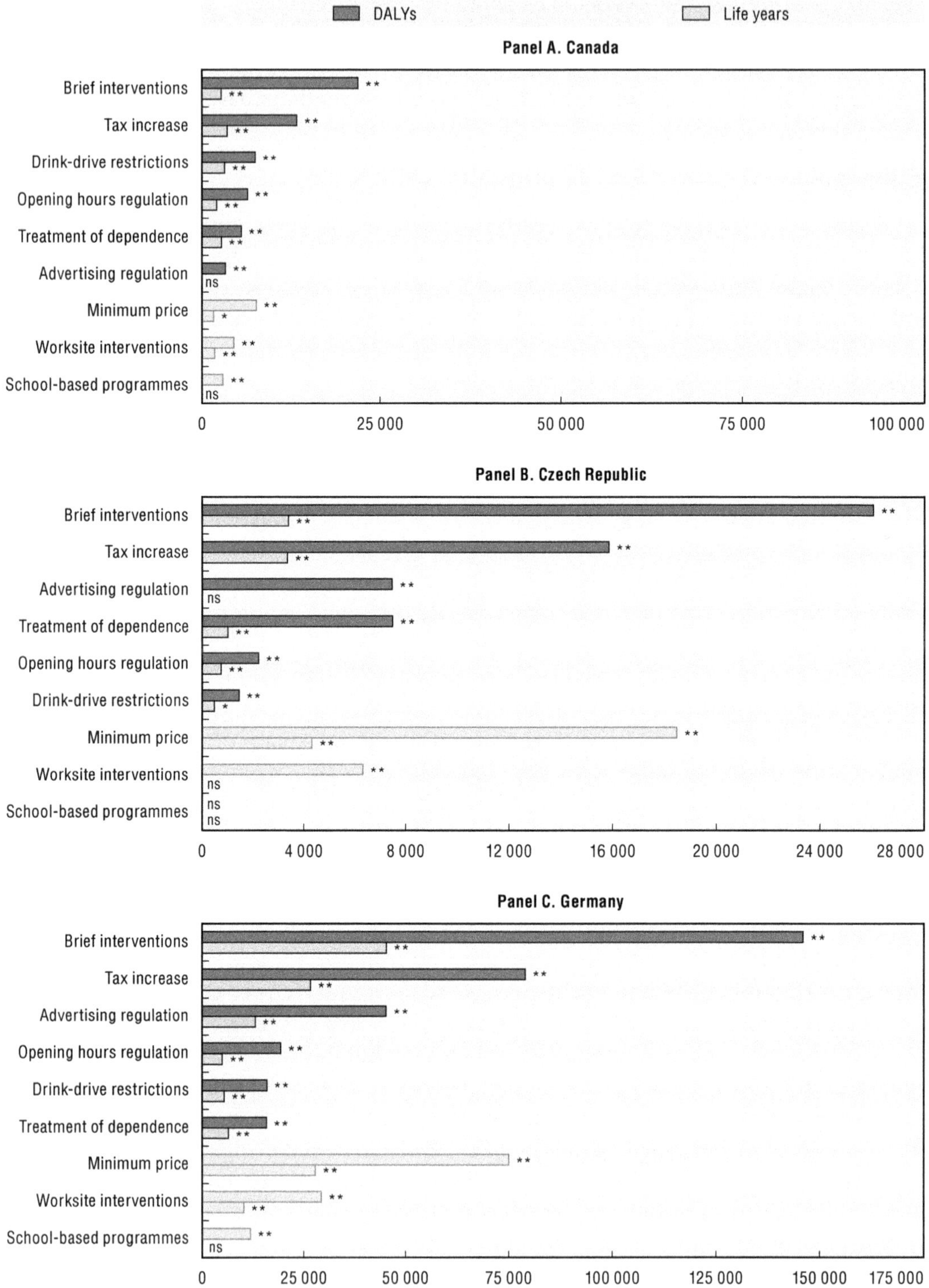


*Note:* ns, not statistically significant, (*) statistically significant at the 10% level, (**) significant at the 5% level. Darker-shaded bars, main analysis; lighter-shaded bars, further analysis.

*Source:* CDP-Alcohol analysis relying on input data from multiple sources, listed in Tables A.4 to A.6 in Annex A.

StatLink http://dx.doi.org/10.1787/888933180448

Figure 5.3. **Number of working-age people freed of alcohol-related diseases, average effect per year**

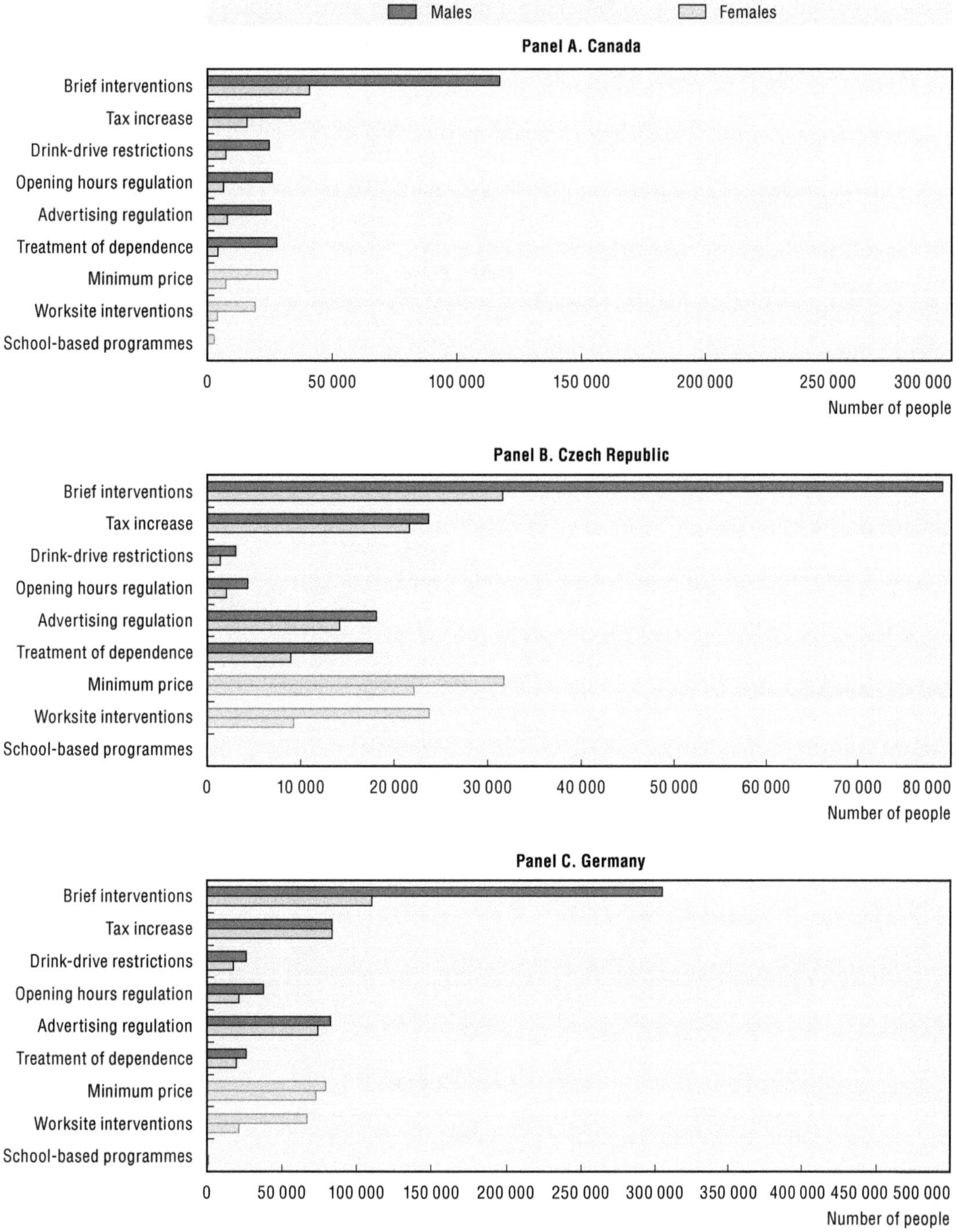


*Note:* Darker-shaded bars, main analysis; lighter-shaded bars, further analysis.

*Source:* CDP-Alcohol analysis relying on input data from multiple sources, listed in Tables A.4 to A.6 in Annex A.

StatLink http://dx.doi.org/10.1787/888933180459

Simply looking at average numbers of life years or DALYs gained through prevention policies, shown in Figure 5.2, is not sufficient when designing a long-term prevention plan. What happens on average is not necessarily what happens in any single year and future outcomes are typically valued less than those occurring in the short term. The health returns of alcohol policies are produced relatively quickly after implementation, compared with other areas of chronic disease prevention policy. The progression is approximately linear over time, but tends to be more rapid in the initial phase with price policies and advertising regulation, with several other policies gaining momentum after five to ten years, as shown in Figure 5.4.

Figure 5.4. **Cumulative DALYs saved over time**

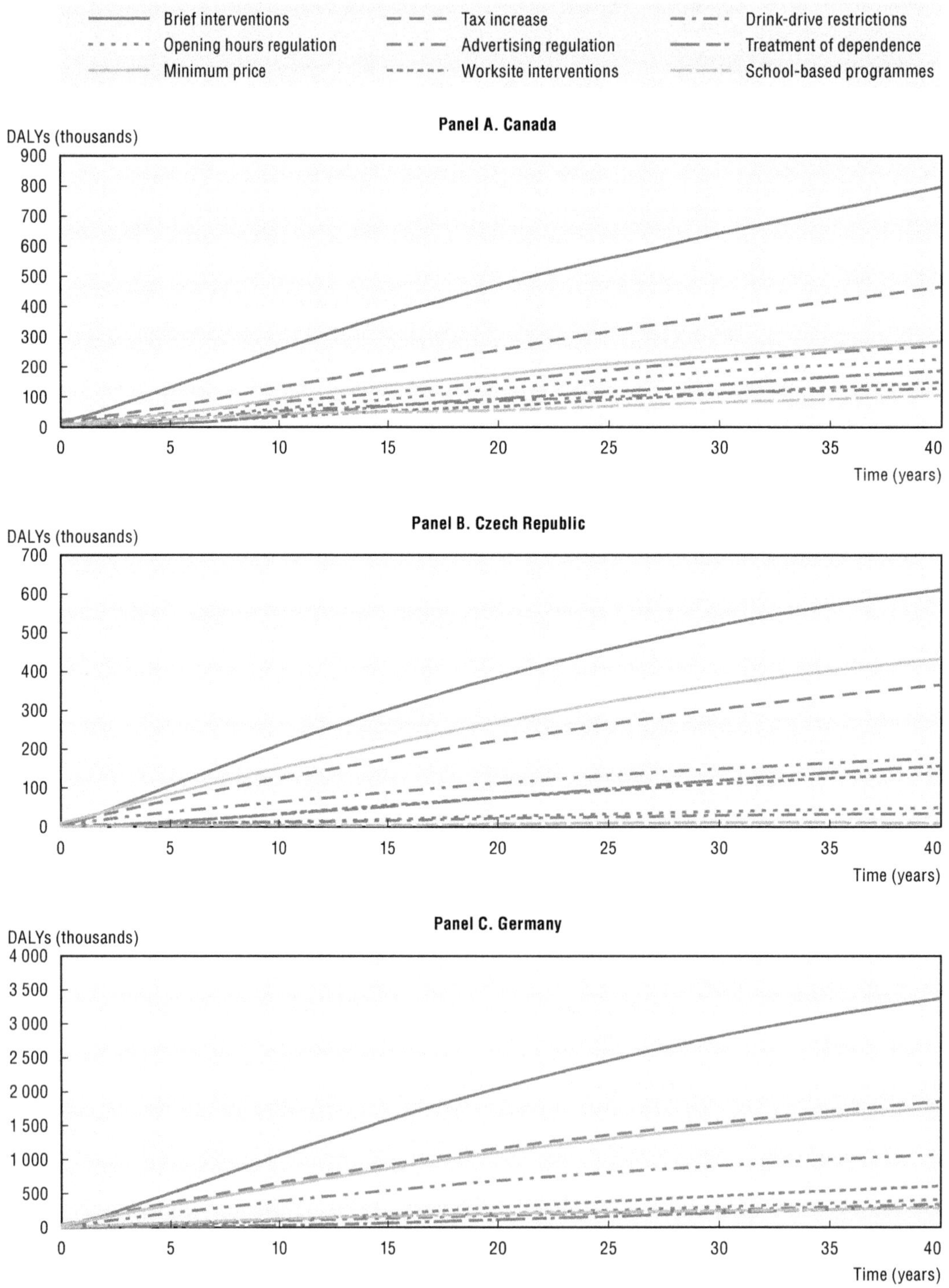


*Source:* CDP-Alcohol analysis relying on input data from multiple sources, listed in Tables A.4 to A.6 in Annex A.

StatLink http://dx.doi.org/10.1787/888933180466

## Policy impacts on the incidence of alcohol-related diseases and injuries

The greatest impact of policies on the occurrence of alcohol-related diseases is seen for alcohol-use disorders, a heterogeneous group of conditions which includes, but is not limited to, alcohol dependence. Alcohol-use disorders account for the largest share of the burden of disease associated with alcohol. The largest proportionate reductions in incidence may be obtained with brief interventions in primary care, as shown in Figure 5.5, mostly through the prevention of dependence. Impacts are larger in the Czech Republic, where dependence is more common. Other policies have smaller, and similar, impacts on the incidence of alcohol-use disorders, with price policies and advertising regulation showing slightly greater effectiveness. Limitations in opening hours and enforcement of drinking-and-driving restrictions have the largest impacts on injuries, with reductions in the order of 1% at the population level. This corresponds, for instance, to 71 000 and 54 000 fewer injuries each year with the two policies, respectively, in Germany, or 37 000 and 41 000 in Canada. However, by design, these policies have no impacts on overall alcohol consumption and other alcohol-related conditions in our analysis.

In the analysis, the greatest impact on cancer incidence are obtained with price policies and brief interventions in primary care and at the workplace. In particular, the occurrence of alcohol-related cancers would be cut by up to 2% following changes in taxation leading to a 10% price hike. This corresponds to 4 200 fewer cases each year in Germany, 1 600 in Canada, and 500 in the Czech Republic.

In the analysis, approximately two thirds of ischemic heart disease cases occur in people who are mild or moderate alcohol users, whose risk is not increased by alcohol. However, the net effect of most policies is an overall reduction in cardiovascular disease. The size of these effects, not shown in the figure, is generally modest.

## Implementation costs, effects on health expenditure, and the cost effectiveness of policies

The estimated costs of implementing alternative alcohol policies and the net effects of the same policies on health care expenditures in the three countries are shown in Figure 5.6 (the latter in the bars below the horizontal axis, the former in the bars above the axis).

- Policies delivered in health care settings, including brief interventions and the treatment of dependence, carry the largest implementation costs by a relatively wide margin. This is in connection with the staff and drug costs involved in delivering those interventions and with the scale at which they have been modelled in the analysis. Brief interventions are also expected to produce the largest reductions in health care expenditures. However, these reductions are sufficiently large to offset implementation costs and make the policy cost saving only in the Czech Republic, where the number of cases of dependence prevented is largest.
- Several policies (especially price policies) are shown to have the potential to generate savings in health care expenditure which more than offset implementation costs. Price policies, especially tax hikes, are shown to be cheaper to implement, relative to other policies, and to produce large savings in health care expenditure, with cumulative gains of up to USD PPP 55 per person after ten years in the Czech Republic, as shown in Figure 5.7.
- Other policies are likely to generate a net increase in government expenditure, although financial savings from possible crime reductions are not accounted for in our analysis.

- The costs of worksite interventions and enforcement of drinking-and-driving restrictions are generally higher than those of regulatory and fiscal policies, and neither of the above produces sufficiently large savings in health care expenditures to offset implementation costs.
- The costs of school-based programmes are modest, but so are their effects too.

Figure 5.5. **Decrease in numbers of disease and injury cases, average per year, 2010-50**

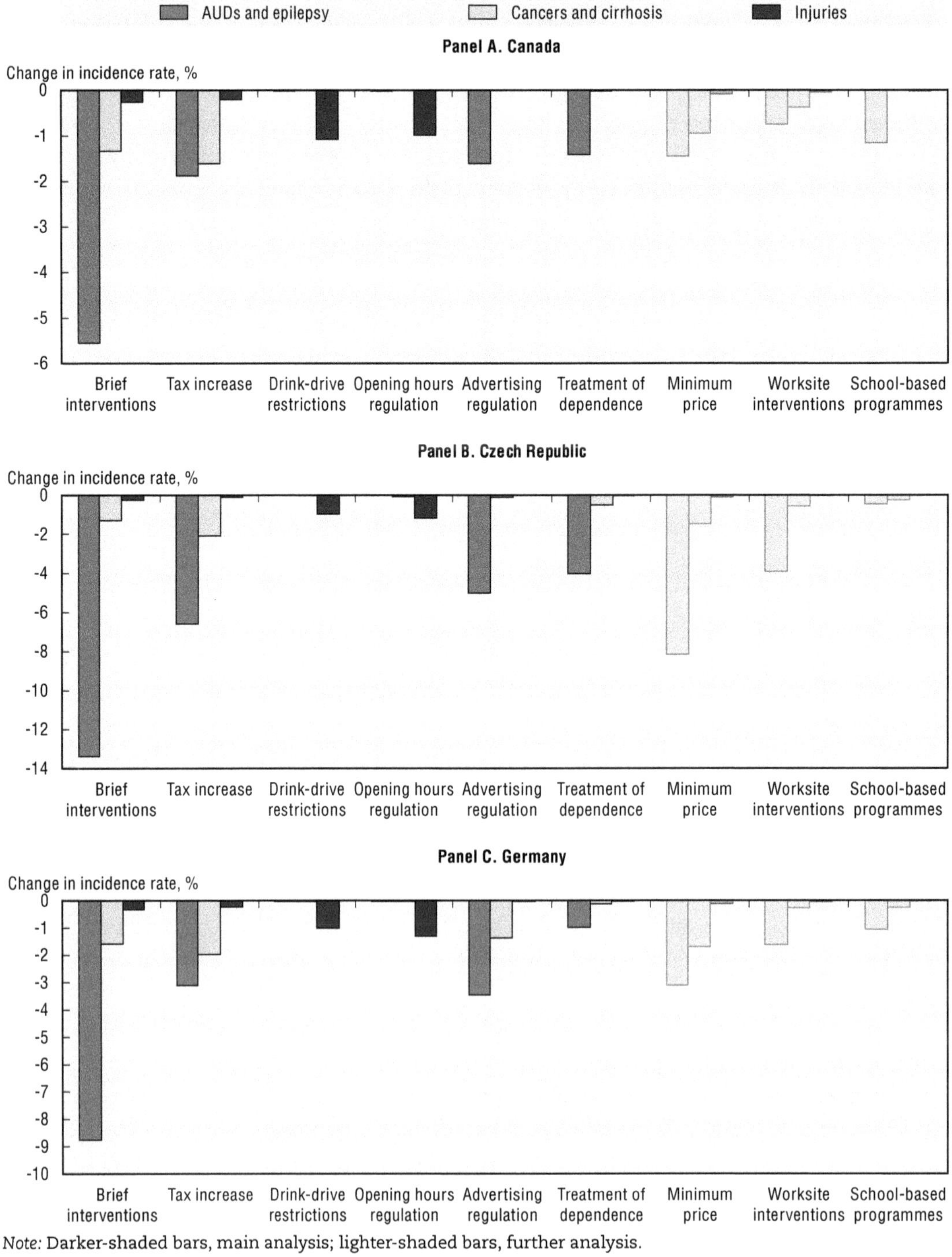


*Note:* Darker-shaded bars, main analysis; lighter-shaded bars, further analysis.

*Source:* CDP-Alcohol analysis relying on input data from multiple sources, listed in Tables A.4 to A.6 in Annex A.

StatLink http://dx.doi.org/10.1787/888933180476

Figure 5.6. **Economic impact at the population level, average per year, 2010-50**

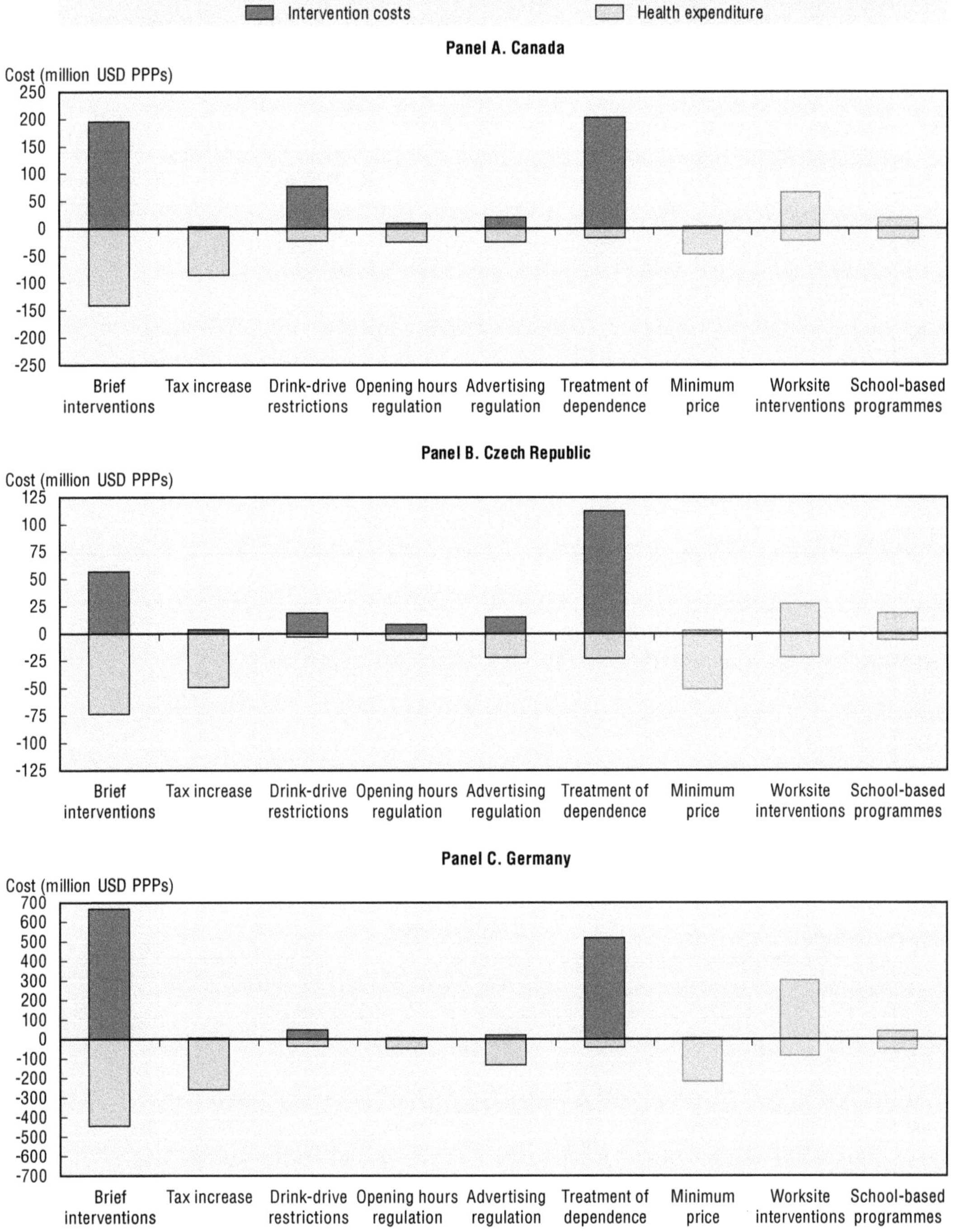


*Note:* Darker-shaded bars, main analysis; lighter-shaded bars, further analysis.

*Source:* CDP-Alcohol analysis relying on input data from multiple sources, listed in Tables A.4 to A.6 in Annex A.

StatLink http://dx.doi.org/10.1787/888933180487

Even after discounting future savings at a 3% rate, reductions in health care expenditures potentially generated by alcohol policies are shown to be substantial and build up linearly over time, as shown in Figure 5.7, contributing to a favourable cost-effectiveness profile for those policies. Figure 5.8 shows the cost-effectiveness ratios of the policies examined over the course of the simulation period. Interventions that do not appear in the three panels

Figure 5.7. **Cumulative impact on health expenditure over time**

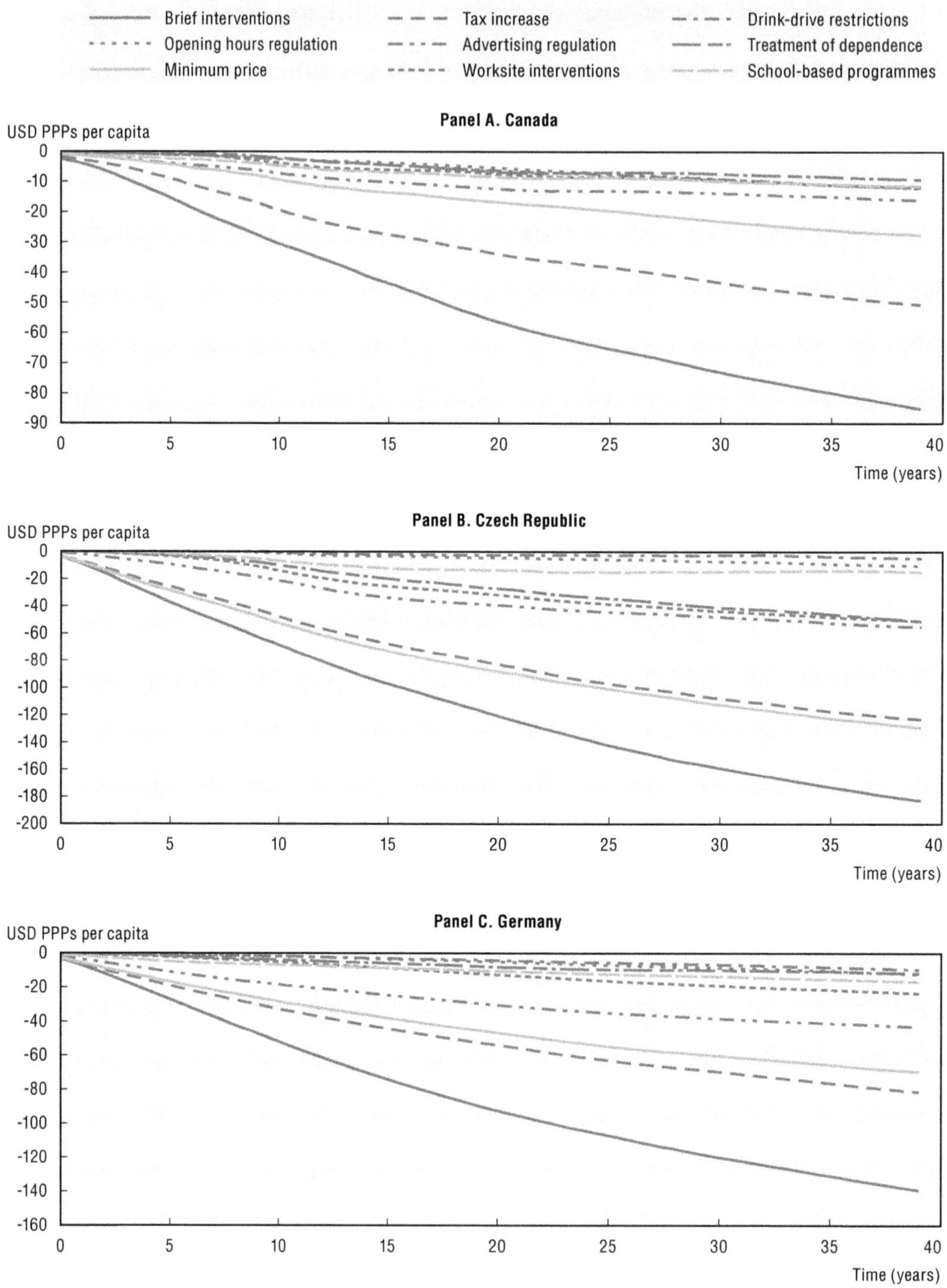


*Source:* CDP-Alcohol analysis relying on input data from multiple sources, listed in Tables A.4 to A.6 in Annex A.

StatLink http://dx.doi.org/10.1787/888933180497

of this figure are cost saving (therefore a cost-effectiveness ratio is not calculated). Policies that are not cost saving have generally favourable cost-effectiveness profiles throughout the simulation, relative to a USD 50 000 per year of life gained in good health, often applied as a reference standard in industrialised economies, although the cost effectiveness of

Figure 5.8. **Cost effectiveness of interventions over time**

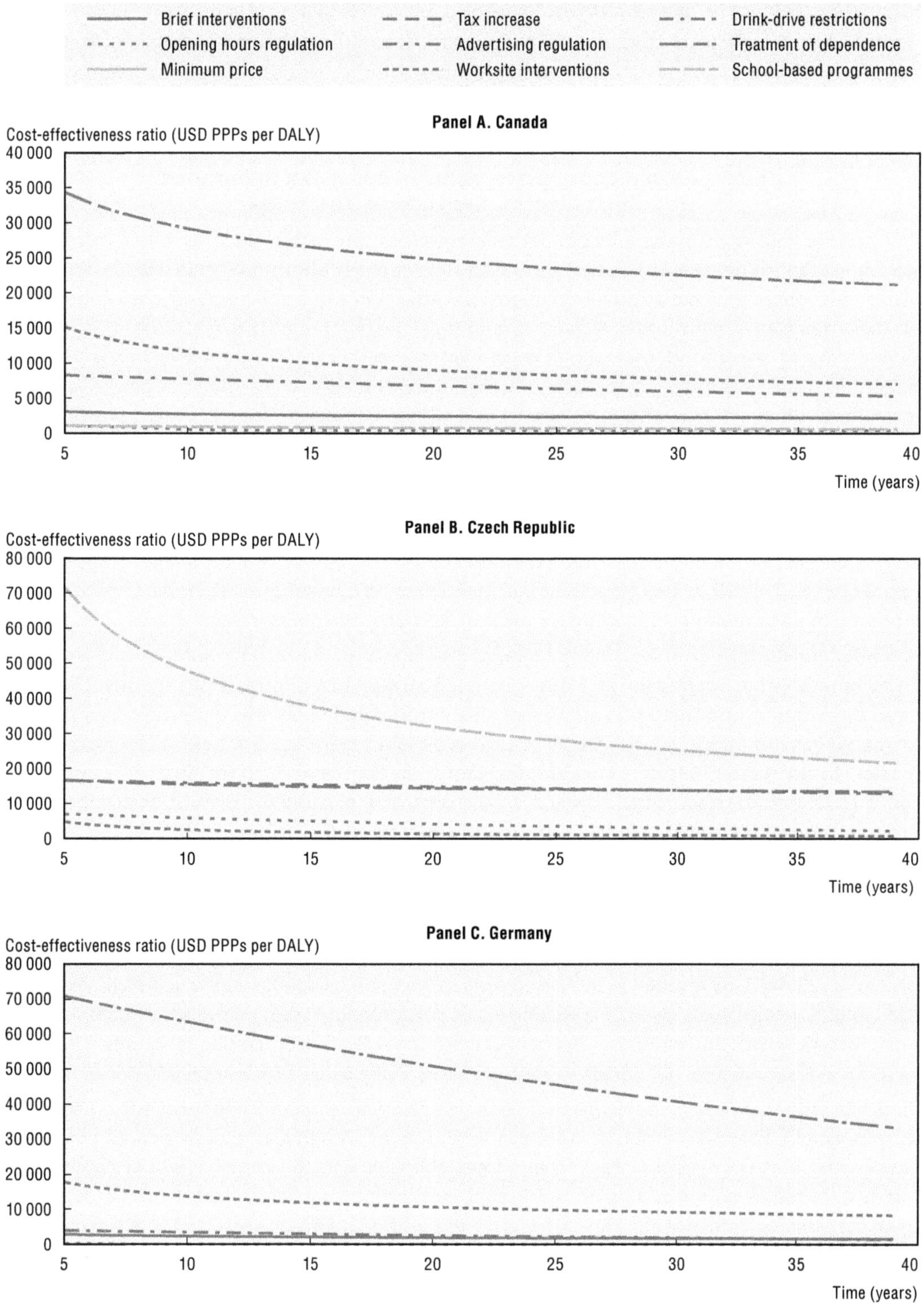


*Note:* Tax increase, advertising regulation and minimum price are cost-saving policies in all three countries; brief interventions are cost-saving in the Czech Republic; in Germany, school-based programmes are cost-saving and opening hours regulation becomes cost-saving eight years after implementation.

*Source:* CDP-Alcohol analysis relying on input data from multiple sources, listed in Tables A.4 to A.6 in Annex A.

StatLink http://dx.doi.org/10.1787/888933180505

school-based programmes in the Czech Republic and treatment of dependence in Germany only drops below the above threshold after 10 and 20 years, respectively. Overall, this picture strongly suggests that alcohol policies represent an efficient use of health system resources, relative to many established health care interventions and medical technologies.

### Box 5.2. **Do alcohol price policies boost tax avoidance and illicit alcohol production and trade?**

Alcohol policies aimed at making alcoholic beverages less affordable, such as hikes in taxation, may generate tax avoidance behaviours or lead people to seek cheaper alternative beverages, possibly of illicit origin. These responses may partly offset the beneficial effects of price policies, and are a cause of concern for their consequences on criminal activities. In principle, illegal phenomena like smuggling and trade of informally produced or counterfeit alcoholic beverages may be boosted by increases in the prices of legal alcohol. Certain forms of tax avoidance, such as cross-border trade, as well as illicit trade thrive on the wide differences in taxation systems and rates across and within countries. They deprive governments of tax revenues and may reinforce criminal organisations and corruption, in addition to exposing the population to health threats when the commodities illegally traded are produced in ways that escape statutory public health controls. However, a recent systematic review of the epidemiology and effects of unrecorded alcohol use concludes that "Very large amounts of alcohol are produced globally that go unrecorded. The primary harm from this kind of alcohol arises from the fact that it is typically much cheaper than licit alcohol" (Rehm et al., 2014). The OECD has established a Task Force on Charting Illicit Trade to contribute to the understanding of illicit markets, including for alcohol, and possible policy responses.

Cross-border and illicit trade of alcoholic beverages are important concerns in some countries, at different levels of income. WHO estimates the size of unrecorded alcohol consumption (which includes also cross-border and illicit trade), and their data show that this varies widely between countries, as a proportion of total estimated consumption. Data for OECD countries are shown in Figure A below. The figure also shows the variation in unrecorded alcohol consumption between 2005 and 2010, in litres of pure alcohol per capita. In most countries, worldwide, unrecorded consumption remained constant or decreased between the two dates, while it increased only in a minority of countries (WHO, 2014).

An instance in which taxation changes led to increases in cross-border trade is the introduction of a single market for alcohol in the European Union in 2003, which triggered a tax competition between member countries (Lockwood and Migali, 2009). Finland decreased its alcohol taxes by one third following the accession of neighbouring Estonia in the European Union, where alcohol could be bought at substantially lower prices (Anderson et al., 2009a). This resulted in increased consumption and alcohol-related deaths (Koski et al., 2007), which led Finland to raise taxes again in 2008 (and again in subsequent years). However, the same effects were not observed in Denmark and southern Sweden, despite the adoption of similar measures (i.e. abolition of stringent quotas and reduction of high tax rates on alcohol) in the same time period (Mäkelä et al. 2008).

Alcoholic beverages are considerably more expensive in Norway than in Sweden, due to a higher taxation in Norway. Despite a strict regulation of cross-border shopping, Norwegian stores located near the border report lower revenues from alcohol sales than stores elsewhere in the country, whilst consumers living in the same area report no lower expenditures, suggesting that they bear a lesser tax burden than other Norwegian consumers (Beatty et al., 2009). On the other hand, a Danish study found that tax hikes and cuts are passed through to similar degrees in areas at different distances from the German border, despite lower price levels in Germany that may incentivise cross-border trade (Bergman and Hansen, 2013).

Smuggling and illicit trade are more complex phenomena, determined by a variety of factors, including, but not limited to, tax differentials between and within countries. A higher incidence of crime and corruption, as well as weaker law enforcement, are among other potential determinants. Illicit production and trade of alcoholic beverages vary widely across countries and tend to be larger in lower-income countries. Commercial data from market research in countries with a relatively high incidence of informal

## Box 5.2. **Do alcohol price policies boost tax avoidance and illicit alcohol production and trade?** *(cont.)*

alcohol drinking in Africa (Tanzania, Nigeria, Botswana and Zimbabwe) provide some insights into the patterns of informal alcohol use and the possible effects of price hikes in those settings. Each country has peculiar alcohol market features, but some common trends include a disproportionate representation of low-income groups among drinkers of informal alcohol, mostly motivated by its greater affordability (the affordability gap is perceived to be relatively large), and a predominance of social off-trade consumption of informal alcohol. Use of informal alcohol tends to be concentrated during daytime and weekdays, at least in the above African countries. A relatively large proportion of informal alcohol drinkers (up to half) drink exclusively informal alcohol. The rest may be more likely to trade between different types of alcohol, if alternatives become more affordable. Low-income drinkers are generally more price-sensitive than other drinkers, which suggests that price increases in the formal sector may lead some of them to trade down to informal alcohol, but more, and direct, evidence is required to assess whether and to what extent this would happen as a result of tax increases.

Estimates for the United Kingdom suggest a tax revenue loss for illicit alcohol trade of just over GBP 1 billion in the fiscal year 2011-12, corresponding to an illicit market share of 3% for spirits, 9% for beer and 6% for wine (HMRC, 2013). Analyses by the UK Treasury show fluctuations in the illicit market share for different beverages, which do not appear to be correlated with changes in taxation. On the other hand, the alcohol tax cut implemented in Finland in 2004 was associated with a reduction in illegal home production and smuggling from 0.27 litres per capita in 2003 to 0.11 in 2004 and 0.08 in 2006. Legal home production also decreased from 0.19 litres in 2003 to 0.09 in 2006 (Mäkelä and Österberg, 2009). However, alcohol statistics show that after taxes increased again, starting in 2008, total unrecorded consumption (no breakdown is available between different forms) went up only slightly, from 2.2 to 2.3 litres per capita in 2009, and remained stable thereafter despite further tax increases (Østhus, 2012).

Figure A. **Unrecorded alcohol consumption in OECD countries**

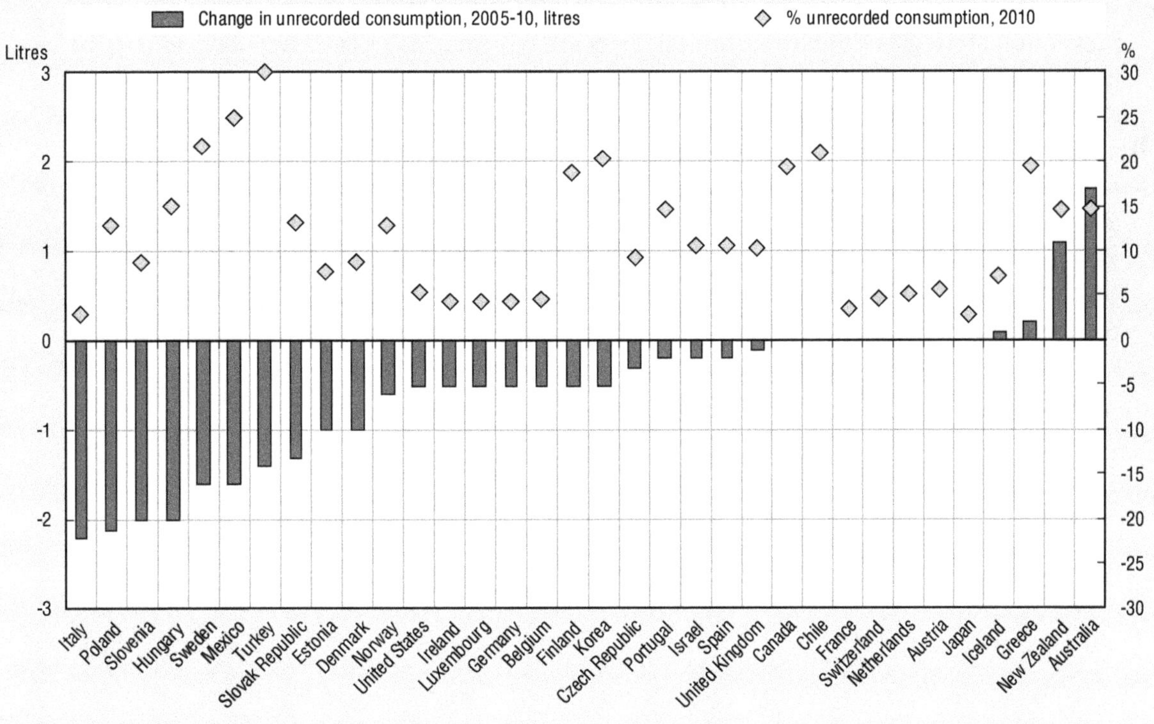


*Source:* WHO Global Information System on Alcohol and Health (GISAH); includes unrecorded consumption from home production, illegal production or import.

StatLink http://dx.doi.org/10.1787/888933180519

## Combining alcohol policies

As often happens in prevention, multi-faceted problems require diversified policy responses. The policies assessed in our analysis typically address different types of drinking behaviours, in different social groups, through different mechanisms. Countries that intend to address effectively the problem of harmful alcohol use cannot rely on individual policies to accomplish their goal. OECD analyses show that the combined impacts of multiple policies will be larger than those of individual policies. In addition, a multi-pronged approach may create a "critical-mass" effect that would make a change in the social norms that regulate alcohol drinking behaviours more likely.

Combining multiple alcohol policies in a broader prevention strategy is shown to generate overall impacts that are close to the sum of the impacts of the individual component policies, in most cases. So, the end result is broadly additive, despite an assumption of less than additive impacts at the individual level, in case of simultaneous exposure to the effects of more than one policy. Figure 5.9 provides an illustration, showing the numbers of life years and DALYs potentially gained with three possible combinations of alcohol policies. In particular, these include a "fiscal and regulatory package", combining tax increases with regulation of advertising and off-trade outlet opening hours; a "health care package", combining brief interventions and treatment of dependence in primary care; and a "mixed package" combining tax increases with treatment of dependence, enforcement of drinking-and-driving restrictions, and limitations in outlet opening hours. The three combined strategies have relatively similar effects in each country (around 37 000 DALYs gained in Canada; 23-29 000 DALYs in the Czech Republic and 119-137 000 DALYs in Germany), with slightly larger impacts from the health care package compared with other combined strategies in the Czech Republic and Germany.

Health care expenditure reductions potentially associated with the three combined prevention strategies can be substantial. They are largest in the Czech Republic, where the health care package can generate yearly savings exceeding USD PPP 8 per person; while the fiscal and regulatory package could save just over USD PPP 6 per person in Germany, and USD 4 in Canada, as shown in Figure 5.10. The implementation costs of the health care and mixed packages are larger than the reductions obtained in health care expenditure (especially those of the former), but the cost-effectiveness profile of both remains very favourable in all three countries, with the highest cost-effectiveness ratios being USD PPP 2 800 per DALY saved for the mixed package and USD PPP 6 600 for the health care package in Canada. The fiscal and regulatory package, on the other hand, has significantly lower implementation costs, and is cost saving overall.

Figure 5.9. **Health outcomes of a multiple-intervention strategy, average number per year**

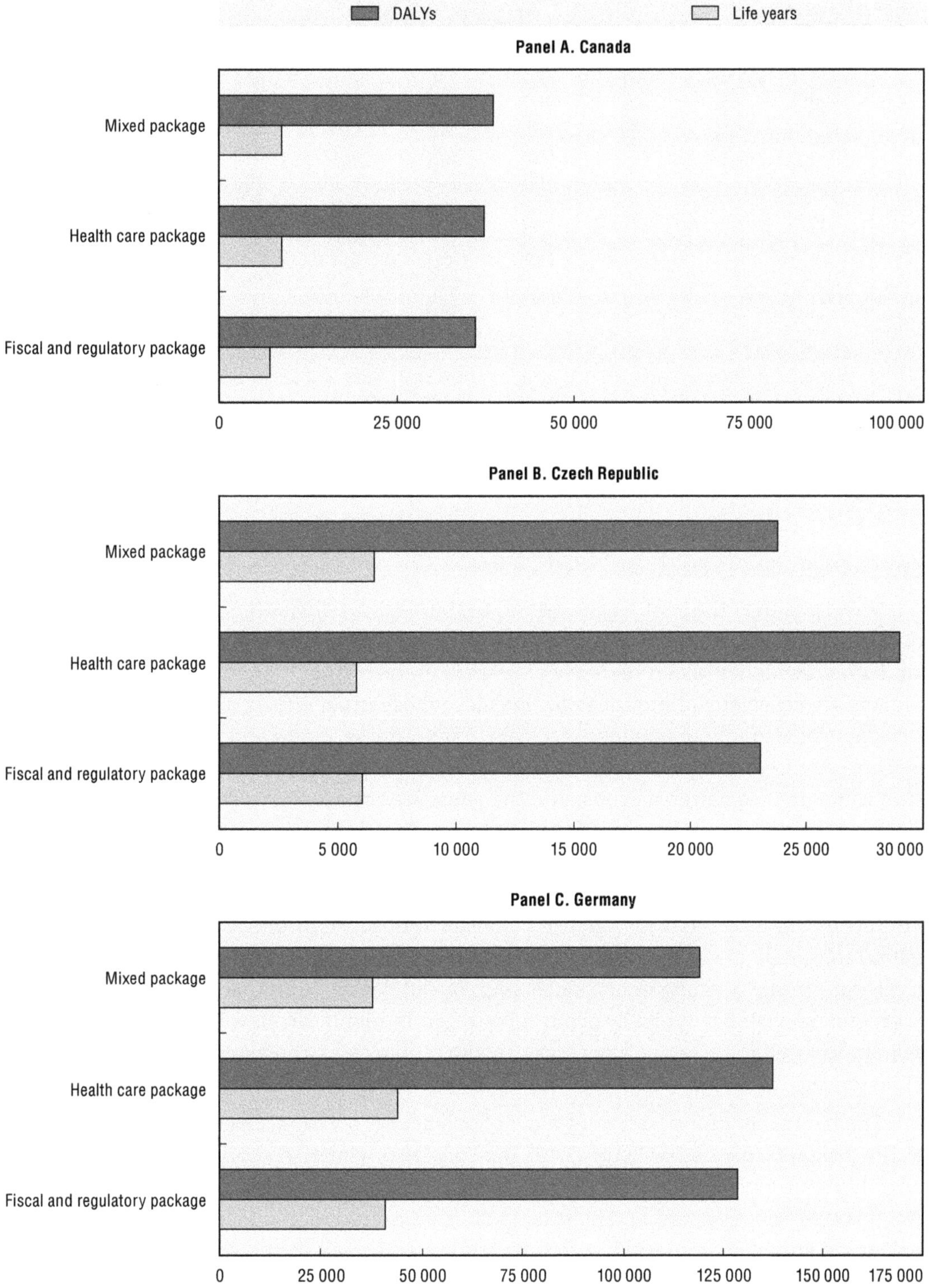


*Source*: CDP-Alcohol analysis relying on input data from multiple sources, listed in Tables A.4 to A.6 in Annex A.

StatLink http://dx.doi.org/10.1787/888933180529

Figure 5.10. **Impact on health expenditure of a multiple-intervention strategy, average per year, 2010-50**

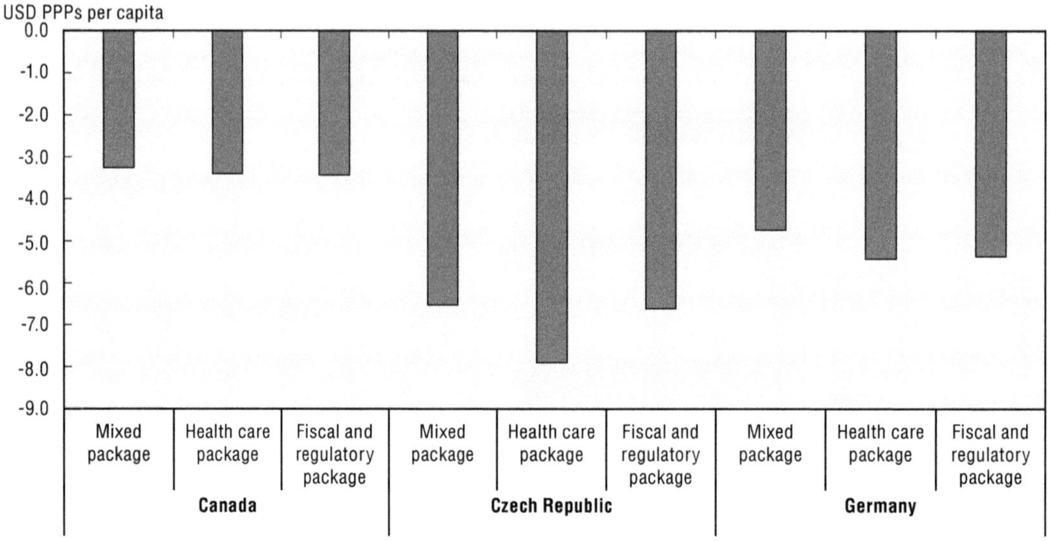


*Source:* CDP-Alcohol analysis relying on input data from multiple sources, listed in Tables A.4 to A.6 in Annex A.

StatLink http://dx.doi.org/10.1787/888933180532

## Who benefits the most from alcohol policies?

Unsurprisingly, the health gains generated by alcohol policies tend to be enjoyed by men more than women, mainly because of the larger prevalence of risky drinking behaviours and higher incidence of certain types of injuries in the former. Gender differences in policy impacts are especially pronounced for policies whose main effects are the prevention and treatment of alcohol dependence (typically, brief interventions and pharmacological and psychosocial treatments for dependence). A larger proportion of men requires, and is the beneficiary of, those interventions, and the gains are consequently larger for men than for women. This is shown clearly in Figure 5.11, in which differences in the relative effects of these interventions in the three countries reflect quite closely the differences observed in the prevalence of alcohol dependence in men and women in the same countries. Gender differences are also relatively large for policies whose main effect is to reduce alcohol-related injuries, such as enforcement of drinking-and-driving restrictions and limitations in off-trade outlet opening hours, since injuries and deaths from road traffic accidents and interpersonal violence typically occur more often in men than in women. Differences are less pronounced for other policies, but gains in men exceed those predicted for women in all instances.

The health benefits of different alcohol policies follow typical age patterns, illustrated by the three examples in Figure 5.12. Tax increases (Panel A, Canada) have effects on mortality and morbidity in all age groups, but effects are larger in adults, especially in the 5$^{th}$ and 6$^{th}$ decades of life. The effects of brief interventions (Panel B, Czech Republic) tend to be stronger on morbidity than mortality and peak in the 4$^{th}$ decade of life (later for mortality). Enforcement of drinking-and-driving restrictions (Panel C, Germany) has its largest effects on morbidity in young adults (mostly in their twenties and early thirties) with smaller effects on mortality. The latter increase with age and peak in the 5$^{th}$ decade of life, while effects on morbidity tend to level off.

Figure 5.11. **DALYs by gender, average number per year**

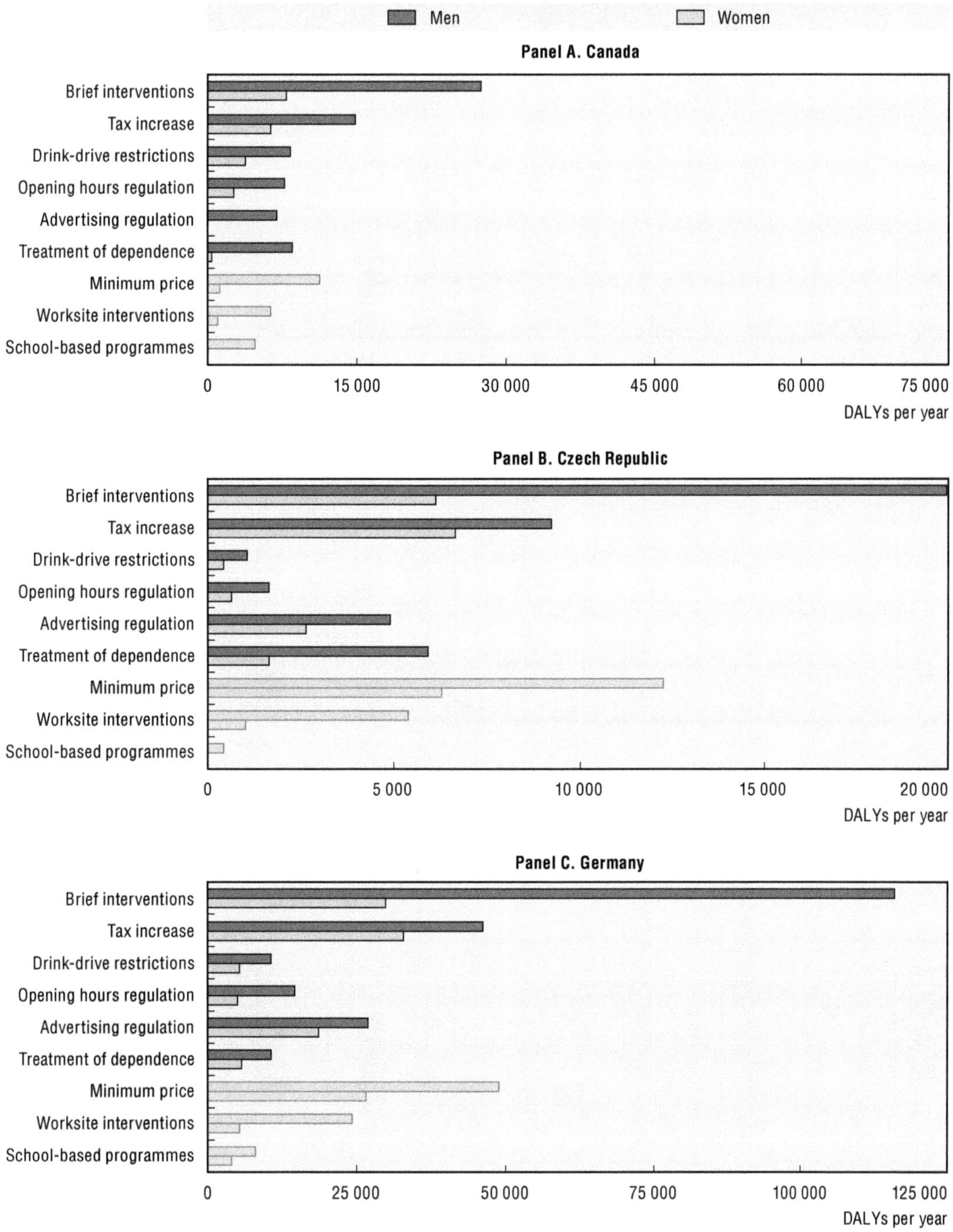


*Note:* Darker-shaded bars, main analysis; lighter-shaded bars, further analysis.

*Source:* CDP-Alcohol analysis relying on input data from multiple sources, listed in Tables A.4 to A.6 in Annex A.

StatLink http://dx.doi.org/10.1787/888933180547

Figure 5.12. **Effects of selected interventions in different age groups**

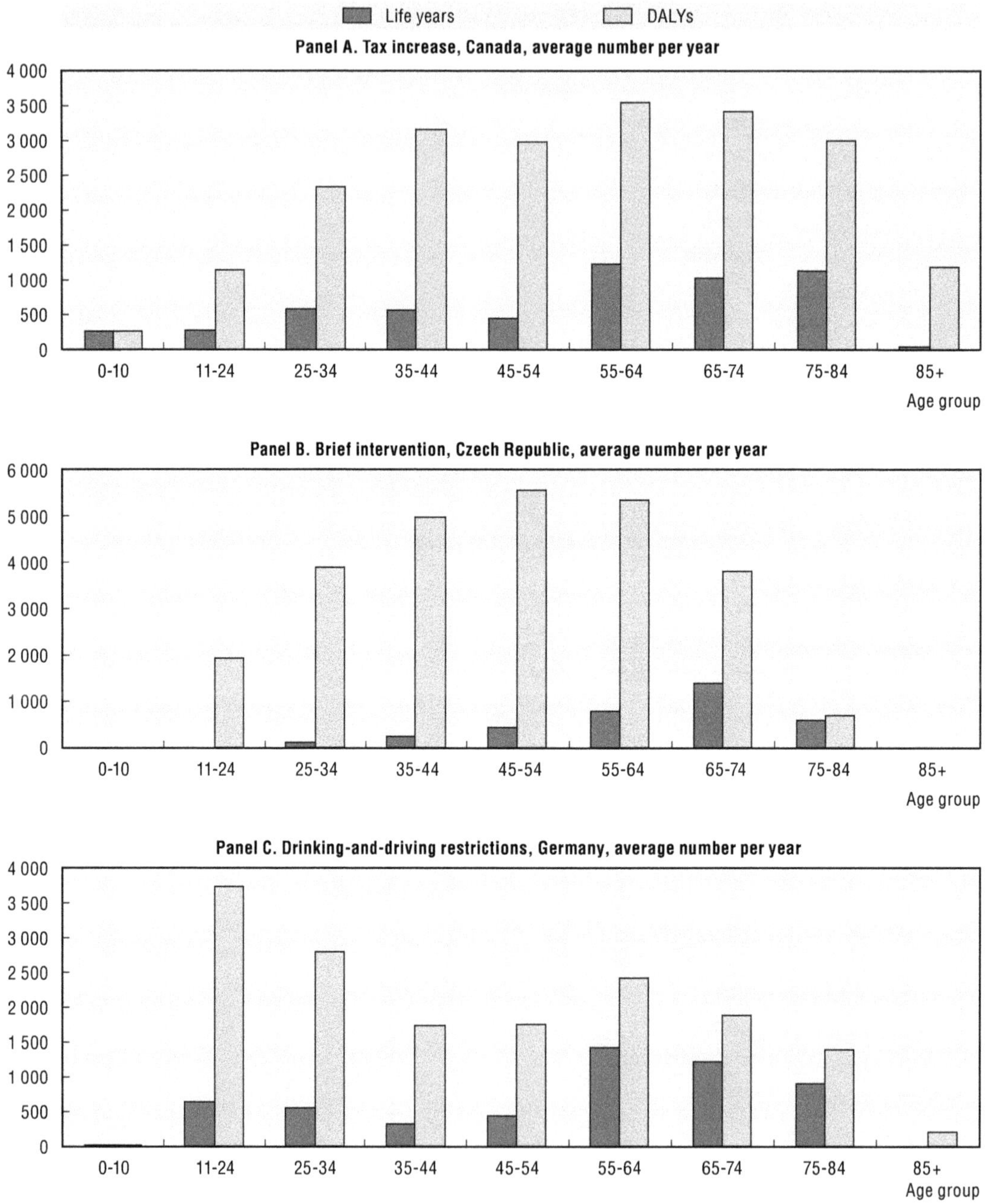


*Source:* CDP-Alcohol analysis relying on input data from multiple sources, listed in Tables A.4 to A.6 in Annex A.

*StatLink* http://dx.doi.org/10.1787/888933180554

## Robustness of findings from the analysis of policy impacts

Models produce their outputs based on data, algorithms and assumptions. Variations in any of those elements will change model predictions. The findings reported in this chapter were tested for robustness in a range of sensitivity analyses based on the WHO software MCLeague, for each intervention, at years 10 and 40 of the simulation. For both costs and effects, input parameters for the sensitivity analyses were derived from the raw output matrices of the CDP-Alcohol model. Probabilistic distributions of outputs were modelled as continuous Gaussian distributions. For health effects, the distributions were constrained (i.e. truncated) at the 95% confidence interval around the mean of CDP-Alcohol model outputs. The degree of covariance between the distributions of costs and health effects was also derived from CDP-Alcohol model outputs. Uncertainty clouds were produced using a Monte Carlo simulation approach involving 1 000 stochastic samplings (i.e. bootstraps).

The sensitivity analyses confirmed the validity of the findings in a relatively broad range of potential variation of both costs and effects for each alcohol policy, with effects not stochastically robust for school-based interventions in the Czech Republic, and treatment of dependence in Germany after 10 years (but with a robustly favourable profile in the longer term), as shown in Figures A.9 to A.14 in Annex A.

The effects of key assumptions were also tested in sensitivity analyses. For instance, coverage of interventions in primary health care (numbers of people who are offered and take up those interventions) is a key driver of the health outcomes produced, and the success of those interventions depends largely on countries' ability to deploy effective incentives for their delivery. The large effects predicted for brief interventions in primary care, for instance, are based on the assumption that the intervention would be offered systematically at all general practices in the countries concerned, and that it would be effective in changing drinkers' behaviour to the same degree observed in experimental conditions in the studies included in an existing meta-analysis (Kaner et al., 2009). For these reasons, the results presented for brief interventions are best interpreted as the impacts that could be achieved in optimal circumstances. At least two economic evaluations of screening and brief intervention programmes in primary care are available, respectively, for England and Italy (Purshouse et al., 2013; Angus et al., 2014). Both are based on the Sheffield Alcohol Policy Model, and reach the conclusion that brief interventions are effective and efficient means of addressing alcohol-related harms, albeit predicting somewhat smaller overall health impacts at the population level. In addition to coverage differences, the assumption made in the above studies that effectiveness at the individual level would be reduced in line with a shorter contact time with health professionals (five minutes) may explain the difference with the results presented in this chapter. Based on the scenario that reflects more closely the approach used in the OECD analysis, the cost-effectiveness ratio of a screening and brief intervention programme in England was estimated in the region of GBP 1 000 per quality adjusted life year (QALY) gained (Purshouse et al., 2012) and in the region of EUR 500 per QALY gained in Italy (Angus et al., 2014). These values match very closely those calculated in our analysis, including USD PPP 1 300 per DALY gained in Canada and 1 500 in Germany; while our analysis suggests that brief interventions are cost saving in the Czech Republic.

Alternative assumptions were also tested concerning the effects of tax increases, particularly in heavy drinkers, as explained in Section 5.4. Model findings in this analysis show that the health gains generated by tax increases are robust even to a dramatic cut of the alcohol price elasticity assumed for heavy drinkers, which would cause a drop in the overall numbers of life years and DALYs gained through tax increases of up to 5% in the three countries examined.

Health gains are larger where risky drinking behaviours are more widespread, and the prevalence of different behaviours may change significantly from one country to another. Since different alcohol policies tend to target different groups of drinkers and drinking behaviours, policy makers can tailor their alcohol strategies in ways that best respond to the specific needs and priorities of their respective countries. In countries where heavy alcohol use and alcohol dependence are especially common, any alcohol strategy would benefit from the inclusion of interventions in primary care for the prevention and treatment of dependence. In countries where HED and the injuries, violence and crime associated with it are of greater concern, regulatory actions imposing restrictions on the availability and marketing of alcohol, and on driving under the influence of alcohol, as well as their enforcement, should take higher priority. Some of these regulatory policies, as well as price policies and school-based programmes, may help delaying drinking initiation.

However, changing the prevalence of the highest-risk drinking behaviours is not the only way of achieving relatively large health gains at the population level. Reductions in alcohol consumptions in less heavy drinkers, including many moderate drinkers (especially young men and young and middle-aged women, for whom even very low quantities of alcohol increase mortality), have the potential to cut mortality and morbidity and generate health gains which may be small at the individual level, but become substantial at the population level given the large numbers of people concerned. Price policies are the best examples of approaches to reduce alcohol consumption overall. Tax increases, in particular, do not specifically target high-risk drinking behaviours. Taxation policies consistently achieve large health gains in all of the three countries examined in our analysis, despite evidence of a lesser response to price changes by heavy drinkers.

### Note

1. Available at: http://www.thecommunityguide.org/alcohol.

### Bibliography

Ames, G.M. and J.B. Bennett (2011), "Prevention Interventions of Alcohol Problems in the Workplace – A Review and Guiding Framework", *Alcohol Research & Health*, Vol. 34, No. 2, pp. 175-187.

Anderson, P. (2015), "Tackling Alcohol-related Harms", in D. McDaid, F. Sassi and S. Merkur (eds.), *Promoting Health, Preventing Disease: The Economic Case*, Open University Press, Maidenhead, United Kingdom.

Anderson, P. (2009), "Is It Time to Ban Alcohol Advertising?", *Clinical Medicine*, Vol. 9, pp. 121–124.

Anderson, P., D. Chisholm and D. Fuhr (2009a), "Effectiveness and Cost-effectiveness of Policies and Programmes to Reduce the Harm Caused by Alcohol", *The Lancet*, Vol. 373, No. 9682, pp. 2234-2246.

Anderson, P., L. Møller and G. Galea (2012), *Alcohol in the European Union: Consumption, Harm and Policy Approaches*, World Health Organization, Copenhagen.

Anderson, P. et al. (2009b), "Impact of Alcohol Advertising and Media Exposure on Adolescent Alcohol Use: A Systematic Review of Longitudinal Studies", *Alcohol and Alcoholism*, Vol. 44, No. 3, pp. 229-243.

Angus, C. et al. (2014), "Cost-effectiveness of a Programme of Screening and Brief Interventions for Alcohol in Primary Care in Italy", *BMC Family Practice*, 15:26.

Ayyagari, P. et al. (2013), "Understanding Heterogeneity in Price Elasticities in the Demand for Alcohol for Older Individuals", *Health Economics*, Vol. 22, No. 1, pp. 89-105

Baltieri, D.A., A. Guerra de Andrade (2004), "Acamprosate in Alcohol Dependence: A Randomized Controlled Efficacy Study in a Standard Clinical Setting", *Journal of Studies on Alcohol*, Vol. 65, pp. 136-139.

Bangert-Drowns, R.L. (1998), "The Effects of School-based Substance Abuse Education – A Meta-Analysis", *Journal of Drug Education*, Vol. 18, No. 3, pp. 243-264.

Beatty, T.K.M., E.R. Larsen and D.E. Sommervoll (2009), "Driven to Drink: Sin Taxes Near a Border", *Journal of Health Economics*, No. 28, pp. 1175-1184.

Bergman, U.M. and N.L. Hansen (2013), "Are Excise Taxes on Beverages Fully Passed Through to Prices? The Danish Experience", Unpublished working paper, University of Copenhagen, available at www.econ.ku.dk/okombe.

Bruvold, W.H. (1988), "A Meta-analysis of the California School-based Risk Reduction Program", *Journal of Drug Education*, Vol. 20, No. 2, pp. 139-152.

Bryden, A. et al. (2012), "A Systematic Review of the Influence on Alcohol Use of Community Level Availability and Marketing of Alcohol", *Health & Place*, Vol. 8, No. 2, pp. 349-357, March.

Burge, S. et al. (1997), "An Evaluation of Two Primary Care Interventions for Alcohol Abuse Among Mexican-American Patients", *Addiction*, Vol. 92, No. 12, pp. 1705-1716.

Cecchini, M. et al. (2010), "Tackling of Unhealthy Diets, Physical Inactivity, and Obesity: Health Effects and Cost-effectiveness", *The Lancet*, Vol. 376, No. 9754, pp. 1775-1784.

Centers for Disease Control and Prevention (2014a), "Vital Signs: Communication Between Health Professionals and their Patients about Alcohol Use – 44 States and the District of Columbia, 2011", *Morbidity and Mortality Weekly Report*, Vol. 63, No. 01, pp. 16-22.

Centers for Disease Control and Prevention (2014b), "Planning and Implementing Screening and Brief Intervention for Risky Alcohol Use: A Step-by-Step Guide for Primary Care Practices", Centers for Disease Control and Prevention, National Center on Birth Defects and Developmental Disabilities, Atlanta, Georgia.

Chisholm, D. et al. (2006), "Comparative Cost-effectiveness of Policy Instruments for Reducing the Global Burden of Alcohol, Tobacco and Illicit Drug Use", *Drug and Alcohol Review*, Vol. 25, pp. 553-565.

Chisholm, D. et al. (2004), "Reducing the Global Burden of Hazardous Alcohol Use: A Comparative Cost-Effectiveness Analysis", *Journal of Studies on Alcohol*, Vol. 65, pp. 782-793.

Cobiac, L. et al. (2009), "Cost-effectiveness of Interventions to Prevent Alcohol-related Disease and Injury in Australia", *Addiction*, Vol. 104, pp. 1646-1655.

Cook, R.F., A.S. Back and J. Trudeau (1996), "Preventing Alcohol Use Problems Among Blue Collar Workers: A Field Test of the Working People Program", *Substance Use and Misuse*, Vol. 31, No. 3, pp. 255-275.

Corrao, G. et al. (2004), "A Meta-analysis of Alcohol Consumption and the Risk of 15 Diseases", *Preventive Medicine*, Vol. 38, No. 5, pp. 613-619.

Dhalwani, N. (2011), "A Review of Alcohol Pricing and Its Effects on Alcohol Consumption and Alcohol-related Harm", *Journal of Pakistan Medical Students*, No. 1.1, pp. 23-27.

Doggett, C., S.L. Burrett and D.A. Osborn (2009), "Home Visits During Pregnancy and After Birth for Women with an Alcohol or Drug Problem", *Cochrane Database of Systematic Reviews*, Vol. 4, Art. No. CD004456.

Elder, R.W. et al. and Task Force on Community Preventive Services (2010), "The Effectiveness of Tax Policy Interventions for Reducing Excessive Alcohol Consumption and Related Harms", *American Journal of Preventive Medicine*, Vol. 38, No. 2, pp. 217-229, February.

Ennet, S.T. et al. (1994), "How Effective Is Drug Abuse Resistance Education? A Meta-Analysis of Project DARE Outcome Evaluations", *American Journal of Public Health*, Vol. 84, No. 9, pp. 1394-1401.

Erke, A., C. Goldenbeld and T. Vaa (2009), "The Effects of Drink-driving Checkpoints on Crashes – A Meta-analysis", *Accident Analysis and Prevention*, Vol. 41, pp. 914-923.

Fogarty, J. (2008), "The Demand for Beer, Wine and Spirits: Insights from a Meta-analysis Approach", *AAWE Working Paper No. 31*, American Association of Wine Economists.

Foxcroft, D.R. and A. Tsertsvadze (2012), "Universal School-based Prevention Programs for Alcohol Misuse in Young People", *Evidence-based Child Health*, Vol. 7, No. 2, pp. 450-575.

Foxcroft, D.R. et al. (2002), "Primary Prevention for Alcohol Misuse in Young People", *Cochrane Database of Systematic Reviews*, Vol. 3, CD003024.

Gallet, C.A. (2007), "The Demand for Alcohol: A Meta-analysis of Elasticities", *Australian Journal of Agricultural and Resource Economics*, Vol. 7, No. 51, pp. 121-135.

Hahn, R.A. et al. (2010), "Effectiveness of Policies Restricting Hours of Alcohol Sales in Preventing Excessive Alcohol Consumption and Related Harms", *American Journal of Preventive Medicine*, Vol. 39, No. 6, pp. 590-604.

Hermansson, U. et al. (2010), "Screening and Brief Intervention for Risky Alcohol Consumption in the Workplace: Results of a 1-year Randomized Controlled Study", *Alcohol and Alcoholism*, Vol. 45, pp. 252-257.

Hill-McManus, D. et al. (2012), "Does Minimum Pricing Reduce the Burden of Disease and Injury Attributable to Alcohol? Model-based Appraisal of Alcohol Minimum Pricing in Ontario and British Columbia", ScHARR, University of Sheffield, available at www.carbc.ca/Portals/0/propertyagent/558/files/240/alcminpricingontbc.pdf.

HM Revenue & Customs (2013), "Measuring Tax Gaps 2013 – Tax Gap Estimates for 2011-12", Official statistics release, 11 October 2013, available at www.gov.uk/government/uploads/system/uploads/attachment_data/file/249537/131010_Measuring_Tax_Gaps_ACCESS_2013.pdf.

Holmes, J. et al. (2012), "The Temporal Relationship Between Per Capita Alcohol Consumption and Harm: A Systematic Review of Time Lag Specifications in Aggregate Time Series Analyses", *Drug and Alcohol Dependence*, Vol. 123, No. 1-3, pp. 7-14.

Jonas, D.E. et al. (2012), "Behavioral Counseling After Screening for Alcohol Misuse in Primary Care: A Systematic Review and Meta-analysis for the U.S. Preventive Services Task Force", *Annals of Internal Medicine*.

Jones, L., E. Stokes and M. Bellis (2007), "A Review of the Effectiveness and Cost-effectiveness of Interventions Delivered in Primary and Secondary Schools to Prevent and/or Reduce Alcohol Use by Young People Under 18 Years Old – Addendum: Additional Economic Evidence Prepared for the Public Health Interventions Advisory Committee (PHIAC)", John Moores University, Liverpool.

Kaner, E. et al. (2013), "Effectiveness of Screening and Brief Alcohol Intervention in Primary Care (SIPS Trial): Pragmatic Cluster Randomized Controlled Trial", *British Medical Journal*, 346:e8501.

Kaner, E.F. et al. (2009), "Effectiveness of Brief Alcohol Interventions in Primary Care Populations", *Cochrane Database of Systematic Reviews*, Vol. 2, Art. No. CD004148.

Khadjesari, Z. et al. (2010), "Can Stand-alone Computer-based Interventions Reduce Alcohol Consumption? A Systematic Review", *Addiction*, Vol. 106, pp. 267-282.

Koski, A. et al. (2007), "Alcohol Tax Cuts and Increase in Alcohol-positive Sudden Deaths: A Time-series Intervention Analysis", *Addiction*, Vol. 102, No. 3, pp. 362-368.

Kraus, L. et al. (2014), "Inanspruchnahme gesundheitlicher Versorgung durch Alkoholabhängige [Health Care Utilization of People with Alcohol Dependence]", *Suchttherapie*, eFirst, http://dx.doi.org/10.1055/s-0034-1376999.

Kypri, K. et al. (2011), "Effects of Restricting Pub Closing Times on Night-time Assaults in an Australian City", *Addiction*, Vol. 106, No. 2, pp. 303-310.

Lai, T. et al. (2007), "Costs, Health Effects and Cost-effectiveness of Alcohol and Tobacco Control Strategies in Estonia", *Health Policy*, Vol. 84, No. 1, pp. 75-88, November.

Leppanen, K. (1979), "Valtakunnallisen lauantaisulkemiskokoeilun vaikutuksista alkoholijuomien myyntiin" (Effects of national Saturday closing experiment on alcohol sales), *Alkoholipolitiikka*, Vol. 44, pp. 20-21.

Lhachimi, S.K. et al. (2012), "DYNAMO-HIA – A Dynamic Modeling Tool for Generic Health Impact Assessments", *PLoS One*, Vol. 7, No. 5, e33317.

Lockwood, B. and G. Migali (2009), "Did the Single Market Cause Competition in Excise Taxes? Evidence from EU Countries", *Economic Journal*, Vol. 119, No. 536, pp. 406-429, March.

Lui, S., M. Terplan and E.J. Smith (2008), "Psychosocial Interventions for Women Enrolled in Alcohol Treatment During Pregnancy", *Cochrane Database of Systematic Reviews*, Vol. 3, Art. No. CD006753.

Mäkelä, P. and E. Österberg (2009), "Weakening of One More Alcohol Control Pillar: A Review of the Effects of the Alcohol Tax Cuts in Finland in 2004", *Addiction*, Vol. 104, No. 4, pp. 554-563.

Mäkelä, P. and T. Paljärvi (2008), "Do Consequences of a Given Pattern of Drinking Vary by Socioeconomic Status? A Mortality and Hospitalisation Follow-up for Alcohol-related Causes of the Finnish Drinking Habits Surveys", *Journal of Epidemiology and Community Health*, Vol. 62, No. 8, pp. 728-733.

Mason, B.J. et al. (2006), "Effect of Oral Acamprosate on Abstinence in Patients with Alcohol Dependence in a Double-blind, Placebo-controlled Trial: The Role of Patient Motivation", *Journal of Psychiatric Research*, Vol. 40, pp. 383-393.

Matano, R.A. et al. (2007), "A Pilot Study of an Interactive Web Site in the Workplace for Reducing Alcohol Consumption", Journal of Substance Abuse Treatment, Vol. 32, pp. 71-80.

McBride, N. et al. (2004), "Harm Minimization in School Drug Education: Final Results of the School Health and Alcohol Harm Reduction Project (SHAHRP)", *Addiction*, Vol. 99, No. 3, pp. 278-291, March.

McBride, N. et al. (2000), "Early Results from a School Alcohol Harm Minimization Study: The School Health and Alcohol Harm Reduction Project", *Addiction*, Vol. 95, No. 7, pp. 1021-1042.

McQueen, J. et al. (2011), "Brief Interventions for Heavy Alcohol Users Admitted to General Hospital Wards", *Cochrane Database of Systematic Reviews*, Vol. 8, Art. No. CD005191.

Meier, P. (2008), "Independent Review of the Effects of Alcohol Pricing and Promotion – Part A: Systematic Review", University of Sheffield, United Kingdom.

Meier, P.S., R. Purshouse and A. Brennan (2010), "Policy Options for Alcohol Price Regulation: The Importance of Modelling Population Heterogeneity", *Addiction*, Vol. 105, No. 3, pp. 383-393.

Meng, Y., D. Hill-McManus and A. Brennan (2012), "Model-based Appraisal of Alcohol Minimum Pricing and Off-licensed Trade Discount Bans in Scotland Using the Sheffield Alcohol Policy Model (v.2) – Second Update, School of Health and Related Research, Sheffield, United Kingdom.

Morley, K.C. et al. (2006), "Naltrexone Versus Acamprosate in the Treatment of Alcohol Dependence: A Multi-centre, Randomized, Double-blind, Placebo-controlled Trial", *Addiction*, Vol. 101, pp. 451-1462.

Nelson, J.P. (2013a), "Meta-analysis of Alcohol Price and Income Elasticities – With Corrections for Publication Bias", *Health Economics Review*, Vol. 3, No. 17.

Nelson, J.P. (2013b), "Gender Differences in Alcohol Demand: A Systematic Review of the Role of Prices and Taxes", *Health Economics*, Published online in Wiley Online Library (wileyonlinelibrary.com).

Nelson, J.P. (2011), "Alcohol Marketing, Adolescent Drinking and Publication Bias in Longitudinal Studies: A Critical Survey Using Meta-analysis", *Journal of Economic Surveys*, Vol. 25, No. 2, pp. 191-232.

NHMRC – National Health and Medical Research Council (1992, *Is There a Safe Level of Alcohol for Men and Women?*, 2nd edition, Australian Government Publishing Service, Canberra.

Nilsen, P. et al. (2008), "A Systematic Review of Emergency Care Brief Alcohol Interventions for Injury Patients", *Journal of Substance Abuse Treatment*, Vol. 35, pp. 184-201.

Nordlund, S. (1984), "Effekten av lørdagsstengningen ved Vinmonopolets butikker" (Effects of Saturday closing of the wine/liquor monopoly outlets), *Alkoholpolitik-Tidsskrift for nordisk alkoholforskning*, Vol. 1, pp. 221-229.

Norstrom, T. and O.J. Skog (2005), "Saturday Opening and Alcohol Retail Shops in Sweden: An Experiment in Two Phases", *Addiction*, Vol. 100, pp. 767-776.

Norstrom, T. and O.J. Skog (2003), "Saturday Opening and Alcohol Retail Shops in Sweden: An Impact Analysis", *Journal of Studies on Alcohol*, Vol. 64, pp. 393-401.

Österberg, E.L. (2011), "Alcohol Tax Changes and the Use of Alcohol in Europe", *Drug and Alcohol Review*, Vol. 30, No. 2, pp. 124-129.

Østhus, S. (2012), "Nordic Alcohol Statistics 2007-2011", *Nordic Studies on Alcohol and Drugs*, Vol. 29, No. 6, pp. 611-623.

Pinsky, I. and S.A. El Jundi (2008), "Alcohol Advertising and Alcohol Consumption Among Youngsters: Review of the International Literature", *Revista Brasileira de Psiquiatria*, Vol. 30, No. 4, pp. 362-374, December.

Popova, S. et al. (2009), "Hours and Days of Sale and Density of Alcohol Outlets: Impacts on Alcohol Consumption and Damage: A Systematic Review", *Alcohol and Alcoholism*, Vol. 44, No. 5, pp. 500-516.

Purshouse, R.C. et al. (2013), "Modelling the Cost-effectiveness of Alcohol Screening and Brief Interventions in Primary Care in England", *Alcohol and Alcoholism*, Vol. 48, No. 2, pp. 180-188.

Purshouse, R.C. et al. (2010), "Estimated Effect of Alcohol Pricing Policies on Health and Health Economic Outcomes in England: An Epidemiological Model", *The Lancet*, Vol. 375, pp. 1355-1364.

Rabinovich, L. et al. (2009), "The Affordability of Alcoholic Beverages in the European Union – Understanding the Link between Alcohol Affordability, Consumption and Harms", Rand Europe Report.

Rehm, J., C.T. Sempos and M. Trevisan (2003), "Alcohol and Cardiovascular Disease – More than One Paradox to Consider. Average Volume of Alcohol Consumption, Patterns of Drinking and Risk of Coronary Heart Disease – A Review", *Journal of Cardiovascular Risk*, Vol. 10, No. 1, pp. 15-20.

Rehm, J. et al. (2014), "A Systematic Review of the Epidemiology of Unrecorded Alcohol Consumption and the Chemical Composition of Unrecorded Alcohol", *Addiction*, Vol. 109, No. 6, pp. 880-893, June.

Rehm, J. et al. (2012), "Alcohol Consumption, Alcohol Dependence and Attributable Burden of Disease in Europe: Potential Gains from Effective Interventions for Alcohol Dependence", Centre for Addiction and Mental Health, Toronto.

Rehm, J. et al. (2003), "The Relationship of Average Volume of Alcohol Consumption and Patterns of Drinking to Burden of Disease: An Overview", *Addiction*, Vol. 98, No. 9, pp. 1209-1228.

Richmond, R. et al. (2000), "Evaluation of a Workplace Brief Intervention for Excessive Alcohol Consumption: The Workscreen Project", *Preventive Medicine*, Vol. 30, pp. 51-63.

Roozen, H.G. et al. (2006), "A Systematic Review of the Effectiveness of Naltrexone in the Maintenance Treatment of Opioid and Alcohol Dependence", *European Neuropsychopharmacology*, Vol. 16, pp. 311-323.

Rösner, S. et al. (2011), "Acamprosate for Alcohol Dependence", *Cochrane Database of Systematic Reviews*, Vol. 9, Art. No. CD004332.

Rösner, S. et al. (2010), "Opioid Antagonists for Alcohol Dependence", *Cochrane Database of Systematic Reviews*, Vol. 12, Art. No. CD001867.

Rossow, I. and T. Norström (2011), "The Impact of Small Changes in Bar Closing Hours on Violence. The Norwegian Experience from 18 Cities", *Addiction*, Vol. 107, pp. 530-537.

Rundall, T. and W. Bruvold (1998), "Meta-analysis of School-based Smoking and Alcohol Use Prevention Programs", *Health Education Quarterly*, pp. 317-334.

Saffer, H. and D. Dave (2006), "Alcohol Advertising and Alcohol Consumption by Adolescents", *Health Economics*, Vol. 15, No. 6, pp. 617-637, June.

Saffer, H. and D. Dave (2002), "Alcohol Consumption and Alcohol Advertising Bans", *Applied Economics*, Vol. 34, No. 11, pp. 1325-1334.

Saitz, R. (2010), "Alcohol Screening and Brief Intervention in Primary Care: Absence of Evidence for Efficacy in People with Dependence or Very Heavy Drinking", *Drug and Alcohol Review*, Vol. 29, No. 6, pp. 631-640.

Sassi, F. (2010), *Obesity and the Economics of Prevention: Fit not Fat*, OECD Publishing, Paris, http://dx.doi.org/10.1787/9789264084865-en.

Scott-Sheldon, L.A. et al. (2014), "Efficacy of alcohol interventions for first-year college students: a meta-analytic review of randomized controlled trials", Journal of Consulting and Clinical Psychology, Vol. 82(2), pp. 177-188.

Shults, R.A. et al. and the Task Force on Community Preventive Services (2001), "Reviews of Evidence Regarding Interventions to Reduce Alcohol-Impaired Driving", *American Journal of Preventive Medicine*, Vol. 21, No. 4S, pp. 66-88.

Siegfried, N. et al. (2014), "Restricting or Banning Alcohol Advertising to Reduce Alcohol Consumption in Adults and Adolescents", *Cochrane Database of Systematic Reviews*, Vol. 11, Art. No. CD010704.

Skara, S. and S. Sussman (2003), "A review of 25 long-term adolescent tobacco and other drug use prevention program evaluations", Preventive Medicine, Vol. 37, No. 5, pp. 451-74.

Smith, L.A. and D.R. Foxcroft (2009), "The Effect of Alcohol Advertising, Marketing and Portrayal on Drinking Behaviour in Young People: Systematic Review of Prospective Cohort Studies", *BMC Public Health*, Vol. 9, No. 51, February.

Spoth, R., M. Greenberg and R. Turrisi (2008), "Preventive Interventions Addressing Underage Drinking: State of the Evidence and Steps Toward Public Health Impact", *Pediatrics*, Vol. 121, pp. S311-336.

Stockwell, T. and T. Chikritzhs (2009), "Do Relaxed Trading Hours for Bars and Clubs Mean More Relaxed Drinking ? A Review of International Research on the Impacts of Changes to Permitted Hours of Drinking", *Crime Prevention and Community Safety*, Vol. 11, pp. 153-170.

Stockwell, T. et al. (2013), "Minimum Alcohol Prices and Outlet Densities in British Columbia, Canada: Estimated Impacts on Alcohol-attributable Hospital Admissions", *American Journal of Public Health*, Vol. 103, No. 11, pp. 2014-2020, November.

Stockwell, T.M. et al. (2012a), "Does Minimum Pricing Reduce Alcohol Consumption? The Experience of a Canadian Province", *Addiction*, Vol. 107, pp. 912-920.

Stockwell, T. et al. (2012b), "The Raising of Minimum Alcohol Prices in Saskatchewan, Canada: Impacts on Consumption and Implications for Public Health", *American Journal of Public Health*, Vol. 102, No. 12, pp. 103-110.

Strøm, H.K. et al. (2014), "Effectiveness of school-based preventive interventions on adolescent alcohol use: a meta-analysis of randomized controlled trials", *Substance Abuse, Treatment, Prevention and Policy*, Vol. 9, No. 48.Tariq, L. et al. (2009), "Cost-effectiveness of an Opportunistic Screening Programme and Brief Intervention for Excessive Alcohol Use in Primary Care", *PLoS One*, Vol. 4, No. 5, e5696.

Sullivan, L.E. et al. (2011), "Meta-analysis of the Efficacy of Nonphysician Brief Interventions for Unhealthy Alcohol Use: Implications for the Patient-Centered Medical Home", *American Journal on Addictions*, Vol. 20, pp. 343-356.

Tobler, N. (1992), "Drug Prevention Programs Can Work: Research Findings", *Journal of Addictive Diseases*, Vol. 11, No. 3, pp. 1-28.

Tobler, N. (1986), "Meta-analysis of 143 Adolescent Drug Prevention Programs: Quantitative Outcome Results of Program Participants Compared to a Control or Comparison Group", *Journal of Drug Issues*, pp. 537-567.

Tobler, N. and H. Stratton (1997), "Effectiveness of School-based Drug Prevention Programs: A Meta-analysis of the Research", *Journal of Primary Prevention*, Vol. 18, No. 1, pp. 71-108.

Tobler, N.S. et al. (2000), "School-based Adolescent Drug Prevention Programs: 1988 Meta-analysis", *Journal of Primary Prevention*, Vol. 20, No. 4, pp. 275-336.

van den Berg, M. et al. (2008), "The Cost-effectiveness of Increasing Alcohol Taxes: A Modelling Study", *BMC Medicine*, 6:36.

VisionGain (2008), "The Global Anti-Addiction Market, 2008-2023", Visiongain, London.

Voas, R.B. (2008), "A New Look at NHTSA's Evaluation of the 1984 Charlottesville Sobriety Checkpoint Program: Implications for Current Checkpoint Issues", *Traffic Injury Prevention*, Vol. 9, No. 1, pp. 22-30.

Vos, T. et al. (2010), "Assessing Cost-Effectiveness in Prevention (ACE–Prevention): Final Report", ACE-Prevention Team, University of Queensland, Brisbane, and Deakin University, Melbourne, available at: www.sph.uq.edu.au/docs/BODCE/ACE-P/ACE-Prevention_final_report.pdf.

Wagenaar, A.C., M.J. Salois and K.A. Komro (2009), "Effects of Beverage Alcohol Price and Tax Levels on Drinking: A Meta-analysis of 1003 Estimates from 112 Studies", Addiction, Vol. 104, No. 2, pp. 179-190.

Wagenaar, A.C., A.L. Tobler and K.A. Komro (2010), "Effects of Tax and Price Policies on Mobility and Mortality: A Systematic Review", *American Journal of Public Health*, Vol. 100, No. 11, pp. 2270-2278.

Webb, G. et al. (2009), "A Systematic Review of Work-place Interventions for Alcohol-related Problems", *Addiction*, Vol. 104, pp. 365-377.

WHO – World Health Organization (2014), *Global Status Report on Alcohol and Health*, WHO, Geneva.

WHO (2008), *The Global Burden of Disease: 2004 Update*, WHO, Geneva.

Wilson, D.B., D.C. Gottfredson and S.S. Najaka (2001), "School-based Prevention of Problem Behaviors: A Meta-analysis", *Journal of Quantitative Criminology*, Vol. 17, No. 3, pp. 247-271.

World Economic Forum and WHO (2011), "From Burden to 'Best Buys': Reducing the Economic Impact of Non-Communicable Diseases in Low- and Middle-Income Countries", World Economic Forum, Geneva.

Wutzke, S.E. et al. (2002), "The Long-term Effectiveness of Brief Interventions for Unsafe Alcohol Consumption: A 10-year Follow-up", *Addiction*, Vol. 97, pp. 665-675.

Young, D.J. and A. Bielinska-Kwapisz (2002), "Alcohol Taxes and Beverage Prices", *National Tax Journal*. Vol. 55, No. 1, pp. 57-73.

Zhao, J. et al. (2013), "The Relationship Between Minimum Alcohol Prices, Outlet Densities and Alcohol-attributable Deaths in British Columbia, 2002-09", *Addiction*, Vol. 108, No. 6, 1059.

Tackling Harmful Alcohol Use
Economics and Public Health Policy


*Special focus V*

# Benefits of population-wide approaches to prevention: The case of minimum alcohol prices

by
Martin McKee
London School of Hygiene and Tropical Medicine

Minimum unit pricing (MUP) for alcohol has been placed on the health policy agenda of many countries following the proposal by the Scottish Government to introduce minimum prices in response to the high and rapidly increasing burden of alcohol-related disease in Scotland. The policy also targets aggressive marketing by large supermarket chains that offer alcohol at prices close to or below the cost of the taxes and duty as a loss-leader to attract customers into stores. It is an explicit recognition of the fact that the most effective health promotion policies are those that take population-wide approaches, instead of targeting only those at highest risk (Rose, 1985).

Where the goal is to influence the consumption of a product that is either harmful (such as alcohol in excess or tobacco) or beneficial (such as fresh fruit and vegetables), policy should focus on price, availability, and marketing, rather than the largely ineffective, and in some cases counterproductive, individual educational interventions (which the producers of harmful substances are most keen to advocate). There are many reasons why a population approach is more desirable, including the following.

- Within a population, the risk is distributed unevenly, with a very small number of people at the highest risk, and many more at moderately increased risk. A policy that tackles only those at very high risk will bring much less overall health benefit than one that shifts the entire distribution of risk in the population (Rose, 1985).
- Policies targeted at individuals assume that people make rational choices when deciding whether to engage in potentially harmful behaviour. This assumes stable preferences, foresight, perfect knowledge, and adequate cognitive abilities to make the decision. These elements are often, and in some cases always, lacking in relation to potentially damaging substances (Song et al., 2014).
- Collective measures, such as regulation, legislation, or fiscal measures, are often cost-neutral or even cost-saving whereas individual interventions, which have to be delivered to each member of the target group, are often expensive.
- There is extensive evidence that policies that include a range of measures are much more effective than any single measure on its own (Anderson and Baumberg, 2006). The Scottish proposal is part of a comprehensive policy to address the poor health of the Scottish people, in which the Scottish government has been in the forefront of progressive policies such as banning smoking in enclosed public spaces.

Before examining the evidence base for this proposal, it is necessary to explain why the Scottish Government focused exclusively on MUP, given that the additional money spent by drinkers will go to alcohol manufacturers and retailers, rather than combining it with the more conventional approach, used so successfully with tobacco in many countries, of increasing taxes. Using minimum prices and tax increases simultaneously would reduce consumption of the very cheap products that appeal to children and heavy drinkers, as well as reduce overall consumption. However, the Scottish Government currently has no powers to raise duties, so unlike many other administrations, it was constrained from implementing a comprehensive pricing strategy including both MUP and progressive increases in alcohol taxes.

The rationale for increasing price is simple. For most goods, an increase in price is associated with a decline in consumption, all else being equal (an exception is what are termed "luxury goods", where the high price is associated with exclusivity and thus greater attraction to those who can afford them; clearly this does not apply to cheap alcohol). The association between price and demand is referred to as the price elasticity of demand, which is the percentage change in demand for alcohol in response to a percentage change in its price. Two recent syntheses of the available data reported overall price elasticities of demand for alcohol of about -0.5, so that that a 10% increase in price would lead to a 5% decrease in demand (Gallet, 2007; Wagenaar et al., 2009), although the precise values vary in different settings and for different products (Meng et al., 2014; Goryakin et al., 2014).

But what does this imply for health? A seminal study by researchers from the University of Sheffield assessed a wide range of pricing policies. It concluded that, in the English population, general increases in price would reduce consumption, health-care costs, and losses of health-related quality of life in all sub-groups of the population that they studied (Purshouse et al., 2010). It also concluded that minimum pricing policies would be most beneficial for harmful drinkers while minimising the impact on moderate drinkers. The study estimated that a MUP of GBP 0.45 (EUR 0.57) could save almost 2 000 deaths per year ten years after implementation of the policy.

Among the main arguments used against MUP is that it will hit moderate drinkers who are at low risk of harm and that the additional costs will fall disproportionately on the poor. This has been examined in further work by the Sheffield group (Holmes et al., 2014). They find that, in England, a MUP of GBP 0.45 would lead to an immediate reduction in consumption of 1.6%, with consumption and spending by moderate drinkers only marginally affected. In contrast, the model estimated a decline in consumption of 3.7% among harmful drinkers, which increased to a 7.6% decline among those in the lowest income quintile. However, the estimated health benefits were also unequally distributed, with those in the lowest socioeconomic group, who comprise 42% of the sample population, accruing 82% of the reduction in premature deaths and 87% of increases in quality-adjusted life-years.

Inevitably, the alcohol industry has challenged the validity of this research, as the estimates are derived from models, rather than actual experience. However, a detailed analysis of data from British Colombia supports the effectiveness of minimum prices. In that setting, minimum prices have been imposed since 1989, and have been increased over time. Research found that a 10% increase in average minimum price for all alcoholic beverages was associated with a 32% reduction in wholly alcohol attributable deaths, with associations still detectable up to three years after price increases (Zhao et al., 2013). These benefits were seen even though minimum prices only affected a small proportion of products. The benefits were, however, undermined to some extent by an increase in sales outlets following liberalisation of the retail alcohol sector, emphasizing the need for a comprehensive response tackling price, availability, and marketing.

Unsurprisingly, given the compelling evidence that a price increase would reduce sales, this proposal has attracted criticism from large parts of the alcohol industry (Hilton et al., 2014), with the Scotch Whiskey Association mounting a legal challenge. This is consistent with the longstanding reluctance of the industry, in common with those selling other potentially hazardous products, to reject population-based approaches, instead favouring less effective measures based on ideas of individual responsibility. The Association lost in the Scottish courts but has appealed to the European Court of Justice; this is likely only to delay implementation, similar to the strategy adopted by the tobacco industry in relation to the European Union's Tobacco Products Directive (Tobacco Tactics, 2013).

## Bibliography

Anderson, P. and B. Baumberg (2006), *Alcohol in Europe: A Public Health Perspective*, EU Health and Consumer Protection Directorate General, Brussels.

Gallet, C.A. (2007), "The Demand for Alcohol: A Meta-analysis of Elasticities", *Australian Journal of Agricultural and Resource Economics*, Vol. 51, No. 2, pp. 121-135.

Goryakin, Y., B. Roberts, and M. McKee (2014), "Price Elasticities of Alcohol Demand: Evidence from Russia", *European Journal of Health Economics*, http://dx.doi.org/10.007/s10198-014-0565-9.

Hilton, S. et al. (2014), "Implications for Alcohol Minimum Unit Pricing Advocacy: What Can We Learn for Public Health from UK Newsprint Coverage of Key Claim-makers in the Policy Debate?", *Social Science & Medicine*, Vol. 102, pp. 157-164.

Holmes, J. et al. (2014), "Effects of Minimum Unit Pricing for Alcohol on Different Income and Socioeconomic Groups: A Modelling Study", *The Lancet*, Vol. 383, No. 9929, pp. 1655-1664.

Meng, Y. et al. (2014), "Estimation of Own and Cross Price Elasticities of Alcohol Demand in the UK. A Pseudo-panel Approach Using the Living Costs and Food Survey 2001-2009", *Journal of Health Economics*, Vol. 34, pp. 96-103.

Purshouse, R.C. et al. (2010), "Estimated Effect of Alcohol Pricing Policies on Health and Health Economic Outcomes in England: An Epidemiological Model", *The Lancet*, Vol. 375, No. 9723, pp. 1355-1364.

Rose, G. (1985), "Sick Individuals and Sick Populations", *International Journal of Epidemiology*, Vol. 14, No. 1, pp. 32-38.

Song, A.V., P. Brown, and S.A. Glantz (2014), "When Health Policy and Empirical Evidence Collide: The Case of Cigarette Package Warning Labels and Economic Consumer Surplus", *American Journal of Public Health*, Vol. 104, No. 2, pp. e42-51

Tobacco Tactics (2013), "PMI's Lobbying Campaign to Undermine the TPD", http://tobaccotactics.org/index.php/PMI%E2%80%99s_Lobbying_Campaign_to_Undermine_the_TPD.

Wagenaar, A.C., M.J. Salois, and K.A. Komro (2009), "Effects of Beverage Alcohol Price and Tax Levels on Drinking: A Meta-Analysis of 1003 Estimates from 112 Studies", *Addiction*, Vol. 104, No. 2, pp. 179-190.

Zhao, J. et al. (2013), "The Relationship Between Minimum Alcohol Prices, Outlet Densities and Alcohol-Attributable Deaths in British Columbia, 2002–09", *Addiction*, Vol. 108, No. 6, pp. 1059-1069.

Tackling Harmful Alcohol Use
Economics and Public Health Policy


# Chapter 6

# Alcohol, the individual and society: A call for coherent alcohol policies

by
Franco Sassi

*While the rationale for government action to tackle harmful alcohol use is strong, the challenges involved in designing, implementing, and building consensus around effective policy measures are daunting. The interests at stake are so powerful and so diverse, and the views of the problem so polarised, that inertia has often been the norm in the past. But action has been gathering new momentum with the emergence of compelling evidence of the health and economic consequences of harmful alcohol use and of the effectiveness of policies to address them. Voices from civil society have been growing stronger, and governments have increasingly recognised their own role in alcohol policy making with major national and international policy initiatives. The evidence available today, to which this book contributes, provides solid foundations for the development of comprehensive, wide-ranging policy strategies to change the social norms upon which long-established harmful drinking habits are based. Initiatives promoted by the alcohol industry may contribute to addressing harmful alcohol use, as part of a multi-stakeholder policy framework, provided that evidence of their impact is available from rigorous and independent evaluations.*

## Key findings

- There is a fresh momentum today for addressing the problem of harmful alcohol use. More evidence of the impacts of alcohol on health and broader social outcomes, such as crime and violence, and of the effectiveness of alcohol policies, is available today than ever before.
- An increase in high-risk drinking behaviours and a progressive concentration of the alcohol industry are also part of a changing scenario.
- Alcohol is an exceptionally complex area for policy making. Difficulties in measuring consumption and its impacts compound the challenges involved in balancing the benefits and harms associated with alcohol use.
- The rationale for government intervention to curb harmful alcohol use, mainly resting on the costs imposed by drinkers on others, is strong and provides wide scope for improving the welfare of drinkers and society as a whole through appropriate policy measures.
- Many alcohol policies have been shown to be effective and efficient, but a critical success factor in tackling harmful alcohol use is governments' ability to design and implement wide-ranging prevention strategies, combining the strengths of different policy approaches adapted to national patterns of drinking.
- Surveys of alcohol consumption are key instruments in the design of sound alcohol policies. Countries and their statistical and public health agencies must step up their efforts to improve the consistency and accuracy of such surveys.
- Initiatives to prevent the harmful use of alcohol promoted by the alcohol industry have the potential to contribute to tackling the problem. Evidence, based on thorough and policy-relevant evaluations of the impacts of such actions, must be gathered more systematically, and replace anecdotes and ideology in the policy debate.

## Harmful alcohol use: An old problem with new dimensions

Few commodities are as deep-rooted in people's cultures and habits as is alcohol. The discovery of Stone Age beer jugs confirmed that fermented beverages already existed about 12 000 years ago, in the Neolithic period (Patrick, 1952), and anthropologists claim that people started growing crops with the aim of brewing alcoholic drinks even before they had expertise and technology to bake, making this ancient form of beer precede bread as a staple food (Katz and Voigt, 1987). Throughout history, and until the present times, alcohol has played a fundamental role in arts and religion, and even became an important public health tool in the medieval age, when the process of brewing was used to purify water from bacteria.

But the side effects of alcohol, too, have been present throughout the history of its use. Excessive alcohol use has traditionally been associated with disease and loss of physical and social function, with crime and violence, with idleness and poverty (although excessive drinking is by no means an exclusive habit of the poor and socially excluded, as discussed in Chapter 3). Governments have been trying for millennia to control the consumption of alcohol. China passed and repealed laws on wine making over 40 times between 1100 BCE and 1400 CE, for instance (ADARFO, 1961).

There are, however, new dimensions to the problems engendered by harmful alcohol use throughout the history of humankind (drinking and driving is one example). Although alcohol consumption has declined in many OECD countries in recent years, there is no room for complacency, as harmful alcohol use continues to be a major public health threat, and one that is growing in size worldwide.

Today's awareness of the health risks associated with harmful alcohol consumption is unprecedented, and evidence of the magnitude and importance of such risks has never been so abundant and detailed. This has generated a momentum for public health action against the harmful use of alcohol, which perhaps for the first time is not associated with a moral or religious drive, and not even exclusively with an economic drive. People's health and welfare have taken centre stage in the conception and design of alcohol policies.

### *Evidence and action*

The World Health Organization (WHO) and, more recently, the Institute for Health Metrics and Evaluation, have produced estimates of the global burden of disease that consistently place alcohol among the top risk factors for death, disease and disability. The estimates discussed in Chapter 1 and in WHO's Special Focus contribution I, showing that alcohol is responsible for over 5% of deaths and for 4% to 5% of DALYs lost worldwide, with a significant increase compared with earlier estimates (Lim et al., 2012; WHO, 2014), amount to a strong call for action. The political declaration adopted by the United Nations following the 2011 "High-level Meeting of the General Assembly on the Prevention and Control of Noncommunicable Diseases" identified harmful alcohol use as one of four leading risk factors behind the current epidemic of non-communicable diseases, along with tobacco use, unhealthy diets and lack of physical activity. The World Health Assembly adopted in 2013 a set of global targets for the prevention and control of non-communicable diseases, which includes a reduction by at least 10% in harmful alcohol use by 2025 ("as appropriate within the national context"). At the same time, a large body of evidence of the effectiveness of a range of alcohol policy options has built up, confirming that harmful alcohol use is not just a high-burden problem, but also one that can be addressed and kept under control with a variety of effective measures. Policies aimed at raising the prices of alcoholic beverages have been studied widely, and thousands of estimates have been produced of consumers' responsiveness to price changes. Regulation and enforcement policies, such as, for instance, advertising restrictions, age limits for alcohol purchases, regulations to prevent motor vehicle driving after drinking alcohol, have been tested and evaluated, and so have policies aimed at delivering information and education on the risks that may be associated with alcohol, and interventions in primary health care to prevent dependence and harmful drinking, as discussed extensively in Chapter 4.

Starting from the above commitments and evidence, the OECD designed a detailed analysis of the health and economic impacts of a range of alcohol policy options with the aim of supporting countries in their efforts to curb harmful alcohol use. The analyses presented in Chapter 5 illustrate a menu of policy options and key facts about the outcomes governments should expect if they decided to implement those policies. For instance, they show that WHO's global target on harmful alcohol use is within countries' reach, as several alcohol policies, including a large scale implementation of screening and brief interventions in primary care, tax increases, or advertising regulation, among others, may reduce hazardous and harmful drinking, as well as alcohol dependence, by between 5% and 10%. Combining multiple policy approaches would further increase impacts.

All of the evidence described was not available only 30 years ago. Even if there are still many gaps in our knowledge, and more evidence needs to be gathered on many dimensions of the effects of alcohol drinking and ways of preventing harms, what we do know today has been sufficient to generate a strong momentum in tackling alcohol-related harms. An increasing number of civil society organisations have focused on this goal, raising public awareness and media attention on the problem. Medicine and public health have become increasingly aware of the size and scope of the risks associated with harmful alcohol use, which extend beyond addiction and dependence. Governments have come to grips with the broader health and social dimensions of alcohol, recognising, for instance, that alcohol taxation may be more than just a source of revenue, and that the value of alcohol production and trade as drivers of economic activity and growth must be assessed in a wider context of benefits and harms. These changing attitudes have also been reflected in the work of international organisations, of which this book is one example.

### *Changing demand, changing supply*

Some of the new dimensions of harmful alcohol use have to do with changes in patterns of alcohol consumption and changes in the alcohol market. While alcohol consumption has decreased in many OECD countries with traditionally high levels of consumption, and especially in major wine-producing countries, the trends examined in Chapter 2 clearly show an increase in certain high-risk drinking behaviours in young people. Heavy drinking, regular or episodic, is increasingly seen in people who, until recently, were less likely to engage in this type of behaviour, such as young and highly-educated women. These emerging trends have prompted concerns about increasing commercial pressures, through pervasive advertising and marketing approaches, which have sought to expand the market for alcoholic beverages to new consumers in the face of an overall decline of the alcohol market in many countries. Women, ethnic minorities and young people have been the targets of product differentiation and branding efforts, promotion of alcoholic beverages as lifestyle commodities, through traditional and less traditional – e.g. Internet-based – channels (de Bruijn et al., 2012). The alcohol industry has become increasingly concentrated, particularly in its beer and spirits segments, to cope with the demands of a globalised market and afford increasing marketing expenses to sustain and develop the business (Jernigan, 2009).

Increased firm size and market concentration have also meant that alcohol beverage manufacturers have been able to expand their corporate social responsibility efforts. There has been a proliferation of initiatives and pledges by individual manufacturers and retailers, by their agencies and trade organisations, aimed at demonstrating the industry's commitment to curbing the harmful use of their products, as discussed in Chapter 4. Whether these initiatives are the result of genuine efforts or marketing tactics, they deserve rigorous evaluation and, if successful, may become part of a broader approach to addressing alcohol-related harms. Some governments have already seized the opportunity and have included business-led initiatives in the frame of national programmes, with jointly set targets and close monitoring of outcomes.

 

## The sheer complexity of addressing harmful alcohol use

An increased emphasis on the public health consequences of harmful alcohol use in the past few decades has raised the importance of alcohol in policy agendas worldwide and broadened the spectrum of actions countries are prepared to consider in fighting the problem. However, governments have seen both public support for, and opposition to, policy initiatives that are perceived by some as undue interference with individual choices. Alcohol-related harms are dreaded and stigmatised, but alcohol is highly valued by many consumers as a source of individual pleasure and social enjoyment, and its production and trade represent an important part of the economy in many countries. Alcohol is "no ordinary commodity" says the title of a landmark book on alcohol policy (Babor et al., 2010), and the complexity that surrounds it is potentially overwhelming for researchers and policy makers alike.

A central economic principle in the context of health promotion and disease prevention (Sassi and Hurst, 2008) is that:

*"Maintaining good health is an important goal for most individuals, but health is by no means the only outcome that individuals value when they choose how to lead their own lives. Individuals wish to engage in activities from which they expect to derive pleasure, satisfaction, or fulfilment, some of which may be conducive to good health, others less or not at all. [...] An assessment of the role of prevention must not ignore those competing goals."*

Alcohol drinking is a case in point. However, there is also good evidence that certain forms of alcohol use lead to poor health, dependence, poor labour market outcomes, anti-social (including criminal and violent) behaviour, and harm to others (from traffic-related injuries to foetal alcohol spectrum disorders). There are strong reasons to believe that these negative consequences of alcohol consumption by some people are not fully reflected, or accounted for, in their individual attitudes to drinking behaviours. This provides a rationale for governments to enact policies aimed at curbing the harms associated with alcohol consumption by creating the conditions that would change individual behaviours. Governments need to balance individual choices with social responsibility.

### *One substance, many commodities*

In his famous prints "Beer Street" and "Gin Lane", painter William Hogarth portrayed two radically different drinking and social cultures in eighteenth century England. Images of addiction, poverty, social degradation and crime in Gin Lane were juxtaposed with images of happiness, prosperity and thriving business in Beer Street, showing how social conditions can shape drinking habits, and are shaped by the latter in turn. The prints were in support of the British Parliament's Sale of Spirits Act of 1751, intended to curb the distillation and consumption of gin, which had turned from an engine of economic growth into a major social scourge over the previous half century (Abel, 2001).

Part of the complexity of alcohol rests precisely in the wide variety of forms in which it can be consumed and in the close links between these and different social cultures. This was true in the 18th century and still is today. Alcohol is one substance, but what people consume are many different commodities that contain alcohol, mostly beverages, but also some solid foods and non-food products. People consume alcoholic beverages in different places, in different ways, in different circumstances and with different people. Each alcoholic beverage is deeply rooted in the history and agricultural and dietary traditions of certain countries and regions, and often represents a non-negligible share of the national economy, especially when its links with tourism, entertainment and hospitality industries are taken into account.

Addressing the harmful use of alcohol in such a wide variety of drinking behaviours and circumstances, and respectfully of the social, cultural and economic dimensions of alcoholic beverages, is a major policy challenge. Many of the policies discussed in Chapter 4 are the result of years of experimentation and evaluation in many settings and countries. For at least some of those policies, evidence has been produced as to whether and how they can be effective in specific population groups, types of drinkers and drinking circumstances. What works in one setting and for a particular type of drinker does not always work in the same way in other settings and for other drinkers. Where such evidence exists, it must be taken into account in the design of the relevant policies in specific countries. Our analysis of policy impacts in Chapter 5 provides important indications of the likely size of the effects to be expected from the implementation of a range of policy options in different countries. It shows that individual alcohol policies can take countries a long way in the pursuit of WHO's target of reducing hazardous alcohol consumption by 10% by 2025, and packages of alcohol policies have the potential to produce health gains in the order of 10% of the burden of alcohol-related diseases estimated for the three countries examined in 2010 (Lim et al., 2012). However, the way the same policies are designed and implemented may play a large role in realising that potential, or otherwise.

### *Can we measure consumption?*

Difficulties in measuring alcohol consumption for individuals and population groups represent a major hurdle on the road towards evidence-based alcohol policies. These difficulties are discussed in detail in Chapter 2, where we provide evidence of common failures of existing measurement tools and their impact on our ability to estimate patterns of alcohol consumption and their consequences.

Aggregate estimates of alcohol consumption at the national level have become increasingly accurate over time. Based on these estimates, organisations like the OECD and WHO have been able to monitor trends in alcohol consumption over time in individual countries and world regions. In Chapter 2 we show that people in OECD countries consume twice as much alcohol as the world average, and that consumption, overall, has declined only slightly in the past 20 years. There have been, however, dramatic falls in alcohol consumption in southern European countries, as well as major increases in some northern and central-eastern European countries. Consumption has also been increasing sharply in major emerging economies like the Russian Federation, India, China and Brazil, all OECD key partners, in the past 20 years. These trends are presented and discussed in Chapter 2.

However, the data continue to have a number of limitations. Unrecorded alcohol consumption is typically outside the scope of such measures, and needs to be estimated separately, often on the basis of difficult assumptions. Inferring consumption from sales data involves many challenges, such as the estimation of waste, alcohol used for cooking or other purposes, consumption by non-residents, and others. Most importantly, aggregate estimates typically do not provide information on patterns of consumption by specific population groups or types of drinkers, which is of critical importance in the design of policies to tackle harmful alcohol use.

Individual-level surveys of alcohol consumption – which may be part of health, lifestyle, substance abuse, household expenditure, or other surveys – provide complementary information to aggregate data. By using survey data from a number of OECD countries, we have been able to show that alcohol consumption is highly concentrated in all of the countries examined, with the heaviest-drinking 20% of the population drinking the majority, sometimes the vast majority, of all alcohol. We have also shown alarming trends in regular or episodic heavy drinking in young people in many countries, with children taking up drinking and experiencing drunkenness at increasingly young ages, and girls catching up with boys in recent years. Based on survey data we have been able to show that the drinking habits of women, particularly those who have better education and highly-paid jobs, are converging to those of men.

Surveys typically make up for the largest shortcomings of aggregate data, shedding light on how individual characteristics and life circumstances may be associated with given levels and patterns of alcohol consumption. However, they have to rely on respondents' self-reports, because no objective measure of alcohol consumption is currently available for use in a survey setting, and self-reports are notoriously biased, as discussed in Chapter 2. They are biased because respondents do not recall accurately their consumption, or wish to conceal it deliberately, due to the social stigma associated with certain drinking behaviours (e.g. Studer et al., 2013), which may be a reason why self-reports by men tend to be less accurate than those made by women. One in five men, and one in ten women, who report drinking "in moderation", in fact drink at hazardous levels (Ely et al., 2001). But surveys are also biased because they rarely include marginalised people, who are often more likely to engage in heavy drinking.

Countries, their statistical and public health agencies, and academic researchers, share responsibility for the lack of progress in developing alcohol consumption surveys, improving the accuracy of reports, evaluating the performance of alternative tools and survey questions, and above all in improving the consistency of definitions, thresholds and survey questions over time and across jurisdictions. Surveys of consumption are key instruments in the design of alcohol policies, and urgent action must be taken to improve their relevance, accuracy and comparability if they are to lend greater support to future efforts to tackle harmful alcohol use.

### *Can we measure health impacts?*

Disease outcomes are among the most important alcohol-related harms, as alcohol is causally linked with more than 200 conditions codified in international disease classification systems (WHO, 2014). Excessive alcohol consumption contributes to a variety of health problems, including chronic diseases like cancer, alcoholic liver disease, cardiovascular disease and mental health conditions, as well as suicide, the sequelae of intoxication and alcohol dependence, and injuries (such as falls and road traffic injuries). In Chapter 5, we have shown that regulating on-trade outlet opening hours, for instance, has the potential to prevent 54 000 injuries each year in Germany, and 41 000 in Canada. A tighter enforcement of regulations against drinking and driving would prevent 71 000 and 37 000 traffic injuries, respectively, including fatalities. A tax increase leading to a 10% hike in alcohol process would cut new cases of alcohol-related cancers by up to 2%, corresponding to 4 200 fewer cases in Germany each year, 1 600 in Canada, and 500 in the Czech Republic.

But more remains to be done to improve our ability to estimate health impacts. Knowledge of the links between alcohol intake, diseases and death is largely based on observational studies, which typically rely on self-reported measures of alcohol use. The problems surrounding these measures, discussed above, often complicate the interpretation of available evidence. And the difficulties are even larger in the estimation of health effects that tend to occur many years later, as a result of alcohol consumption over a long period of time. Similar difficulties exist in assessing the impacts of changes in drinking behaviour, an important dimension in any evaluation of alcohol policies, which may also occur with delays (Rehm et al., 2007; Holmes et al., 2012).

The use of findings from observational studies in the assessment of causal links between alcohol use and diseases is generally challenging. Researchers typically look for dose-response relationships as a sign of causality, or seek to design their studies as natural experiments, but these options are not always viable. Estimating a causal link between alcohol use and disease outcomes requires a comparison between people who are virtually the same, except for their drinking habits, and if they are not the same, it should at least be possible to account for their differences in a statistical analysis. In the context of a meta-analysis of the impact of alcohol on overall mortality, alternative forms of statistical adjustment to account for selected differences between the people observed were shown to have a significant impact on estimates of the relationship between alcohol use and mortality (Di Castelnuovo et al., 2006). An especially challenging bias associated with heterogeneity between people in observational studies is the "healthy drinker" phenomenon, i.e. an increased likelihood of drinking by people in good health, and a correspondingly lower likelihood of drinking by people whose health has deteriorated because of disease which may or may not be related with alcohol use. Some people quit drinking because of their ill health. In addition, many people who drink heavily and die prematurely are not observed in studies. This means that the correlation between alcohol use, disease and death may be underestimated, especially at older ages, in studies that do not accurately account for the above effects.

### *Balancing harms and benefits*

Many studies point to a beneficial effect of moderate alcohol consumption on overall mortality among middle-aged and older men and, for more modest volumes of alcohol consumed, in older women. This is mostly because of lower rates of ischemic heart disease. However, rates for other conditions increase steadily with consumption, which means that drinkers in the above age groups have to trade off a reduced chance of death from, say, myocardial infarction, with an increased chance of death from, say, cancer or accidental injury. According to one of the most detailed studies of alcohol consumption and mortality, any level of consumption increases the risk of death in all men aged up to 35 and all women aged up to 55, for whom ischemic heart disease does not represent a significant health threat (White et al., 2002). As discussed in Chapter 1, we have estimated that between 78% and 83% of drinkers in Canada, the Czech Republic and Germany, would reduce their risk of death from all causes if they gave up one unit of alcohol (10 grams) per week.

The health benefits of alcohol use, however large or small, add to important welfare benefits, such as the pleasure and social networking often associated with drinking. These benefits set alcohol apart from some of the other commodities that are typically the target of public health action. While it is legitimate for governments to consider alcohol policy options affecting all drinkers, as discussed in Chapter 4, the design of such policies should account for the potential losses associated with restrictions imposed on moderate drinkers, which may offset some of the gains made by curbing harmful drinking.

However, the impact of harmful alcohol use extends well beyond its direct health consequences for drinkers. A broader assessment of social impacts, including criminal damage, violence and lost productivity in the workplace, demonstrates the considerable harm imposed on society as a result of excessive alcohol consumption. Social cost studies have been carried out in a number of countries (Rehm et al., 2009). Estimates for the United States, for instance, point to extra health care costs of USD 25.6 billion, and broader societal costs exceeding USD 220 billion, almost ten times the health costs alone (Bouchery et al., 2011).

Making sense of these different messages regarding the effects of alcohol consumption is one of the goals of this book, and especially of the modelling work discussed in Chapter 5, aimed at quantifying those effects and balancing the main harms and benefits associated with alcohol use and with alcohol policies.

## Should governments intervene? And what can they achieve?

The OECD's work on the economics of prevention has focused on people's ability to maximise their own and societal welfare through their free choice of behaviour and consumption of health-related commodities. Where the conditions in which such choices are made are not conducive to optimal outcomes, government intervention may provide a solution. Of the leading risk factors for major chronic diseases, harmful alcohol use is the one that provides the strongest economic justification for government action, as discussed in Chapter 1. While most people cherish their drinking habits and regard their alcohol consumption choices as an eminently private domain, several factors, only some of which under drinkers' control, conjure up a failure to achieve the most desirable individual and societal outcomes.

The greatest failure derives from the costs imposed by drinkers on others, which are not factored into the price people pay for their drinks at the counter, although taxation is one way in which governments make people pay for at least part of those external costs. Injuries and fatalities from accidents caused by drivers under the influence of alcohol, as well as the physical and social consequences of domestic violence fuelled by alcohol, are examples of costs imposed on others, major liabilities for any country and society. Similarly to other health-related behaviours, alcohol drinking also involves "social externalities" as some people engage in hazardous drinking behaviours following the examples provided by family, friends and peers.

If people do not perceive the potential consequences of their own drinking on others when they consume alcoholic beverages, they are also likely to have a biased perception of the consequences of drinking on themselves. Beyond a generic understanding that drinking large quantities of alcohol is bad for one's health, consumers have a very imprecise knowledge of the exact ways in which alcohol poses a risk to the health of men and women. Not only most people ignore the full range of potential disease consequences, but even identifying quantities, frequencies and patterns of drinking that may be dangerous for health generally may be a challenge for many drinkers. Countries' lack of consistency in defining high-risk drinking behaviours, as discussed in Chapter 2, may well be a contributor to people's poor perception of the risks associated with alcohol drinking.

Information failures have an even larger impact when combined with the addictive properties of alcohol, which themselves contribute to the justification for external intervention. Whether addiction to alcohol is biological, as in alcohol dependence, or "rational" as theorised by economists, its synergistic effect with poor information and biased risk perception makes many people unable to make drinking choices that will lead to optimal health and welfare outcomes for themselves. Insights from behavioural research, particularly in relation to myopic (present-oriented) consumption, make addiction and information failures even more of a concern in a welfare perspective. Behavioural research has also provided insights on people's tendency to constantly defer behaviour change, even when aware of the risks associated with the behaviour in question, due to inconsistent time preferences in the consumption of health-related commodities like alcoholic beverages (Sassi and Hurst, 2008).

The recognition of a strong rationale for action is reflected in countries' commitments on alcohol policy. In 1979, the World Health Assembly called upon WHO member states to develop and adopt appropriate legislation and measures to tackle alcohol misuse (WHO, 1979). These efforts culminated with the endorsement, in 2010, of the Global Strategy on the Harmful Use of Alcohol (WHO, 2010) that supports ten target areas for national actions, including: health sector response, community actions, drinking-and-driving policies, limitation of the availability of alcohol, action on marketing and price policies, reducing the negative consequences of intoxication and reducing the public health effect of illegally and informally produced alcohol. There is widespread recognition that tackling harmful drinking requires a range of policies from the different areas identified in the global strategy.

Governments need evidence of the population-level health and economic impacts of alternative policy options in order to ensure an efficient use of public funds in tackling harmful alcohol use. Much of this book is devoted precisely to providing policy makers with the evidence required to design and implement sound alcohol policies that would provide the best value for the resources available. The findings presented in Chapter 5, in particular, are the results of original computer-based simulations of a range of policy scenarios in Canada, the Czech Republic and Germany. The focus of these analyses is on policies whose effectiveness has been assessed in soundly designed and adequately powered studies, and policies that hold promise in addressing harmful alcohol use.

### *Effective and efficient alcohol policies*

The findings produced consistently show that national programmes to deliver screening and brief interventions for heavy drinkers in primary health care, as well as increases in the taxation of alcoholic beverages, have the potential to deliver large health returns by reducing high-risk drinking behaviours, alcohol-related diseases and overall mortality. These policies would reduce the demand for medical care and produce meaningful savings in health care expenditures, for example up to USD PPP 70 per person with brief interventions and USD PPP 55 per person with tax increases in the Czech Republic over 10 years, which would more than offset the costs involved in implementing several of the policies examined. Just by scaling up brief interventions in primary care, each year, 5% of working-age men in the Czech Republic, 3% in Germany and 1.5% in Canada, would avoid alcohol-related disabilities, likely leading to significant productivity gains.

A tighter enforcement of existing legislation against drinking and driving, and regulation limiting on-trade outlet opening hours – even if assumed to have an impact exclusively on accidents and injuries and not on overall alcohol consumption – have the potential to generate health benefits in all of the countries examined. Furthermore, they are cost-effective, despite the relatively high cost of strengthening law enforcement. Regulation of advertising may also achieve important reductions in high-risk alcohol consumption and related harms as shown in Chapter 5, likely to increase with larger cuts in advertising expenditures, provided that regulation is effective in limiting new forms of advertising that tend to escape traditional regulatory measures. Saffer's Special Focus contribution II shows that advertising regulation may provide effective means to tackle high-risk drinking behaviours, and not just alcohol consumption in general.

Improving access to pharmacological and psychosocial treatments for alcohol dependence may also significantly reduce alcohol-related morbidity and mortality, especially in countries with a higher prevalence of problem drinking. However, these programmes tend to involve higher implementation costs than regulatory and fiscal policies.

Several studies in Canada suggest that minimum price policies can reduce alcohol consumption (Stockwell et al., 2012a; 2012b). If this were confirmed in other settings, it would mean that minimum price policies could produce significant health gains and reductions in health care expenditure, at a low implementation cost. While minimum price policies do not yield significant fiscal revenues, Ludbrook's Special Focus contribution III shows that that they may be better suited to targeting heavy drinkers than taxation policies. The minimum price policy scenario assessed in Chapter 5 involves the setting of a generalised price threshold that would raise prices in the cheapest segment of the alcohol market. However, governments can effectively set minimum prices in a variety of ways, discussed in Box 4.1 in Chapter 4, which may be equally or more effective. The goal of the analyses presented in Chapter 5 is to provide broad guidance as to what health and economic impacts should be expected from a range of widely experimented policy options. Fine-tuning the design of a policy in a specific setting will require higher-resolution studies, accounting for policy constraints and interactions with dimensions of the relevant market and policy environments.

Other policies supported by a more conflicting evidence base, such as school-based and workplace programmes, if implemented in line with successful existing examples, also have the potential to improve health outcomes with a favourable cost-effectiveness profile, albeit in a longer time frame (school-based programmes) or at a higher cost than some of the other policy options (workplace programmes).

The pros and cons of alcohol policies that aim at reducing harmful alcohol use by targeting all drinkers and those that target harmful drinkers alone will continue to be debated, now and in the future. The views on this subject held by relevant stakeholders, including the alcohol industry, the public health community, and advocacy groups, will remain polarised. In Chapter 4, we review the evidence and the arguments, and we conclude that, ultimately, the targeting of alcohol policies is a political decision. As long as the objectives and the outcomes are measurable and transparent, it is a government's responsibility to build consensus around a strategy to tackle harmful alcohol use. However, based on the evidence reviewed in this book, if a government is seriously committed to curbing harmful drinking, the targeting of policies is not an "either-or" question, as that government will need to use a variety of policy tools and exploit their synergies and complementarities. The strategy that will result will likely include relatively blunt tools, perhaps poorly targeted, but effective in reaching large numbers of potential harmful drinkers and relatively inexpensive, with more sophisticated and better targeted tools.

The deep cultural and economic roots of alcohol, and the inextricable links of drinking behaviours with broader social norms, are such that individual measures will hardly make a dent in the harmful drinking problem. Like other major public health issues in today's world, harmful alcohol use can only be addressed through pervasive action and society-wide efforts.

## The scope for a multi-stakeholder approach to harmful alcohol use

The alcohol industry and its spinoffs represent an important share of the economy in a number of countries, and the scale of the fiscal revenues associated with the sale of alcoholic beverages contributes to placing the industry in a position of special regard for many governments. In the United Kingdom, for instance, the combined value added of the different segments of the alcohol industry and linked economic activities (e.g. in the hospitality sector) accounts for about 1.7% of the country's gross domestic product, according to estimates commissioned by the alcohol industry (Brink et al., 2011; Ernst & Young, 2013). Estimates of the social costs associated with alcohol, however, also amount to a meaningful share of GDP, as discussed in Chapter 1.

Partly due to its size and economic importance, the alcohol industry was described by the American Medical Association as "politically powerful and able to influence and guide many national, state and local alcohol control policies", and as "effective in influencing how the media, public and decision makers think about alcohol, alcohol consumption, and alcohol problems" (Yoast and Williams, 2004). The Director General of the World Health Organization publicly emphasized in a recent statement that "the alcohol industry has no role in formulating policies, which must be protected from distortion by commercial or vested interests" (Chan, 2013). However, there is no doubt that parts of the alcohol industry, in many countries and world regions, have significantly stepped up their corporate social responsibility initiatives, as a response to the sharpening of the alcohol policy debate. And several countries have been open to co-operating with those parts of the industry in tackling the problem of harmful alcohol use. For example, the UK Department of Health's own account of the initiatives undertaken by the alcohol industry as part of the Responsibility Deal, discussed in Chapter 4, provides a compelling view of the recent proliferation of initiatives (Department of Health, 2014). These initiatives include, among others, a pledge to remove one billion units of alcohol sold annually from the market by December 2015.

Examples of practices which have gone in the opposite direction to the thrust of public policy include the widespread use of price promotions and the adoption of ever more sophisticated marketing techniques, and media, often targeting groups that are most vulnerable to alcohol-related harms. The effectiveness of self-regulation approaches in the marketing of alcohol has been questioned (WHO, 2007; Anderson et al., 2009). Some evaluations have shown poor participation and compliance, and numerous breaches of self-imposed standards (Jones et al., 2008; KPMG LLP, 2008). Product reformulation to reduce alcohol content is a promising area for industry action. Many of the pledges in the context of the UK Responsibility Deal have precisely this objective. The beer industry has a long tradition of marketing low-alcohol and alcohol-free products. But initiatives have been sporadic otherwise, and often triggered by specific economic incentives. For instance, the alcohol content of many beers sold in the United Kingdom was reduced in 2012 to prevent the application of higher rate duties (Moylan, 2012).

Limited evidence is available today in support of, or against, the effectiveness of business-led initiatives as contributors to the fight against harmful alcohol use. Some evaluations are under way, including as part of the UK Responsibility Deal programme, but the debate so far is mostly centred on anecdotes and ideology. As in other key areas of public health action, a pragmatic approach is required, involving serious investment in the assessment of the potential for all types of initiatives to become part of an effective and efficient policy toolkit.

In its work on the economics of prevention, the OECD has invoked the adoption of a multi-stakeholder approach as the most sensible way forward in the prevention of chronic diseases linked with lifestyles (see, for example, Sassi, 2010). While it must be recognised that the interests at stake are often in conflict with each other, it must also be acknowledged that no party is in a position to produce meaningful changes in health-related behaviours and in the chronic diseases associated with them without co-operation from other stakeholders. An open dialogue and co-operation with alcohol manufacturers, as well as major retailers and other related industries, may be, and has already been in some countries, part of an effective policy approach in fighting the harms associated with alcohol consumption. However, there remains scope for broader and more incisive private sector actions, and for a more thorough and policy-relevant evaluation of the impacts of such actions.

## Bibliography

Abel, E.L. (2001), "The Gin Epidemic: Much Ado About What?", *Alcohol and Alcoholism*, Vol. 36, No. 5, pp. 401-405.

ADARFO – Alcoholism and Drug Addiction Research Foundation of Ontario (1961), *It's Best to Know about Alcoholism*, ADARFO, Toronto.

Anderson, P. et al. (2009), "Impact of Alcohol Advertising and Media Exposure on Adolescent Alcohol Use: A Systematic Review of Longitudinal Studies", *Alcohol and Alcoholism*, Vol. 44, pp. 229-243.

Babor, T.F. et al. (2010), "Alcohol: No Ordinary Commodity", *Research and Public Policy*, Oxford University Press.

Bouchery, E.E. et al. (2011), "Economic Costs of Excessive Alcohol Consumption in the U.S., 2006", *American Journal of Preventive Medicine*, Vol. 41, No. 5, pp. 516-524.

Brink, M. et al. (2011), *The Contribution Made by Beer to the European Economy*, Report commissioned by the Brewers of Europe and conducted by Ernst & Young Tax Advisors and Regioplan Policy Research, Amsterdam, September

Chan, M. (2013), "WHO's Response to Article on Doctors and the Alcohol Industry", *British Medical Journal*, Vol. 1, No. 346, p. f2647, May.

Department of Health (2014), "Responsibility Deal Alcohol Network – Pledge to Remove 1 Billion Units of Alcohol from the Market by End 2015 – First Interim Monitoring Report", Department of Health, Public Health Directorate, Health and Wellbeing Division, Alcohol and Drugs Branch, United Kingdom.

de Bruijn, A., E. van den Wildenberg and A. van den Broeck (2012), "Commercial Promotion of Drinking in Europe: Key Findings of Independent Monitoring of Alcohol Marketing in Five European Countries", Dutch Institute for Alcohol Policy (STAP), available at http://amphoraproject.net/w2box/data/AMPHORA%20Reports/Ammie_repport_2012.pdf?PHPSESSID=35ci20qg5dv9k73h8ugq6dho71.

Di Castelnuovo, A. et al. (2006), "Alcohol Dosing and Total Mortality in Men and Women: An Updated Meta-analysis of 34 Prospective Studies", *Archives of Internal Medicine*, Vol. 166, pp. 2437-2445.

Ely, M. et al. (2001), "Methods of Estimating Individual Levels of Alcohol Consumption in the General Population", *Alcohol Insight No. 9*, Alcohol Research UK.

Ernst & Young (2013), "The Wine and Spirit Trade Association – Economic Impact Assessment", December.

Holmes, J. et al. (2012), "The Temporal Relationship Between Per Capita Alcohol Consumption and Harm: A Systematic Review of Time Lag Specifications in Aggregate Time Series Analyses", Drug and Alcohol Dependence, Vol. 123, No. 1-3, pp. 7-14.

Jernigan, D.H. (2009), "The Global Alcohol Industry: An Overview", *Addiction*, Vol. 104, Suppl. 1, pp. 6–12.

Jones, S.C., D. Hall and G. Munro (2008), "How Effective Is the Revised Regulatory Code for Alcohol Advertising in Australia?", *Drug and Alcohol Review*, Vol. 27, pp. 29-38.

Katz, S.H. and M.M. Voigt (1987), "Bread and Beer: The Early Use of Cereals in the Human Diet", *Expedition*, Vol. 28, No. 2, pp. 23-34.

KPMG LLP (2008), "Review of the Social Responsibility Standards for the Production and Sale of Alcoholic Drinks", KPMG, London.

Lim, S.S. et al. (2012), "A Comparative Risk Assessment of Burden of Disease and Injury Attributable to 67 Risk Factors and Risk Factor Clusters in 21 Regions, 1990-2010: A Systematic Analysis for the Global Burden of Disease Study 2010", *The Lancet*, Vol. 15, No. 380(9859), pp. 2224-2260, December.

Moylan, J. (2012), "Will Weaker Beers Help the Brewing Industry?", BBC website, available at www.bbc.co.uk/news/business-17399368, accessed on 4 September 2012.

Patrick, C.H. (1952), *Alcohol, Culture, and Society*, Duke University Press, Durham, North Carolina, 1952, pp. 12-13, Reprint edition by AMS Press, New York, 1970.

Rehm, J., J. Patra and S. Popova (2007), "Alcohol Drinking Cessation and Its Effect on Esophageal and Head and Neck Cancers: A Pooled Analysis", *International Journal of Cancer*, Vol. 121, pp. 1132-1137.

Rehm, J. et al. (2009), "Global Burden of Disease and Injury and Economic Cost Attributable to Alcohol Use and Alcohol Use Disorders", *The Lancet*, Vol. 373, No. 9682, pp. 2223-2233.

Sassi, F. (2010), *Obesity and the Economics of Prevention: Fit not Fat*, OECD Publishing, Paris, http://dx.doi.org/10.1787/9789264084865-en.

Sassi, F. and J. Hurst (2008), "The Prevention of Lifestyle-Related Chronic Diseases: An Economic Framework", *OECD Health Working Papers*, No. 32, OECD Publishing, Paris, http://dx.doi.org/10.1787/243180781313.

Stockwell, T.M. et al. (2012a), "Does Minimum Pricing Reduce Alcohol Consumption? The Experience of a Canadian Province", *Addiction*, Vol. 107, pp. 912-920.

Stockwell, T.M. et al. (2012b), "The Raising of Minimum Alcohol Prices in Saskatchewan, Canada: Impacts on Consumption and Implications for Public Health", *American Journal of Public Health*, Vol. 102, No. 12, pp. 103-110.

Studer, J. et al. (2013), "Examining Non-response Bias in Substance Use Research – Are Late Respondents Proxies for Non-respondents?", *Drug and Alcohol Dependence*, Vol. 132, pp. 316-323.

White, I.R., D.R. Altmann and K. Nanchahal (2002), "Alcohol Consumption and Mortality: Modelling Risks for Men and Women at Different Ages", *British Medical Journal*, Vol. 325, No. 191.

WHO – World Health Organization (2014), "Global Status Report on Alcohol and Health", World Health Organization, Geneva.

WHO (2010), "Global Alcohol Strategy to Reduce the Harmful Use of Alcohol", World Health Organization, Geneva.

WHO (2007), "WHO Expert Committee on Problems Related to Alcohol Consumption (second report)", *WHO Technical Report Series No. 944*, World Health Organization, Geneva.

WHO (1979), "Resolution WHA32.40. Development of the WHO Programme on Alcohol-related Problems", *Thirty-ninth World Health Assembly*, World Health Organization, Geneva, 25 May 1979.

Yoast, R.A. and J. Williams (2004), "Reducing Underage Drinking Through Coalitions", *Alcohol Industry 101: Its Structure & Organization*, American Medical Association, Chicago, United States.

# ANNEX A

# *Supplementary figures and tables*

## 1. Supplementary tables and figures associated with Chapters 2 and 3

Table A.1 contains a list of national survey datasets used in the analyses reported in Chapters 2 and 3. Table A.2 contains information on drinking guidelines in OECD countries, as reported by national representatives in April 2014. Guidelines in Table A.2 are for the general population and not for specific population groups (e.g. pregnant women, alcohol dependent people).

## Table A.1. **Description of the national health survey data used in the analyses reported in Chapters 2 and 3**

| | Survey name | Available survey waves | Data provider |
|---|---|---|---|
| Australia | National Health Survey | 1989-90, 1995, 2001, 2004-05, 2007-08 | Australian Bureau of Statistics |
| Canada | National Health Population Survey and Canadian Community Health Survey | 1994/95, 2000/01, 2003, 2005, 2007/08, 2009/10, 2011/12 | Statistic Canada |
| Chile | Servicio Nacional de Drogas y Alcohol (ex-CONACE) | 2008, 2010 | Ministry of Interior and Public Security |
| Czech Republic | European Health Interview Survey in the Czech Republic (EHIS) | 2008 | Institute of Health Information and Statistics (UZIS) |
| England | Health Survey for England | 1991-2011 (every year) | Office for Population Censuses and Surveys (1991-1993), then (since 1994) conducted jointly by the National Centre for Social Research (NatCen) and the Health and Social Survey Research group at the Department of Epidemiology at University College London |
| Finland | Finrisk | 1997, 2002, 2007 | National Institute for Health and Welfare (THL) |
| France | Enquête Santé et Protection Sociale | 2002, 2004, 2006, 2008, 2010 | Institute for Reseach and Information in Health Economics |
| Germany | Epidemiological Survey on Substance Abuse | 1995, 1997, 2000, 2003, 2006, 2009 | GESIS - Leibniz Institutes for the Social Sciences |
| Hungary | European Health Interview Survey (EHIS) | 2009 | Hungarian Central Statistical Office |
| Ireland | Survey on Lifestyle And Nutrition | 1998, 2002, 2007 | Irish Social Science Data Archive |
| Italy | Multiscopo Aspect of Daily Life | 2005,2006, 2007, 2008, 2009, 2010 | Italian National Institute of Statistic |
| Japan | National Survey on Alcohol Drinking and Lifestyle | 2003, 2008 | Tottori University |
| Korea | Korean National Health and Nutrition Examination Survey | 2008 | Jointly carried out by the Korean Institute for Health and Social Affairs and the Korean Health Industry Develpment Institute |
| New Zealand | National Health Survey | 1996/97, 2002/03, 2006/07 | Ministry of Health |
| Portugal | General Population Survey on Psychoactive Substances | 2007 | carried out by PhD. C. Balsa from CESNova/ Sociology and Human Sciences School/ NOVA University of Lisbon, after a call from the Instituto da Droga e da Toxicodependência, IP. |
| Slovak Republic | Európsky prieskum zdravia 2009 (EHIS) | 2009 | National Health Information Centre (Ministry of Health) |
| Slovenia | Anketa o zdravju in zdravstvenem varstvu 2007 (EHIS) | 2007 | Institute of Public Health |
| Spain | Encuesta Nacional de Salud de Espana | 2006 | Instituto Nacional de Estadistica and Ministry of Public Health, Social Services and Equality |
| Switzerland | Swiss Health Survey | 1992, 1997, 2002, 2007 | Swiss Federal Statistical Office |
| United States | National Health and Nutrition Examination Survey/ and National Survey on Drug Use and Health | NHANES: 1999/2000, 2001/02, 2003/04, 2005/06, 2007/08, 2009/10 NSDUH: 1999-2009 | NHANES: National Center for Health Statistics (NCHS - CDC)/ NSDUH: Substance Abuse and Mental Health Services Administration (SAMHSA) |

*Note:* Trends analysis used all survey years whereas inequality analysis used the most recent years (underlined).

## Table A.2. National drinking guidelines

| | Quantity in grams of pure alcohol contained in a standard drink | Hazardous drinking limit (limit above which people are at risk for their health) | Heavy episodic drinking limit (maximum recommendations for the number of drinks per drinking occasion) |
|---|---|---|---|
| | National definition | National guideline | National guideline and definition in national survey |
| Australia | 10 g | > 2 drinks per day (20 g) | Guideline: > 4 drinks per occasion (40 g)<br>Questionnaire NHS: men: 7+/women: 5+ drinks in a day (70/50g); more recently: 4+ drinks per occasion (40 g) |
| Austria (1) | 8 g | Men: > 3 drinks/day (> 24 g/day)<br>Women: > 2 drinks/day (> 16 g/day) | Guideline: not defined |
| Belgium | not defined | Not defined | Guideline: not defined |
| Canada | 13.6 g | Men: > 3 drinks/day and up to 15 drinks/week (> 30 g/day)<br>Women: > 2 drinks/day and up to 10 drinks/week (> 20 g/day) | Guideline (2012): men: 4+/women: 3+ drinks per occasion (54/41 g)<br>Questionnaire: 5+ drinks per occasion (68 g) |
| Chile | 13-15.5 g | Men: > 4 drinks per day (> 52-62 g/day)<br>Women: > 3 drinks per day (> 39-46.5 g/day) | Guideline: 5+ drinks per occasion (> 69g);<br>Questionnaire SENDA: 6+ drinks per occasion, other survey: 5+ drinks per occasion |
| Czech Republic (2) | 16 g | Men: > 40 g/day<br>Women: > 20 g/day | Guideline: not defined<br>Questionnaire: 5+ drinks per occasion (80 g) |
| Denmark (3) | 12 g | Men: > 2 drinks per day (24 g)<br>Women: > 1 drinks per day (12 g) | Guideline: 4+ drinks per occasion (48 g) |
| Estonia | 10 g | Men: > 4 drinks per day (40 g), at least 3 alcohol-free days in a week, Women: > 2 drinks per day (20 g), at least 3 alcohol-free days in a week | Guideline: not defined<br>Questionnaire: 6+ drinks per occasion (60 g) |
| Finland | 12 g | Men: 2 drinks per day (24 g)<br>Women: 1 drink per day (12 g)<br>*High risk in clinical guidelines issued by Medical Association: Men: > 24 drinks/week (> 40 g/day)*<br>*Women: > 16 drinks/week (> 27 g/day)* | Guideline: no guideline *but men: 7+/women: 5+ defined as high risk in clinical guidelines issued by Medical Association*<br>Questionnaire: men 7+/women 5 + drinks per occasion (84/60 g) |
| France (4) | 10 g | Men: > 3 drinks per day (30 g)<br>Women: > 2 drinks per day (20 g) | Guideline: not defined<br>Questionnaire: 6+ drinks per occasion |
| Germany | 12 g | Men: > 24 g per day<br>Women: > 12 g per day, no more than 5 days a week | Guideline: not defined<br>Questionnaire: 5+ drinks per occasion (60 g) |
| Greece | 10 g | Men: > 3 drinks per day (30 g)<br>Women: > 2 drinks per day (20 g) | Guideline: not defined |
| Hungary | 12 g/16 g | Men: > 3 drinks per day (36-48 g)<br>Women: > 2 drinks per day (24-32 g) | Guideline: not defined<br>Questionnaire: 6+ drinks per occasion (72-96 g) |
| Iceland | 12 g | not defined (5) | Guideline: not defined |
| Ireland | 10 g | Men: > 17 drinks per week ~2.4 drinks per day (24 g)<br>Women: > 11 drinks per week ~1.6 drinks per day (16 g) | Guideline: 6+ drinks per occasion (60 g)<br>Questionnaire: 6+ drinks per occasion (60 g) |
| Israel | 14 g | Men: > 3 drinks per day (30 g)<br>Women: > 2 drinks per day (20 g) | Guideline: not defined |
| Italy | 12 g | Men: > 2-3 drinks per day (24-36 g)<br>Women: > 1-2 drinks per day (12-24 g) | Guideline: not defined<br>Questionnaire: 5/6+ drinks per occasion (60-72 g) |
| Japan | 10 g | Men: > = 4 drinks per day (40 g)<br>Women: > = 2 drinks per day (20 g) | Guideline: not defined<br>Questionnaire: 7+ drinks per occasion |
| Korea (6) | 8.5 g | Men: 14 unit per one week<br>Women: 10 unit per one week | Guideline: not defined<br>Questionnaire: men: 7+/women: 5+ drinks per occasion |
| Luxembourg | 12 g | Men: > 2 drinks per day (24 g)<br>Women: > 1 drinks per day (12 g) | Guideline: 5+ drinks per occasion (60 g)<br>Questionnaire: 5+ drinks per occasion (60 g) |
| Mexico | Not defined (7) | Not defined (7) | Guideline: not defined<br>Questionnaire: 5 or more drinks per one occasion for male; 4 or more drinks per one occasion for female |
| Netherlands | 10 g | Men: > 2 drinks per day (20 g)<br>Women: > 1 drinks per day (10 g) | Guideline: not defined |

Table A.2. **National drinking guidelines** *(cont.)*

| | Quantity in grams of pure alcohol contained in a standard drink | Hazardous drinking limit (limit above which people are at risk for their health) | Heavy episodic drinking limit (maximum recommendations for the number of drinks per drinking occasion) |
|---|---|---|---|
| | National definition | National guideline | National guideline and definition in national survey |
| New Zealand | 10 g | Men: > 3 drinks per day (30 g) and no more than 15 per week<br>Women: > 2 drinks per day (20 g) and no more than 10 per week | Guideline: men: 5+/women: 4+ drinks per occasion (50/40 g)<br>Questionnaire: men: 6+/women: 4+ drinks per occasion |
| Norway | not defined (8) | not defined | Guideline: not defined<br>Questionnaire: 6+ drinks per occasion |
| Poland | 10 g | Men: > 4 drinks per day (40 g)<br>Women: > 2 drinks per day (20 g) | Guideline: men: 6+/women: 4+ drinks per occasion (60/40 g)<br>Questionnaire: 6+ drinks per occasion |
| Portugal | 12 g | Men: > 2-3 drinks per day (24-36 g)<br>Women: > 1-2 drinks per day (12-24 g) | Guideline: men: 6+/women: 5+ drinks per occasion (72/60 g) |
| Slovak Republic (9) | no official definition | no mandatory national recommendation | Guideline: not defined<br>Questionnaire: 6+ drinks per occasion |
| Slovenia | 10 g | Men: > 2 drinks per day (> 20 g/day),<br>Women: > 1 drink per day (> 10 g/day), | Guideline: men: 50 g/women: 30 g per occasion<br>Questionnaire: men: 6+/women: 4+ drinks per occasion |
| Spain | 10 g | Men: > 4 drinks per day (40 g)<br>Women: > 2 drinks per day (20 g) | Guideline: men: 6+/women: 4+ per occasion (60/40 g)<br>Questionnaire: 6+ drinks per occasion |
| Sweden (10) | 12 g | Men: > 14 drinks/week (> 24 g/day)<br>Women: > 9 drinks/week (> 15 g/day) | Guideline: men: 5+/women: 4+ drinks per occasion (60/48 g)<br>Questionnaire: 60 g per occasion |
| Switzerland | 10-12 g | Guideline (2008):<br>Men: > 4 drinks per day (40 g - 48 g)<br>Women: > 2 drinks per day (20 g - 24 g) | Guideline (2008): men: 5+/women: 4+ drinks per occasion (50-60/40-48 g)<br>Questionnaire (Swiss Health Survey): 6+ drinks per occasion (60-72) |
| Turkey | not defined | not defined | Guideline: not defined |
| United Kingdom (England) | 8 g | Men: > 21 drinks/week (> 24 g/day)<br>Women: > 14 drinks/week (> 16 g/day) | Guideline: men: 8+/women: 6+ drinks per occasion (64/48 g)<br>Questionnaire: idem. |
| United States | (11) | (11) | (11) |

*Note:* National guidelines for hazardous drinking limit relate to general population and may not refer to specific groups (like pregnant women).

1. In Austria, no official definition of the content of standard drink and drinking limits.
2. No official guideline, the only relevant limits can be deducted from national survey questionnaires.
3. Denmark has low-risk and high-risk drinking limits. Definition of hazardous drinking here corresponds to low-risk drinking.
4. In France, the quantity mentioned is the maximum quantity but less is better. For pregnant women, the recommendation is zero alcohol.
5. In Iceland, in clinical guidelines for primary health care, there is a criteria for reference at 21 units for male and 14 units for female a week. However, these recommendations are not published or advertised.
6. In Korea, no national definition. Limits reported here correspond to the Korea National Health & Nutrition Examination Survey.
7. In Mexico, no official definition of the standard alcoholic drink, although a 2001 study estimated the Mexican standard drink contains 13 g of pure alcohol (available at: www.alcoholinformate.org.mx/seminarios/Cuaderno11.pdf). There is no national guideline that refers to the hazardous drinking limit. However, there is a Mexican Official Norm that specifies the relation between the level of ethanol in blood and the intoxication level through the symptoms (available at: www.cofepris.gob.mx/MJ/Paginas/NormasPorTema/Alcohol.aspx). Such norm applies for workers that manipulate ethanol but it also appears in the national guideline for treatment of acute intoxication with ethanol among adult population.
8. The Norwegian Institute of Public Health defined a standard drink as 12-15 g.
9. In Slovak Republic no official definition of the content of standard drink and drinking limits.
10. In Sweden, the recommendation to general public for risk-free consumption is zero alcohol.
11. In the United States, answers may vary since State and local jurisdictions set the policies. More information is available on the NIAAA Policy Information System: https://alcoholpolicy.niaaa.nih.gov.

*Source:* OECD National correspondents; HED limits derived from national survey questionnaires, listed in Table A.1.

Figures A.1 to A.6 present the adjusted probabilities of three drinking patterns: any drinking in the past 12 months; hazardous drinking in the past 12 months; and, heavy episodic drinking (HED) at least once a week in the past 12 months. Figures A1 to A.3 show probabilities by education level, while Figures A.4 to A.6 show probabilities by socioeconomic status (SES, either measured by occupation or household income as mentioned in the figure notes). A clear gradient emerges from Figures A.1 and A.4, with more educated and higher SES people more likely to consume alcohol in the past 12 months. Mixed patterns emerge for hazardous drinking and HED. Men with less education and lower SES are more likely to drink at risk in most countries, whereas the opposite is observed in women: those with more education and higher SES are more likely to drink at risk, although with some exceptions.

Figure A.1. **Any drinking in the past 12 months by education level, selected OECD countries**

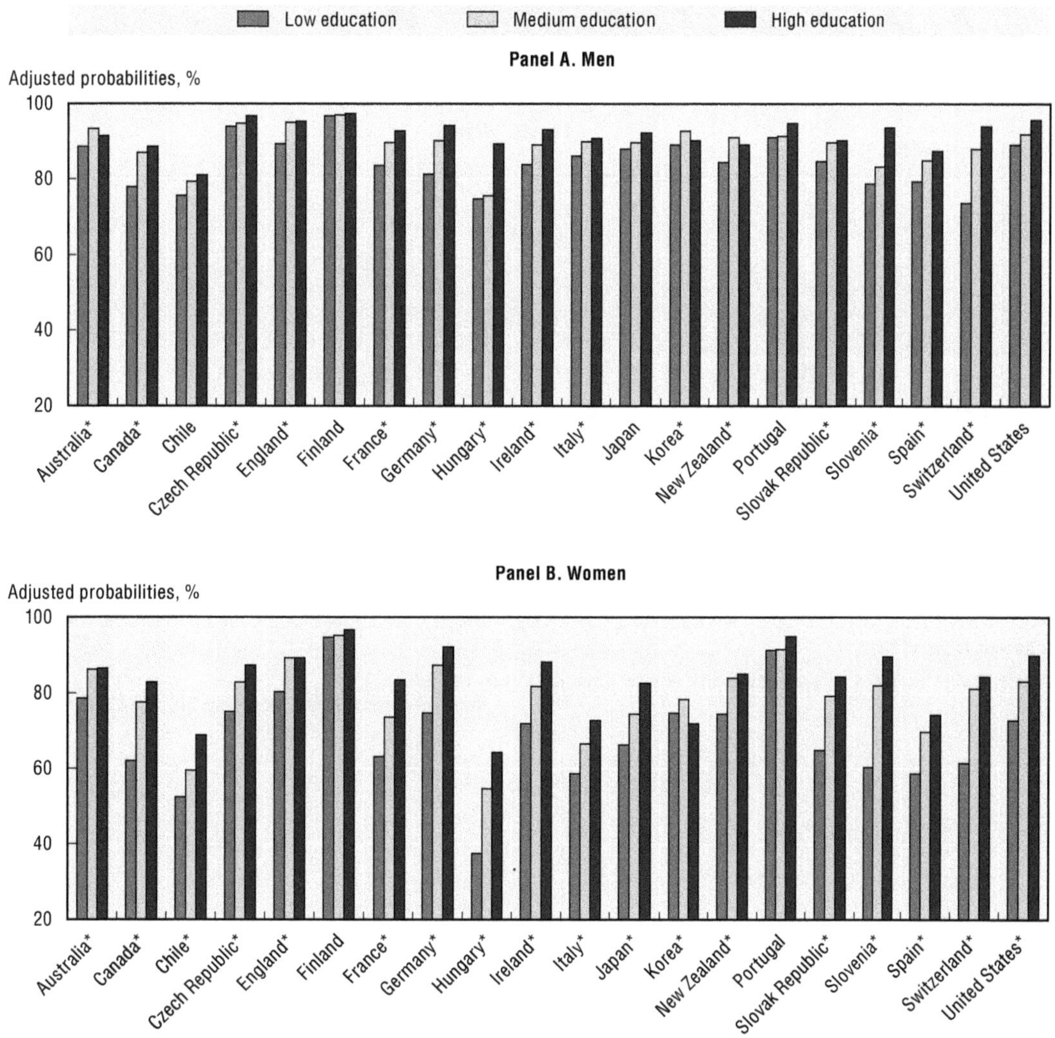


*Note:* Analysis covering people aged 25+, except in the Czech Republic, the Slovak Republic and Slovenia where people are aged 16+. Adjusted probabilities are computed for an average individual aged 40, with all covariates (marital status, working status, smoking, ethnicity) set at the sample mean. (*) means the overall gradient is significant.

*Source:* OECD analyses of national health survey data (details in Table A.1).

StatLink http://dx.doi.org/10.1787/888933180591

Figure A.2. **Hazardous drinking in the past 12 months by education level, selected OECD countries**

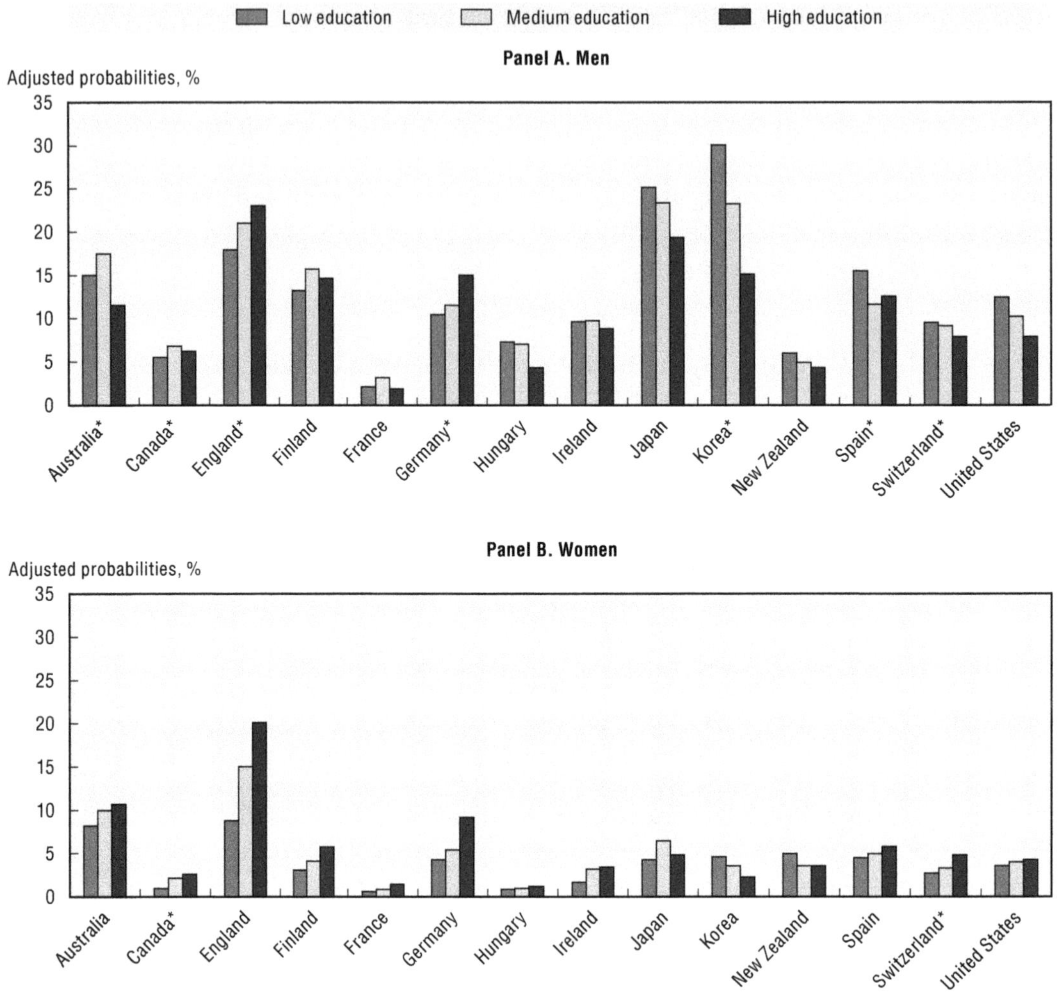


*Note*: Analysis covering people aged 25+. Adjusted probabilities are computed for an average individual aged 40, with all covariates (marital status, working status, smoking, ethnicity) set at the sample mean. (*) means the overall gradient is significant.

*Source*: OECD analyses of national health survey data (details in Table A.1).

StatLink http://dx.doi.org/10.1787/888933180608

Figure A.3. **Heavy episodic drinking at least once a week in the past 12 months by education level, selected OECD countries**

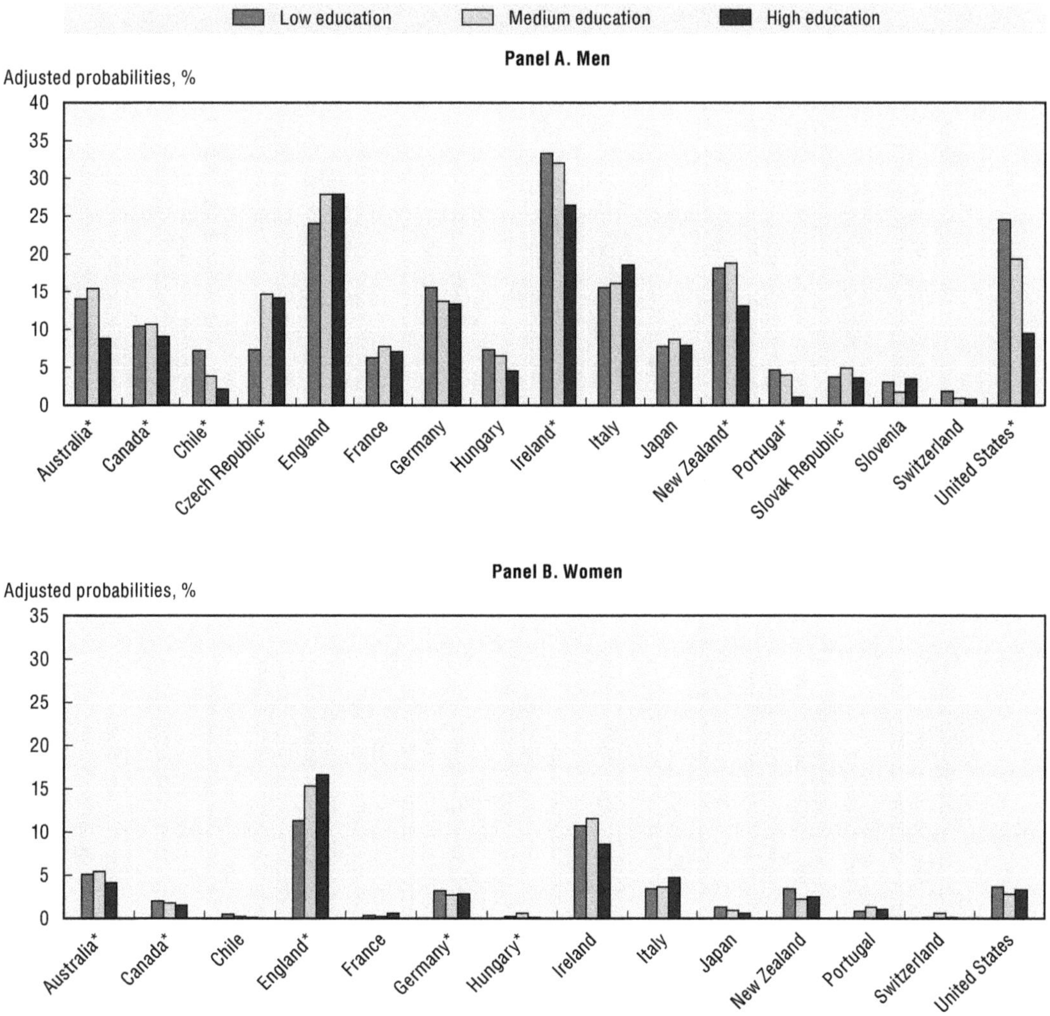


*Note:* Analysis covering people aged 25+, except in the Czech Republic, the Slovak Republic and Slovenia where people are aged 16+. Adjusted probabilities are computed for an average individual aged 40, with all covariates (marital status, working status, smoking, ethnicity) set at the sample mean. (*) means the overall gradient is significant.

*Source:* OECD analyses of national health survey data (details in Table A.1).

StatLink http://dx.doi.org/10.1787/888933180611

Figure A.4. **Any drinking in the past 12 months by socioeconomic status (SES), selected OECD countries**

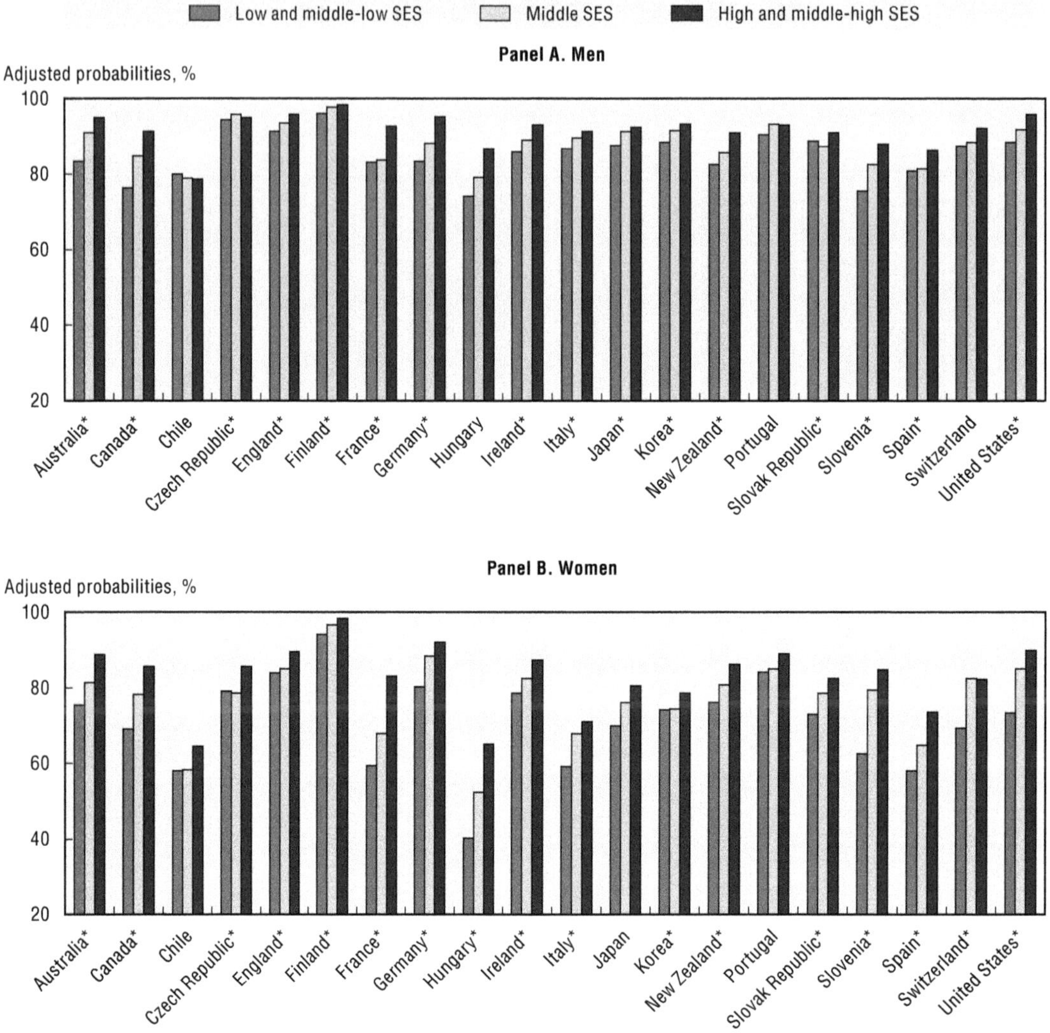


*Note:* Analysis covering people aged 25+, except in the Czech Republic, the Slovak Republic and Slovenia where people are aged 16+. Adjusted probabilities are computed for an average individual aged 40, with all covariates (marital status, working status, smoking, ethnicity) set at the sample mean. SES is based on occupation-based social class in Chile, England, France, Hungary, Italy, Japan, Portugal, Spain, and Switzerland, and on household income in other countries. (*) means the overall gradient is significant.

*Source:* OECD analyses of national health survey data (details in Table A.1).

StatLink http://dx.doi.org/10.1787/888933180624

 

Figure A.5. **Hazardous drinking in the past 12 months by socioeconomic status (SES), selected OECD countries**

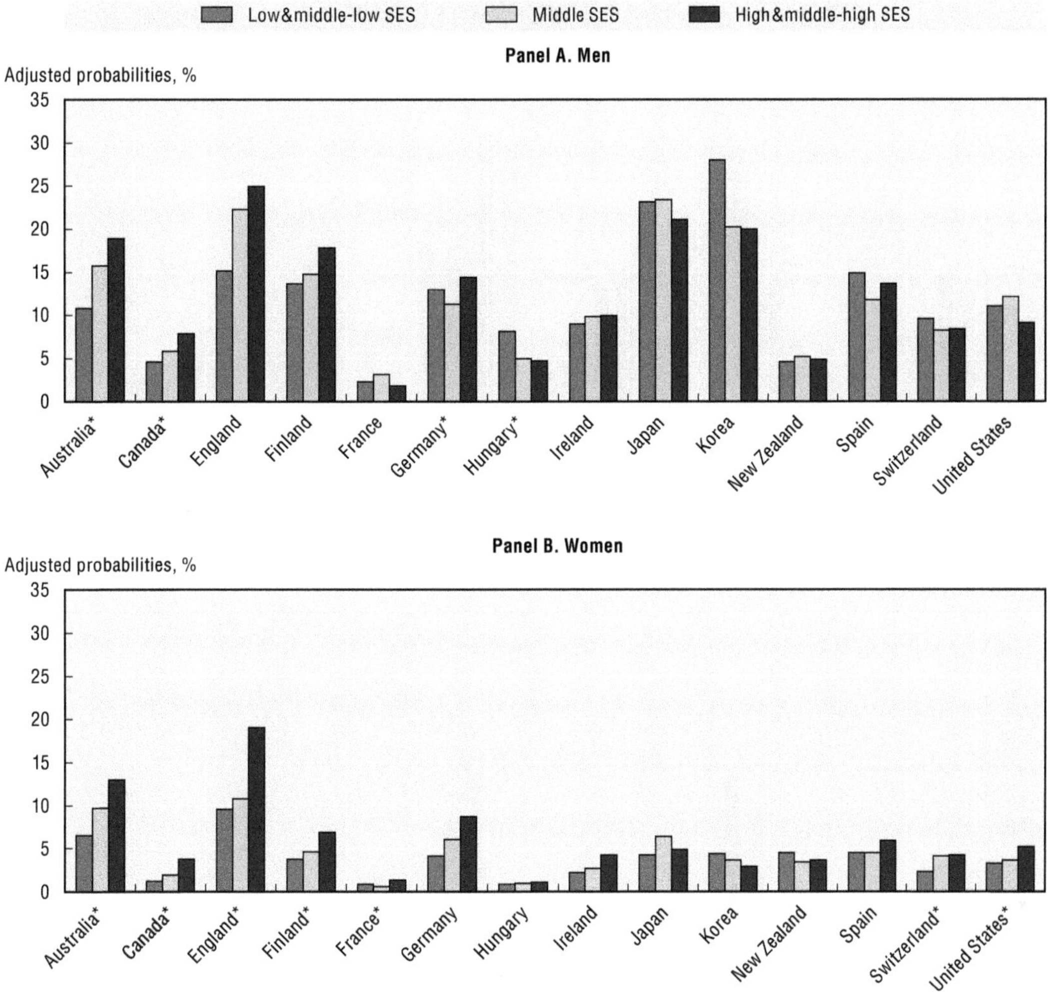


*Note:* Analysis covering people aged 25+. Adjusted probabilities are computed for an average individual aged 40, with all covariates (marital status, working status, smoking, ethnicity) set at the sample mean. SES is based on occupation in England, France, Hungary, Japan, Spain and Switzerland, and on household income in other countries. (*) means the overall gradient is significant.

*Source:* OECD analyses of national health survey data (details in Table A.1).

StatLink http://dx.doi.org/10.1787/888933180638

Figure A.6. **Heavy episodic drinking at least once a week in the past 12 months by socioeconomic status (SES), selected OECD countries**

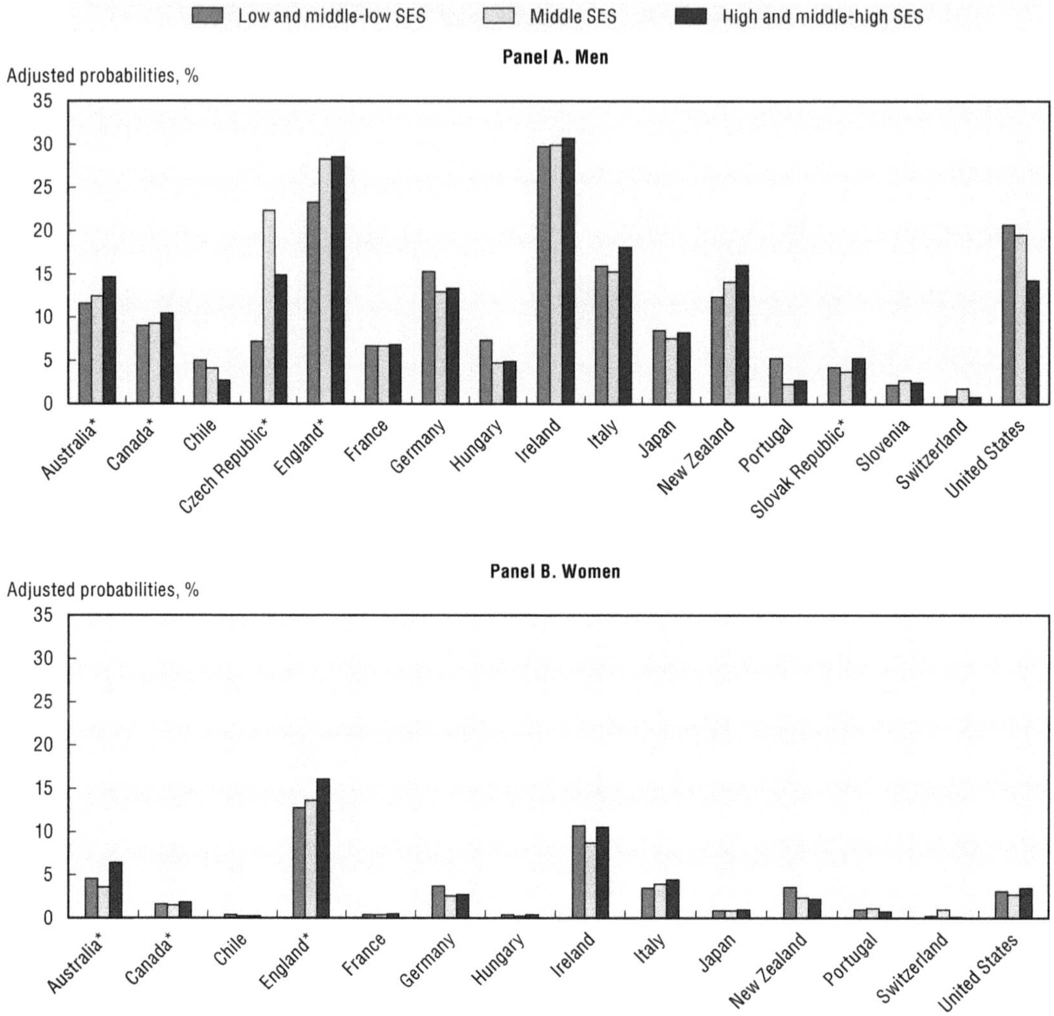


*Note*: Analysis covering people aged 25+, except in the Czech Republic, the Slovak Republic and Slovenia where people are aged 16+. Adjusted probabilities are computed for an average individual aged 40, with all covariates (marital status, working status, smoking, ethnicity) set at the sample mean. SES is based on occupation-based social class in Chile, England, France, Hungary, Italy, Japan, Portugal and Switzerland, and on household income in other countries. (*) means the overall gradient is significant.

*Source*: OECD analyses of national health survey data (details in Table A.1).

StatLink http://dx.doi.org/10.1787/888933180643

## 2. Supplementary tables and figures associated with Chapter 4

Table A.3 presents country-specific information about key alcohol policy areas, including: national legal minimum age for off- and on-trade sales of beer, wine and spirits; restrictions for off- and on-trade sales of alcoholic beverages; national maximum legal blood alcohol concentration; and, legally binding regulations on alcohol advertising. The main source of information is *WHO's Global Status Report on Alcohol and Health 2014*. However, the information was validated, and in some cases amended, by OECD national correspondents. Only national policies, or those consistently applied by all subnational jurisdictions in a country, are reported in the table. However, in some countries subnational jurisdictions have different policies in place, and these are not reflected in the table.Further information and narrative descriptions of the policies listed in the table can be found in Chapter 4.

## Table A.3. **Summary of selected alcohol policies in OECD countries and partner economies**

| | Australia | Austria | Belgium | Brazil | Canada | Chile | China | Czech Republic | Denmark | Estonia |
|---|---|---|---|---|---|---|---|---|---|---|
| **National legal minimum age for off-premise sales** | | | | | | | | | | |
| Beer | 18 | 16 | 16 | 18 | subn | 18 | N | 18 | 16 | 18 |
| Wine | 18 | 16 | 16 | 18 | subn | 18 | N | 18 | 16 | 18 |
| Spirits | 18 | subn | 18 | 18 | subn | 18 | N | 18 | 18 | 18 |
| **National legal minimum age for on-premise sales** | | | | | | | | | | |
| Beer | 18 | 16 | 16 | 18 | subn | 18 | N | 18 | 18 | 18 |
| Wine | 18 | 16 | 16 | 18 | subn | 18 | N | 18 | 18 | 18 |
| Spirits | 18 | subn | 18 | 18 | subn | 18 | N | 18 | 18 | 18 |
| **Restrictions for on-/off-premise sales of alcoholic beverages** | | | | | | | | | | |
| Time (hours/day) | Y/Y | Y/Y | N/N | N/N | Y/Y | Y/N | N/N | N/N | Y/Y | Y/N |
| Location (place/density) | Y/Y | Y/N | N/N | N/N | Y/Y | Y/Y | N/N | Y/N | N/N | Y/N |
| Specific events | Y | N | Y | Y | Y | Y | N | Y | N | N |
| Intoxicated persons | Y | Y | Y | Y | Y | Y | Y | Y | Y | Y |
| Petrol stations | Y | N | Y | Y | Y | Y | N | N | N | N |
| **National maximum legal blood alcohol concentration (%)** | | | | | | | | | | |
| General | 0.05 | 0.05 | 0.05 | 0.02 | subn | 0.03 | 0.02 | 0 | 0.05 | 0.02 |
| Young | 0 | 0.01 | 0.05 | 0.02 | 0 | 0.03 | 0.02 | 0 | 0.05 | 0.02 |
| Professional | 0 | 0.01 | 0.05 | 0.02 | subn | 0.03 | 0.02 | 0 | 0.05 | 0.02 |
| **Legally binding regulations** | | | | | | | | | | |
| Advertisement | Y | Y | N | Y | Y | N | Y | Y | Y | Y |
| Product placement | N | Y | N | Y | N | N | N | Y | Y | N |
| Sponsorship | N | N | N | N | N | N | N | Y | N | N |
| Sales promotion | Y | N | N | N | N | N | N | N | N | N |
| Health warnings (advert/containers) | N/N | N/N | N/N | Y/Y | N/N | N/N | N/N | N/N | N/N | Y/N |

| | Finland | France | Germany | Greece | Hungary | Iceland | India | Indonesia | Ireland | Israel |
|---|---|---|---|---|---|---|---|---|---|---|
| **National legal minimum age for off-premise sales** | | | | | | | | | | |
| Beer | 18 | 18 | 16 | 18 | 18 | 20 | subn | 21 | 18 | 18 |
| Wine | 18 | 18 | 16 | 18 | 18 | 20 | subn | 21 | 18 | 18 |
| Spirits | 20 | 18 | 18 | 18 | 18 | 20 | subn | 21 | 18 | 18 |
| **National legal minimum age for on-premise sales** | | | | | | | | | | |
| Beer | 18 | 18 | 16 | 18 | 18 | 20 | subn | 21 | 18 | 18 |
| Wine | 18 | 18 | 16 | 18 | 18 | 20 | subn | 21 | 18 | 18 |
| Spirits | 18 | 18 | 18 | 18 | 18 | 20 | subn | 21 | 18 | 18 |
| **Restrictions for on-/off-premise sales of alcoholic beverages** | | | | | | | | | | |
| Time (hours/day) | Y/Y | N/N | N/N | N/N | N/N | Y/Y | Y/Y | Y/N | Y/Y | Y/N |
| Location (place/density) | Y/Y | Y/Y | N/N | N/N | Y/N | N/N | Y/Y | Y/N | Y/Y | N/N |
| Specific events | Y | Y | N | Y | Y | Y | Y | N | Y | N |
| Intoxicated persons | Y | Y | Y | N | Y | Y | N | N | Y | N |
| Petrol stations | Y | Y | N | N | N | Y | Y | N | Y | N |
| **National maximum legal blood alcohol concentration (%)** | | | | | | | | | | |
| General | 0.05 | 0.05 | 0.05 | 0.05 | 0 | 0.05 | 0.03 | 0 | 0.05 | 0.05 |
| Young | 0.05 | 0.05 | 0 | 0.02 | 0 | 0.05 | 0.03 | 0 | 0.02 | 0.01 |
| Professional | 0.05 | 0.05/0.02† | 0.05/0† | 0.02 | 0 | 0.05 | 0.03 | 0 | 0.02 | 0.01 |
| **Legally binding regulations** | | | | | | | | | | |
| Advertisement | Y | Y | Y | N | Y | Y | Y | Y | Y | Y |
| Product placement | Y | Y | Y | N | Y | Y | Y | Y | Y | N |
| Sponsorship | Y | Y | N | N | N | Y | Y | Y | N | N |
| Sales promotion | Y | Y | Y | N | N | Y | Y | Y | Y | Y |
| Health warnings (advert/containers) | N/N | Y/Y | N/N | N/N | N/N | N/N | Y/Y | Y/Y | N/N | Y/Y |

Table A.3. **Summary of selected alcohol policies in OECD countries and partner economies** *(cont.)*

| | Italy | Japan | Korea | Luxembourg | Mexico | Netherlands | New Zealand | Norway | Poland | Portugal |
|---|---|---|---|---|---|---|---|---|---|---|
| **National legal minimum age for off-premise sales** | | | | | | | | | | |
| Beer | 18 | 20 | 19 | 16 | 18 | 18 | 18 | 18 | 18 | 16 |
| Wine | 18 | 20 | 19 | 16 | 18 | 18 | 18 | 18 | 18 | 16 |
| Spirits | 18 | 20 | 19 | 16 | 18 | 18 | 18 | 20 | 18 | 18 |
| **National legal minimum age for on-premise sales** | | | | | | | | | | |
| Beer | 18 | 20 | 19 | 16 | 18 | 18 | 18 | 18 | 18 | 16 |
| Wine | 18 | 20 | 19 | 16 | 18 | 18 | 18 | 18 | 18 | 16 |
| Spirits | 18 | 20 | 19 | 16 | 18 | 18 | 18 | 20 | 18 | 18 |
| **Restrictions for on-/off-premise sales of alcoholic beverages** | | | | | | | | | | |
| Time (hours/day) | Y/N | N/N | N/N | Y/N | Y/N | N/N | Y/Y | Y/Y | N/N | Y/N |
| Location (place/density) | Y/N | N/N | N/N | N/Y | Y/N | Y/N | Y/N | N/N | Y/N | Y/N |
| Specific events | Y | N | N | N | Y | Y | N | N | Y | Y |
| Intoxicated persons | Y | N | N | Y | Y | Y | Y | Y | Y | Y |
| Petrol stations | Y | N | N | N | N | Y | Y | Y | N | Y |
| **National maximum legal blood alcohol concentration (%)** | | | | | | | | | | |
| General | 0.05 | 0.03 | 0.05 | 0.05 | subn | 0.05 | 0.05 | 0.02 | 0.02 | 0.05 |
| Young | 0 | 0.03 | 0.05 | 0.02 | subn | 0.02 | 0 | 0.02 | 0.02 | 0.02 |
| Professional | 0 | 0.03 | 0.05 | 0.02 | subn | 0.05 | 0.05 | 0.02 | 0.02 | 0.02 |
| **Legally binding regulations** | | | | | | | | | | |
| Advertisement | Y | N | Y | N | Y | Y | Y | Y | Y | Y |
| Product placement | N | N | N | N | Y | N | N | Y | Y | Y |
| Sponsorship | Y | N | N | N | Y | N | N | Y | Y | Y |
| Sales promotion | Y | N | N | N | Y | N | Y | Y | Y | Y |
| Health warnings (advert/containers) | N/N | N/N | N/Y | N/N | Y/Y | N/N | N/N | N/N | Y/N | N/N |

| | Russian Federation | Slovakia | Slovenia | South Africa | Spain | Sweden | Switzerland | Turkey | United Kingdom | United States |
|---|---|---|---|---|---|---|---|---|---|---|
| **National legal minimum age for off-premise sales** | | | | | | | | | | |
| Beer | 18 | 18 | 18 | 18 | 16 | 18* | 16 | 18 | 18 | 21 |
| Wine | 18 | 18 | 18 | 18 | 16 | 20 | 16 | 18 | 18 | 21 |
| Spirits | 18 | 18 | 18 | 18 | 16 | 20 | 18 | 18 | 18 | 21 |
| **National legal minimum age for on-premise sales** | | | | | | | | | | |
| Beer | 18 | 18 | 18 | 18 | 16 | 18 | 16 | 18 | 18 | 21 |
| Wine | 18 | 18 | 18 | 18 | 16 | 18 | 16 | 18 | 18 | 21 |
| Spirits | 18 | 18 | 18 | 18 | 16 | 18 | 18 | 18 | 18 | 21 |
| **Restrictions for on-/off-premise sales of alcoholic beverages** | | | | | | | | | | |
| Time (hours/day) | Y/N | N/N | Y/N | Y/N | N/N | Y/Y | N/N | Y/N | Y/N | subn |
| Location (place/density) | Y/N | Y/N | Y/N | Y/N | Y/N | Y/Y | Y/N | Y/N | N/Y | subn |
| Specific events | Y | Y | Y | N | Y | Y | Y | Y | Y | subn |
| Intoxicated persons | N | Y | Y | Y | N | Y | N | N | Y | subn |
| Petrol stations | N | N | Y | N | Y | Y | N | Y‡ | Y | subn |
| **National maximum legal blood alcohol concentration (%)** | | | | | | | | | | |
| General | 0 | 0 | 0.05 | 0.05 | 0.05 | 0.02 | 0.05 | 0.05 | 0.08 | 0.08 |
| Young | 0 | 0 | 0 | 0.05 | 0.03 | 0.02 | 0.01 | 0.05 | 0.08 | subn |
| Professional | 0 | 0 | 0 | 0.05 | 0.03 | 0.02 | 0.01 | 0.02 | 0.08 | 0.04 |
| **Legally binding regulations** | | | | | | | | | | |
| Advertisement | Y | Y | Y | N | Y | Y | Y | Y | Y | N |
| Product placement | N | Y | N | N | N | Y | N | Y | Y | N |
| Sponsorship | N | Y | N | N | N | Y | Y | Y | N | N |
| Sales promotion | N | N | N | N | N | Y | Y | Y | N | N |
| Health warnings (advert/containers) | Y/Y | N/N | Y/N | N/Y | N/N | Y/N | N/N | N/N | N/N | Y/Y |

*Notes:* (†) In France and Germany, professional drivers of vehicles transporting passengers have a lower BAC limit compared to other professional drivers; (*) minimum age in Sweden is 18 for beers with less than 3.5% of alcohol content; (‡) in Turkey, the sale of alcoholic beverages in petrol stations is not allowed, except for beer.

*Sources:* WHO Global Status Report on Alcohol and Health 2014 and OECD national correspondents.

## 3. Supplementary tables and figures associated with Chapter 5

Table A.4 to A.6 provide the list of the main input parameters used in the model-based analyses presented in Chapter 5, along with references to the respective sources. References are listed next to the input parameters.

Table A.7 shows the cost per capita (per unit of population) of the interventions assessed in the OECD analyses. Only costs associated with the delivery of the interventions are included, expressed in USD PPPs.

Figure A.7 shows the cumulative effectiveness of multiple-intervention strategies over time in the three countries concerned. The vertical axis shows the number of disability adjusted life years (DALYs) gained (thousands), while the horizontal axis corresponds to the time frame of the analysis. DALYs are discounted exponentially at a 3% rate.

Figure A.8 describes the cumulative impact of multiple-intervention strategies on health expenditure over time in the three countries concerned. The vertical axis shows the cumulative impact of interventions on health expenditure (USD PPPs per capita), while the horizontal axis corresponds to the time frame of the analysis. Figures are discounted exponentially at a 3% rate.

Figures A.9, A.11 and A.13 illustrate the average annual cost-effectiveness ratios of different policies after they have been in place for 10 years. The vertical axis shows intervention costs (millions of USD PPPs), while the horizontal axis shows intervention effects (thousands of DALYs). Clouds of points for each intervention reflect the stochastic uncertainty surrounding cost and effect estimates in model simulations. Clouds resting mostly or entirely beneath the threshold lines indicate favourable cost-effectiveness profiles.

Figures A.10, A.12 and A.14 illustrate the average annual cost-effectiveness ratios of different policies after they have been in place for 40 years. These figures have the same characteristics as Figures A.9, A.11 and A.13.

## Table A.4. **Input parameters used in CDP-alcohol model and relevant sources – Canada**

| | | |
|---|---|---|
| | Population distribution | United States Census Bureau. International Data Base. Available at: *www.census.gov/population/international/data/idb/region.php.* |
| | Total mortality | Human Mortality Database. University of California, Berkeley (United StatesA) and Max Planck Institute for Demographic Research (Germany). Available at *www.mortality.org.* |
| | Fertility rates | UN population division. On-line Population Database, detailed indicators. Available at: *http://esa.un.org/unpd/wpp/unpp/panel_indicators.htm.* |
| | Migration rates | OECD calculations on population distribution and mortality data. |
| | RR SES – residual mortality | Mackenbach, J.P., A.E. Kunst, A.E. Cavelaars, F. Groenhof and J.J. Geurts (1997), "Socioeconomic Inequalities in Morbidity and Mortality in Western Europe", *The Lancet*, Vol. 349, No. 9066, pp. 1655-1659.<br>Pappas, G., S. Queen, W. Hadden and G. Fisher (1993), "The Increasing Disparity in Mortality Between Socioeconomic Groups in the United States, 1960 and 1986", *New England Journal of Medicine*, Vol. 329, No. 2, pp. 103-109. |
| | Disability weights | Lopez, A.D., C.D. Mathers, M. Ezzati, D.T. Jamison and C.J.L. Murray (2006), Global Burden of Disease and Risk Factors, Oxford University Press/The World Bank. New York. |
| Alcohol consumption | Probability of initiation | Statistics Canada. Canadian Community Health Survey. Ottawa: Statistics Canada, 2012. Available at: *www.statcan.gc.ca/concepts/health-sante/index-eng.htm.* |
| | Volume<br>Pattern | Statistics Canada. National Population Health Survey. Ottawa: Statistics Canada, 2012. Available at: *www.statcan.gc.ca/concepts/nphs-ensp/index-eng.htm.* |
| Cancers | Incidence<br>Prevalence<br>Mortality | IARC. Globocan database. Website *http://globocan.iarc.fr/.* |
| | Fatality | OECD calculations on mortality/prevalence data. |
| | Remission/duration | OECD calculations using CDP model. |
| | RR alcohol – incidence | Corrao, G., V. Bagnardi, A. Zambon and C. La Vecchia (2004), "A Meta-analysis of Alcohol Consumption and the Risk of 15 Diseases", *Preventive Medicine*, Vol. 38, No. 5, pp. 613-619.<br>Lhachimi, S.K., K.J. Cole, W.J. Nusselder, H.A. Smit, P. Baili, K. Bennett, J. Pomerleau, M. McKee, K. Charlesworth, M.C. Kulik, J.P. Mackenbach and H. Boshuizen (2012), "Health Impacts of Increasing Alcohol Prices in the European Union: A Dynamic Projection", *Preventive Medicine*, Vol. 55, No. 3, pp. 237-243. |
| | RR SES – incidence [oropharynx, breast] | van Loon, A.J., J. Brug, R.A. Goldbohm, P.A. van den Brandt and J. Burg (1995), "Differences in Cancer Incidence and Mortality Among Socio-economic Groups", *Scandinavian Journal Social Medicine*, Vol. 23, No. 2, pp. 110-120. |
| | RR SES – incidence [liver, oesophagus] | Ferraroni, M., E. Negri, C. La Vecchia, B. D'Avanzo and S. Franceschi (1989), "Socioeconomic Indicators, Tobacco and Alcohol in the Aetiology of Digestive Tract Neoplasms", *International Journal of Epidemiology*, Vol. 18, No. 3, pp. 556-562. |
| | RR cirrhosis – cancer [liver] | Ha, N.B., N.B. Ha, A. Ahmed, W. Ayoub, T.J. Daugherty, E.T. Chang, G.A. Lutchman, G. Garcia, A.D Cooper, E.B. Keeffe and M.H. Nguyen (2012), "Risk Factors for Hepatocellular Carcinoma in Patients with Chronic Liver Disease: A Case-control Study", *Cancer Causes Control*, Vol. 23, No. 3, pp. 455-462. |
| Ischaemic heart disease | Incidence | Statistics Canada. Vital statistics morbidity database. Ottawa: Statistics Canada. |
| | Prevalence | OECD calibration on PHAC calculations using DisMod II. |
| | Mortality | Statistics Canada. Vital statistics mortality database. Ottawa: Statistics Canada. |
| | Fatality | OECD calculation on mortality/prevalence data. |
| | Remission/duration | OECD calculations using CDP model. |
| | RR alcohol – incidence | Corrao, G., V. Bagnardi, A. Zambon and C. La Vecchia (2004), "A Meta-analysis of Alcohol Consumption and the Risk of 15 Diseases", *Preventive Medicine*, Vol. 38, No. 5, pp. 613-619.<br>Roerecke, M. and J. Rehm (2010), "Irregular Heavy Drinking Occasions and Risk of Ischemic Heart Disease: A Systematic Review and Meta-analysis", *American Journal of Epidemiology*, Vol. 171, No. 6, pp. 633-644. |
| | RR SES – incidence | Forssas, E.H., I.T. Keskimäki, A.R. Reunanen AND S.V. Koskinen (2008), "Coronary Heart Disease Among Diabetic and Nondiabetic People – Socioeconomic Differences in Incidence, Prognosis and Mortality", *Journal of Diabetes and its Complications*, Vol. 22, No. 1, pp. 10-17.<br>Salomaa, V., M. Niemelä, H. Miettinen, M. Ketonen, P. Immonen-Räihä, S. Koskinen, M. Mähönen, S. Lehto, T. Vuorenmaa, P. Palomäki, H. Mustaniemi, E. Kaarsalo, M. Arstila, J. Torppa, K. Kuulasmaa, P. Puska, K. Pyörälä and J. Tuomilehto (2000), "Relationship of Socioeconomic Status to the Incidence and Prehospital, 28-day, and 1-year Mortality Rates of Acute Coronary Events in the FINMONICA Myocardial Infarction Register Study", *Circulation*, Vol. 101, No. 16, pp. 1913-1918. |
| | RR SES – mortality | Haan, M., G.A. Kaplan and T. Camacho (1987), "Poverty and Health. Prospective Evidence from the Alameda County Study", *American Journal of Epidemiology*, Vol. 125, No. 6, pp. 989-998.<br>Logue, E.E. and D. Jarjoura (1990), "Modeling Heart Disease Mortality with Census Tract Rates and Social Class Mixtures", *Social Science & Medicine*, Vol. 31, No. 5, pp. 545-550.<br>Kaplan, G.A. and J.E. Keil (1993), "Socioeconomic Factors and Cardiovascular Disease: A Review of the Literature", *Circulation*, Vol. 88(4Pt1), pp. 1973-1998. |

Table A.4. **Input parameters used in CDP-alcohol model and relevant sources – Canada** *(cont.)*

| | | |
|---|---|---|
| Stroke | Incidence | Statistics Canada. Vital statistics morbidity database. Ottawa: Statistics Canada. |
| | Prevalence | OECD calibration on PHAC calculations using DisMod II. |
| | Mortality | Statistics Canada. Vital statistics mortality database. Ottawa: Statistics Canada. |
| | Fatality | OECD calculations on mortality/prevalence data. |
| | Remission/duration | OECD calculations using CDP model. |
| | RR alcohol – incidence | Corrao, G., V. Bagnardi, A. Zambon and C. La Vecchia (2004), "A Meta-analysis of Alcohol Consumption and the Risk of 15 Diseases", *Preventive Medicine*, Vol. 38, No. 5, pp. 613-619.<br>Lhachimi, S.K., K.J. Cole, W.J. Nusselder, H.A. Smit, P. Baili, K. Bennett, J. Pomerleau, M. McKee, K. Charlesworth, M.C. Kulik, J.P. Mackenbach and H. Boshuizen (2012), "Health Impacts of Increasing Alcohol Prices in the European Union: A Dynamic Projection", *Preventive Medicine*, Vol. 55, No. 3, pp. 237-243. |
| | RR SES – incidence | Kuper, H., H.O. Adami, T. Theorell and E. Weiderpass (2007), "The Socioeconomic Gradient in the Incidence of Stroke: A Prospective Study in Middle-aged Women in Sweden", *Stroke*, Vol. 38, No. 1, pp. 27-33.<br>Hart, C.L., D.J. Hole and G.D. Smith (2000), "The Contribution of Risk Factors to Stroke Differentials, by Socioeconomic Position in Adulthood: The Renfrew/Paisley Study", *American Journal of Public Health*, Vol. 90, No. 11, pp. 1788-1791. |
| | RR SES – mortality | Arrich, J., W. Lalouschek and M. Müllner (2005), "Influence of Socioeconomic Status on Mortality After Stroke: Retrospective Cohort Study", *Stroke*, Vol. 36, No. 2, pp. 310-314.<br>Arrich, J., M. Müllner, W. Lalouschek, S. Greisenegger, R. Crevenna and H. Herkner (2008), "Influence of Socioeconomic Status and Gender on Stroke Treatment and Diagnostics", *Stroke*, Vol. 39, No. 7, pp. 2066-2072.<br>Jakovljević, D., C. Sarti, J. Sivenius, J. Torppa, M. Mähönen, P. Immonen-Räihä, E. Kaarsalo, K. Alhainen, K. Kuulasmaa, J. Tuomilehto, P. Puska and V. Salomaa (2001), "Socioeconomic Status and Ischemic Stroke: The FINMONICA Stroke Register", *Stroke*, Vol. 32, No. 7, pp. 1492-1498. |
| Alcohol use disorders | Incidence | OECD calculations using DisMod II. |
| | Prevalence | WHO. WHO Global Health Observatory Data Repository. Available at: *http://apps.who.int/gho/data/view.main.58000.* |
| | Mortality | WHO. Mortality and burden of disease for member states. Geneva: WHO (2011).<br>WHO. Causes of death summary tables. Geneva: WHO (2011). |
| | Fatality | OECD calculation on mortality/prevalence data. |
| | Remission/duration | Hasin, D.S., F.S. Stinson, E. Ogburn and B.F. Grant (2007), "Prevalence, Correlates, Disability, and Comorbidity of DSM-IV Alcohol Abuse and Dependence in the United States: Results from the National Epidemiologic Survey on Alcohol and Related Conditions", *Archives of General Psychiatry*, Vol. 64, No. 7, pp. 830-842.<br>Dawson, D.A., B.F. Grant, F.S. Stinson, P.S. Chou, B. Huang and W.J. Ruan (2006), "Recovery from DSM-IV Alcohol Dependence: United States, 2001-2002", *Alcohol Research and Health*, Vol. 29, No. 2, pp. 131-142. |
| | RR alcohol – incidence | Meier, P. (2008), "Independent Review of the Effects of Alcohol Pricing and Promotion – Part B: Modeling the Potential Impact of Pricing and Promotion Policies for Alcohol in England: Results from the Sheffield Alcohol Policy Model, Sheffield: University of Sheffield.<br>Dawson, D.A., T.K. Li and B.F. Grant (2008), "A Prospective Study of Risk Drinking: At Risk for What?", *Drug and Alcohol Dependence*, Vol. 95, No. 1-2, pp. 62-72. |
| Liver cirrhosis | Incidence | OECD calculations. |
| | Prevalence | OECD calculations using DisMod II. |
| | Mortality | WHO. Mortality and burden of disease for member states. Geneva: WHO (2011).<br>WHO. Causes of death summary tables. Geneva: WHO (2011). |
| | Fatality | OECD calculation on mortality/prevalence data. |
| | Remission/duration | Fauci, A.S., E. Braunwald, D.L. Kasper, S.L. Hauser, D.L. Longo, J.L. Jameson and J. Loscalzo (2009), Harrison's Manual of Medicine, McGraw Hill Professional, London. |
| | RR alcohol – incidence | Corrao, G., V. Bagnardi, A. Zambon and C. La Vecchia (2004), "A Meta-analysis of Alcohol Consumption and the Risk of 15 Diseases", *Preventive Medicine*, Vol. 38, No. 5, pp. 613-619. |
| | RR SES – incidence | Najman, J.M., G.M. Williams and R. Room (2007), "Increasing Socioeconomic Inequalities in Male Cirrhosis of the Liver Mortality: Australia 1981-2002", *Drug and Alcohol Review*, Vol. 26, No. 3, pp. 273-278.<br>Crombie, I.K. and E. Precious (2011), "Changes in the Social Class Gradient of Cirrhosis Mortality in England and Wales Across the 20th Century", *Alcohol and Alcoholism*, Vol.46, No. 1, pp. 80-82. |

Table A.4. **Input parameters used in CDP-alcohol model and relevant sources – Canada** *(cont.)*

| | | |
|---|---|---|
| Epilepsis | Incidence | OECD calculations using DisMod II. |
| | Prevalence | Statistics Canada. CANSIM on-line database; neurological conditions, by age group and sex. Available at: *www5.statcan.gc.ca/cansim/.* |
| | Mortality | WHO. Mortality and burden of disease for member states. Geneva: WHO (2011).<br>WHO. Causes of death summary tables. Geneva: WHO (2011). |
| | Fatality | OECD calculation on mortality/prevalence data. |
| | RR alcohol – incidence | Meier, P. (2008), "Independent Review of the Effects of Alcohol Pricing and Promotion – Part B: Modeling the Potential Impact of Pricing and Promotion Policies for Alcohol in England: Results from the Sheffield Alcohol Policy Model", Sheffield: University of Sheffield. |
| | RR SES – incidence | Heaney, D.C., B.K. MacDonald, A. Everitt, S. Stevenson, G.S. Leonardi, P. Wilkinson and J.W. Sander (2002), "Socioeconomic Variation in Incidence of Epilepsy: Prospective Community Based Study in South East England", *British Medical Journal*, Vol. 325, No. 7371, pp. 1013-1016.<br>Benn, E.K., W.A. Hauser, T. Shih, L. Leary, E. Bagiella, P. Dayan, R. Green, H. Andrews, D.J. Thurman and D.C. Hesdorffer (2008), "Estimating the Incidence of First Unprovoked Seizure and Newly Diagnosed Epilepsy in the Low-income Urban Community of Northern Manhattan, New York City", *Epilepsia*, Vol. 49, No. 8, pp. 1431-1439. |
| Injuries | Incidence | Smartrisk. The burden of injury in Canada. Toronto: Smartrisk (2009). |
| | Prevalence | OECD calculations using DisMod II. |
| | Mortality | Statistics Canada. Mortality, summary list of causes. Ottawa: Statistics Canada (2009). |
| | Fatality | OECD calculations. |
| | Remission/duration | Smartrisk. The burden of injury in Canada. Toronto: Smartrisk (2009). |
| | RR alcohol – incidence | Corrao, G., V. Bagnardi, A. Zambon and C. La Vecchia (2004), "A Meta-analysis of Alcohol Consumption and the Risk of 15 Diseases", *Preventive Medicine*, Vol. 38, No. 5, pp. 613-619. |
| | RR alcohol – mortality | White, I.R., D.R. Altmann and K. Nanchahal (2002), "Alcohol Consumption and Mortality: Modelling Risks for Men and Women at Different Ages", *British Medical Journal*, Vol. 325, No. 7357, p. 191. |
| | RR SES – incidence | Cubbin, C., F.B. LeClere and G.S. Smith (2000), "Socioeconomic Status and the Occurrence of Fatal and Nonfatal Injury in the United States", *American Journal of Public Health*, Vol. 90, No. 1, pp. 70-77. |

## Table A.5. **Input parameters used in CDP-alcohol model and relevant sources – Czech Republic**

| | | |
|---|---|---|
| | Population distribution | United States Census Bureau. International Data Base. Available at: *www.census.gov/population/international/data/idb/region.php*. |
| | Total mortality | UN Populavion Division. World population prospects, extended dataset. Available at: *http://esa.un.org/unpd/wpp/ASCII-Data/DISK_NAVIGATION_ASCII.htm*.<br>UN population division. On-line Population database, detailed indicators. Available at: *http://esa.un.org/unpd/wpp/unpp/panel_indicators.htm*. |
| | Fertility rates | UN population division. On-line Population database, detailed indicators. Available at: *http://esa.un.org/unpd/wpp/unpp/panel_indicators.htm*. |
| | Migration rates | OECD calculations on population distribution and mortality data. |
| | RR SES – residual mortality | Mackenbach, J.P., A.E. Kunst, A.E. Cavelaars, F. Groenhof and J.J. Geurts (1997), "Socioeconomic Inequalities in Morbidity and Mortality in Western Europe", *The Lancet*, Vol. 349, No. 9066, pp. 1655-1659.<br>Pappas, G., S. Queen, W. Hadden and G. Fisher (1993), "The Increasing Disparity in Mortality Between Socioeconomic Droups in the United States, 1960 and 1986", *New England Journal of Medicine*, Vol.329, No. 2, pp. 103-109. |
| | Disability weights | Lopez, A.D., C.D. Mathers, M. Ezzati, D.T. Jamison and C.J.L. Murray (2006), Global Burden of Disease and Risk Factors, Oxford University Press/The World Bank, New York. |
| Alcohol consumption | Probability of initiation | Institute for Therapy Research. Epidemiological Survey of Substance Abuse (1995, 1997, 2000, 2003, 2006, and 2009). Available at: *http://www.gesis.org*. |
| | Volume<br>Pattern | Czech National Institute of Public Health own analyses on: 2012 National Survey on Tobacco smoking and Alcohol Consumption in the Czech Republic; 2005 Czech National Survey on Mental Health; 2002 GENACIS study. |
| Cancers | Incidence<br>Prevalence<br>Mortality | IARC. Globocan database. Website *http://globocan.iarc.fr/*. |
| | Fatality | OECD calculations on mortality/prevalence data. |
| | Remission/duration | OECD calculations using CDP model. |
| | RR alcohol – incidence | Corrao, G., V. Bagnardi, A. Zambon and C. La Vecchia (2004), "A Meta-analysis of Alcohol Consumption and the Risk of 15 Diseases", *Preventive Medicine*, Vol. 38, No. 5, pp. 613-619.<br>Lhachimi, S.K., K.J. Cole, W.J. Nusselder, H.A. Smit, P. Baili, K. Bennett, J. Pomerleau, M. McKee, K. Charlesworth, M.C. Kulik, J.P. Mackenbach and H. Boshuizen (2012), "Health Impacts of Increasing Alcohol Prices in the European Union: A Dynamic Projection", *Preventive Medicine*, Vol. 55, No. 3, pp. 237-243. |
| | RR SES – incidence [oropharynx, breast] | van Loon, A.J., J. Brug, R.A. Goldbohm, P.A. van den Brandt and J. Burg (1995), "Differences in Cancer Incidence and Mortality Among Socio-economic Groups", *Scandinavian Journal Social Medicine*, Vol. 23, No. 2, pp. 110-120. |
| | RR SES – incidence [liver, oesophagus] | Ferraroni, M., E. Negri, C. La Vecchia, B. D'Avanzo and S. Franceschi (1989), "Socioeconomic Indicators, Tobacco and Alcohol in the Aetiology of Digestive Tract Neoplasms", *International Journal of Epidemiology*, Vol. 18, No. 3, pp. 556-562. |
| | RR cirrhosis – cancer [liver] | Ha, N.B., N.B. Ha, A. Ahmed, W. Ayoub, T.J. Daugherty, E.T. Chang, G.A. Lutchman, G. Garcia, A.D. Cooper, E.B. Keeffe and M.H. Nguyen (2012), "Risk Factors for Hepatocellular Carcinoma in Patients with Chronic Liver Disease: A Case-control Study", *Cancer Causes Control*, Vol. 23, No. 3, pp. 455-462. |

## Table A.5. **Input parameters used in CDP-alcohol model and relevant sources – Czech Republic** *(cont.)*

| | | |
|---|---|---|
| Ischaemic heart disease | Incidence | WHO Europe. European Hospital Morbidity Database. Available at: *http://data.euro.who.int/hmdb/index.php.* |
| | Prevalence | OECD calculations using DisMod II. |
| | Mortality | WHO. Mortality and burden of disease for member states. Geneva: WHO (2011).<br>WHO. Causes of death summary tables. Geneva: WHO (2011). |
| | Fatality | OECD calculation on mortality/prevalence data. |
| | Remission/duration | OECD calculations using CDP model. |
| | RR alcohol – incidence | Corrao, G., V. Bagnardi, A. Zambon and C. La Vecchia (2004), "A Meta-analysis of Alcohol Consumption and the Risk of 15 Diseases", *Preventive Medicine*, Vol. 38, No. 5, pp. 613-619.<br>Roerecke, M. and J. Rehm (2010), "Irregular Heavy Drinking Occasions and Risk of Ischemic Heart Disease: A Systematic Review and Meta-analysis", *American Journal of Epidemiology*, Vol. 171, No. 6, pp. 633-644. |
| | RR SES – incidence | Forssas, E.H., I.T. Keskimäki, A.R. Reunanen AND S.V. Koskinen (2008), "Coronary Heart Disease Among Diabetic and Nondiabetic People – Socioeconomic Differences in Incidence, Prognosis and Mortality", *Journal of Diabetes and its Complications*, Vol. 22, No. 1, pp. 10-17.<br>Salomaa, V., M. Niemelä, H. Miettinen, M. Ketonen, P. Immonen-Räihä, S. Koskinen, M. Mähönen, S. Lehto, T. Vuorenmaa, P. Palomäki, H. Mustaniemi, E. Kaarsalo, M. Arstila, J. Torppa, K. Kuulasmaa, P. Puska, K. Pyörälä and J. Tuomilehto (2000), "Relationship of Socioeconomic Status to the Incidence and Prehospital, 28-day, and 1-year Mortality Rates of Acute Coronary Events in the FINMONICA Myocardial Infarction Register Study", *Circulation*, Vol. 101, No. 16, pp. 1913-1918. |
| | RR SES – mortality | Haan, M., G.A. Kaplan and T. Camacho (1987), "Poverty and Health. Prospective Evidence from the Alameda County Study", *American Journal of Epidemiology*, Vol. 125, No. 6, pp. 989-998.<br>Logue, E.E. and D. Jarjoura (1990), "Modeling Heart Disease Mortality with Census Tract Rates and Social Class Mixtures", *Social Science & Medicine*, Vol. 31, No. 5, pp. 545-550.<br>Kaplan, G.A. and J.E. Keil (1993), "Socioeconomic Factors and Cardiovascular Disease: A Review of the Literature", *Circulation*, Vol. 88(4Pt1), pp. 1973-1998. |
| Stroke | Incidence<br>Prevalence | Truelsen, T., B. Piechowski-Jóźwiak, R. Bonita, C. Mathers, J. Bogousslavsky and G. Boysen (2006), "Stroke Incidence and Prevalence in Europe: A Review of Available Data", *European Journal of Neurology*, Vol. 13, No. 6, pp. 581-598. |
| | Mortality | WHO. Mortality and burden of disease for member states. Geneva: WHO (2011).<br>WHO. Causes of death summary tables. Geneva: WHO (2011). |
| | Fatality | OECD calculations on mortality/prevalence data. |
| | Remission/duration | OECD calculations using CDP model. |
| | RR alcohol – incidence | Corrao, G., V. Bagnardi, A. Zambon and C. La Vecchia (2004), "A Meta-analysis of Alcohol Consumption and the Risk of 15 Diseases", *Preventive Medicine*, Vol. 38, No. 5, pp. 613-619.<br>Lhachimi, S.K., K.J. Cole, W.J. Nusselder, H.A. Smit, P. Baili, K. Bennett, J. Pomerleau, M. McKee, K. Charlesworth, M.C. Kulik, J.P. Mackenbach and H. Boshuizen (2012), "Health Impacts of Increasing Alcohol Prices in the European Union: A Dynamic Projection", *Preventive Medicine*, Vol. 55, No. 3, pp. 237-243. |
| | RR SES – incidence | Kuper, H., H.O. Adami, T. Theorell and E. Weiderpass (2007), "The Socioeconomic Gradient in the Incidence of Stroke: A Prospective Study in Middle-aged Women in Sweden", *Stroke*, Vol. 38, No. 1, pp. 27-33.<br>Hart, C.L., D.J. Hole and G.D. Smith (2000), "The Contribution of Risk Factors to Stroke Differentials, by Socioeconomic Position in Adulthood: The Renfrew/Paisley Study", *American Journal of Public Health*, Vol. 90, No. 11, pp. 1788-1791. |
| | RR SES – mortality | Arrich, J., W. Lalouschek and M. Müllner (2005), "Influence of Socioeconomic Status on Mortality After Stroke: Retrospective Cohort Study", *Stroke*, Vol. 36, No. 2, pp. 310-314.<br>Arrich, J., M. Müllner, W. Lalouschek, S. Greisenegger, R. Crevenna and H. Herkner (2008), "Influence of Socioeconomic Status and Gender on Stroke Treatment and Diagnostics", *Stroke*, Vol. 39, No. 7, pp. 2066-2072.<br>Jakovljević, D., C. Sarti, J. Sivenius, J. Torppa, M. Mähönen, P. Immonen-Räihä, E. Kaarsalo, K. Alhainen, K. Kuulasmaa, J. Tuomilehto, P. Puska and V. Salomaa (2001), "Socioeconomic Status and Ischemic Stroke: The FINMONICA Stroke Register", *Stroke*, Vol. 32, No. 7, pp. 1492-1498. |
| Alcohol use disorders | Incidence | OECD calculations using DisMod II. |
| | Prevalence | WHO. WHO Global Health Observatory Data Repository. Available at: *http://apps.who.int/gho/data/view.main.58000.* |
| | Mortality | WHO. Mortality and burden of disease for member states. Geneva: WHO (2011). |
| | Fatality | WHO. Causes of death summary tables. Geneva: WHO (2011).<br>OECD calculation on mortality/prevalence data |

## Table A.5. **Input parameters used in CDP-alcohol model and relevant sources – Czech Republic** *(cont.)*

| | | |
|---|---|---|
| | Remission/duration | Hasin, D.S., F.S. Stinson, E. Ogburn and B.F. Grant (2007), "Prevalence, Correlates, Disability, and Comorbidity of DSM-IV Alcohol Abuse and Dependence in the United States: Results from the National Epidemiologic Survey on Alcohol and Related Conditions", *Archives of General Psychiatry*, Vol. 64, No. 7, pp. 830-842.<br>Dawson, D.A., B.F. Grant, F.S. Stinson, P.S. Chou, B. Huang and W.J. Ruan (2006), "Recovery from DSM-IV Alcohol Dependence: United States, 2001-2002", *Alcohol Research and Health*, Vol. 29, No. 2, pp. 131-142. |
| | RR alcohol – incidence | Meier, P. (2008), "Independent Review of the Effects of Alcohol Pricing and Promotion – Part B: Modeling the Potential Impact of Pricing and Promotion Policies for Alcohol in England: Results from the Sheffield Alcohol Policy Model", Sheffield: University of Sheffield.<br>Dawson, D.A., T.K. Li and B.F. Grant (2008), "A Prospective Study of Risk Drinking: At Risk for What?", *Drug and Alcohol Dependence*, Vol. 95, No. 1-2, pp. 62-72. |
| Liver cirrhosis | Incidence | WHO Europe. European Hospital Morbidity Database. Available at: *http://data.euro.who.int/hmdb/index.php*. |
| | Prevalence | OECD calculations using DisMod II. |
| | Mortality | WHO. Mortality and burden of disease for member states. Geneva: WHO (2011).<br>WHO. Causes of death summary tables. Geneva: WHO (2011). |
| | Fatality | OECD calculation on mortality/prevalence data. |
| | Remission/duration | Fauci, A.S., E. Braunwald, D.L. Kasper, S.L. Hauser, D.L. Longo, J.L. Jameson and J. Loscalzo (2009), Harrison's Manual of Medicine, McGraw Hill Professional, London. |
| | RR alcohol – incidence | Corrao, G., V. Bagnardi, A. Zambon and C. La Vecchia (2004), "A Meta-analysis of Alcohol Consumption and the Risk of 15 Diseases", *Preventive Medicine*, Vol. 38, No. 5, pp. 613-619. |
| | RR SES – incidence | Najman, J.M., G.M. Williams and R. Room (2007), "Increasing Socioeconomic Inequalities in Male Cirrhosis of the Liver Mortality: Australia 1981-2002", *Drug and Alcohol Review*, Vol. 26, No. 3, pp. 273-278.<br>Crombie, I.K. and E. Precious (2011), "Changes in the Social Class Gradient of Cirrhosis Mortality in England and Wales Across the 20th Century", *Alcohol and Alcoholism*, Vol.46, No. 1, pp. 80-82. |
| Epilepsy | Incidence | OECD calculations using DisMod II. |
| | Prevalence | Pugliatti, M., E. Beghi, L. Forsgren, M. Ekman and P. Sobocki (2007), "Estimating the Cost of Epilepsy in Europe: A Review with Economic Modeling", *Epilepsia*, Vol. 48, No. 12, pp. 2224-2233. |
| | Mortality | WHO. Mortality and burden of disease for member states. Geneva: WHO (2011).<br>WHO. Causes of death summary tables. Geneva: WHO (2011). |
| | Fatality | OECD calculation on mortality/prevalence data. |
| | RR alcohol – incidence | Meier, P. (2008), "Independent Review of the Effects of Alcohol Pricing and Promotion – Part B: Modeling the Potential Impact of Pricing and Promotion Policies for Alcohol in England: Results from the Sheffield Alcohol Policy Model", Sheffield: University of Sheffield. |
| | RR SES – incidence | Heaney, D.C., N.K. MacDonald, A. Everitt, S. Stevenson, G.S. Leonardi, P. Wilkinson and J.W. Sander (2002), "Socioeconomic Variation in Incidence of Epilepsy: Prospective Community Based Study in South East England", *British Medical Journal*, Vol. 325, No. 7371, pp. 1013-1016.<br>Benn, E.K., W.A. Hauser, T. Shih, L. Leary, E. Bagiella, P. Dayan, R. Green, H. Andrews, D.J. Thurman and D.C. Hesdorffer (2008), "Estimating the Incidence of First Unprovoked Seizure and Newly Diagnosed Epilepsy in the Low-income Urban Community of Northern Manhattan, New York City", *Epilepsia*, Vol. 49, No. 8, pp. 1431-1439. |
| Injuries | Incidence | EuroSafe. Injuries in the European Union, Report on injury statistics 2008-2010. Amsterdam: EuroSafe (2013). |
| | Prevalence | OECD calculations using DisMod II. |
| | Mortality | WHO. Mortality and burden of disease for member states. Geneva: WHO (2011).<br>WHO. Causes of death summary tables. Geneva: WHO (2011). |
| | Fatality | OECD calculations. |
| | Remission/duration | Smartrisk. The burden of injury in Canada. Toronto: Smartrisk (2009). |
| | RR alcohol – incidence | Corrao, G., V. Bagnardi, A. Zambon and C. La Vecchia (2004), "A Meta-analysis of Alcohol Consumption and the Risk of 15 Diseases", *Preventive Medicine*, Vol. 38, No. 5, pp. 613-619. |
| | RR alcohol – mortality | White, I.R., D.R. Altmann and K. Nanchahal (2002), "Alcohol Consumption and Mortality: Modelling Risks for Men and Women at Different Ages", *British Medical Journal*, Vol. 325, No. 7357, p. 191. |
| | RR SES – incidence | Cubbin, C., F.B. LeClere and G.S. Smith (2000), "Socioeconomic Status and the Occurrence of Fatal and Nonfatal Injury in the United States", *American Journal of Public Health*, Vol. 90, No. 1, pp. 70-77. |

Table A.6. **Input parameters used in CDP-alcohol model and relevant sources – Germany**

| | | |
|---|---|---|
| | Population distribution | Statistisches Bundesamt. Bevölkerungsvorausberechnung. Available at: *destatis.de.* |
| | Total mortality | Statistisches Bundesamt. Bevölkerung Deutschlands bis 2060 Ergebnisse der 12. koordinierten Bevölkerungsvorausberechnung. Available at: *www.destatis.de/DE/Publikationen/Thematisch/Bevoelkerung/VorausberechnungBevoelkerung/BevoelkerungDeutschland2060.html.* |
| | Fertility rates | UN population division. On-line Population database, detailed indicators. Available at: *http://esa.un.org/unpd/wpp/unpp/panel_indicators.htm.* |
| | Migration rates | OECD calculations on population distribution and mortality data. |
| | RR SES – residual mortality | Mackenbach, J.P., A.E. Kunst, A.E. Cavelaars, F. Groenhof and J.J. Geurts (1997), "Socioeconomic Inequalities in Morbidity and Mortality in Western Europe", *The Lancet*, Vol. 349, No. 9066, pp. 1655-1659.<br>Pappas, G., S. Queen, W. Hadden and G. Fisher (1993), "The Increasing Disparity in Mortality Between Socioeconomic Groups in the United States, 1960 and 1986", *New England Journal of Medicine*, Vol. 329, No. 2, pp. 103-109. |
| | Disability weights | Lopez, A.D., C.D. Mathers, M. Ezzati, D.T. Jamison and C.J.L. Murray (2006), Global Burden of Disease and Risk Factors, Oxford University Press/The World Bank, New York. |
| Alcohol | Probability of initiation<br>Volume<br>Pattern | Institute for Therapy Research. Epidemiological Survey of Substance Abuse (1995, 1997, 2000, 2003, 2006, and 2009). Available at: *http://www.gesis.org.* |
| Cancers | Incidence<br>Prevalence<br>Mortality | IARC. Globocan database. Website *http://globocan.iarc.fr/.* |
| | Fatality | OECD calculations on mortality/prevalence data. |
| | Remission/duration | OECD calculations using CDP model. |
| | RR alcohol – incidence | Corrao, G., V. Bagnardi, A. Zambon and C. La Vecchia (2004), "A Meta-analysis of Alcohol Consumption and the Risk of 15 Diseases", *Preventive Medicine*, Vol. 38, No. 5, pp. 613-619.<br>Lhachimi, S.K., K.J. Cole, W.J. Nusselder, H.A. Smit, P. Baili, K. Bennett, J. Pomerleau, M. McKee, K. Charlesworth, M.C. Kulik, J.P. Mackenbach and H. Boshuizen (2012), "Health Impacts of Increasing Alcohol Prices in the European Union: A Dynamic Projection", *Preventive Medicine*, Vol. 55, No. 3, pp. 237-243. |
| | RR SES – incidence [oropharynx, breast] | van Loon, A.J., J. Brug, R.A. Goldbohm, P.A. van den Brandt and J. Burg (1995), "Differences in Cancer Incidence and Mortality Among Socio-economic Groups", *Scandinavian Journal Social Medicine*, Vol. 23, No. 2, pp. 110-120. |
| | RR SES – incidence [liver, oesophagus] | Ferraroni, M., E. Negri, C. La Vecchia, B. D'Avanzo and S. Franceschi (1989), "Socioeconomic Indicators, Tobacco and Alcohol in the Aetiology of Digestive Tract Neoplasms", *International Journal of Epidemiology*, Vol. 18, No. 3, pp. 556-562. |
| | RR cirrhosis – cancer [liver] | Ha, N.B., N.B. Ha, A. Ahmed, W. Ayoub, T.J. Daugherty, E.T. Chang, G.A. Lutchman, G. Garcia, A.D Cooper, E.B. Keeffe and M.H. Nguyen (2012), "Risk Factors for Hepatocellular Carcinoma in Patients with Chronic Liver Disease: A Case-control Study", *Cancer Causes Control*, Vol. 23, No. 3, pp. 455-462. |

Table A.6. **Input parameters used in CDP-alcohol model and relevant sources – Germany** *(cont.)*

| | | |
|---|---|---|
| Ischaemic heart disease | Incidence | WHO Europe. European Hospital Morbidity Database. Available at: *http://data.euro.who.int/hmdb/index.php.* |
| | Prevalence | Robert Koch Institute. GEDA 2010: Coronary heart disease facts and figures. Available at: *www.rki.de/DE/Content/Gesundheitsmonitoring/Gesundheitsberichterstattung/GesundAZ/Content/K/KoronHerzKH/KoronHerzKH.html?nn=2370692.* |
| | Mortality | WHO. Mortality and burden of disease for member states. Geneva: WHO (2011).<br>WHO. Causes of death summary tables. Geneva: WHO (2011). |
| | Fatality | OECD calculation on mortality/prevalence data. |
| | Remission/duration | OECD calculations using CDP model. |
| | RR alcohol – incidence | Corrao, G., V. Bagnardi, A. Zambon and C. La Vecchia (2004), "A Meta-analysis of Alcohol Consumption and the Risk of 15 Diseases", *Preventive Medicine*, Vol. 38, No. 5, pp. 613-619.<br>Roerecke, M. and J. Rehm (2010), "Irregular Heavy Drinking Occasions and Risk of Ischemic Heart Disease: A Systematic Review and Meta-analysis", *American Journal of Epidemiology*, Vol. 171, No. 6, pp. 633-644. |
| | RR SES – incidence | Forssas, E.H., I.T. Keskimäki, A.R. Reunanen AND S.V. Koskinen (2008), "Coronary Heart Disease Among Diabetic and Nondiabetic People – Socioeconomic Differences in Incidence, Prognosis and Mortality", *Journal of Diabetes and its Complications*, Vol. 22, No. 1, pp. 10-17.<br>Salomaa, V., M. Niemelä, H. Miettinen, M. Ketonen, P. Immonen-Räihä, S. Koskinen, M. Mähönen, S. Lehto, T. Vuorenmaa, P. Palomäki, H. Mustaniemi, E. Kaarsalo, M. Arstila, J. Torppa, K. Kuulasmaa, P. Puska, K. Pyörälä and J. Tuomilehto (2000), "Relationship of Socioeconomic Status to the Incidence and Prehospital, 28-day, and 1-year Mortality Rates of Acute Coronary Events in the FINMONICA Myocardial Infarction Register Study", *Circulation*, Vol. 101, No. 16, pp. 1913-1918. |
| | RR SES – mortality | Haan, M., G.A. Kaplan and T. Camacho (1987), "Poverty and Health. Prospective Evidence from the Alameda County Study", *American Journal of Epidemiology*, Vol. 125, No. 6, pp. 989-998.<br>Logue, E.E. and D. Jarjoura (1990), "Modeling Heart Disease Mortality with Census Tract Rates and Social Class Mixtures", *Social Science & Medicine*, Vol. 31, No. 5, pp. 545-550.<br>Kaplan, G.A. and J.E. Keil (1993), "Socioeconomic Factors and Cardiovascular Disease: A Review of the Literature", *Circulation*, Vol. 88(4Pt1), pp. 1973-1998. |
| Stroke | Incidence<br>Prevalence | Truelsen, T., B. Piechowski-Jóźwiak, R. Bonita, C. Mathers, J. Bogousslavsky and G. Boysen (2006), "Stroke Incidence and Prevalence in Europe: A Review of Available Data", *European Journal of Neurology*, Vol. 13, No. 6, pp. 581-598. |
| | Mortality | WHO. Mortality and burden of disease for member states. Geneva: WHO (2011).<br>WHO. Causes of death summary tables. Geneva: WHO (2011). |
| | Fatality | OECD calculations on mortality/prevalence data. |
| | Remission/duration | OECD calculations using CDP model. |
| | RR alcohol – incidence | Corrao, G., V. Bagnardi, A. Zambon and C. La Vecchia (2004), "A Meta-analysis of Alcohol Consumption and the Risk of 15 Diseases", *Preventive Medicine*, Vol. 38, No. 5, pp. 613-619.<br>Lhachimi, S.K., K.J. Cole, W.J. Nusselder, H.A. Smit, P. Baili, K. Bennett, J. Pomerleau, M. McKee, K. Charlesworth, M.C. Kulik, J.P. Mackenbach and H. Boshuizen (2012), "Health Impacts of Increasing Alcohol Prices in the European Union: A Dynamic Projection", *Preventive Medicine*, Vol. 55, No. 3, pp. 237-243. |
| | RR SES – incidence | Kuper, H., H.O. Adami, T. Theorell and E. Weiderpass (2007), "The Socioeconomic Gradient in the Incidence of Stroke: A Prospective Study in Middle-aged Women in Sweden", *Stroke*, Vol. 38, No. 1, pp. 27-33.<br>Hart, C.L., D.J. Hole and G.D. Smith (2000), "The Contribution of Risk Factors to Stroke Differentials, by Socioeconomic Position in Adulthood: The Renfrew/Paisley Study", *American Journal of Public Health*, Vol. 90, No. 11, pp. 1788-1791. |
| | RR SES – mortality | Arrich, J., W. Lalouschek and M. Müllner (2005), "Influence of Socioeconomic Status on Mortality After Stroke: Retrospective Cohort Study", *Stroke*, Vol. 36, No. 2, pp. 310-314.<br>Arrich, J., M. Müllner, W. Lalouschek, S. Greisenegger, R. Crevenna and H. Herkner (2008), "Influence of Socioeconomic Status and Gender on Stroke Treatment and Diagnostics", *Stroke*, Vol. 39, No. 7, pp. 2066-2072.<br>Jakovljević, D., C. Sarti, J. Sivenius, J. Torppa, M. Mähönen, P. Immonen-Räihä, E. Kaarsalo, K. Alhainen, K. Kuulasmaa, J. Tuomilehto, P. Puska and V. Salomaa (2001), "Socioeconomic Status and Ischemic Stroke: The FINMONICA Stroke Register", *Stroke*, Vol. 32, No. 7, pp. 1492-1498. |
| Alcohol use disorders | Incidence | OECD calculations using DisMod II. |
| | Prevalence | WHO. WHO Global Health Observatory Data Repository. Available at: *http://apps.who.int/gho/data/view.main.58000.* |
| | Mortality | WHO. Mortality and burden of disease for member states. Geneva: WHO (2011).<br>WHO. Causes of death summary tables. Geneva: WHO (2011). |
| | Fatality | OECD calculation on mortality/prevalence data. |
| | Remission/duration | Hasin, D.S., F.S. Stinson, E. Ogburn and B.F. Grant (2007), "Prevalence, Correlates, Disability, and Comorbidity of DSM-IV Alcohol Abuse and Dependence in the United States: Results from the National Epidemiologic Survey on Alcohol and Related Conditions", *Archives of General Psychiatry*, Vol. 64, No. 7, pp. 830-842.<br>Dawson, D.A., B.F. Grant, F.S. Stinson, P.S. Chou, B. Huang and W.J. Ruan (2006), "Recovery from DSM-IV Alcohol Dependence: United States, 2001-2002", *Alcohol Research and Health*, Vol. 29, No. 2, pp. 131-142. |
| | Remission/duration | Meier, P. (2008), "Independent Review of the Effects of Alcohol Pricing and Promotion – Part B: Modeling the Potential Impact of Pricing and Promotion Policies for Alcohol in England: Results from the Sheffield Alcohol Policy Model, Sheffield: University of Sheffield.<br>Dawson, D.A., T.K. Li and B.F. Grant (2008), "A Prospective Study of Risk Drinking: At Risk for What?", *Drug and Alcohol Dependence*, Vol. 95, No. 1-2, pp. 62-72. |

Table A.6. **Input parameters used in CDP-alcohol model and relevant sources – Germany** *(cont.)*

| | | |
|---|---|---|
| Liver cirrhosis | Incidence | WHO Europe. European Hospital Morbidity Database. Available at: *http://data.euro.who.int/hmdb/index.php.* |
| | Prevalence | OECD calculations using DisMod II. |
| | Mortality | WHO. Mortality and burden of disease for member states. Geneva: WHO (2011).<br>WHO. Causes of death summary tables. Geneva: WHO (2011). |
| | Fatality | OECD calculation on mortality/prevalence data. |
| | Remission/duration | Fauci, A.S., E. Braunwald, D.L. Kasper, S.L. Hauser, D.L. Longo, J.L. Jameson and J. Loscalzo (2009), *Harrison's Manual of Medicine*, McGraw Hill Professional, London. |
| | RR alcohol – incidence | Corrao, G., V. Bagnardi, A. Zambon and C. La Vecchia (2004), "A Meta-analysis of Alcohol Consumption and the Risk of 15 Diseases", *Preventive Medicine*, Vol. 38, No. 5, pp. 613-619. |
| | RR SES – incidence | Najman, J.M., G.M. Williams and R. Room (2007), "Increasing Socioeconomic Inequalities in Male Cirrhosis of the Liver Mortality: Australia 1981-2002", *Drug and Alcohol Review*, Vol. 26, No. 3, pp. 273-278.<br>Crombie, I.K. and E. Precious (2011), "Changes in the Social Class Gradient of Cirrhosis Mortality in England and Wales Across the 20th Century", *Alcohol and Alcoholism*, Vol.46, No. 1, pp. 80-82. |
| Epilepsy | Incidence | Deutsche Epilepsievereinigung. Prevalence of Epilepsy in Germany. Available at: *www.epilepsie.sh/Haeufigkeit.319.0.html.* |
| | Prevalence | Kamtsiuris, P., K. Atzpodien, U. Ellert, R. Schlack and M. Schlaud (2007), "Prevalence of Somatic Diseases in German Children and Adolescents. Results of the German Health Interview and Examination Survey for Children and Adolescents (KiGGS)", *Bundesgesundheitsblatt – Gesundheitsforschung – Gesundheitsschutz*, Vol. 50, No. 5-6, pp. 686-700.<br>Deutsche Epilepsievereinigung. Prevalence of Epilepsy in Germany. Available at: *www.epilepsie.sh/Haeufigkeit.319.0.html.* |
| | Mortality | WHO. Mortality and burden of disease for member states. Geneva: WHO (2011).<br>WHO. Causes of death summary tables. Geneva: WHO (2011). |
| | Fatality | OECD calculation on mortality/prevalence data. |
| | RR alcohol – incidence | Meier, P. (2008), "Independent Review of the Effects of Alcohol Pricing and Promotion – Part B: Modeling the Potential Impact of Pricing and Promotion Policies for Alcohol in England: Results from the Sheffield Alcohol Policy Model, Sheffield: University of Sheffield. |
| | RR SES – incidence | Heaney, D.C., B.K. MacDonald, A. Everitt, S. Stevenson, G.S. Leonardi, P. Wilkinson and J.W. Sander (2002), "Socioeconomic Variation in Incidence of Epilepsy: Prospective Community Based Study in South East England", *British Medical Journal*,<br>Vol. 325, No. 7371, pp. 1013-1016.<br>Benn, E.K., W.A. Hauser, T. Shih, L. Leary, E. Bagiella, P. Dayan, R. Green, H. Andrews, D.J. Thurman and D.C. Hesdorffer (2008), "Estimating the Incidence of First Unprovoked Seizure and Newly Diagnosed Epilepsy in the Low-income Urban Community of Northern Manhattan, New York City", *Epilepsia*, Vol. 49, No. 8, pp. 1431-1439. |
| Injuries | Incidence | Robert Koch Institut. GEDA-10 Survey. Robert Koch Institut: Berlin; 2014.<br>Kahl, H., R. Dortschy and G. Ellsäßer (2007), "Verletzungen bei Kindern und Jugendlichen (1-17 Jahre) und Umsetzung von persönlichen Schutzmaßnahmen Ergebnisse des bundesweiten Kinder- und Jugendgesundheitssurveys (KiGGS)", *Bundesgesundheitsbl – Gesundheitsforsch – Gesundheitsschutz*, Vol. 5/6, pp. 718-727.<br>Varnaccia, G., A.C. Saß nd A. Rommel (2014), "Das Unfallgeschehen bei Kindern und Jugendlichen in Deutschland. Datenquellen und Ergebnisse", *Bundesgesundheitsblatt – Gesundheitsforschung – Gesundheitsschutz*, Vol. 57, No. 6. |
| | Prevalence | OECD calculations using DisMod II. |
| | Mortality | Federal Health Monitoring Database. Deaths by external causes and their sequelae. Available at: *www.gbe-bund.de.* |
| | Fatality | OECD calculations. |
| | Remission/duration | Smartrisk. The burden of injury in Canada. Toronto: Smartrisk (2009). |
| | RR alcohol – incidence | Corrao, G., V. Bagnardi, A. Zambon and C. La Vecchia (2004), "A Meta-analysis of Alcohol Consumption and the Risk of 15 Diseases", *Preventive Medicine*, Vol. 38, No. 5, pp. 613-619. |
| | RR alcohol – mortality | White, I.R., D.R. Altmann and K. Nanchahal (2002), "Alcohol Consumption and Mortality: Modelling Risks for Men and Women at Different Ages", *British Medical Journal*, Vol. 325, No. 7357, p. 191. |
| | RR SES – incidence | Cubbin, C., F.B. LeClere and G.S. Smith (2000), "Socioeconomic Status and the Occurrence of Fatal and Nonfatal Injury in the United States", *American Journal of Public Health*, Vol. 90, No. 1, pp. 70-77. |

### Table A.7. **Per-capita costs of selected alcohol policies (USD PPPs)**

| | Canada | Czech Republic | Germany |
|---|---|---|---|
| Brief interventions | 5.11 | 6.02 | 8.96 |
| Tax increase | 0.13 | 0.42 | 0.06 |
| Drink-drive restrictions | 2.05 | 2.05 | 0.63 |
| Opening hours regulation | 0.26 | 0.90 | 0.13 |
| Advertising regulation | 0.54 | 1.66 | 0.30 |
| Treatment of dependence | 5.26 | 12.21 | 7.10 |
| Minimum price | 0.12 | 0.30 | 0.08 |
| Worksite interventions | 1.70 | 2.96 | 4.09 |
| School-based programmes | 0.51 | 2.05 | 0.56 |
| Mixed package | 5.37 | 9.38 | 6.22 |
| Health care package | 9.19 | 17.01 | 14.00 |
| Fiscal and regulatory package | 0.93 | 2.97 | 0.49 |

*Source:* OECD analysis using the WHO-CHOICE approach (http://www.who.int/choice/cost-effectiveness/inputs/en/).

StatLink http://dx.doi.org/10.1787/888933180654

Figure A.7. **Cumulative DALYs saved over time**

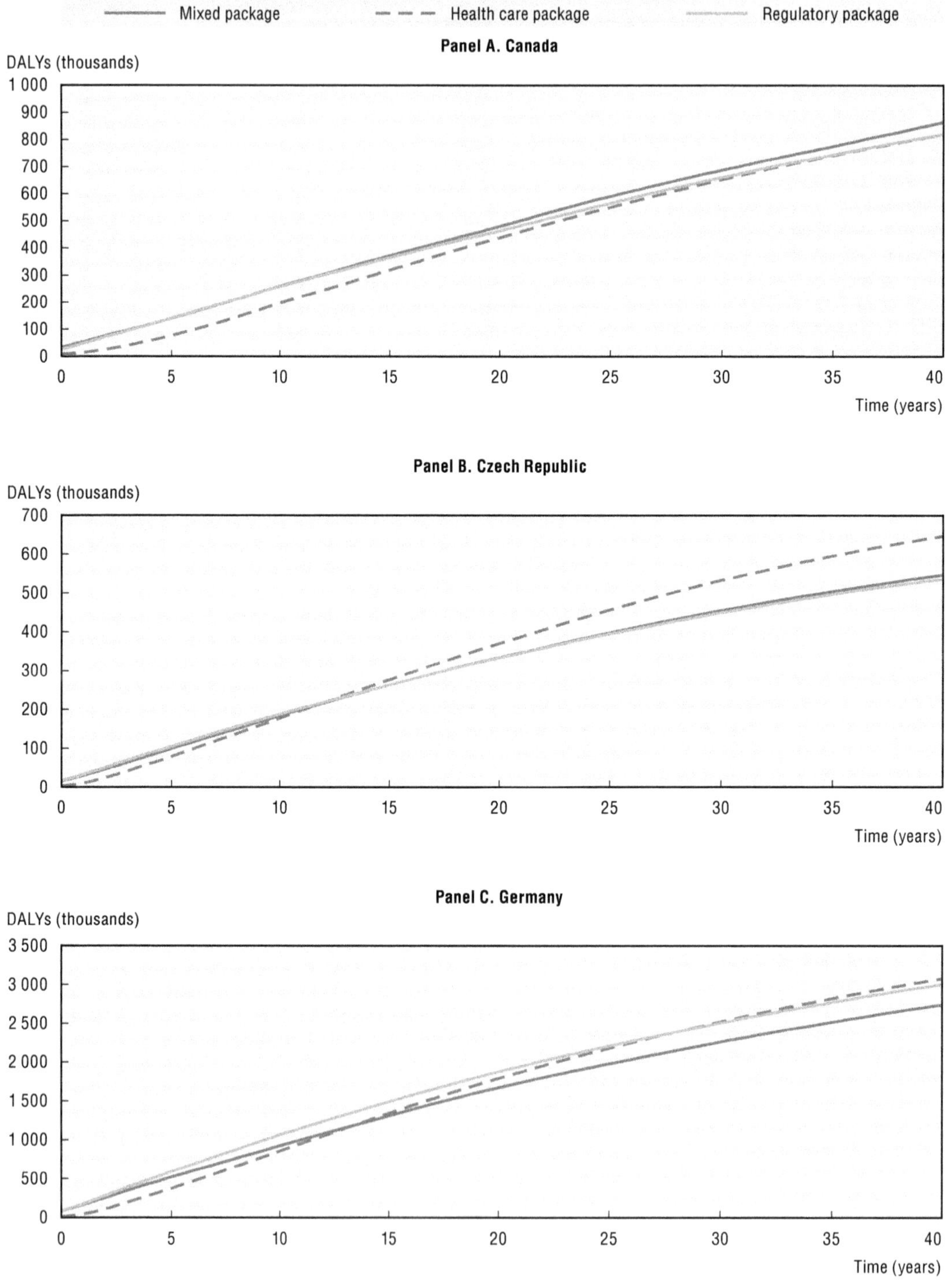


*Source:* CDP-Alcohol analysis relying on input data from multiple sources, listed in Tables A.4 to A.6.

StatLink http://dx.doi.org/10.1787/888933180661

Figure A.8. **Cumulative impact on health care expenditure over time**

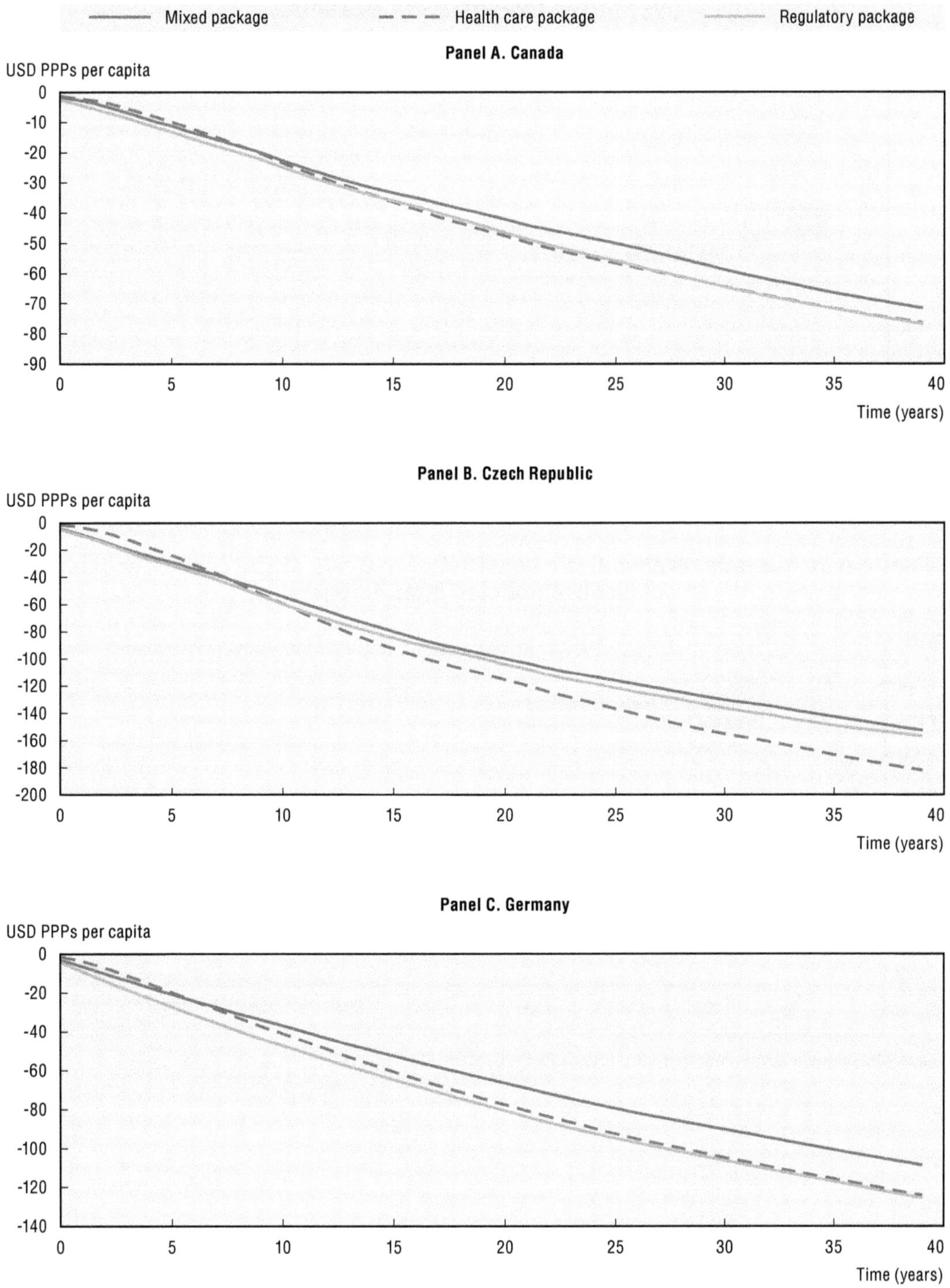


*Source:* CDP-Alcohol analysis relying on input data from multiple sources, listed in Tables A.4 to A.6.

StatLink http://dx.doi.org/10.1787/888933180675

Figure A.9. **Canada: Probabilistic sensitivity analysis of the cost-effectiveness of alcohol policies after 10 years**

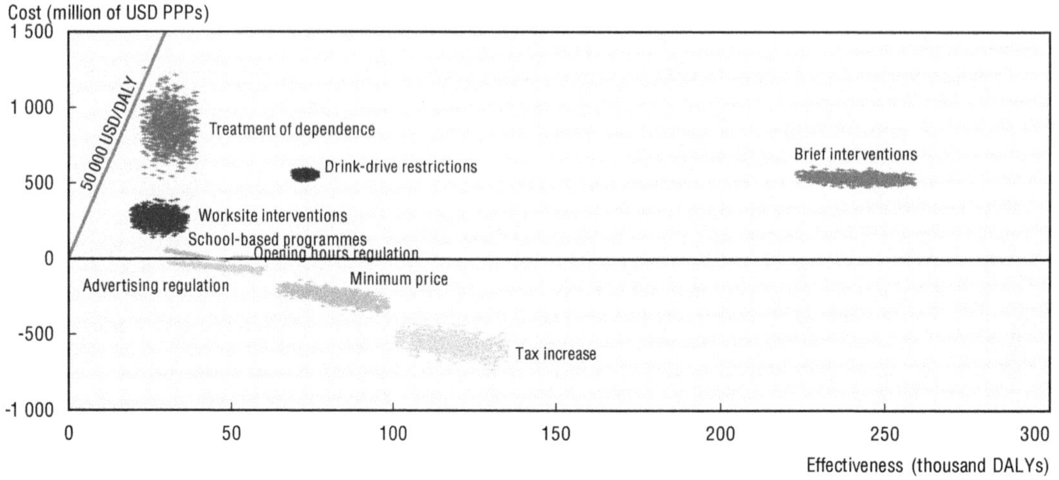


*Source:* MCLeague analysis relying on input data from the CDP-Alcohol model.

StatLink http://dx.doi.org/10.1787/888933180685

Figure A.10. **Canada: Probabilistic sensitivity analysis of the cost-effectiveness of alcohol policies after 40 years**

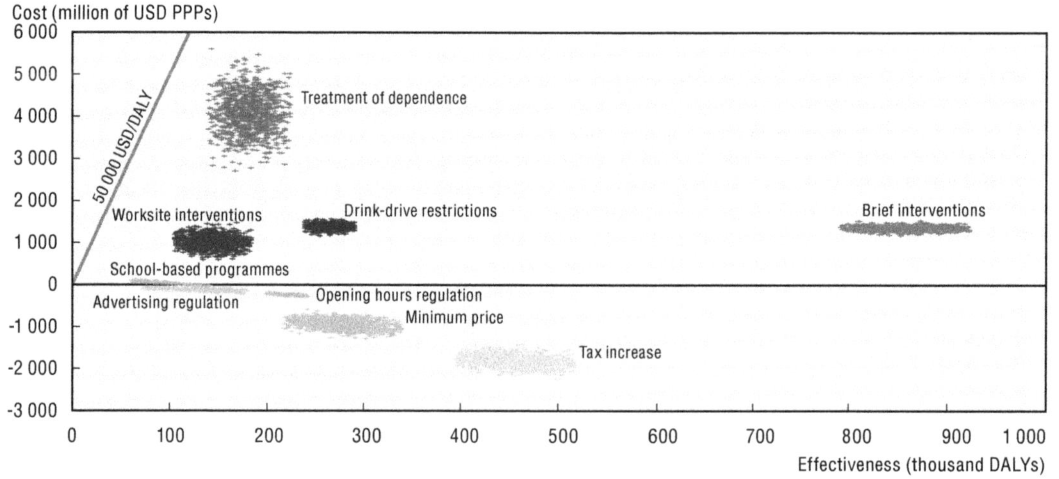


*Source:* MCLeague analysis relying on input data from the CDP-Alcohol model.

StatLink http://dx.doi.org/10.1787/888933180697

Figure A.11. **Czech Republic: Probabilistic sensitivity analysis of the cost-effectiveness of alcohol policies after 10 years**

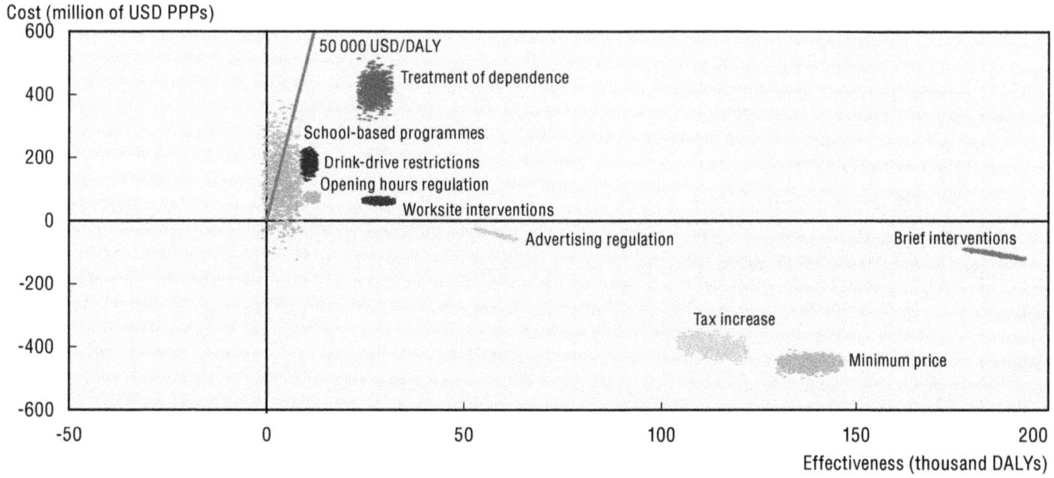


*Source*: MCLeague analysis relying on input data from the CDP-Alcohol model.

StatLink http://dx.doi.org/10.1787/888933180707

Figure A.12. **Czech Republic: Probabilistic sensitivity analysis of the cost-effectiveness of alcohol policies after 40 years**

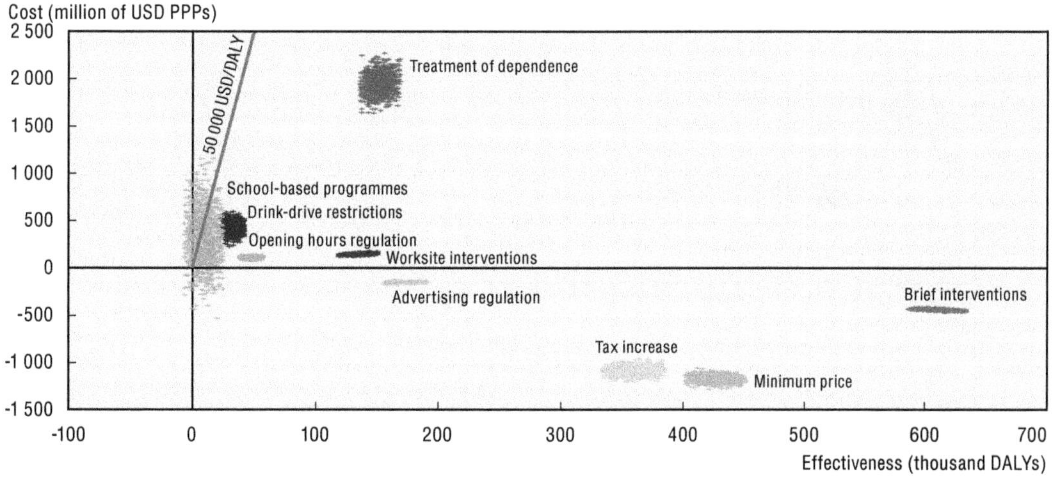


*Source*: MCLeague analysis relying on input data from the CDP-Alcohol model.

StatLink http://dx.doi.org/10.1787/888933180715

Figure A.13. **Germany: Probabilistic sensitivity analysis of the cost-effectiveness of alcohol policies after 10 years**

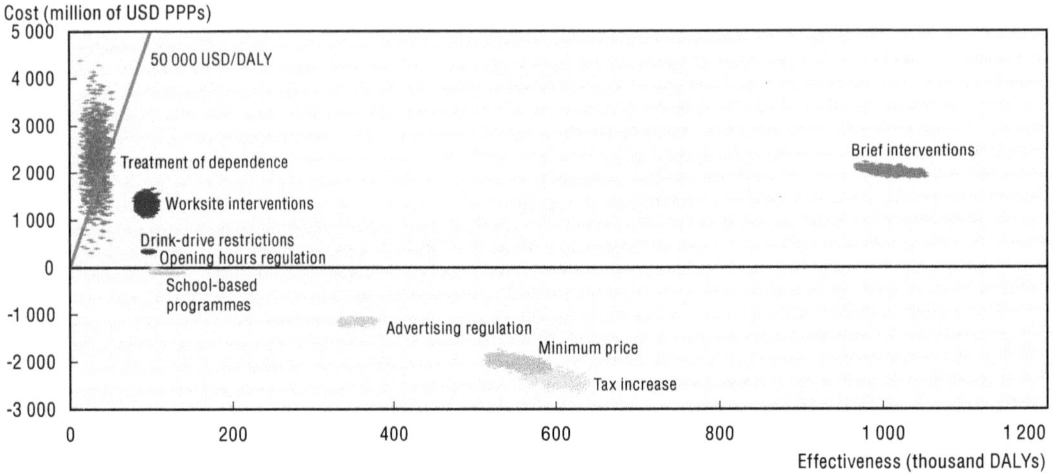


*Source:* MCLeague analysis relying on input data from the CDP-Alcohol model.

StatLink http://dx.doi.org/10.1787/888933180727

Figure A.14. **Germany: Probabilistic sensitivity analysis of the cost-effectiveness of alcohol policies after 40 years**

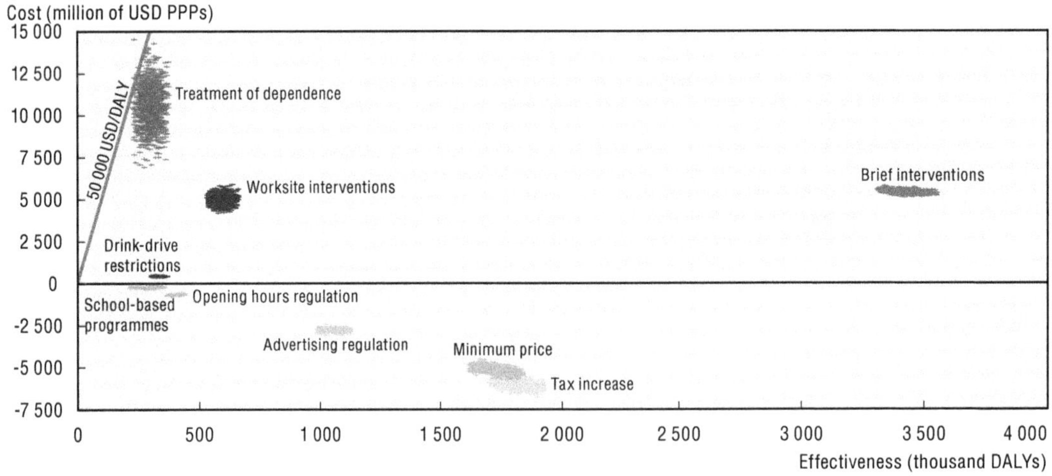


*Source:* MCLeague analysis relying on input data from the CDP-Alcohol model.

StatLink http://dx.doi.org/10.1787/888933180733

 

# ANNEX B

## *Authors' and contributors' biographies*

**Franco Sassi** is responsible for the OECD Public Health Programme. He is a senior health economist in the OECD Health Division. He is the lead author of *Obesity and the Economics of Prevention: Fit not Fat* (2010), and of a large number of publications on the economics of chronic disease prevention. Previously, he was a senior lecturer in health policy at the London School of Economics and Political Science (LSE) and director of the graduate programme in Health Policy, Planning and Financing run jointly by the LSE and the London School of Hygiene & Tropical Medicine, for eight years. Franco has an undergraduate degree from Bocconi University (Milan) and obtained his doctorate in health economics from the University of London. The overarching theme of his research and publications, throughout his career, has been the evaluation of health interventions. He has held adjunct and visiting positions at a number of universities in the United States, including the University of California at Berkeley, Harvard University, the University of California at San Francisco, and Duke University, as well as at the at the Université de Montréal in Canada, and at the Catholic University of Rome. He was awarded a 2000-01 Commonwealth Fund Harkness Fellowship in Health Care Policy.

**Marion Devaux** is a health policy analyst in the OECD Health Division. She holds a master's degree in statistics from the Ecole Nationale de la Statistique et Analyse de l'Information (ENSAI, France) and a Ph.D. in Health Economics from Université Paris Dauphine. She previously worked on the intergenerational transmission of health inequalities at the Institute for research and information in health economics (IRDES, Paris), and published in many academic journals. At the OECD since 2008, Marion has contributed to a range of projects on the prevention of obesity, health systems characteristics, inequality in health, and inequities in health care utilisation. She is responsible for a project on the labour market outcomes of chronic diseases and associated risk factors, including on employment, productivity, wages, sickness absence, receipt of welfare benefits and early retirement.

**Michele Cecchini** is a health economist and policy analyst in the OECD Health Division, where he has been working on the Economics of Prevention programme since 2007. His research interests include priority setting and programme evaluation in the health sector, in particular with regards to the health and economic assessment of policies influencing non-medical determinants of health (e.g. nutrition, physical activity and alcohol consumption). Michele holds a position of adjunct professor in applied health economics at the School of Public Health of the University of Siena and held a visiting position at the Health Services & Systems Research Centre of the Duke-NUS Graduate Medical School in

Singapore. He has also served as a temporary advisor to a number of government and international agencies, including WHO and IARC, on a range of diet- and physical-activity related issues. After obtaining a degree in Medicine and Surgery from the University of Genoa, Michele completed his specialist training in Public Health at the University of Siena. He also obtained a master's degree in Health Policy, Planning and Financing from the London School of Economics and the London School of Hygiene and Tropical Medicine.

**Roberto Astolfi** is an economist and statistician at the OECD. He is currently the head of the Composite Leading Indicators and Environmental Accounts Unit in the Statistics Directorate. Previously, he was responsible for Health Expenditure data collection and analysis at the OECD Health Division where he also contributed to the Economics of Prevention programme. Before joining the OECD he was a researcher in the National Accounts department at ISTAT in Italy and a business cycle analyst at Eurostat in Luxembourg. Roberto received his Ph.D. in Economic, Mathematical and Statistical Analysis of Social Phenomena from the University of Rome "La Sapienza". His main research interests lie in the fields of econometrics of time series analysis, model selection and forecasting, and applied macro-economics and health economics.

**Annalisa Belloni** is a health policy analyst in the OECD Health Division, where she has been working since 2010. She holds a master's degree in Health Economics and Management from the Catholic University of the Sacred Heart (UCSC, Rome). At the OECD, she has been working on the Economics of Prevention programme and particularly on the analysis of the role of fiscal measures in health promotion reviewing the theoretical arguments and empirical evidence on the key factors that governments must address when considering the adoption of fiscal measures in areas such as tobacco, alcohol, food and non-alcoholic beverages. She also contributed to a range of projects on pharmaceutical pricing and reimbursement policies, and on geographical variations in health care in OECD countries.

**Anne Ludbrook** is theme leader on health behaviours and inequalities in the Health Economics Research Unit (HERU), University of Aberdeen. Her current research interests are focused around the use of economics in health improvement, with a particular interest in alcohol, obesity and smoking. Anne led the review of the health and economic impacts of smoking in public places that supported the introduction of smoke-free legislation in Scotland. Other recent studies have focused on minimum unit pricing for alcohol; inequalities in the distribution of alcohol related harms; economic factors influencing food choice; physical activity effects of promoting active travel; and the use of incentives for quitting smoking. Anne is a graduate of the University of York and has worked in HERU for more than 30 years.

**Marjana Martinic** is the deputy president of the International Alliance for Responsible Drinking, where she is responsible for all scientific programmes, research activities, and policy work. Marjana has published extensively on alcohol policy and serves on the Science Group of the European Commission's Alcohol and Health Forum. She received her A.B. in Biology from Harvard University and her doctorate in Neuroscience from Northwestern University. Previously she worked in basic research on the development of the central nervous system at the University of Virginia School of Medicine and the U.S. National Institutes of Health.

**Martin McKee** qualified in medicine in Belfast, Northern Ireland, with subsequent training in internal medicine and public health. He is Professor of European Public Health at the London School of Hygiene and Tropical Medicine where he founded the European

Centre on Health of Societies in Transition (ECOHOST), a WHO Collaborating Centre. He is also research director of the European Observatory on Health Systems and Policies and president-elect of the European Public Health Association. He has published over 760 academic papers and 42 books and his contributions to European health policy have been recognised by, among others, election to the UK Academy of Medical Sciences, the Romanian Academy of Medical Sciences, and the US Institute of Medicine, by the award of honorary doctorates from Hungary, The Netherlands, and Sweden and visiting professorships at universities in Europe and Asia, the 2003 Andrija Stampar medal for contributions to European public health, the 2014 Alwyn Smith Prize for outstanding contributions to the health of the population, and in 2005 was made a Commander of the Order of the British Empire (CBE). He has an active following on Twitter as @martinmckee.

**Henry Saffer** received a Ph.D. in Economics from the City University of New York in 1977. He has published a number of papers on public policy and substance abuse. These include papers on the effects of alcohol and tobacco advertising, prescription drug advertising, the effects of alcohol pricing and other alcohol control policies, and the effects of illicit drug control policies. His current work includes a study of self-regulation and health choices. He has been the principal investigator on a number of grants from the National Institute on Alcohol Abuse and Alcoholism, and on grants from the National Institute of Cancer, the National Institute on Drug Abuse, the National Institute of Mental Health, the J.M. Foundation and the Robert Wood Johnson Foundation. Saffer is currently a Research Associate at the National Bureau of Economic Research in New York and is ranked in the top 100 health economists in the world by the World Bank.

**Patrick Love**, senior editor at OECD Publishing, helped edit the book. He is the author or co-author of five books in the OECD Insights series and is editorial advisor for the other titles in the series. He manages and writes for the OECD Insights blog.

# ORGANISATION FOR ECONOMIC CO-OPERATION AND DEVELOPMENT

The OECD is a unique forum where governments work together to address the economic, social and environmental challenges of globalisation. The OECD is also at the forefront of efforts to understand and to help governments respond to new developments and concerns, such as corporate governance, the information economy and the challenges of an ageing population. The Organisation provides a setting where governments can compare policy experiences, seek answers to common problems, identify good practice and work to co-ordinate domestic and international policies.

The OECD member countries are: Australia, Austria, Belgium, Canada, Chile, the Czech Republic, Denmark, Estonia, Finland, France, Germany, Greece, Hungary, Iceland, Ireland, Israel, Italy, Japan, Korea, Luxembourg, Mexico, the Netherlands, New Zealand, Norway, Poland, Portugal, the Slovak Republic, Slovenia, Spain, Sweden, Switzerland, Turkey, the United Kingdom and the United States. The European Union takes part in the work of the OECD.

OECD Publishing disseminates widely the results of the Organisation's statistics gathering and research on economic, social and environmental issues, as well as the conventions, guidelines and standards agreed by its members.

OECD PUBLISHING, 2, rue André-Pascal, 75775 PARIS CEDEX 16
(81 2013 02 1P) ISBN 978-92-64-18085-7 – 2015

www.ingramcontent.com/pod-product-compliance
Ingram Content Group UK Ltd.
Pitfield, Milton Keynes, MK11 3LW, UK
UKHW051500290926
15471UKWH00008B/1318

9 789264 180857